*Latin American Populism
in the Twenty-First Century*

Latin American Populism in the Twenty-First Century

Edited by

Carlos de la Torre and
Cynthia J. Arnson

Woodrow Wilson Center Press
Washington, D.C.

The Johns Hopkins University Press
Baltimore

EDITORIAL OFFICES

Woodrow Wilson Center Press
One Woodrow Wilson Plaza
1300 Pennsylvania Avenue, N.W.
Washington, D.C. 20004-3027
Telephone: 202-691-4029
www.wilsoncenter.org

ORDER FROM

The Johns Hopkins University Press
Hampden Station
P.O. Box 50370
Baltimore, Maryland 21211
Telephone: 1-800-537-5487
www.press.jhu.edu/books/

2 4 6 8 9 7 5 3 1

Library of Congress Cataloging-in-Publication Data

Latin American populism in the twenty-first century / edited by Carlos de la Torre
and Cynthia J. Arnson.
    pages   cm
    Includes index.
    ISBN 978-1-4214-1009-8
    1. Populism—Latin America.   2. Latin America—Politics and government.
I. Torre, Carlos de la (Carlos de la Torre Espinosa)
JL966.L363 2013
320.56′62098—dc23
                                                        2013005972

Wilson Center

Contents

Tables and Figures

Tables

Figures

Acknowledgments

A book of this nature is always a collective endeavor. Behind the contributions of the many chapter authors stand the sweat, labor, and support of research assistants, interns, and colleagues. We are grateful to Latin American Program interns Julie Anderson, Adam Drolet, Lisa Hartland, Smith Monson, and Elizabeth Pierson for excellent research and logistical support. No one was more critical in bringing the manuscript to completion than intern Melissa Nolan. Former Latin American Program assistant Nikki Nichols also provided excellent research assistance. As with other activities of the Latin American Program, the success of this book rests on the professionalism and assistance of program associate Adam T. Stubits and program assistant Verónica Colón-Rosario. Joe Brinley and Cherie Worth, of the Woodrow Wilson Center Press, and Alfred Imhoff, the project editor, provided the outstanding support for which they are known and appreciated.

We wish to thank Diego Abente Brun of the International Forum for Democracy Studies of the National Endowment for Democracy, Julio F. Carrión of the University of Delaware, and Jorge Lanzaro of Uruguay's

Universidad de la República and a former Wilson Center scholar for their participation in the 2009 conference on which this book is based.

This book represents the culmination of the Latin American Program's three-year project on "Democratic Governance and the 'New Left' in Latin America." Previous publications of the project can be found at http://www.wilsoncenter.org/publication-series/democratic-governance-and-the-new-left. We are grateful to the Ford Foundation and the Open Society Foundation for their generous support of our work. Carlos de la Torre also thanks the John Simon Guggenheim Memorial Foundation for a 2010–11 fellowship in support of his project "Understanding Popular Support for Populist and Authoritarian Regimes."

Cynthia J. Arnson
Woodrow Wilson International Center for Scholars

Carlos de la Torre
University of Kentucky

October 2012

*Latin American Populism
in the Twenty-First Century*

Chapter 1

Introduction: The Evolution of Latin American Populism and the Debates Over Its Meaning

Carlos de la Torre and
Cynthia J. Arnson

Late on the night of October 7, 2012, tens of thousands of flag-waving supporters of Venezuelan president Hugo Chávez flooded into the streets of Caracas, chanting and singing the national anthem as they celebrated Chávez's victory in that day's presidential elections. With more than 80 percent of eligible voters casting their ballots—one of the highest turnouts in Venezuelan history—Chávez triumphed over his opponent, Henrique Capriles Radonski, by 55.4 percent to 44.5 percent, winning in twenty-two of the country's twenty-four states. Following the announcement of his victory by the National Electoral Council (Consejo Nacional Electoral), Chávez addressed the crowd from "the people's balcony" of the presidential palace. Invoking the name of the nineteenth-century hero of Latin American independence, Simón Bolívar, he vowed to continue Venezuela's transition toward the "democratic and Bolivarian socialism of the twenty-first century."

The authors wish to thank Latin American Program intern Melissa Nolan for outstanding research assistance.

1

The reemergence of populism as part of the discussion of contemporary politics in Latin America is, for the most part, a product of the regime and persona of Hugo Chávez. Elected as president for the fourth time since 1998, he created and commanded a huge and loyal following among Venezuela's poor and marginalized, using the country's lavish oil revenues to finance extensive social programs. Under his charismatic leadership—which blended authoritarianism with new forms of grassroots participation—Venezuela drafted a new Constitution that demolished the political institutions of the country's pacted democracy, creating new ones subject to Chávez's control. His policies and discourse fostered polarization within Venezuela and throughout the region. And in a way that was particularly vexing for both Venezuela's neighbors and the United States, he claimed to be part of—indeed, to lead—a worldwide movement against imperialism and in solidarity with oppressed peoples. Until his diagnosis with cancer in mid-2011, he appeared set to govern indefinitely, under provisions of a constitutional reform that did away with term limits. But health issues prevented him from taking office in January 2013. Before leaving for Cuba for his fourth cancer surgery in eighteen months, Chávez designated Vice President Nicolás Maduro as his successor in case new elections needed to be called. Chávez's long absence from Venezuela launched a period of uncertainty about the country's political future and the direction of *chavismo* without Chávez.

The election of the indigenous leader Evo Morales as president of Bolivia in 2005 and of Rafael Correa in Ecuador in 2006 lent credence to the notion that populism was indeed resurgent in the Western Hemisphere. Similarities in the style of governance and the close personal and political affinities among Chávez, Morales, and Correa nourished a temptation to view Andean populism as one homogenous bloc, despite important differences: the unique dynamics of social mobilization in each country, the distinct nature of linkages between social movements and the state, and the role of ethnicity in shaping politics at the national level.[1] The similarities and differences among the so-called radical populists of the left are explored in detail in chapters 9, 10, and 11 of this book.

Predictably, the emergence of Chávez, Morales, and Correa at a similar point in history sparked new rounds of debate and controversy in

1. Cynthia J. Arnson with José Raúl Perales, eds., *Democratic Governance and the "New Left" in Latin America* (Washington, D.C.: Latin American Program, Woodrow Wilson International Center for Scholars, 2007), 4, http://www.wilson center.org/sites/default/files/NewLeftDemocraticGovernance.pdf.

both scholarly and policy circles. Indeed, the wave of leftist electoral victories in Latin America in the late 1990s and early 2000s in such diverse countries as Chile, Uruguay, Brazil, Bolivia, Argentina, and Venezuela focused unprecedented attention on the so-called rise of the left,[2] in which scholars and policymakers distinguished between the social-democratic leaders of institutionalized democracies such as Chile and Brazil and "the rebirth of an influential Latin American political tradition"[3]—populism—in the Andean region.[4]

Adopting narratives that link populism to irrationality, some depicted the Chávez, Morales, and Correa regimes as dangerous and irresponsible. Critics decried the resurgence of free-spending populist economic policies that defy the logic of the market, the risk to democracy itself posed by personalistic demagogues, and the dangers of an explicit anti–United States foreign policy agenda.[5] Others had less catastrophic views but, drawing on an extensive literature on Latin America populism,

2. A rich literature on the "new left" in Latin America attempted to make sense of the wave of leftist governments that came to power in Latin America in the late 1990s and 2000s, and their implications for democracy as well as social inclusion. See, e.g., Kurt Weyland, Raúl L. Madrid, and Wendy Hunter, eds., *Leftist Governments in Latin America: Successes and Shortcomings* (Cambridge: Cambridge University Press, 2010); Maxwell Cameron and Eric Hershberg, eds., *Latin America's Left Turns: Politics, Policies, and Trajectories of Change* (Boulder, Colo.: Lynne Rienner, 2010); Steven Levitsky and Kenneth M. Roberts, eds., *The Resurgence of the Latin American Left* (Baltimore: Johns Hopkins University Press, 2011); Jorge G. Castañeda and Marco A. Morales, eds., *Leftovers: Tales of the Latin American Left* (New York: Routledge, 2008); and Cynthia J. Arnson et al., eds., *La "Nueva Izquierda" en América Latina: Derechos Humanos, Participación Política, y Sociedad Civil* (Washington, D.C., and Buenos Aires: Woodrow Wilson International Center for Scholars, Universidad Torcuato di Tella, and Centro de Estudios Legales y Sociales, 2009), http://www.wilsoncenter.org/topics/pubs/Nueva%20Izquierda%20Enero%2020091.pdf. For other publications of the Latin American Program's project on "Democratic Governance and the 'New Left' in Latin America," see http://www.wilsoncenter.org/publication-series/democratic-governance-and-the-new-left-bulletins.

3. "The Return of Populism," *The Economist*, April 12, 2006.

4. For a critique of the simplistic division between the social-democratic and populist lefts, see Kenneth M. Roberts, "Repoliticizing Latin America: The Revival of Populist and Leftist Alternatives," *Woodrow Wilson Center Update on the Americas*, November 2007, http://www.wilsoncenter.org/sites/default/files/repoliticizing.roberts.lap.pdf.

5. See, e.g., the special issue on populism in *Letras Libres* (Mexico City) 7, no. 75 (March 2005); and Hal Brands, *Dealing with Political Ferment in Latin America: The Populist Revival, the Emergence of the Center, and the Implications for U.S. Policy* (Carlisle, Pa.: Strategic Studies Institute, 2009).

nonetheless shared a pessimistic and pejorative portrayal of these governments' authoritarian qualities.[6] The regimes of Chávez, Morales, and Correa were distinguished from and contrasted with the pragmatic, moderate, "responsible" left—Michelle Bachelet in Chile, Tabaré Vázquez in Uruguay, Luiz Inácio Lula da Silva in Brazil—who embraced the fundamentals of liberal democracy as well as the precepts of the market economy. Critics of the populist left pointed especially to the instrumental use of laws, the concentration of power in the executive, the gutting of institutions that provide for checks and balances, and the restriction of fundamental freedoms (particularly freedom of the press) that foster and preserve democratic pluralism. Critics also decried the return of populist economic policies that sacrificed macroeconomic stability and the logic of the market economy for political or social goals pursued by an inefficient and bloated, albeit redistributionist, state.[7]

Others, however, portrayed the Chávez, Correa, and Morales regimes in a radically different light. They were depicted as democratic innovators whose credentials were rooted in a commitment to social justice and to the expansion of participation by previously excluded groups.[8] The dramatic break with neoliberal orthodoxy, the state's increased involvement in the economy, the implementation of new social programs targeted at the poor, and the renewed sense of nationalism and pride were

6. Jorge Castañeda, "Latin America's Left Turn," *Foreign Affairs* 85 (May 2006): 28–43. For a critique of Castañeda that builds on the concept of populism, see John French, "Understanding the Politics of Latin America's Plural Lefts (Chávez/Lula): Social Democracy, Populism and Convergence on the Path to a Post-Neoliberal World," *Third World Quarterly* 30 (2009): 349–70; see also René Antonio Mayorga, "Outsiders and Neopopulism: The Road to Plebiscitarian Authoritarianism," paper presented at the conference "The Crisis of Democratic Representation in the Andes," Kellogg Institute for International Affairs, University of Notre Dame, May 13–14, 2002.

7. Sebastian Edwards, *Left Behind: Latin America and the False Promise of Populism* (Chicago: University of Chicago Press, 2010).

8. D. L. Raby, *Democracy and Revolution: Latin America and Socialism Today* (London: Pluto Press, 2006); Gregory Wilpert, *Changing Venezuela by Taking Power: The History and Policies of the Chávez Government* (London: Verso, 2007); Pablo Stefanoni and Herve do Alto, *La Revolución De Evo Morales: De La Coca Al Palacio, Claves Para Todos* (Buenos Aires: Capital Intelectual, 2006); Ernesto Laclau, "Consideraciones sobre el Populismo Latinoamericano," *Cuadernos del CENDES* 23, no. 64 (2006): 115–20; Franklin Ramírez Gallegos, "Post-neoliberlismo indocile: Agenda pública y relaciones socio-estatales en el Ecuador de la Revolución Ciudadana," *Temas y Debates* 20 (2010): 175–94.

all seen as positive developments. In this more sanguine view of populist governance, Chávez, Morales, and Correa democratized their societies, promoting new constitutions that expanded citizenship rights and established models of direct democracy with the potential to lead to better forms of participation and representation. All three presidents won elections and referenda using populist rhetoric that emphasized the empowerment of *el pueblo* (the people) as the embodiment of the nation. As a consequence of new policies, previously excluded citizens became more actively involved in politics and showed increasing levels of support for democracy. These regimes were portrayed as examples for leftists around the world that alternatives to neoliberalism and liberal democracy were possible and desirable.[9] As Enrique Peruzzotti writes in chapter 3, many contemporary scholars have viewed the expansion of citizenship under populist regimes "as a necessary antidote to the ills of representative politics."

Our goal in this book is not to sidestep the intense polarization that exists over the issue of populism; nor do we pretend that our own scholarship is free of normative bias. Our principal aim is to explain populism's reemergence, place it in historical context, and explore the continuities and differences between past and current populist leaders. We thus compare classical populist regimes such as those of Argentina's Juan Domingo Perón and Brazil's Getúlio Vargas with neoliberal neopopulists like those of Peru's Alberto Fujimori and Argentina's Carlos Menem, and radical nationalist populists such as Chávez, Correa, and Morales. This historical lens helps us to understand more deeply the underlying conditions that give rise to populism in Latin America, its continuities and changing expressions over time, and, ultimately, its consequences for the meaning and content of democracy.

The chapters in this book explore the historical patterns of populism in the specific cases of Argentina, Bolivia, Brazil, Colombia, Ecuador, Peru, and Venezuela. And they also examine comparatively such broad themes as populism and the party system, the nature of populist discourse and appeals, the social policies of populist regimes, and the characteristics of populist democracy. Through this comparative and historical approach, we focus on the ambiguities of past and current populist

9. Tariq Ali, *Pirates of the Caribbean: Axis of Hope* (London: Verso, 2008); Raby, *Democracy and Revolution.*

regimes with respect to liberal democracy. We focus on such questions as:

- Theoretically and empirically, what explains the revival of populism?
- What are the differences and continuities between the "classical" populism of the 1930s and 1940s and its current manifestations?
- What are the social bases of populism, and how do they differ from the past?
- How do leaders mobilize followers?
- How viable are these regimes, and what are their prospects for enduring over time?
- Are they developing alternative forms of democratic participation and citizenship that will improve democratic forms or ultimately undermine them as an authoritarian regime consolidates itself?

Populism itself is a contested concept. As the chapters in this volume illustrate, scholars still debate its definition—whether to employ a structuralist approach that links populism to a particular historical period and set of economic policies—notably, the import-substitution industrialization policies of the 1930s and 1940s—or to decouple politics from economics.[10] In chapter 6, Hector Schamis adopts a structuralist approach to the understanding of Peronism in Argentina, anchors it in a particular historical moment in the aftermath of the Great Depression, and rejects political and discursive definitions of populism. Other chapters in the book give primacy to populism's political and discursive aspects, or to what Kurt Weyland defines in chapter 5 as a political *strategy* for "winning and exercising power."[11]

10. In a classic work on the subject, the economists Rudiger Dornbusch and Sebastian Edwards examined the macroeconomics of populist regimes, defining economic populism in terms of a set of policies that emphasized growth and redistribution and downplayed the risks of inflation, unsustainable fiscal deficits, wage increases not accompanied by increases in productivity, and the reaction of important economic actors to non-market policies. See Rudiger Dornbusch and Sebastian Edwards, eds., *The Macroeconomics of Populism in Latin America* (Chicago: University of Chicago Press, 1991).

11. For Kurt Weyland, populism is political strategy for "winning and exercising power" based on the direct, unmediated, noninstitutional support of large numbers of people. Elections, plebiscites, mass demonstrations, and public opinion polls serve to mobilize supporters and demonstrate power capabilities. See Kurt Weyland, "Clarifying a Contested Concept: Populism in the Study of Latin American Politics," *Comparative Politics* 34, no. 1 (2001): 1–22. See also Kenneth Roberts, "Neo-

Although a common definition is elusive, we can agree on some of populism's central characteristics. As a form of governance, discourse, and political representation, populism posits and fosters division between "the people" and "the oligarchy." The role of charismatic, personalistic leadership is central, such that the direct or quasi-direct relationship between the leader and the masses preempts and at times overrides the role of institutions in the day-to-day functioning of government. (The British historian Alan Knight has called this relationship a "particularly intense form of 'bonding.'")[12] Populist discourse is used to obtain office and subsequently to consolidate and hold on to power. Though mass mobilization is a feature of populism, populist manifestations differ with respect to the composition of their social base, the methods of mobilizing followers, and the nature of linkages between leaders and followers. The level of polarization generated by populist discourse and practice also varies from case to case. These variations and exceptions are research questions we aim to explore.

As Francisco Panizza indicates in chapter 4, "populism is not so much the direct relationship between the leader and the people but the leader's ability to reach those who regard themselves as having no voice in the political system." According to Panizza, populist leaders construct popular identities by claiming to speak "for" the people, and in so doing they combine the "politics of recognition to the politically excluded" with the politics of distribution to those disadvantaged by the economic system. Panizza uses the term "populist intervention" to capture the use of populist appeals in combination with other forms of political identification.

Under populism, politics becomes a quasi-religious and ethical struggle between good and evil, redemption and downfall.[13] Populists characterize their rivals—of both the left and the right—as enemies of the leader, the people, and by extension, the nation. For example, in one of their

liberalism and the Transformation of Populism in Latin America: The Peruvian Case," *World Politics* 48 (October 1995): 82–116.

12. Alan Knight, "Populism and Neo-Populism in Latin America, Especially Mexico," *Journal of Latin American Studies* 30 (1998): 223–48.

13. José Álvarez Junco, "Magia y Ética en la Retórica Política," in *Populismo, caudillaje y discurso demagógico*, edited by José Álvarez Junco (Madrid: Centro de Investigaciones Sociológicas and Siglo XXI, 1987), 219–271; Loris Zanatta, "El populismo, entre la religión y la política: Sobre las raíces históricas del antiliberalismo en América Latina," *Estudios Interdisciplinarios de América Latina y el Caribe* 19, no. 2 (2008): 29–45; José Pedro Zúquete, "The Missionary Politics of Hugo Chávez," *Latin American Politics and Society* 50, no. 1 (2008): 91–122.

more defining political dimensions, populist regimes construe politics as a moral and Manichaean struggle between the people and the oligarchy.[14] Populism appears as a revolt against institutions, such as political parties and the legislature, that are perceived as corrupt and out of touch with the needs and demands of ordinary people. Populism appeals to the principle of a sovereign people in order to simultaneously overhaul decaying institutions and replace them with a new institutional order.[15] Paraphrasing the political and economic theorist Joseph Schumpeter, Kenneth Roberts in chapter 2 identifies populist mobilization as a "force of 'creative destruction' that can break down, realign, and (potentially) rebuild more institutionalized forms of mass political representation."

Moreover, as Panizza argues, populist interventions can occur in different types of political systems:

> In a context of crisis of representation—such as occurred in Bolivia, Ecuador, and Venezuela in the late 1990s and early 2000s—the foundational aspects of populism become dominant, whereas in other more institutionalized contexts, populist antagonisms were mediated and constrained by the involvement of political institutions.

Hugo Chávez, Evo Morales, and Rafael Correa are heirs to and innovators with respect to Latin America's populist tradition. As César Montúfar argues in chapter 11, today's radical populist regimes do not see themselves as "another government, subject to democratic alternation, but as a new political regime that will endure over time, opening a new epoch."

Despite important differences, leaders in Venezuela, Bolivia, and Ecuador came to power in countries that had experienced deep crises of

14. José Álvarez Junco, *El Emperador del Paralelo: Lerroux y la Demagogia Populista* (Madrid: Alianza Editorial, 1990); Carlos de la Torre, *Populist Seduction in Latin America*, 2nd ed. (Athens: Ohio University Press, 2010); Kirk Hawkins, *Venezuela's Chavismo and Populism in Comparative Perspective* (Cambridge: Cambridge University Press, 2010); Knight, "Populism and Neopopulism"; Cas Mudde, "The Populist Zeitgeist," *Government and Opposition* 39, no. 4, (2004): 541–63; Francisco Panizza, "Introduction: Populism and the Mirror of Democracy," in *Populism and the Mirror of Democracy*, edited by Francisco Panizza (London: Verso, 2005), 1–32; Ignacio Walker, *Democracy and Populism in Latin America*, Working Paper 347 (Notre Dame, Ind.: Kellogg Institute for International Studies, University of Notre Dame, 2008).

15. Ernesto Laclau, *On Populist Reason* (London: Verso, 2005).

political representation; since taking power, they have contributed to the further erosion of political parties.[16] In a distinguishing feature of contemporary radical populism, Chávez, Morales, and Correa lead self-described revolutionary governments that aim to "refound" the political and cultural institutions of their respective countries. Invoking the name and legacy of the nineteenth-century liberator Simón Bolívar, for example, Chávez speaks of leading a "Bolivarian Revolution," understood as the second and definitive struggle for independence. Morales, the first indigenous president of Bolivia since the Spanish conquest, is at the forefront of what he describes as a cultural, democratic, and postcolonial revolution to empower indigenous peoples. Rafael Correa is the leader of what his supporters understand as a "Citizens' Revolution."

These self-described revolutionary processes differ from past revolutions in Latin America and, in our view, constitute a new and distinct phase of radical populism in the region—in five main ways. First, the "revolutions" are carried out through elections, not armed struggle. Chávez and Correa in particular engage in permanent political campaigns, using the convening of frequent elections to displace older elites, rally supporters, and consolidate their hegemony.[17] In the case of Venezuela, for example, Margarita López Maya and Alexandra Panzarelli write in chapter 9 that in the first thirteen years under Chávez, Venezuelans voted in fifteen different electoral processes. All these elections—even those for municipal and legislative posts—amounted essentially to plebiscites on Chávez's rule. Correa also appeared to be following Chávez's example by using frequent elections as vehicles to ratify and consolidate power, outside the constitutionally mandated schedule of presidential, legislative, and municipal elections.

Second, these revolutions are carried out in the name of democracy, a contested concept that leaders interpret in substantive rather than procedural terms. For Correa, for example, the essence of democratic citizenship resides in the socioeconomic sphere and depends on state policies to

16. Paul Drake and Eric Hershberg, eds., *State and Society in Conflict: Comparative Perspectives on Andean Crises* (Pittsburgh: University of Pittsburgh Press, 2006); Scott Mainwaring, Ana María Bejarano, and Eduardo Pizarro, eds., *The Crisis of Democratic Representation in the Andes* (Palo Alto, Calif.: Stanford University Press, 2006).

17. Catherine Conaghan and Carlos de la Torre, "The Permanent Campaign of Rafael Correa: Making Ecuador's Plebiscitary Presidency," *International Journal of Press/Politics* 13 (2008): 267–84.

advance social justice. For Chávez (whose policies have likewise aimed at fostering social inclusion), advancing democracy depends on replacing the unresponsive institutions of liberal democracy with new forms of direct, participatory democracy. And for Morales, as John Crabtree indicates in chapter 10, democracy means replacing and/or complementing liberal institutions with forms of indigenous and other autonomies designed to enhance grassroots, particularly indigenous, participation.[18]

Third, the political projects of these three leaders do not aim to improve or correct the deficits of liberal democracy. Rather, constituent assemblies that have drafted new constitutions in all three countries have sought to "refound" the nation, creating expanded mechanisms for direct and semidirect citizen participation and elaborately enshrining the role of the state in providing for social welfare.[19] In practice, as César Montúfar writes in chapter 11, the goal is to establish a different kind of democracy, based on elections but also on a new constitutional order that concentrates power in the hands of the president and, more broadly, the executive branch. Similarly, majoritarian mobilization led by a personalistic leader takes precedence over the checks and balances and respect for basic civil rights inherent in liberal democracy.[20] Mechanisms of "horizontal accountability" by other branches of government and an independent press have been replaced by a variant of "vertical accountability" involving frequent elections, referenda, and plebiscites.[21] As Montúfar underscores, democratic deinstitutionalization is accompanied by a process of reinstitutionalization along the lines spelled out in new constitutions.

18. See Luis Tapia, "Representación, participación y democratización en las relaciones Estado-sociedad civil en Bolivia," in *La "Nueva Izquierda,"* ed. Arnson et al., 119–30.

19. See, e.g., Margarita López Maya, "Venezuela: Hugo Chávez and the Populist Left," in *Resurgence*, ed. Levitsky and Roberts, 214–38; and Edwards, *Left Behind*, 185–90.

20. Raúl L. Madrid, Wendy Hunter, and Kurt Weyland, "The Policies and Performances of the Contestatory and Moderate Lefts," in *Leftist Governments*, ed. Weyland, Madrid, and Hunter, 140–81.

21. As opposed to the "vertical accountability" imposed by citizens who vote in regular elections, "horizontal accountability" refers to intra-state actions to prevent, sanction, or redress the unlawful activities of other state agencies. Examples are attorneys general, ombudsmen, and comptrollers. See Guillermo O'Donnell, "Horizontal Accountability: The Legal Institutionalization of Mistrust," in *Democratic Accountability in Latin America*, edited by Scott Mainwaring and Christopher Welna (Oxford: Oxford University Press, 2003), 34–44.

Fourth, in emphasizing substantive democracy, all three regimes rely on state intervention in the economy in the name of distributing wealth and reducing poverty and inequality. Although this statist, redistributionist aspect of populism is not new, governments in Venezuela, Bolivia, and Ecuador are rich in hydrocarbons and have reaped huge benefits from the commodity boom of the 2000s that sent oil and natural gas prices to record levels. (The discovery of huge oil and gas reserves in Argentina's Patagonia region created potential windfalls for Argentina as well.) Vastly expanded commodity rents have facilitated ambitious programs of state-led redistribution, coupled with varying degrees of antipathy and bargaining vis-à-vis the domestic private sector and foreign, especially private, capital.[22]

Chávez went the farthest, expropriating hundreds of domestic companies in sectors ranging from telecommunications to construction, agriculture, and retail. Nationalizations focused primarily on the energy sector have been more limited but nonetheless significant in Bolivia, Ecuador, and Argentina.[23] Increased state intervention in the economies of Venezuela, Bolivia, Ecuador, and Argentina and uncertain rules of the game regarding the private sector have served to depress domestic and foreign private investment overall.[24] That said, given high energy

22. All three countries have withdrawn from the World Bank's International Center for Settlement of Investment Disputes, which arbitrates such conflicts. On broader questions of commodity rents and their impact on governance, see Sebastián Mazzuca, "Natural Resource Boom and Institutional Curses in the New Political Economy of South America," in *Constructing Democratic Governance in Latin America*, edited by Jorge Domínguez and Michael Shifter (Baltimore: Johns Hopkins University Press, forthcoming).

23. See Paul Alexander Haslam, "Foreign Investors Over a Barrel: Nationalizations and Investment Policy," in *Latin America's Left Turns*, ed. Cameron and Hershberg, 209–30. Haslam indicates that the Morales government increased taxes on companies involved in the oil and gas sector and obliged them to provide services to the state oil company, Yacimientos Petrolíferos Fiscales Bolivianos. Brazil's Petrobras and Spain's REPSOL were among the companies affected. Other nationalizations covered railroads, power, private pension funds, and the local telephone company. As in Venezuela, constitutional provisions codified the role of the state in the hydrocarbons sector. Haslam indicates that "the governments of Bolivia and Venezuela have paid compensation that has been considered adequate in most cases." In April 2012, Argentine president Cristina Fernández de Kirchner expropriated 51 percent of YPF, an oil company belonging to Spain's REPSOL.

24. E.g., after the 2006 renationalization of natural gas in Bolivia and the large increases in royalties demanded of foreign companies, overall foreign direct investment declined by 41 percent in 2007. In subsequent years, and despite measures such

prices and huge proven reserves of oil and natural gas in such places as Venezuela, Bolivia, and Argentina, state-owned energy companies from around the globe as well as some private multinational energy companies have rushed to do business.

As a result of enhanced revenues, public investment and social spending have skyrocketed and poverty rates and, to a lesser extent, inequality, have fallen dramatically.[25] As Kurt Weyland argues in chapter 5, populist social programs have the advantage of rapidly targeting the poor; such programs serve to boost the popularity of presidents and function as a visible instrument for maintaining power. At the same time, however, they suffer from major flaws in design. Social programs are haphazard and politicized, lacking in efficiency, transparency, and institutionalization. Because they are tied to the persona of the president—who distributes benefits primarily to his or her political supporters rather than on the basis of universal, objective criteria—programs are unlikely to survive beyond the mandate of a particular government. (In Ecuador, as Montúfar notes, benefits have been universal and not tied to support for the president.) Weyland argues that the fiscal foundation of social programs, especially those that rely so heavily on oil and other windfall commodity rents, is unsustainable in the long run.[26] This is as true for the radical populists of the twenty-first century as it had been for populist regimes in earlier eras.

as the 2012 nationalization of the country's Spanish-owned power company, the Bolivian government appeared interested in attracting private investment to develop its natural resources. For example, beginning in 2010, the government signed agreements with companies in Japan, South Korea, China, and Finland to develop Bolivia's lithium resources. See Cynthia J. Arnson and Jessica Varat, "Introduction," in *Energy and Development in South America: Conflict and Cooperation*, edited by Cynthia J. Arnson, Claudio Fuentes, and Francisco Rojas Aravena, with Jessica Varat (Washington, D.C., and Quito: Woodrow Wilson International Center for Scholars and FLACSO, 2008), 2, http://www.wilsoncenter.org/sites/default/files/lap.energy devsa.pdf; and Eurasia Group, "Bolivia: Nationalization of Power Utility Not a Harbinger of a New Wave of Nationalization," May 2, 2012, 1-2.

25. See Nora Lustig, "Poverty, Inequality, and the New Left in Latin America," *Woodrow Wilson Center Update on the Americas*, October 2009, http://www.wilson center.org/sites/default/files/LAP_090716_Lustig%20Bulletin%20ENG_1.pdf; and Nora Lustig and Darryl McLeod, "Are Latin America's New Left Regimes Reducing Inequality Faster? Addendum to *Poverty, Inequality and the New Left in Latin America*," http://www.wilsoncenter.org/sites/default/files/LUSTIG%2526MCLEOD _INEQ%2526LEFT_JUL%2027_09.pdf.

26. Kurt Weyland, "The Rise of Latin America's Two Lefts: Insights from Rentier State Theory," *Comparative Politics* 41, no. 2 (2006): 145–64.

Fifth, and finally, in the foreign policy arena, Chávez, Morales, and Correa view their governments as part of a continental or even world-wide movement aimed at the realignment of international politics. In Chávez's words, "Latin America is at the vanguard of a new world."[27] Or, as Morales declared, "We want Bolivia, . . . with its political, economic, programmatic, cultural and ecological proposals, to be a hope for the entire world."[28] Although earlier manifestations of Latin American populism involved heavy doses of nationalism (and in the Argentine case, defiance of the United States), contemporary radical populists have antiglobalization, antiliberal, and to varying degrees, anti–United States postures at the core of their foreign policy rhetoric and strategies.[29] Chávez's leadership in forging relationships outside the Western Hemisphere with regimes hostile to the United States, particularly Iran, brought national security considerations into the debates over United States–Latin American relations in a way not seen since the end of the Cold War.[30]

27. Quoted by Charles Lindholm and José Pedro Zúquete, *The Struggle for the World: Liberation Movements for the 21st Century* (Palo Alto, Calif: Stanford University Press, 2010), 32.

28. Ibid., 47.

29. The United States supported an attempted coup against Chávez in 2002. But despite growing ideological confrontation between Chávez and the administration of George W. Bush, Venezuela continued to send some 40 percent of its oil exports to the United States for the remainder of the decade. Bolivia ended cooperation on counterdrug matters with the U.S. Drug Enforcement Administration and expelled the U.S. Agency for International Development, which had been involved in, among other things, crop substitution programs in areas of coca cultivation. The United States, Venezuela, and Bolivia expelled each other's ambassadors in 2008, and Ecuador followed suit in 2011, leaving diplomatic representation in the hands of lower-ranking officials. Ecuador and the United States renamed ambassadors in mid-2012, and the country continued to receive trade benefits through the Andean Trade Preferences and Drug Eradication Act. Those benefits were called into question as Ecuador considered granting asylum to WikiLeaks founder Julian Assange, wanted in Sweden on sexual assault charges. For an excellent overview of the foreign policies of social-democratic and populist left-wing governments in Latin America, see Carlos Pérez Llana, "Modelos politicos internos y alianzas externas," in *América Latina: Integración o Fragmentación?* edited by Ricardo Lagos (Buenos Aires: Edhasa, 2008), 51–88.

30. See Stephen Johnson, *Iran's Influence in the Americas* (Washington, D.C.: Center for Strategic and International Studies, 2012); the testimonies of Cynthia J. Arnson, Douglas Farah, Roger Noriega, and Ilan Berman, U.S. Senate Committee on Foreign Relations, Subcommittee on the Western Hemisphere, Peace Corps, and Global Narcotics Affairs, February 16, 2012, http://www.foreign.senate.gov/hearings/ irans-influence-and-activity-in-latin-america; and Cynthia J. Arnson, Haleh Esfan-

Classical Populism: The Origins and Legacies

The current wave of populism in the Andean region is heir to a long tradition in Latin American politics. Leaders such as Juan Domingo Perón and Eva Perón in Argentina, Getúlio Vargas in Brazil, Víctor Raúl Haya de la Torre in Peru, José María Velasco Ibarra in Ecuador, and Jorge Eliécer Gaitán in Colombia were either celebrated as the embodiment of democratic principles or vilified as authoritarian demagogues. During their time in office, previously excluded populations were incorporated into the national community and leaders achieved near-mythical status in the eyes of their followers.[31] Consider, for example, the suicide letter written by Brazil's Getúlio Vargas, quoted by Leslie Bethell in chapter 7. Vargas maintained that he was always "a slave of the people." He had returned to power in 1950–51 "*nos braços do povo*" (in the arms of the people) and had sought to defend the people and particularly the very poor against powerful interests. Now, old and tired, he was "serenely" taking the first step on the road to eternity, "leaving life to enter History."

Classical populists of the 1930s and 1940s fought against electoral fraud, expanded the franchise, and, in Kenneth Roberts's words, mobilized "the excluded or the alienated behind a new political leadership in frontal opposition to the status quo." Populist leaders were exalted as the embodiment of the nation's true, uncorrupted traditions and values against those of foreign-oriented elites. The appeal of these leaders bordered on the religious. Aprismo, for example, named for the Alianza Popular Revolucionaria Americana (American Popular Revolutionary Alliance, APRA), was a moral-religious crusade seeking the regeneration of the Peruvian people and nation. As McClintock indicates in chapter 8, Aprista political meetings always included the party anthem, the "Marsellesa Aprista":

diari, and Adam Stubits, eds., *Iran in Latin America: Threat or "Axis of Annoyance"?* Woodrow Wilson Center Reports on the Americas 23, 2009, http://www.wilson center.org/sites/default/files/Iran_in_LA.pdf. In July 2012, President Barack Obama told a Spanish-language television station in Miami that "what Mr. Chávez has done over the last several years has not had a serious national security impact on us." Senator Marco Rubio (R-Fla.) accused Obama of "living under a rock," downplaying the Iranian government's "attempts to expand its intelligence network throughout the hemisphere." David Jackson, "Obama: Chavez Doesn't Pose Serious Threat to U.S.," *USA Today*, July 11, 2012.

31. Gaitán was assassinated before taking office; see chapter 12.

> Peruvians embrace the new religion;
> The Popular Alliance
> Will conquer our longed-for redemption![32]

APRA was not only identified as a religious movement during political meetings; when party members met, they greeted each other with the phrase "Only Aprismo will save Peru"—a slogan that also appeared on campaign posters. Haya de la Torre, steeped in a personal history of real as well as perceived sacrifice and persecution, took on an aura of martyrdom and sainthood, identifying political action with a call to the priesthood and political success with the ability to communicate a mystical sentiment. The religiosity of APRA was reinforced by biblical references in his speeches, as well as by a campaign song comparing the suffering and persecution of Apristas with that of the early Christians:

> Men who suffer
> A cruel pain
> Let us make
> APRA a legion.
> March! March!
> Brothers in pain!
> Fight! Fight!
> With the banner of love
> With faith and unity.[33]

In more economically developed nations such as Argentina, Brazil, and Mexico, populist presidents pursued nationalist and redistributive social policies that coincided with the period of import-substitution industrialization (ISI). Such was the fit between ISI and populism that widely used textbooks on Latin America explained ISI and populism as organically linked.[34] In chapter 6, Hector Schamis adopts this structuralist interpretation, interpreting the emergence of Argentine populism as a response to the Great Depression that was anchored in ISI. Peronism, he explains, was based on the rise of a new, urban industrial working class

32. Steve Stein, *Populism in Peru* (Madison: University of Wisconsin Press, 1980), 175.

33. Ibid., 178.

34. Thomas Skidmore and Peter Smith, *Modern Latin America* (Oxford: Oxford University Press, 1984, and subsequent editions).

and its alliance with a rising industrial bourgeoisie and the middle class against rural elites. Peronist policies were nationalist, redistributive, and inclusionary. Once the material foundation of the populist alliance was undermined in Argentina, Schamis argues, populism ceased to exist.

Schamis builds on modernization and dependency theories that, despite their different emphases, understood politics and societies as derivative of deeper social and economic processes.[35] Gino Germani, an Italian-born sociologist who moved to Argentina in the 1930s, is perhaps the most representative scholar of modernization theory; for him, populism was a phase in the history of Latin America, characterized by the social mobilization and political incorporation of previously excluded masses during the transition to modernity.[36] Germani's critics, working within a dependency paradigm, shared his view of populism as a stage closely tied to broader social and economic transformations. In dependency theory, however, populism was linked to the crisis of agro-export-led development and the emergence of ISI.[37] Hence, though dependency theory built on Marxist class categories, Germani emphasized modernization and mass society; both approaches shared a historicist view, in which populism constituted a phase in Latin American history, linked to structural social and economic processes such as ISI and modernization.

Not all scholars accepted a structuralist approach that viewed political phenomena as tied to and reflective of deeper economic trends. Researchers noted that the fit between ISI and populism was not that tidy, even in the major republics. The British historian and sociologist Ian Roxborough, for example, argued that whereas ISI began in Brazil before the 1930s, populist politics were not inaugurated until the late 1940s during Vargas's second term (1950–54).[38] Other scholars have

35. Kurt Weyland, "Clarifying a Contested Concept," *Comparative Politics* 34, no. 1 (2001): 8.

36. Germani emigrated from Italy to Argentina, following the rise of fascist leader Benito Mussolini. See esp. Gino Germani, *Autoritarismo, Fascismo y Populismo Nacional* (Buenos Aires: Temas, 2003), 43–70; and his biography by Ana Alejandra Germani, *Antifascism and Sociology: Gino Germani, 1911–1979* (New Brunswick, N.J.: Transaction Books, 2008).

37. Octavio Ianni, *La Formación del Estado Populista en América Latina* (Mexico City: ERA, 1975); Guillermo O'Donnell, *Modernization and Bureaucratic Authoritarianism* (Berkeley: University of California Press, 1973).

38. Ian Roxborough, "Unity and Diversity in Latin American History," *Journal of Latin American Studies* 16 (1984): 1–26.

noted that populism also emerged in agrarian contexts and that it was not necessarily tied to one particular set of economic policies. In Bolivia, Ecuador, and Peru, populism was not linked to ISI, even though, as in the industrializing republics, it occasioned the political inclusion of previously excluded electors. Many scholars felt uneasy with models of historical development that were based on generalizations about larger countries such as Argentina and Brazil, to the exclusion of the experiences of smaller nations.

In many countries, populist leaders built enduring political organizations, such as Peru's APRA, Bolivia's Movimiento Nacionalista Revolucionario (Nationalist Revolutionary Movement, MNR), and Argentina's Peronist party (formally, the Partido Justicialista). In other countries, leaders did not create or institutionalize formal parties, and electoral coalitions were assembled for different electoral contests. In chapter 2, Kenneth Roberts explains these different approaches to institution building in terms of the levels of polarization and confrontation provoked by different populist experiences.[39] In some cases, such as Argentina and Peru, the polarized construction of politics ends in a total and fundamental struggle or cleavage between "the people" and "the oligarchy." To sustain conflict with the elite, leaders needed to organize followers in political parties and in civil society organizations. In other experiences, such as that of Ecuador's Velasco Ibarra, there was political but not social polarization. The level of confrontation was not as intense in Ecuador, and Velasco Ibarra did not feel impelled to create formal political and social organizations.

Populist leaders both repressed and co-opted existing labor groups. The Brazilian case is illustrative in this regard. Under the Estado Novo (1937–45), repression was replaced by co-optation. As Leslie Bethell explains,

> Unions lacked autonomy and were subordinate to the state; workers were not permitted to engage in political activity, nor to strike. On the other hand, unions were legally recognized, union leaders had some (limited) political influence, and wage increases and social welfare benefits (pensions, medical care, etc.) were extended to increasing numbers of industrial workers, civil servants, and their dependents.

39. See also Kenneth Roberts, "Populism, Political Conflict, and Grass-Roots Organization in Latin America," *Comparative Politics* 38, no. 2 (2006): 127–48.

As pressure for political "democratization" increased toward the end of World War II, the Estado Novo moved from co-optation to mobilization. *Trabalhismo* was invented by a regime that began to recognize the future *political* potential of organized labor. State propaganda increasingly emphasized the economic and social gains made by workers under the Estado Novo and projected Vargas as "*o pai dos pobres*" (the father of the poor).

Social historians have shown that workers strategically used populist political openings to press autonomous demands against specific bosses and elites. The labor historian Joel Wolfe describes a form of workers' populism under Vargas.[40] Similarly, Daniel James shows how Argentine workers used the Peronist opening and discourse to attack the symbols of their exclusion from the public sphere and to demand their recognition as workers and citizens. He describes how, in Perón's name, workers in 1945 burned newspapers, attacked the clubs of the elites, and simultaneously occupied urban spaces such as main plazas from which they had previously been excluded.[41]

Most studies of populism have argued that it emerges in times of crisis. Modernization theorists focus on the crisis occasioned by the transition to modernity, and dependency theorists emphasize the crisis of agro-export-led development and the rise of ISI. Kenneth Roberts, building on the notion of "critical juncture" put forward by the political scientists Ruth Berins Collier and David Collier, has written the most systematic study of the social conditions that produce populism.[42] In chapter 2, Roberts defines critical junctures as "periods of decisive political change and uncertainty, when established institutional arrangements begin to erode and a range of different outcomes become viable possibilities." At the critical juncture that led to the activation and incorporation of workers, peasants, and the middle class, strong institutions and long-lasting political parties were created. In several countries, this period coincided with a state-centric development model.

40. Joel Wolfe, "'Father of the Poor' or 'Mother of the Rich'? Getúlio Vargas, Industrial Workers, and Constructions of Class, Gender, and Populism in São Paulo, 1930–1954," *Radical History Review* 58, no. 80 (1994): 102–3.

41. Daniel James, "October Seventeenth and Eighteenth, 1945: Mass Protest, Peronism, and the Argentinean Working Class," *Journal of Social History*, Spring 1988, 441–61.

42. Ruth Berins Collier and David Collier, *Shaping the Political Arena* (Princeton, N.J.: Princeton University Press, 1991).

Although Roberts rightly identifies different critical junctures in which populism emerges, it is also true that populism has arisen in Latin America during "noncritical junctures" not marked by crises. Whenever populist leaders have been allowed to participate in elections in countries such as Argentina, Bolivia, Peru, Ecuador, and Venezuela, they have acquired significant followings and/or won elections. Indeed, the British historian Alan Knight has emphasized the degree to which populism is not an extraordinary phenomenon linked to crises but rather one that can emerge in periods of apparent normalcy.[43]

Military populism constitutes a classical variant that warrants further study.[44] In chapter 8, McClintock analyzes the military reformism of General Juan Velasco Alvarado (1968–75), who spearheaded fundamental structural transformations in Peru, including a sweeping agrarian reform. McClintock argues that, like classical populists, Velasco Alvarado divided Peruvians between the people and the oligarchy, favored ISI policies, and proclaimed "fully participatory social democracy" as an alternative to liberal democracy.[45]

Even though national populist regimes were democratizing insofar as they incorporated previously excluded masses into political life, Gino Germani and others have called attention to these regimes' authoritarian traits. Referring in part to the precedent of Benito Mussolini's Italy, Germani observed that "the political incorporation of the popular masses started under totalitarianism. It gave workers an experience of political and social participation in their personal lives, annulling at the same time political organizations and the basic rights that are the pillars for any genuine democracy."[46]

As Enrique Peruzzotti argues in chapter 3, classical populists equated democracy with free elections. Hector Schamis indicates in chapter 6, for example, that women in Argentina were granted political rights and voter turnout grew from 18 to 50 percent of the population during the first Perón government. However, Peruzzotti argues that this model of democracy, though inclusionary, was at odds with notions of account-

---

43. Knight, "Populism and Neopopulism," 227.

44. Michael Conniff, "Neopopulismo en América Latina: La década de los noventa y después," *Revista de Ciencia Política* 22, no. 1 (2003): 35–37.

45. Chávez, who visited Peru under Velasco Alvarado, was deeply influenced by its model of participatory democracy. See Bart Jones, *Hugo!* (Hanover, N.H.: Steerforth Press, 2007).

46. Gino Germani, *Política y Sociedad en una Época de Transición* (Buenos Aires: Paidós, 1962), 337.

ability and the divisions of powers and bypassed mechanisms of checks and balances. As Peruzzotti indicates, "the popularly elected president appears as the institutional power that directly expresses the democratic will of the people, while the legislative and judicial powers symbolize constitutional constraints on the majority." One of the principal legacies of classical populism was its deep ambivalence toward liberal democracy. That is, classical populism was democratizing to the extent that previously excluded groups were brought into the political system; at the same time, however, populist leaders refused to accept the constraints and limitations of liberal constitutional principles that served to constrain state power, guarantee the political autonomy of civil society, and assure pluralism.

Neoliberal Neopopulism

If structuralist approaches to populism had possessed fully predictive powers, populism would have ended following the military dictatorships of the 1970s: The bureaucratic-authoritarian military regimes that took power in the Southern Cone dismantled the social and economic foundations of populism—ISI, the industrial bourgeoisie, and working-class organizations. Yet, as Bethell indicates, with the "third wave" of democratization, old populists such as Leonel Brizola became governor of the state of Rio de Janeiro in 1982 and again in 1990, and Jânio Quadros became major of São Paulo in 1985. Traditional populist parties, such as the Concentración de Fuerzas Populares in Ecuador, won the first democratic election in 1979, and President Alan García of Peru's APRA was elected in a landslide in 1985.

Most intriguingly, a new generation of politicians such as Alberto Fujimori in Peru, Fernando Collor de Mello in Brazil, Carlos Menem in Argentina, and Abdalá Bucaram in Ecuador adopted the strategies, symbols, and discourses of their populist predecessors while implementing neoliberal economic policies that reduced the role of the state in the economy in favor of the free market. To make sense of the continuities and differences between classical and new populists, U.S. and Latin American scholars coined the term "neopopulism."[47] To explain the re-

47. José Nun, "Populismo, representación, y menemismo," *Sociedad* 5 (1994): 93–121; Marcos Navaro, *Pilotos de Tormentas. Crisis de representación y personal-*

emergence of populism in neoliberal contexts, and to account for the synergies between neoliberalism and populism, scholars decoupled politics and economics, focusing on the political characteristics of populism without linking it to specific historical periods or particular social and economic policies. Kurt Weyland, for example, redefined populism "as a political strategy through which a personalistic leader seeks or exercises government power based on direct, unmediated, uninstitutionalized support from large numbers of mostly unorganized followers."[48] Theorists underscored the centrality of the competition for and exercise of power—not social and economic processes—as the defining element of populist politicians. Rather than hewing to any particular political ideology, populists were pragmatic as well as opportunistic in their quest to retain power.

Scholars bitterly contested the concept of neopopulism. Arguing that populism was a redistributive and democratizing force, many scholars rejected the notion that populism was a concept that could apply to neoliberal, right-wing politicians who slashed social spending, thereby undermining democracy in their nations.[49] Structuralists such as Schamis argued that the "conceptual stretching" of the definition of populism to include neoliberal presidents caused problems of theoretical and conceptual consistency.[50] Political theorists responded at two levels. At the theoretical level, they argued that instead of understanding politics as derivative of socioeconomic processes, it was more fruitful to explore how the economy and politics were related in different historical periods. At the empirical and historical level, these scholars demonstrated the extent to which structuralist approaches exaggerated the redistributive face of classical populism. Perón, for example, followed both expansion-

ización de la política en Argentina 1989–1993 (Santo Dumont, Argentina: Letra Buena, 1994); Roberts, "Neoliberalism and the Transformation of Populism"; Kurt Weyland, "Neopopulism and Neoliberalism in Latin America: Unexpected Affinities," *Studies in Comparative International Development* 35, no. 1 (1996): 3–31; Knight, "Populism and Neopopulism."

48. Weyland, "Clarifying a Contested Concept," 14.

49. Nicolás Lynch, "El Neopopulismo: Un Concepto Vacío," *Socialismo y Participación* 86 (December 1999): 63–80; Aníbal Quijano, "Populismo y fujimorismo," in *El fantasma del populismo: Aproximación a un tema [siempre] actual*, edited by Felipe Burbano (Caracas: Nueva Sociedad, 1998), 171–207.

50. Hector Schamis, "Populism, Socialism, and Democratic Institutions," in *Latin America's Struggle for Democracy*, edited by Larry Diamond, Marc Plattner, and Diego Abente (Baltimore: Johns Hopkins University Press, 2008), 60–61.

ary and conservative monetarist policies at different moments of his tenure. Scholars underscored the problems inherent in associating or reducing populism to its social and economic policy dimensions and highlighted the advantages for comparative analysis of a definition rooted in the consideration of politics or political economy.[51]

For example, Kenneth Roberts shows that neopopulism emerged out of a new critical conjuncture linked to the crises of ISI and to the crises of political party representation in the final decades of the twentieth century. During this neoliberal critical conjuncture, parties were undermined by the severity of economic crises, the weakening of labor unions, and the embrace by many parties—including populist ones—of the neoliberal credo. Under neopopulism, which was as polarizing as its classical predecessor, political parties and elites were portrayed not only as out of touch with the needs and desires of the electorate but also as enemies of "the people." The leaders who emerged were antiparty and antiestablishment. Leaders such as Carlos Menem in Argentina (and later, Álvaro Uribe in Colombia) had made their careers within political parties; subsequently, they denied their links to parties, condemning them as corrupt and inept, and they created new, personalistic electoral vehicles. This "politics of antipolitics" was nourished by broad popular dissatisfaction with rampant hyperinflation (caused in part by the failure of ISI), bloated and inefficient states, the privileges and reach of corrupt special interests, and, as the Peruvian case indicates, by the profound security crisis of the 1980s. Left-wing and center-left parties that were linked to the old regime fell into disrepute. A new wave of politicians, backed by a technocratic elite enjoying the support and encouragement of the international financial institutions based in Washington, embraced neoliberalism as the panacea for the economic ills of their country and the region.

Neoliberal neopopulists met with differing degrees of success in exercising and holding onto power. Abdalá Bucaram in Ecuador lasted scarcely six months; lacking an institutional base, he was removed by the Congress on the dubious legal grounds that he was mentally incapable of governing.[52] Collor de Mello similarly had a weak support base in the legislature and, as Leslie Bethell indicates, could not survive corruption

51. Kurt Weyland, "Neopopulism and Neoliberalism in Latin America: How Much Affinity?" *Third World Quarterly*, 2003, 1095–1116.
52. De la Torre, *Populist Seduction*, chap. 3.

scandals. By contrast, Carlos Menem and Alberto Fujimori were both reelected to second terms. Their success is explained by the populist politics of patronage and clientelism financed by the privatization of state-owned enterprises. Ultimately, the Fujimori regime collapsed under the weight of scandals related to corruption and electoral fraud (he is currently serving time in a Peruvian prison for his involvement in corruption and human rights abuses).[53] And Menem's quest for a third term was ruled unconstitutional; many blame his policies for plunging Argentina into the severest economic crisis of its modern history, which brought the country to the brink of financial collapse in 2001–2.

Neopopulist leaders had a variety of effects on democratization in their respective countries. In Bolivia, the neopopulist challengers of Conciencia de Patria (Conscience of the Homeland), led by the radio talk host Carlos Palenque, and the Unión Cívica Solidaridad (Civic Solidarity Union) of the beer magnate Max Fernández were absorbed by the party system; some argue that these parties contributed to the democratization of Bolivia.[54] Under Menem, the transformation of Peronist identity from an antagonistic opposition between the people and the oligarchy into a more amorphous and less confrontational version with broader appeal made neopopulism,[55] in Kurt Weyland's view, "more representative than classical populism and more compatible with liberal democracy."[56] Elsewhere, as in Fujimori's Peru, Cynthia McClintock shows how liberal democratic institutions were attacked and destroyed. Fujimori "denounced members of Congress as 'unproductive charlatans,' Congress as a 'large, heavy, thick-skinned pachyderm,' and judges as 'jackals.' Just like Velasco, Fujimori belittled not only existing political parties but also the concept of parties; they were '*palabrería*' (all talk and no action)."

Without characterizing these regimes as a variant of populism, Guillermo O'Donnell coined the term "delegative democracy" to refer

53. See Carlos Basombrío, "Peace in Peru, but Unresolved Tasks," in *In the Wake of War: Democratization and Internal Armed Conflict in Latin America*, edited by Cynthia J. Arnson (Washington, D.C., and Palo Alto, Calif.: Woodrow Wilson Center Press and Stanford University Press, 2012), 215–38.

54. Fernando Mayorga, *Neopopulismo y Democracia: Compadres y Padrinos en la política boliviana, 1988–1999* (Cochabamba, Bolivia: CESU-UMSS, 2002).

55. Marcos Novaro, "Populismo y gobierno: Las transformaciones en el peronismo y la consolidación democrática argentina," in *Fantasma del populismo*, ed. Burbano, 25–49.

56. Weyland, "Clarifying a Contested Concept," 16.

to their particular blend of authoritarian and democratizing traits.[57] In O'Donnell's view, delegative democracies do not respect civil rights and democratic procedures. They are based on the idea that whoever wins an election has the popular mandate to govern according to his or her interpretation of the people's will and interests, constrained not by institutions but by raw power relations. The president's policies are unconnected to promises made during the campaign or to the agreements made with organizations and associations who supported his or her election. According to O'Donnell, "the president is taken to be the embodiment of the nation and the main custodian and definer of its interests."[58] To "save the country" in the context of economic crises that constrain the institutionalization of democracy, he or she looks for neoliberal technocrats who can design and implement the required economic therapy. Because the government needs to rescue the nation from crisis, its actions do not always respect democratic institutions and procedures or compromises with the opposition.

In chapter 3, Enrique Peruzzotti argues that delegative democracy differs from classical populism in that the mobilization of the popular sector, a crucial component of classical populism, is absent. Delegative democracies tend to be characterized by significant levels of political apathy; by contrast, when corruption scandals eroded the image and standing of neopopulist presidents in Brazil, Ecuador, and Peru, citizens took to the streets to demand the presidents' resignations. Peruzzotti also argues that delegative democracy is associated with countries that experienced transitions from repressive bureaucratic authoritarian rule; hence, citizens value human and civil rights, constitutional procedures, and pluralism. By contrast, populism, not delegative democracy, is more associated with countries such as Venezuela and Ecuador that did not experience the same periods of democratic breakdown as their Southern Cone neighbors.

Political theories of populism correctly emphasize the lack of institutions that mediate between leaders and followers but also tend to exaggerate followers' lack of autonomous organizational capacity. Ethnographic research on poor people who work in the informal sector has demonstrated that they create organizations with strategic capacities to

57. Guillermo O'Donnell, "Delegative Democracy," *Journal of Democracy* 4, no. 1 (1994): 55–69.
58. Ibid., 59–60.

negotiate with the state and with political parties.[59] Populist parties and movements are organized through clientelistic, informal networks that distribute resources, information, and jobs to the poor.[60] Studies of political clientelism, for example, demonstrated that poor people voted instrumentally for the candidate with the best capacity to deliver goods and services.[61] Others have argued that clientelist exchanges are not based solely on instrumental rationality; they also generate identities.

Kenneth Roberts argues that when political parties decomposed during the neoliberal critical juncture of the final decades of the twentieth century, serial populism emerged in Peru and Ecuador until the advent of Rafael Correa. (In chapter 8, McClintock concurs regarding serial populism in Peru.) Roberts writes that these two countries have witnessed a "cycling of dominant personalities in highly fluid competitive arenas that were structured neither by party institutions nor by a central pragmatic divide." In Peru, leaders as diverse as Alberto Fujimori, Alejandro Toledo, Ollanta Humala, and Keiko Fujimori have used populist rhetoric and strategies to rally support. In Ecuador, Montúfar argues that Bucaram and Lucío Gutiérrez constitute examples of failed neoliberal neopopulism, given that they could not complete their terms.

In analyzing the Colombian case in chapter 12, Ana María Bejarano highlights Álvaro Uribe's politicization of the country's security crisis, employing tactics potentially appealing to would-be right-wing populists in other national contexts. Unlike other cases in which socioeconomic or political exclusion gave rise to populist mobilization, under Uribe, "insecurity became the main axis of polarization within society and the cen-

59. Javier Auyero, *Poor People's Politics* (Durham, N.C.: Duke University Press, 2001); John Cross, *Informal Politics: Street Vendors and the State in Mexico City* (Stanford, Calif: Stanford University Press, 1998); Patricia Fernández-Kelly and Jon Shefner, eds., *Out of the Shadows: Political Action and the Informal Economy in Latin America* (University Park: Pennsylvania State University Press, 2006); Sian Lazar, *El Alto, Rebel City: Self and Citizenship in Andean Bolivia* (Durham, N.C.: Duke University Press, 2008).

60. Auyero, *Poor People's Politics*; Amparo Menéndez-Carrión, *La Conquista del Voto* (Quito: Corporación Editora Nacional, 1986); Steven Levitsky, "An 'Organized Disorganization': Informal Organization and the Persistence of Local Party Structures in Argentine Peronism," *Journal of Latin American Studies* 33 (2001): 29–65; Flavia Freidenberg and Steven Levitsky, "Informal Institutions and Party Organizations in Latin America," in *Informal Institutions and Democracy: Lessons from Latin America*, edited by Gretchen Helmke and Steven Levitsky (Baltimore: Johns Hopkins University Press, 2006), 178–201.

61. Menéndez-Carrión, *La Conquista del Voto*.

tral issue around which new political loyalties came to be articulated." The politicization of citizens' legitimate fears was part of a strategy to achieve, concentrate, and attempt to retain power. Uribe's discourse drew from the populist tool kit, polarizing Colombia by identifying political opponents and groups in civil society as terrorists or terrorist sympathizers and by using illegal means to spy on critics, including opposition politicians, Supreme Court magistrates, nongovernmental organizations, and journalists. In Colombia, however, and unlike in other Andean nations, strong institutions constrained Uribe's ambitions; the Constitutional Court ruled his third bid for office unconstitutional, and he was unable to run for a third consecutive term.

Radical Populism and the Refounding of the Nation

As the chapters by Margarita López Maya and Alexandra Panzarelli, John Crabtree, and César Montúfar illustrate, Chávez, Morales, and Correa share with each other, and with earlier populist manifestations in Latin America, the use of a Manichaean discourse of confrontation between the people and the oligarchy. To greater or lesser degrees, their speech politicizes relations of class and ethnic inequality, polarizes their respective societies, and transforms politics into struggles over higher moral values. The continuous activation of common people in elections and plebiscites and the attacks on elites in the name of "the people" allow supporters of these regimes to feel that they are living in a revolutionary moment and writing new chapters in history. This environment forces people to take sides and reduces the space for skeptical bystanders. Society becomes polarized and simplified into two antagonistic blocs: the camps of history and antihistory, of the people and their leader against the enemies of the homeland.

Montúfar and López Maya and Panzarelli argue that to achieve these transformations, Chávez, Correa, and Morales employ two strategies: (1) the use of permanent campaigns and other communication strategies to link leaders with citizens, bypassing existing institutional channels; and (2) direct transfers or subsidies to the poor, provided in a clientelistic fashion and linked to government windfalls from high commodity prices. (As John Crabtree indicates, however, referenda and *consultas* (consultations) were common in Bolivia in the several years preceding Morales's presidency.) Permanent campaigning, according to Montúfar, signifies that the administrative acts of governing are fused with political marketing that goes beyond the public relations strategies employed by virtually all governments. Elections are used as strategies to displace the *partidocracia*, manufacture enemies (political parties, the privately owned media, imperialism, etc.), and ratify in plebiscitary fashion the president's continuing efforts to combat enemies, both domestic and foreign.[62] Characteristic of this process is the restriction of rights of opponents to compete on a level playing field. In a feature shared with classical populism and delegative democracy, the vote—understood as the voice of the sovereign people—becomes the embodiment of the democratic act. Issues of democratic accountability, the separation of powers, and checks and balances become secondary or wholly nonexistent.

In places such as Ecuador, experts in communications occupy important positions in the government. Like right-wing neopopulists such as Fujimori, radical populists in Venezuela and Ecuador have aimed to control the media, regulating content, nationalizing privately owned outlets, and harassing and attempting to discredit prominent journalists.[63] The attacks on media freedoms represent blatant attempts to control the public sphere by restricting the free flow of ideas critical to an informed citizenry.

Chávez's television show *Aló Presidente* (Hello, Mr. President) and Rafael Correa's show *Enlaces Cuidadanos* (Citizens' Ties) have aimed to enhance the charisma of a president who talks directly and without intermediaries to citizens. Morales is an important exception in this regard, because Bolivia has no television show comparable to the ones in Venezuela and Ecuador.[64] Unlike town halls or other gatherings in which politicians engage directly with constituents, the presidential media programs in Venezuela and Ecuador serve to reinforce the vertical, hierarchical linkage between leader and subject, in the absence of other more

62. The term *partidocracia,* which has no precise English translation, is a pejorative one which connotes a political system that, though in theory democratic, is dominated by self-interested or corrupt party elites who act on behalf of their party rather than the constituents they are supposed to represent. The behavior of such elites is understood to be an important source of popular dissatisfaction with democracy overall.

63. Catherine Conaghan, *Fujimori's Peru: Deception in the Public Sphere* (Pittsburgh: University of Pittsburgh Press, 2005).

64. Laurence Whitehead, "Conclusion: Bolivia's Latest 'Refoundation,'" in *Unresolved Tensions: Bolivia Past and Present*, edited by John Crabtree and Laurence Whitehead (Pittsburgh: University of Pittsburgh Press, 2008), 259.

institutionalized forms of communication and exchange. In discussing the Colombian case, Ana María Bejarano argues that Uribe's Consejos Comunales de Gobierno (Communal Councils of Government) also served "to create and recreate the illusion of a direct link between the president and the local communities."

Venezuela, Bolivia, and Ecuador have increased the direct transfer of subsidies to the poor, benefiting from high commodity prices to expand social programs. In Venezuela, World Bank figures indicate that the poverty rate fell from 55.4 percent of the population in 2002 to 28.5 percent in 2009.[65] Poverty in Ecuador fell more modestly, from 37 percent in 2006 to 32.8 percent in 2010.[66] The data available for Bolivia show that the poverty rate dropped from 60 percent in 2006 to 50.6 percent in 2009, with an even greater decrease in levels of extreme poverty.[67] Montúfar shows how Correa spent more in his first three years in office than governments during the entire decade of the 1990s, and more than his immediate predecessors during the six-year period between 2000 and 2006; the 2010 budget alone represented an increase of 29 percent. The goal of these policies, he argues, is to consolidate a "clientelistic base of support."

In Bolivia, revenues from the hydrocarbons sector have financed social transfer programs for school-age children (Bono Juancito Pinto) and the elderly (Renta Dignidad), accounting for approximately 2 percent of Bolivian gross domestic product in 2007.[68] The political scientist Javier Corrales has indicated that per capita social spending in Venezuela increased 314 percent between 1998 and 2006.[69] Yet, as Weyland argues in chapter 5, these social programs would suffer from problems of qual-

65. World Bank, "Poverty Headcount Ratio at National Poverty Line (% of Population), 2001," data retrieved from World Development Indicators Database, http://data.worldbank.org/indicator/SI.POV.NAHC/countries/VE?display=graph. For an analysis of trends in poverty and inequality under leftist governments in Latin America, see also Lustig, "Poverty, Inequality and the New Left"; and Lustig and McLeod, "Are Latin America's New Left Regimes Reducing Inequality Faster?"

66. World Bank, "Poverty Headcount Ratio"; see also Juan Ponce and Alberto Acosta, "¿Pobreza en la Revolución Ciudadana O pobreza de revolución?" *Ecuador Debate* 81 (December, 2010): 7–20.

67. The data are from Bolivia's Unidad de Análisis de Políticas Sociales y Económicas, http://www.udape.gob.bo/index.php?option=com_wrapper&view=wrapper&Itemid=104.

68. George Gray Molina, "The Challenge of Progressive Change under Morales," in *Leftist Governments*, ed. Weyland, Madrid, and Hunter, 66.

69. Javier Corrales, "The Repeating Revolution: Chávez's New Politics and Old Economics," in *Leftist Governments*, ed. Weyland, Madrid, and Hunter, 45.

ity, efficiency, and long-term sustainability if commodity rents were to diminish.

Democracy as understood and practiced by Chávez, Correa, and Morales bears little if any resemblance to the liberal republican tradition. Crabtree argues that although aspects of direct democracy were in place in Bolivia before Morales's election, the Movimiento al Socialismo has seen itself "as building a political system that supplanted what it saw as a corrupted system of liberal democracy." Strong communitarian traditions have persisted, Crabtee indicates, "with problems discussed and decisions taken collectively." Morales adheres to these long-standing traditions when he consults with the leaders of social movements on policy issues ranging from education to the regulation of coca cultivation and social security.[70]

For some, Bolivia represents a democracy of social movements.[71] Other scholars have contested the extent to which these consultations signify broad participation in shaping outcomes or simply reflect Morales's attempt to impose his own criteria. Critics charge that the regime uses its followers to intimidate the opposition through mass rallies and other forms of collective action. According to the scholar of indigenous movements Donna Lee Van Cott, "Morales's political vision, and his party's, emphasizes economic equality and popular power at the expense of oppositional rights and the rule of law."[72] In this same vein, others maintain that Morales has failed to respect the rule of law or the independence of the judiciary.[73] Indeed, as Crabtree indicates, during Morales's second term, when the government also controlled both houses of Congress, an antagonistic discourse toward real or imagined enemies—traditional political parties, elites of the "*media luna*" in the eastern part of the country, and the U.S. government—shrunk "the spaces for active opposition" even further.

Unlike Morales, who must constantly negotiate and connect with powerful bottom-up influences, Rafael Correa is leading what César

70. Álvaro García Linera, *Biografía Política e Intelectual: Conversaciones con Pablos Stefanoni, Franklin Ramírez y Maritsella Svampa* (La Paz: Le Monde Diplomatique, 2009), 90.

71. Ibid.

72. Donna Lee Van Cott, "Indigenous Movements Lost Momentum," *Current History* 108, no. 715 (2009): 85.

73. Franz Xavier Barrios, "The Weakness of Excess: The Bolivian State in an Unbounded Democracy," in *Unresolved Tensions*, ed. Crabtree and Whitehead, 125–41.

Montúfar calls "a revolution from above, a revolution created by the executive branch." Correa's regime is more technocratic than participatory, and his Alianza País lacks organic ties to any social sector. Correa understands democracy in substantive terms as the provision of social justice. In an address in Oxford, he distinguished formal democracy—understood as the right to vote—from real democracy, based on "equity, justice, and dignity" and the "rights to education, health, and housing."[74] Downplaying or ignoring liberal democratic principles such as pluralism, civil rights, and the separation of powers, he declared in a speech in Havana that Cuba constitutes an example of real democracy and human rights. The Cuban Revolution "is extraordinary," he said,

> because it secured the reestablishment of human rights for all Cuban men and women. It is the recognition that the first constitutional right of all human beings is their full dignity.[75]

As Montúfar indicates, Correa has eroded the independence of other branches of government, aggressively concentrated power in the executive branch, and increasingly personalized the political arena.

If Morales's style of government includes strong participatory elements and Correa's is top-down, Chávez's was somewhere in the middle. In chapter 9, Margarita López Maya and Alexandra Panzarelli distinguish three phases in Chávez's effort to organize the poor through models of participatory democracy. The first phase was marked by the organization of supporters around Chávez's charismatic leadership and the failure of efforts to organize a political party. During the second phase, between 1999 and 2007, the regime created a series of participatory institutions aimed at defending Chávez, generating enthusiasm "from below," and contributing to the president's legitimacy among the poor. After 2007, the regime made a more concerted and explicit effort to build a socialist democracy; hence, participatory democracy has become more top-down and clientelistic.

Despite similarities, the regimes of Chávez, Correa, and Morales differ in important ways, particularly with respect to the political autonomy

74. Rafael Correa, "Experiencia de un Cristiano de Izquierda en un Mundo secular," Oxford Union Society, October 26, 2009.

75. Digital Granma internacional, January 9, 2009, http://www.granma.cubaweb.cu/2009/01/09/nacional/artic10.html.

of social movements and the independence of civil society from the state. In Venezuela in the 1980s, scholars have argued, middle-class citizens organized neighborhood associations that excluded the poor; these groups adopted an explicitly anti-Chávez agenda, and some went so far as to support an attempted coup against Chávez in 2002.[76] Lopéz Maya and Panzarelli describe how Chávez responded by organizing the poorer members of civil society from the top down, through new organizations such as the Bolivarian Circles, the Electoral Battalions, and, later, the Communal Councils. These groups were mobilized during electoral periods and took an active role in rescuing Chávez from the attempted coup in 2002. It is an open question as to whether these groups created "from above" can or do act autonomously of Chávez or how they would function in the aftermath of a Chávez presidency.

In chapter 10, John Crabtree demonstrates how powerful working-class union and indigenous organizations elected Morales as the first indigenous head of state since the Spanish conquest.[77] The Morales regime has given symbolic and institutional empowerment to indigenous organizations, appealing to the hope and promise of overcoming the legacies of centuries-old colonialism. As the anthropologist Nancy Postero describes,

On January 21, [2006], Morales participated in a popular ceremony at Tiwanaku, a pre-Inca site near La Paz, where, after walking barefoot over coca leaves, he was blessed by Andean religious leaders and recognized as the Apamallku, the highest indigenous authority. To the thousands of admirers shivering in the freezing Altiplano morning, he declared, "a new millennium has arrived for the original peoples of the world."[78]

76. María Pilar García-Guadilla, "Civil Society: Institutionalization, Fragmentation, Autonomy," in *Venezuelan Politics in the Chávez Era: Class, Polarization, and Conflict*, edited by Steve Ellner and Daniel Hellinger (Boulder, Colo.: Lynne Rienner, 2003), 179–97; Margarita López Maya, *Del viernes negro al referendo revocatorio* (Caracas: Alfadil, 2005).

77. See also Raúl Madrid, "The Rise of Ethnopopulism in Latin America," *World Politics* 60, no. 3 (2008): 475–509; Forrest Hylton and Sinclair Thompson, *Revolutionary Horizons: Past and Present in Bolivian Politics* (London: Verso, 2007); and Pablo Stefanoni and Herve do Alto, *La Revolución De Evo Morales: De La Coca Al Palacio* (Buenos Aires: Capital Intelectual, 2005).

78. Nancy Postero, "Morales's MAS Government: Building Indigenous Popular Hegemony in Bolivia," *Latin American Perspectives* 37, no. 3 (2010): 18.

Simultaneously, however, within the government's erstwhile support base, regionally based, powerful elites have built organizations and movements with which Morales must negotiate. As a result, in Morales's Bolivia, there is more conflict but also more negotiation between the regime and social movements.[79] Crabtree argues that Morales's "extraordinary legitimacy" is at times directly challenged by the power of the social movements that sustain him politically.

In chapter 11, César Montúfar illustrates the degree to which Ecuador differs from Bolivia with respect to the relationship between the government and social movements. Rather than creating new participatory spaces or enhancing longstanding ones, Correa has tried to exclude and dismantle the genuinely participatory spaces of indigenous groups.[80] Correa came to power after the indigenous movement—the most powerful in the Americas during the 1990s—entered into a crisis. Correa was the ultimate political outsider, without a party or base in social movements, and has constituted Alianza País as an efficient apparatus for proselytizing and organizing elections; in so doing, however, he has struggled simultaneously against both conservative opponents of the regime and organized social movements of indigenous peoples, teachers, students, civil servants, and environmental groups. In advancing a "citizen's revolution," his regime has attempted to replace independent social movements with top-down organizations loyal to the president.

Historically, populist leaders have undermined the autonomy of civil society and thus the possibility that independent forms of citizenship would thrive.[81] As noted above, classical as well as radical populists

---

79. Molina, "Challenge of Progressive Change."

80. Mark Becker, ¡Pachakutick! Indigenous Movements and Electoral Politics in Ecuador (New York: Rowman & Littlefield, 2011), 103–213; Carmen Martínez Novo, "The Indigenous Movement and the Citizen's Revolution in Ecuador: Advances, Ambiguities, and Turn Backs," unpublished paper delivered at the conference "Outlook for Indigenous Politics in the Andean Region," Center for Strategic and International Studies, Washington, 2009; Pablo Ospina, "Corporativismo, Estado y Revolución Ciudadana: El Ecuador de Rafael Correa," unpublished manuscript.

81. Phillip Oxhorn, "The Social Foundation of Latin America's Recurrent Populism: Problems of Popular Sector Class Formation and Collective Action," Journal of Historical Sociology 11, no. 2 (1998): 212–46; and Phillip Oxhorn, "Beyond Neoliberalism? Latin America's New Crossroads," in Beyond Neoliberalism in Latin America: Societies and Politics at a Crossroads, edited by John Burdick, Kenneth Roberts, and Philip Oxhorn (New York: Palgrave Macmillan, 2009), 217–33.

equated citizenship with social rights and directed social programs to loyal supporters. Venezuela and Ecuador are continuing down the path forged by their predecessors, undermining the organizational spaces for autonomous citizenship. In Bolivia, the empowerment of indigenous peoples and the strength of social movements may allow for a novel form of pluricultural citizenship that recognizes indigenous legal frameworks and codes of justice. Yet conflicts continue in the arena of natural resource extraction between the state and the indigenous population living in areas of actual or potential commodity exploitation.[82]

In Bolivia, as Crabtree argues, social movements might be able to counter the authoritarian temptation to concentrate power in the hands of Morales. López Maya, Panzarelli, and Montúfar show that in Venezuela and Ecuador, new populist caudillos of the twenty-first century are concentrating power in their own hands and are undermining both the separation of powers as well as the institutional spaces that guarantee civil society's autonomy from the state. If under neoliberalism the market penetrated and weakened a fragile civil society, under twenty-first-century socialism, the state attempts to control or co-opt social movements. In Venezuela and Ecuador, and to a lesser extent in Bolivia, citizens' rights to form independent political associations or organizations and to express themselves without fear of reprisal are being undermined and attacked at the same time that press and media freedoms are being curtailed.

Populism and Democracy

As the discussion above indicates, disputes over the meaning of populism are closely intertwined with debates over the meaning of democracy.[83] Viewed through a liberal lens, populism and democracy are incompatible and antagonistic.[84] Gino Germani was one of the first to analyze Peronism as a form of working-class authoritarianism; in later years, Fujimori and Chávez have been portrayed as examples of competitive

---

82. Anthony Bebbington, "The New Extraction: Rewriting the Political Ecology of the Andes?" *NACLA Report of the Americas*, September–October 2009, 12–20.

83. Nadia Urbinati, "Democracy and Populism," *Constellations* 5, no. 1 (1998): 116.

84. Koen Abts and Stefan Rummens, "Populism versus Democracy," *Political Studies* 55 (2007): 405–24.

authoritarianism.[85] Describing Venezuela, for example, the political scientist Javier Corrales wrote:

The executive branch has concentrated power, eroded the autonomy of checks and balances, reduced press freedoms, imposed costs on actors situated in the opposition, showing little interest in guaranteeing pluralism.[86]

But viewing populism as a form of authoritarianism has its limits; such criticism is based on an idealized notion of liberal democracy, cannot explain rising levels of popular satisfaction with democracy in nations such as Venezuela,[87] and does not take into account the sheer numbers of people who have found new forms of political expression through participatory institutions created by the regime.[88]

Rather than arguing that the logic of populism is inherently antidemocratic, it is more fruitful to analyze its ambiguous relationship with democratization. As Francisco Panizza argues in chapter 4, the relationship between populism and democracy cannot be established in abstract terms but depends, rather, on the political context in which populism and democracy interact. The political theorist Margaret Canovan sustains that populism and democracy are closely related, emphasizing democracy's pragmatic as well as redemptive aspects:

From a pragmatic point of view, corresponding to the ordinary, everyday diversity of people-as-population, modern democracy is a complex set of institutions that allow us to coexist with other people and their divergent interests with as little coercion as possible. But democracy is also a repository of one of the redemptive visions (characteristic of modernity) that promises salvation through politics. The promised savior is "the people," a mysterious collectivity somehow composed of us, ordinary people, and yet capable of transfiguration

85. Steven Levitsky and Lucan A. Way, "The Rise of Competitive Authoritarianism," *Journal of Democracy* 13, no. 2 (2002): 51–65.

86. Corrales, "Repeating Revolution," 28.

87. See Corporación Latinobarómetro, Informe 2010, 26, http://www.infoamerica .org/primera/latinobarometro_2010.pdf.

88. See Ana María Sanjuán, "La esencia social de la revolución bolivariana en Venezuela: Una Mirada preliminar sobre sus fortalezas y debilidades," in *La "Nueva Izquierda,"* ed. Arnson et al., 131–62.

into an authoritative entity that can make dramatic and redeeming political appearances.[89]

Latin American populists have privileged a notion of democracy that is based more on the quasi-liturgical incorporation of common people through mass rallies than on the institutionalization of popular participation through the rule of law.[90] Because populist politicians claim to embody the people, and the people's will is not given institutional channels of expression, populist regimes have replaced traditional forms of political deliberation with plebiscitary acclamation.

As Peruzzotti indicates in chapter 3, however, Latin American populists also view expressions of popular sovereignty as taking place through elections.[91] Whereas classical populist leaders expanded the franchise, contemporary radical populists such as Chávez, Correa, and Morales use permanent political campaigns to both refound the nation and continually ratify their own rule. That is, once coming to power through electoral means, such leaders continually organize elections and referenda: for constituent assemblies to write new constitutions, for the approval of new constitutions, and for the election of public officials, including the president, typically under ever-more restrictive rules of the game. An electoral logic based on confrontation keeps alive the myth of a redeeming people struggling against local elites, imperialism, and other enemies. As a result—and as Germani forcefully argued decades ago—even though populism continues to mobilize and incorporate previously excluded populations, its understandings of sovereignty and participation deinstitutionalize democratic politics, at times even in the name of creating new and better participatory institutions. The chapters that follow elucidate this central tension in contemporary Latin American politics: between, on the one hand, mediated, institutionalized competition, and, on the other, politics ultimately centered on the plebiscitary acclamation of a caudillo.

---

89. Margaret Canovan, *The People* (Cambridge: Polity Press, 2005), 89–90.

90. De la Torre, *Populist Seduction.*

91. Enrique Peruzzotti, "Populismo y representación democrática," in *El retorno del pueblo: El populismo y nuevas democracias en América Latina,* edited by Carlos de la Torre and Enrique Peruzzotti (Quito: FLACSO, 2008), 97–125.

Chapter 2

Parties and Populism in Latin America

Kenneth M. Roberts

Since the onset of mass politics in early-twentieth-century Latin America, populism has exerted a transforming effect on party systems and political representation. Populism has contributed to the breakdown of party systems in some countries, the realignment of political competition in others, and the recomposition of party systems in a number of cases. It has brought new voters into the political arena, shifted the political loyalties of old ones, and altered the associational bases of civil society. Populism has created new social and political cleavages, and it has forged new patterns of linkage between parties, citizens, and social actors. Much of what we recognize in the political landscape of Latin America can traced to the impact of populist movements.

Clearly, populism's political effects are highly varied, and they are often unpredictable. Populism sometimes erupts with little or no warning, and though some populist movements are ephemeral in character, leaving few traces behind, others become embedded in political institutions, with remarkably durable effects. Given this variability and unpredictability, it is inherently difficult to develop generalizable theories about the causes and consequences of populism. Indeed, scholars have struggled even to reach a consensus on the meaning of the concept and its essential empirical properties.[1]

Populism, however, is not a random political occurrence. Neither is it a simple product of political voluntarism, despite its frequent association with charismatic leadership. By focusing on the relationship between populism and party system transformation, this chapter tries to advance our theoretical understanding of the causal conditions that give rise to populism and the political effects of different variants of populist mobilization. Populism, I argue, is a permanent possibility where representative institutions are weak, fragile, or ineffective at articulating and responding to social concerns. The prospects for populism, however, are magnified during the "critical junctures" that have marked the transition from one political and economic era to another in modern Latin America. Critical junctures are periods of decisive political change and uncertainty, when established institutional arrangements are challenged and a range of different outcomes become viable possibilities. These turning points in the region's political development are characterized by institutional crises or de-alignment, the undermining of established elites and political actors, and the political mobilization of new social and political subjects—conditions that are especially conducive to the rise of populist movements.

In turn, the institutional effects of populism—that is, whether it contributes to the breakdown, realignment, or recomposition of party systems—depend on the relative mobilizational capacities of populist figures and their opponents, as well as the character of the socio-political cleavages they form. In general, the labor-incorporating variants of populism associated with the critical juncture that marked the onset of industrialization and mass politics in early-twentieth-century Latin America produced patterns of party system realignment and recomposition with highly durable institutional legacies, largely because they built strong, mass-based forms of association in both partisan and civic arenas.[2] The late-twentieth-century critical juncture triggered by the demise of import-substitution industrialization and the transition to market liberal-

1. Kurt Weyland, "Clarifying a Contested Concept: Populism in the Study of Latin American Politics," *Comparative Politics* 34, no. 1 (2001): 1–22.
2. Ruth Berins Collier and David Collier, *Shaping the Political Arena: Critical Junctures, the Labor Movement, and Regime Dynamics in Latin America* (Princeton, N.J.: Princeton University Press, 1991).

ism had quite different effects. Although it also spawned new variants of populism, these tended to be embedded in larger processes of social dislocation and political deinstitutionalization, even where significant political cleavages were formed. The institutional legacies of contemporary populist movements, therefore, remain highly uncertain, and they are unlikely to be as durable as those spawned by the first cycle of populism.

As the preceding suggests, populism is not bound to a fixed set of economic policies or a specific stage of socioeconomic development. It is, instead, a mode of political representation characterized by an antielite or antiestablishment ideological discourse and the top-down mobilization of mass constituencies that lack a capacity for autonomous political expression.[3] As Carlos de la Torre states, populist discourse "dichotomizes politics as a struggle between two irreconcilable and antagonistic camps: the people against the oligarchy."[4] Populist leaders, therefore, invoke a politically righteous (but ill-defined) "people" in a redemptive struggle against entrenched, corrupt, or unresponsive elites. Where populist discourse identifies these elites in both political and economic terms —that is, as a ruling oligarchy backed by economic power—populism may lean to the left, generate class-based sociopolitical cleavages, and support redistributive economic policies. Alternatively, where populist discourse identifies elites in more narrowly defined political terms—as a corrupt political establishment or *partidocracia*—populism may lean to the right, protect economic elites, and avoid threats to the larger social order.

Either way, however, populism nearly always poses a challenge to established party systems. Rarely, if ever, is populist mobilization effectively channeled into or contained by well-established parties; where it does emerge within an established party, it represents the rise of an alternative or insurgent leadership that challenges the organizational hierarchy.[5] Populism, in short, is the quintessential expression of outsider

3. See Kenneth M. Roberts, "Neoliberalism and the Transformation of Populism in Latin America: The Peruvian Case," *World Politics* 48, no. 1 (October 1995): 82–116; Kurt Weyland, "Neopopulism and Neoliberalism in Latin America: Unexpected Affinities," *Studies in Comparative International Development* 32 (Fall): 3–31; Robert Barr, "Populists, Outsiders, and Anti-Establishment Politics," *Party Politics* 15, no. 1 (2009): 29–48; and Carlos de la Torre, *Populist Seduction in Latin America* (Athens: Ohio University Center for International Studies, 2010).

4. De la Torre, *Populist Seduction*, xiv.

5. An interesting exception is the populist movement led by Jorge Gaitán in Colombia, who built his political career largely within the traditional Liberal Party. Tellingly, however, Gaitán's charismatic leadership, antioligarchic discourse, and

politics. As such, it tends to undermine established party systems by mobilizing the excluded or the alienated behind a new political leadership in
frontal opposition to the status quo. In the process, however, it may
spawn new parties, civic groups, or social networks that thoroughly
transform the political landscape. To paraphrase Schumpeter, then,
populist mobilization is a force of "creative destruction" that can break
down, realign, and (potentially) rebuild more institutionalized forms of
mass political representation. Populism may leave party systems standing in some sort of altered form, but it rarely leaves them unscathed.

Populism, Party Systems,
and Critical Junctures in Latin America

To understand why populism tends to thrive during critical junctures in
Latin America, it is useful to first identify two different mechanisms
whereby populist figures can become serious competitors in the electoral
arena. To achieve electoral success as a populist outsider, a political entre-
preneur must either (1) mobilize support among nonparticipants, or (2)
win over voters who previously supported an established party. The first
mechanism, which might be labeled an *activation* process, can be viable in
a context of widespread political exclusion or withdrawal. In such contexts, large blocs of potential voters, or latent constituencies, are available
for mobilization, conditional upon their electoral enfranchisement and
the capacity of a populist leader to activate nonparticipants around an
agenda of political inclusion and/or social reform. By definition, then, an
activation process entails a significant expansion of electoral participation, unless (hypothetically) the mobilization of new voters is offset by a
demobilization of traditional voters. In the latter case, a basic shift would
occur in the social composition but not the size of the electorate.

The second mechanism, which might be labeled a *conversion* process,
requires that a populist outsider win over voters who are alienated from

---

support for popular mobilization proved highly divisive within the Liberal Party,
and his career was cut short by an assassin's bullet in 1948 when he was the frontrun-
ner in a presidential election campaign. More recently, populist tendencies under
Honduran president Manuel Zelaya were also controversial within his Liberal Party.
After being removed from power in a military coup in 2009 and spending a period of
time in exile, Zelaya returned to Honduras and tried to build a new left-leaning populist movement outside the country's two traditional parties.

established parties that they previously supported. Conversion assumes that voters are potentially mobile and that partisan loyalties are contingent rather than fixed. As such, it challenges the notion that electoral mobilization under conditions of universal suffrage will "freeze" partisan alignments as sociopolitical cleavages become institutionalized and voting behavior becomes habituated.[6] Conversion may occur if a populist outsider articulates new issues that are salient to voters but neglected by established parties, or that otherwise fail to map onto existing cleavage lines.[7] Conversion may also occur when a populist outsider mobilizes disillusioned voters against the political class and the established parties they lead. Where support for established parties has been eroded by economic crises, perceptions of widespread corruption, or a chronic inability to resolve social and economic hardships, populist outsiders can employ antisystem appeals to mobilize newly detached or alienated voters.[8] The programmatic content of such appeals may be opaque or even vacuous; running for office on a platform of "change" or "throw the bums out," after all, tells voters nothing about what a candidate might do in public office. Nevertheless, in contexts of widespread dissatisfaction with the performance of incumbents, antiestablishment appeals may resonate widely and pry voters away from traditional parties.

Clearly, activation and conversion processes are not mutually exclusive. An astute populist outsider may well prove capable of both mobilizing nonparticipants and converting erstwhile but alienated supporters of established parties. What matters, however, is that both these strategies pose formidable challenges to established party systems. At a minimum, populist mobilization by outsiders realigns party systems by forcing established parties to share the electoral arena with a major new power contender. Under conversion, realignment occurs as votes are transferred from an established party or parties to an emerging populist rival, invariably weakening the former. Under activation, established par-

6. Seymour Martin Lipset and Stein Rokkan, "Cleavage Structures, Party Systems, and Voter Alignments: An Introduction," in *Party Systems and Voter Alignments: Cross-National Perspectives*, edited by Seymour Martin Lipset and Stein Rokkan (New York: Free Press, 1967).

7. Simon Hug, *Altering Party Systems: Strategic Behavior and the Emergence of New Political Parties in Western Democracies* (Ann Arbor: University of Michigan Press, 2001).

8. The role of corruption in feeding antiestablishment politics is driven home by Kirk Hawkins, *Venezuela's Chavismo and Populism in Comparative Perspective* (New York: Cambridge University Press, 2010).

ties may retain their votes but lose vote shares as a populist rival captures a slice of an expanded electorate.

Such forms of realignment, though disruptive for established party systems, at least leave one or more traditional parties intact to compete against a rising populist alternative. As such, they represent a process of change that comes mixed with elements of continuity. More thorough patterns of change are found, however, when populist mobilization is associated with a wholesale rejection of the political establishment, culminating not in systemic realignment but rather in a breakdown or decomposition of the party system. Under decomposition, voters abandon traditional parties en masse, relegating them to the margins of the political system, if not causing their extinction altogether. Decomposition may, of course, be only a temporary stage before the recomposition of a new party system—an interregnum, so to speak, between two quite different party systems. Party systems that decompose, however, generally do not quickly recompose. Indeed, it is not clear that they must recompose at all, in any but the most minimal sense of providing partisan labels to register candidates running for public office. What follows decomposition, therefore, is highly uncertain, as organizational constraints on political choices are relaxed at both elite and mass levels, and the maneuvering space of political entrepreneurs is magnified.

What is it about critical junctures, then, that makes them susceptible to these mechanisms of populist mobilization and party system change? Critical junctures are watershed periods of political change, when political institutions across a range of countries adjust—in different ways—to a common set of societal pressures or challenges. More specifically, as used here, critical junctures correspond to major, cross-national shifts in the logic of capitalist development that realign states, markets, and social actors. These realignments, in turn, alter the ways in which party systems organize and represent societal interests, define programmatic alternatives, and mediate between states and citizens. These changes often prove disruptive for established party systems, while providing opportunities for emerging competitors, including populist movements.

For example, the labor-incorporating critical junctures studied by Collier and Collier were tailor-made for the activation mechanism of populist mobilization outlined above.[9] The oligarchic party systems that emerged during the era of agroexport development in the nineteenth

9. Collier and Collier, *Shaping the Political Arena.*

century were predicated on elite domination and the political exclusion of popular sectors. This exclusion was grounded in both institutional and structural conditions—namely, suffrage restrictions that denied citizenship rights to popular sectors, and a preindustrial social order in which an urban working class was still in gestation and peasants were subjected to semifeudal forms of landlord control. The critical juncture that marked the onset of mass politics in the early decades of the twentieth century, therefore, was triggered by underlying patterns of economic modernization and social mobilization: Industrialization and urbanization created new middle and working classes, whereas trade unionization generated powerful pressures for an extension of social and political citizenship rights. In many countries, populist movements took the lead in activating urban (and sometimes rural) popular sectors and articulating their socioeconomic and political claims. In the process, they often eclipsed traditional oligarchic parties and realigned party systems along a new axis of competition that divided elite and popular sectors. They also played a central role in the adoption of import-substitution industrialization (ISI) policies that sharply expanded the developmental, regulatory, and social welfare functions of capitalist states following the collapse of the agroexport development model in the Great Depression of the 1930s.

This process of activation and political incorporation proved highly conducive to institution building, and it bequeathed highly durable institutional legacies in many countries. Labor-incorporating critical junctures transformed civil society by creating new class-based collective actors—most prominently, labor unions, but also peasant movements in a number of countries. These societal actors, in turn, were linked to parties and sometimes states via new corporatist institutions of interest intermediation that provided representation and material rewards in exchange for a measure of political control. In the process, states developed new and stronger institutional capacities to promote industrialization, regulate markets, provide social services, and mediate social conflicts.

Most important for our purposes, this critical juncture spawned the formation of new populist parties—such as the Partido Revolucionario Institucional (Institutional Revolutionary Party) in Mexico, the Peronist party in Argentina, the Alianza Popular Revolucionaria Americana (APRA; the American Popular Revolutionary Alliance) in Peru, the Movimiento Nacionalista Revolucionario (Revolutionary National Movement) in Bolivia, and Acción Democrática (Democratic Action)

in Venezuela—that challenged traditional elites with antioligarchic discourses and mobilizing appeals to traditionally excluded working- and
lower-class constituencies. In contrast to traditional oligarchic parties,
which were loosely knit networks of notables with limited clientelistic
linkages to the lower classes, populist parties were centralized mass organizations that mobilized diverse popular sectors around charismatic figures and programmatic claims for political inclusion, social reform, and
state-led developmentalist and redistributive policies. But in contrast to
the partisan left, which also employed an antioligarchic discourse, populist parties were ideologically eclectic and ill defined; they typically promised some sort of "third way" between capitalism and socialism, while
aiming their appeals at diverse national and popular constituencies
rather than a predefined working-class subject.[10]

In short, the classical expressions of populism in Latin America were
generally associated with institution building in the civic, partisan, and
state arenas, despite the centrality of charismatic figures such as Perón
(Argentina), Vargas (Brazil), Cárdenas (Mexico), and Haya de la Torre
(Peru). These leaders served as unifying figures to help weave together
the heterogeneous strands of populist coalitions, but their appeals to
mass constituencies were mediated by representative institutions, even if
these institutions were ultimately subordinated to the personal authority
and political interests of dominant personalities.[11] Where charismatic
appeals were more direct and unmediated—most prominently, under
José María Velasco Ibarra in Ecuador—populist leadership was highly
unstable, and it bequeathed very fluid institutional legacies. In Ecuador's
more agrarian economy, Velasco Ibarra did not mobilize a strong labor
union base, and he made little effort to develop a party organization to
encapsulate his followers. His antioligarchic discourse allowed him to
capture the presidency five times with shifting sociopolitical constituencies, but he only succeeded in completing one term in office, and his charismatic authority did not leave behind a solid party organization or a
political cleavage to structure competition after his departure.

In much of the region, however, the institutional legacies of populism
were deeply embedded in a state-centric matrix of development that en-

10. Michael L. Conniff, ed., *Latin American Populism in Comparative Perspective*
(Albuquerque: University of New Mexico Press, 1982); Michael L. Conniff, ed.,
Populism in Latin America (Tuscaloosa: University of Alabama Press, 1999).

11. See Ernesto Laclau, *On Populist Reason* (London: Verso, 2005).

dured for half a century, until the ISI model exhausted its dynamism and eventually collapsed in the debt crisis of the early 1980s.[12] With the demise of ISI and the adoption of neoliberal stabilization and structural adjustment policies, the representative institutions associated with nationalistic, state-led capitalist development—many of them forged during earlier cycles of populist mobilization—were plunged into crisis, and a new critical juncture emerged to realign states, markets, and social actors for a new era of globalized economic liberalism. Labor movements were dramatically weakened, and their corporatist linkages to parties and states were loosened or severed as economies were opened to international competition.[13] Meanwhile, historic populist parties were pummeled by economic crises and the social dislocations that accompanied market restructuring; in a strange twist of fate, many of those saddled with governing responsibilities during the critical juncture actually took the lead in the imposition of structural adjustment policies, further scrambling traditional alignments of support and opposition in party systems.[14] These parties were once synonymous with antioligarchic discourses and antiestablishment political mobilization, but they gradually turned into conservative pillars of the political order and defenders of market orthodoxy—and in so doing, they became increasingly detached from the popular constituencies whose loyalties they had once commanded.

In short, neoliberal critical junctures during the final decades of the twentieth century produced fundamental shifts in the social moorings and sociopolitical alignments of Latin American party systems. Party systems were undermined by three primary features of the critical junc-

12. Marcelo Cavarozzi, "Politics: A Key for the Long Term in South America," in *Latin American Political Economy in the Age of Neoliberal Reform*, edited by William C. Smith, Carlos Acuña, and Eduardo Gamarra (New Brunswick, N.J.: Transaction Books, 1994).

13. Philip Oxhorn, "Is the Century of Corporatism Over? Neoliberalism and the Rise of Neopluralism," in *What Kind of Democracy? What Kind of Market? Latin America in the Age of Neoliberalism*, edited by Philip Oxhorn and Graciela Ducatenzeiler (University Park: Pennsylvania State University Press, 1998); Kenneth M. Roberts, "Social Inequalities without Class Cleavages in Latin America's Neoliberal Era," *Studies in Comparative International Development* 36, no. 4 (2002–3): 3–34.

14. María Victoria Murillo, *Labor Unions, Partisan Coalitions, and Market Reforms in Latin America* (Cambridge: Cambridge University Press, 2001); Katrina Burgess, *Parties and Unions in the New Global Economy* (Pittsburgh: University of Pittsburgh Press, 2004).

ture. First, severe and in some cases prolonged economic crises—including recessions, financial crises, and hyperinflationary cycles—imposed
heavy political costs on incumbent parties throughout the region following the democratic transitions of the 1980s. Where crises were iterative
or prolonged, retrospective voting patterns produced anti-incumbent
vote shifts that progressively weakened successive governing parties
and undermined entire party systems. Second, traditional forms of
party-society linkage were eroded by economic crises, market reforms,
and their attendant social dislocations. With unions in decline and austerity imposed by fiscal and balance-of-payments constraints, states re-
treated from a broad range of regulatory and social welfare functions
that had previously allowed parties to secure the support of popular constituencies. Corporatist, clientelist, and programmatic linkages between
parties and voters all suffered erosion during this period. Finally, as the
"Washington Consensus" for market liberalization spread across the
region, and even historic populist and leftist parties converged on promarket policies, the programmatic distinctions that had undergirded
competitive alignments and provided a basis for partisanship became
increasingly blurred.[15] Parties could compete for support on the basis of
competence and good governance in the management of market reforms, but they were hard-pressed to offer viable alternatives to a neoliberal model that appeared to be secured by global market constraints
and the economic and political leverage of international financial institutions like the World Bank and the International Monetary Fund.

Although these features of the critical juncture were especially disruptive for historic populist and labor-based parties, their effects were hardly
limited to them. Even conservative, business-allied, and promarket parties were challenged by the political costs of economic crises, the erosion
of clientelist linkages to low-income voters, and the blurring of programmatic distinctions that occurred when their erstwhile populist competitors assumed political responsibility for the adoption of market reforms.
Indeed, remarkably few traditional conservative parties took the lead in
the process of market liberalization, and even fewer reaped political rewards from the decisive shift in public policies toward their ideological
preferences in the 1980s and 1990s. As such, the destabilizing effects of

15. John Williamson, "What Washington Means by Policy Reform," in *Latin
American Adjustment: How Much Has Happened?* edited by John Williamson (Washington, D.C.: Institute for International Economics, 1990).

neoliberal critical junctures for party systems were truly systemic in character, rather than concentrated on the parties that were the most deeply embedded in the state-centric logic of the ISI era.

These multipronged destabilizing effects proved highly conducive to new cycles of populist mobilization, demonstrating that populism was not restricted to an earlier stage of state-capitalist development, and that it would not be extinguished by the transition to neoliberalism. In contrast to earlier patterns of populist mobilization, however, which had capitalized on the initial activation and political incorporation of excluded latent constituencies, new expressions of populism during the neoliberal critical juncture operated in an institutional environment where universal suffrage was already the norm and low-income voters had been previously mobilized by established parties. Consequently, although new populist outsiders might hope to reactivate disenchanted citizens who had withdrawn from politics, successful electoral mobilization inevitably required the conversion of voters who were accustomed to supporting established parties.

Typically, this conversion operated through rhetorical attacks on the political establishment or its alleged *partidocracia*, which was blamed for a plethora of societal ills—in particular, political corruption and economic mismanagement. In the discourse of populist outsiders, party elites were an entrenched and self-serving oligarchy that monopolized power and grew increasingly detached from *el pueblo*, whose political redemption could only be secured by a new leadership that emerged from outside the established system. In a context where statist development models were in crisis, and the parties and interest groups (including labor) associated with them were widely discredited, populist outsiders could easily launch attacks on the establishment from the political right. Indeed, they could even adapt their populist discourse to neoliberal reforms that promised to level the playing field by eliminating the political influence of special interests, as demonstrated by leaders like Fujimori in Peru and Collor de Mello in Brazil (see chapters 7, 8, and 11).

Nevertheless, populist outsiders did not emerge as major power contenders throughout the region during neoliberal critical junctures, as party systems survived and adapted to the economic transition in a number of countries. Furthermore, where populist outsiders did arise—in countries like Peru, Venezuela, and Ecuador—they varied widely in their policy orientations and patterns of political mobilization and organization. As such, new populist leaders had disparate effects on sociopolitical

cleavages and the nature of political competition. To explain this variation, a more in-depth comparative analysis of political dynamics during
neoliberal critical junctures is required.

Populism and the Political Outcomes
of Neoliberal Critical Junctures

The collapse of ISI and the transition to market liberalism posed formidable challenges to party systems throughout Latin America, but they
did not foreordain their demise. Whereas party systems in several countries thoroughly decomposed, in other countries they weathered the
storm more or less intact, typically by adapting their programmatic orientations and party-society linkages, and sometimes through significant
realignments of electoral competition. By the end of the 1990s, the neoliberal critical juncture had drawn to a close, as the momentum for market reform waned and the region entered a new, postadjustment political
era. Indeed, the Washington Consensus was placed on the political defensive by the fallout of the Asian financial crisis, the revival of social protest movements, and the beginnings of a dramatic political shift to the
left. The latter included the rise of new types of left-wing populism that
were strikingly different from the conservative populism of the market
reform period. These factors weighed heavily on the "reactive sequences"
of the aftermath period that followed the critical juncture—sequences
that were often driven by strengthening societal resistance to market liberalism and were heavily conditioned by the institutional legacies of the
critical juncture itself.

These institutional outcomes and their political legacies are analyzed
in greater detail in other work, and thus are only briefly summarized
here.[16] The key point is that neoliberal critical junctures differentiated
political outcomes along two primary dimensions: first, the extent to
which party systems survived or decomposed during the transition to
market liberalism; and second, the extent to which political competition
was structured by a stable programmatic divide between supporters and
critics of the neoliberal model. The first dimension was shaped by both

---

16. Kenneth M. Roberts, *Changing Course: Parties, Populism, and Political Representation in Latin America's Neoliberal Era* (in progress).

historic features of the party systems that developed during the ISI era and by shorter-term political and economic dynamics during the critical juncture itself. Where strong labor movements and labor-mobilizing party systems emerged during the ISI era, the state-centric matrix of development tended to be more advanced, and the transition to market liberalism was more traumatic and politically disruptive in the 1980s and 1990s. Economic crises were more severe and prolonged, social dislocation and deunionization were more pronounced, and party systems were plagued by massive anti-incumbent vote shifts and generalized electoral volatility that opened political space for the rise of new populist outsiders.

By contrast, where traditional oligarchic parties of the nineteenth century remained electorally dominant during the ISI era, the state-centric logic of development was generally less advanced, and the transition to market liberalism was accompanied by less severe economic crises and higher levels of party system continuity. These conditions made the rise of new populist outsiders less likely. Antecedent party system characteristics and development trajectories thus weighed heavily on the fate of party systems and the prospects for populist outsiders during neoliberal critical junctures, although they were not fully deterministic; where massive social protests accompanied the process of market reform, as in Ecuador in the 1990s, party system decomposition was also a likely outcome of the critical juncture.

Considerable variation also existed on the second key dimension, related to the extent of programmatic structuring of party systems around support and opposition to the neoliberal model. In some countries, electoral competition pivoted on an axis that consistently divided supporters and critics of the neoliberal model, or at least provided voters with a relatively coherent choice between promarket orthodoxy and alternatives that favored a stronger role for the state in reducing inequalities and protecting citizens from market insecurities. In other countries, alternatives to neoliberal orthodoxy were poorly defined or electorally insignificant, and no consistent programmatic divide structured electoral competition. In particular, programmatic alignments were undermined during the critical juncture in many countries because historic center-left or labor-based populist parties took the lead in the adoption of neoliberal stabilization and structural adjustment policies. Where market reforms were adopted "by surprise"—that is, by candidates who ran for office as opponents of neoliberalism—party competition became divorced from

coherent and consistent programmatic alternatives, and electoral victories largely ceased to produce policy mandates.[17]

These two dimensions were not tightly coupled together, as the degree
of programmatic structuring was at least partially independent of the
level of party system adaptation and decomposition. As such, these two
dimensions can be combined in a diagram—given as figure 2.1—that
identifies four different political outcomes of neoliberal critical junctures
in the 1980s and 1990s, each of which established a new institutional
baseline for the aftermath period. Where established parties remained
electorally dominant at the end of the critical juncture and competed
along a programmatic axis, as depicted in the top left cell in figure 2.1,
the outcome might be labeled *contested liberalism*. Under this outcome,
market reforms adopted during the critical juncture were defended by
relatively well-organized, orthodox supporters within the party system,
and they were challenged by organized rivals that advocated more expansive state developmental or social welfare roles.

Brazil, Uruguay, Chile, Mexico, and El Salvador provide examples of
this institutional outcome. In these countries, the critical juncture ended
with a programmatic divide between an intact partisan center and/or
right wing that defended market reforms, and a strengthening partisan
left wing that had largely abandoned socialist objectives and accepted
core elements of market liberalism, but that nonetheless gave expression
to societal claims for redistributive measures and expanded social citizenship. Crucially, in all these countries centrist or conservative parties
—or, in the Chilean case, military rulers—had overseen the process of
market liberalization during the critical juncture, allowing leftist parties
to mark off their programmatic differences and align electoral competition even as they moderated historic commitments to socialist reform. In
all these countries, relatively stable electoral competition continued in
the aftermath period, with the main leftist party eventually capturing the
presidency everywhere but in Mexico, where it fell just short in 2006.
Outsider populist pressures have been notably absent or modest in this
group of countries; where populist tendencies have emerged, as in
Mexico with Manuel López Obrador in the 2006 election, they did so
within an established party (the leftist Partido de la Revolución Democrática) rather than in opposition to the entire party system.

17. Susan Stokes, *Mandates and Democracy: Neoliberalism by Surprise in Latin
America* (Cambridge: Cambridge University Press, 2001).

Programmatic structuring of partisan competition	Adaptation of established parties	Decomposition of party system
Contestation of neoliberal orthodoxy	Contested liberalism (Chile, Uruguay, Brazil, Mexico, El Salvador)	Polarized populism (Venezuela, Ecuador under Correa)
Low contestation of neoliberal orthodoxy	Neoliberal convergence (Honduras, Costa Rica, Argentina, Colombia, Paraguay, Bolivia)	Serial populism (Peru, Ecuador before Correa)

Figure 2.1. Party Systems during Neoliberal Critical Junctures, 1980s to 1990s

Alternatively, where established parties remained electorally dominant at the end of the critical juncture, but none consistently challenged the neoliberal model, the outcome might be called *neoliberal convergence.* This outcome is found in the lower left cell in figure 2.1. Pluralist competition between established parties existed under this outcome, but it was weakly structured programmatically, given that all the major parties had supported or managed the process of market liberalization. Honduras, Costa Rica, Colombia, Argentina, Bolivia, and Paraguay provide examples of this outcome. In these countries, established party systems—in most cases, with two primary parties—survived the critical juncture, with the major parties participating in the reform process and adapting their societal linkages and programmatic positions to the new socioeconomic landscape.

Paradoxically, although most of these party systems were relatively stable during the critical juncture—that is, through the late 1990s—they proved to be highly prone to disruption in the reactive sequences of the aftermath period. In particular, in the absence of an established party capable of channeling societal opposition to market liberalization, they were vulnerable to the rise of new populist and leftist competitors in the aftermath period. Left-leaning populist outsiders eroded support for the established parties in Costa Rica and Paraguay, with Fernando Lugo breaking the historic stranglehold of the Colorado Party in the latter case. In Honduras, the iconoclastic populist leadership of Manuel Zelaya emerged within and deeply split the traditional Liberal Party, culminating in a military coup that cut short his presidential term. In Argentina, the reactive sequences that followed in the wake of the 2001 financial crisis and the mass protests that toppled President Fernando de la Rúa caused a breakdown of the anti-Peronist side of the party system, whereas Peronism itself veered back toward the political left under Néstor Kirchner and Cristina Fernández de Kirchner. New leftist alternatives also emerged in Colombia, although the demise of that country's historic two-party oligarchic system and its displacement by a conservative independent running on a national security platform had more to do with Colombia's failed peace process than with its relatively smooth transition to market liberalism.[18] Most dramatic of all, the three established parties that took turns managing Bolivia's neoliberal model were all wiped out by a sequence of massive social protests after 2000. These protests toppled two presidents and spawned the formation of a new leftist party with deep roots in Bolivia's indigenous, *cocalero*, and labor movements.

These patterns of instability strongly suggest that neoliberal critical junctures produced more durable institutional legacies where they bequeathed a party system with at least one major contender that consistently offered a programmatic alternative to market liberalism—that is, where contested liberalism rather than neoliberal convergence was the outcome. Whereas the competitive alignments of party systems under contested liberalism remained quite stable in the aftermath period, those of neoliberal convergence suffered major electoral realignments (in Costa Rica, Paraguay, and possibly Honduras), partial party system breakdowns (Argentina), or more thorough patterns of party system decomposition and recomposition (Bolivia and Colombia). As such, the outcome of neoliberal convergence was not a stable institutional equilibrium; indeed, reactive sequences in the aftermath period tended to push countries toward one of the other cells in figure 2.1.

In two of those cells, located on the right-hand side of figure 2.1, party system decomposition sometimes occurred not in the aftermath period but during the critical juncture itself. In each case, some form of populist leadership emerged in the representational void left by the demise of

18. Although Álvaro Uribe broke with Colombia's historic Liberal Party and cultivated a highly personalistic base of support in capturing the presidency, his leadership fell short of conventional populist benchmarks; see chapter 12 in this volume, and John C. Dugas, "The Emergence of Neopopulism in Colombia? The Case of Álvaro Uribe," *Third World Quarterly* 24, no. 6 (December 2003): 1117–36.

traditional parties. Where dominant personalities did not consistently structure competition along an axis of support and opposition to market liberalism, *serial populism* was the result. This outcome, found in the lower right cell of figure 2.1, was characterized by a cycling of dominant personalities in highly fluid competitive arenas that were structured neither by party institutions nor by a central programmatic divide. Peru and Ecuador are the paradigmatic examples of this phenomenon.[19] In these countries, new populist figures emerged during the critical juncture and in the immediate aftermath period to challenge traditional parties and political elites. Although leaders like Fujimori and Toledo in Peru and Bucaram and Gutiérrez in Ecuador were not necessarily full-fledged populists in their discursive and mobilizational practices, they nevertheless made highly personalistic appeals to diverse popular constituencies that were detached from traditional ruling elites. Because these leaders generally supported market reforms, however—in office, if not always on the campaign trail—they did not sharply polarize the political arena along programmatic lines or an elite/mass cleavage. Likewise, all either eschewed party organization or led parties that were little more than vehicles for their personal political aspirations. Consequently, serial populism produced neither durable political alignments nor stable representative institutions; once a dominant personality lost popular support, he was quickly replaced by another.

In Ecuador, where market reforms triggered (and were limited by) the rise of powerful protest movements led by indigenous groups, serial populism eventually veered to the left under Rafael Correa in the aftermath of the critical juncture.[20] Although Correa's populist leadership was largely detached from the country's indigenous movement, his attempts to refound the constitutional order and steer economic policies in a more statist direction sharply polarized the political arena. As such, a new and potentially more durable political cleavage grounded in both leadership and programmatic distinctions began to form in the aftermath period. The rise of Ollanta Humala in Peru as a more polarizing populist figure

19. Ecuador experienced a pattern of neoliberal convergence for much of the critical juncture, but shifted toward serial populism as the party system broke down.

20. Deborah Yashar, *Contesting Citizenship in Latin America: The Rise of Indigenous Movements and the Postliberal Challenge* (Cambridge: Cambridge University Press, 2005); Donna Lee Van Cott, *From Movements to Parties in Latin America: The Evolution of Ethnic Politics* (Cambridge: Cambridge University Press, 2005).

in the 2006 elections had clear parallels, suggesting that serial populism
—like neoliberal convergence—may not be a stable competitive equilibrium in an aftermath period where the neoliberal consensus has broken
down and leftist alternatives have reemerged. Humala was subsequently elected to the presidency in 2011 and charted a relatively moderate course after taking office; it remains unclear, then, whether he represents a new cycle of serial populism or a shift toward a more polarizing
variant of populist leadership.

Ecuador's reactive sequences, however, clearly pushed the country
toward the cell of *polarized populism* found in the upper right quadrant
of figure 2.1, where Venezuela is also located. Under polarized populism,
the demise of traditional parties during the critical juncture clears the
slate for the rise of new dominant personalities who sharply contest the
neoliberal model. Electoral competition is thus poorly institutionalized
but highly structured by a central political and programmatic divide that
has at least some grounding in elite/mass distinctions. Venezuela under
Hugo Chávez clearly provides the paradigmatic example of this outcome, with popular mobilization being heavily directed from above by a
charismatic figure who rose to power as a populist outsider. The Bolivian
case has also clearly moved out of the cell of neoliberal convergence
toward higher levels of polarization under Evo Morales in the aftermath period, but it differs from Venezuela and Ecuador in one fundamental respect: Unlike Chávez and Correa, Morales's leadership was
spawned by a more autonomous, bottom-up pattern of social mobilization during the anti-neoliberal protest movements that followed the
country's critical juncture. Morales's leadership, therefore, may have
some populist tendencies and an antielite populist discourse, but its origins lie in a pattern of autonomous, bottom-up social mobilization that
is not conventionally understood in Latin America as populist.[21]

Populism and the Reconstruction
of Party Systems

What are the implications, then, of serial and polarized forms of populism for the rebuilding of party systems that decomposed during neo-

---

21. Raúl L. Madrid, "The Rise of Ethnopopulism in Latin America," *World Politics* 60, no. 3 (April 2008): 475–508.

liberal critical junctures or the reactive sequences of their aftermath periods? Clearly, party systems that decompose and get displaced by populist figures are very difficult to piece back together. A party like the Alianza Popular Revolucionaria Americana in Peru might retreat to the political margins and then reemerge to compete down the road, but APRA's revival under a chastened and more conservative Alan García in 2006 is better understood as yet another cycle in the personalistic politics of serial populism than as a return to prominence by the party itself. It is far from clear that APRA remains a viable contender for power in the absence of its dominant leader, as the party's dismal showing in 2011 elections suggests (despite rapid economic growth throughout García's second term). Likewise, there is little to indicate that the traditional parties in Venezuela, Bolivia, and Ecuador are capable of leading the conservative establishment's opposition to the more polarizing populist and leftist leaders who have emerged in those countries. Instead, opposition forces have relied heavily on fluid electoral coalitions and extrapartisan forms of political expression, from the mass media to social protests and, in the Venezuelan case, an oil sector strike and short-lived military coup.

In contrast to serial populism, the more polarizing forms of leadership in these latter countries at least create a central sociopolitical and programmatic cleavage along which party systems could be aligned and rebuilt. To date, however, conservative oppositions in these countries have failed to congeal around new party organizations, although Venezuela has shown signs of building a broad center-right electoral coalition. In part, this may reflect the fact that conservative oppositions tend to be the mirror image of their populist rivals; if diverse popular constituencies are held together by their loyalty to a dominant personality, fractious conservative opponents may share little in common other than their antipathy for that leader. The failure of conservative party-building efforts, however, may also reflect a lack of confidence in their ability to compete in the electoral arena against the crushing popular majorities that have been mobilized by the likes of Chávez, Morales, and Correa. Indeed, the willingness of these leaders to employ plebiscitary measures to sideline opponents, concentrate power, and refound constitutional orders has raised serious doubts about whether the institutional safeguards are in place to ensure opposition rights and effective electoral contestation. This is especially the case in Venezuela, where *chavismo* not only monopolized the executive and legislative branches after rewriting the rules of the game but also gained control over the judiciary and the electoral machinery, while placing a variety of constraints on regime opponents.

Consequently, rather than invest in party building efforts with highly uncertain electoral payoffs, conservative elites may well opt to employ other power resources—such as their economic leverage, media influence, or military ties—to destabilize populist rulers and precipitate their downfall by extra-institutional means. Needless to say, this type of polarized conflict—where neither side of the political cleavage makes an unqualified commitment to liberal democratic norms and procedures— is not likely to culminate in institutionalized forms of partisan and electoral competition.

Likewise, new populist figures themselves have mixed incentives for engaging in party-building activities. Party organizations inevitably constrain a leader's political autonomy; they create bureaucratic interests that may be distinct from those of a leader, and they establish a tier of secondary officials with political interests that need to be accommodated. Indeed, parties provide organizational and human resources that can be utilized by potential political rivals to challenge a leader.[22] Furthermore, organization building is a costly, long-term process that may pay few dividends for leaders with short time horizons dictated by electoral calendars or more immediate political battles. Historic populist figures may have needed party organizations to mobilize voters when electoral campaigns were labor-intensive affairs, but in an era of mass communication technologies, leaders can appeal directly to popular constituencies without an expansive network of grassroots party branches. In Latin America, as elsewhere, mass party organizations are increasingly dispensable instruments for electoral mobilization and public administration; a wide range of civic groups, professional campaign managers, media outlets, survey tools, and technocratic networks have assumed political roles that were once the primary domain of party organizations—often supplanting the latter in democratic processes of interest articulation, political socialization, and public policymaking.

Not surprisingly, then, populist figures often dispense with significant party-building activities and opt for direct and unmediated relations with popular constituencies. This is especially the case where populist outsiders challenge established political elites but adopt policy orienta-

---

22. James McGuire, *Peronism without Perón: Unions, Parties, and Democracy in Argentina* (Stanford, Calif.: Stanford University Press, 1997).

tions that pose little threat to economic elites. In Ecuador, for example, the legendary populist José María Velasco Ibarra adopted an antioligarchic discourse and railed against the Liberal and Conservative party establishments. In contrast to other populist figures in the ISI era, however, he did not mobilize workers or peasants behind a reformist agenda that would threaten elite economic interests, and he made no serious attempt to form a party organization. In more recent times, Alberto Fujimori waged a battle against Peru's party establishment, but he allied himself with business elites in the implementation of neoliberal reforms. He famously created a new party label for each of his four national election campaigns, but he did little to build a party organization beyond a tight circle of technocrats, political collaborators, and congressional leaders. For these populist figures, political mobilization was largely limited to the electoral arena and did not entail the mass organization of followers in either civil society or the partisan sphere.

Where populist leaders do build party organizations—or, for that matter, labor unions and other mass-based civic associations—it is typically because they are contesting both political and economic elites and need to mobilize popular majorities both inside and outside the electoral arena as a counterweight to elite power resources.[23] For this reason, more polarizing populist and leftist leaders like Chávez, Morales, and Correa—all staunch critics of neoliberalism who support statist, nationalist, and redistributive development projects—have made more serious efforts to organize parties than did the neoliberal populists of the 1990s like Fujimori and Collor de Mello. Not surprisingly, party building proceeded most rapidly in Bolivia, where the bottom-up pattern of social mobilization was less classically populist. In Bolivia, the social movements that toppled two governments and brought down the party establishment provided a dense network of activists that could be readily incorporated into a new "movement party" led by Evo Morales, the Movimiento al Socialismo (MAS). As the electoral expression of highly mobilized civic groups, the MAS competed in municipal and legislative elections before its meteoric rise allowed Morales to capture the presidency in 2005. With deep roots in organized popular movements, the MAS has thus given partisan expression to one side of the sociopolitical cleavage that emerged after 2000 in Bolivia, although the other side of

23. Kenneth M. Roberts, "Populism, Political Conflict, and Grass-Roots Organization in Latin America," *Comparative Politics* 38, no. 2 (January 2006): 127–48.

the cleavage remains poorly institutionalized for partisan and electoral competition.[24]

In contrast to the MAS, party building in Venezuela and Ecuador has been much more of a top-down affair, reflecting the independence of Chávez and Correa from social movements at the time they took office. Indeed, both leaders have sought to build party organizations from the heights of state power, in contrast to the civic origins of the MAS in Bolivia. Chávez came into power with a long-standing network of collaborators but little in the way of a party organization. He formed an official party, the Movimiento V (Quinta) República (MVR; Fifth Republic Movement), as an electoral vehicle, but he ran highly personalistic campaigns at the head of broad coalitions that included other small leftist parties. In power, he engaged in extensive grassroots organizational work, creating a diverse and constantly shifting set of community organizations to mobilize voters and administer social programs, but much of this organizational energy was deployed outside the ranks of the MVR.[25] In 2007, he attempted to consolidate and institutionalize his partisan base by folding the MVR and allied leftist parties into the Partido Socialista Unido de Venezuela (United Socialist Party of Venezuela), although several of the smaller parties opted to maintain their independence.[26] His conservative opposition has found it even more difficult to congeal behind an institutionalized partisan expression, and it is forced to compete in an electoral arena that is highly skewed by the concentration of power in the executive branch. Consequently, polarized populism in Venezuela displaced the historic party system and created a profound political cleavage that aligns the relevant actors. But thus far it has not institutionalized this alignment through a reconfigured and fully competitive party system.

In Ecuador, Rafael Correa launched his populist bid for the presidency in 2006 with even less in the way of a party organization. He relied on a small circle of academic contacts and political collaborators to organize his campaign, and he proved highly effective at using mass media

24. Raúl Madrid, "Bolivia: Origins and Policies of the *Movimiento al Socialismo*," in *The Resurgence of the Latin American Left*, edited by Steven Levitsky and Kenneth M. Roberts (Baltimore: Johns Hopkins University Press, 2011), 239–59.

25. Kirk Hawkins, *Venezuela's Chavismo and Populism in Comparative Perspective* (New York: Cambridge University Press, 2010).

26. Margarita López Maya, "Venezuela: Hugo Chávez and the Populist Left," in *Resurgence*, ed. Levitsky and Roberts, 213–38.

appeals to mobilize the electorate. To highlight his independence and outsider status, he did not even organize a slate of legislative candidates to run on his ticket. After taking office, sacking opposition legislators, and convoking new constituent assembly elections, however, he made a concerted effort to organize a new party and thus consolidate his legislative bloc and popular base. In the process, he repeatedly clashed with indigenous and other popular movements that, in contrast to Bolivia, played little role in the gestation of his leadership.[27]

In short, new populist leaders and movements have sometimes been grounded in deep sociopolitical cleavages, but they have been slow to institutionalize these competitive alignments in civic or partisan spheres. Once they have broken down, party systems have proven difficult to reconstitute; in contrast to an earlier generation of populist leaders who sponsored the initial political incorporation of mass constituencies, contemporary populists compete on a landscape where citizens have already developed and renounced partisan loyalties, and parties confront a plethora of rival societal actors who perform basic representative functions. In the aftermath of market liberalization, highly pluralistic civil societies rarely provide centralized labor and secondary associations that can be grafted onto (or transformed into) mass party organizations, as was customary during the early stages of industrialization, when populist leaders built parties around corporatist linkages to labor and peasant unions. As such, the institutional legacies of contemporary populist movements are unlikely to be as durable as those that followed the onset of mass politics in early-twentieth-century Latin America.

Conclusion

The critical juncture that marked Latin America's transition to market liberalism in the 1980s and 1990s undermined many traditional party systems and thus opened political space for a variety of new populist leaders and movements. In contrast to the classical forms of populism that emerged during the early stages of industrialization and mass politics in the first half of the twentieth century, these new expressions of populism did not readily construct party organizations around labor

27. Catherine Conaghan, "Ecuador: Rafael Correa and the Citizens' Revolution," in *Resurgence*, ed. Levitsky and Roberts, 260–82.

unions or other mass-based civic associations.[28] Indeed, they often mobilized support in the electoral arena among highly fragmented and largely disorganized popular constituencies, relying on charismatic authority to unify the disparate strands of a citizenry alienated from established parties.

Where dominant personalities cycled, producing a pattern of serial populism, political deinstitutionalization occurred in the party system and, to some extent, in democratic regimes as well. Under more polarizing types of leadership, regimes were refounded and new political cleavages formed, with party systems being at least partially reconstituted around this cleavage alignment. To date, it is not clear whether these reconfigured party systems will become fully competitive and pluralistic, as opposed to being merely the hegemonic extensions of populist autocrats. What is clear is that contemporary populism, like its historical antecedents, exists in uneasy tension with party systems—as it does with other democratic institutions—and often acts as a force of creative destruction in the transformation of political representation. Populism may well arise from a generalized crisis of representation in Latin American democracies, and it often provides alternative forms of democratic leadership that are more responsive to popular interests and sentiments. On its own, however, it is unlikely to resolve such a crisis of representation.

28. Bolivia might be an exception, but as explained above, the bottom-up pattern of social mobilization that spawned the political leadership of Evo Morales and the MAS was not conventionally populist. For this reason, Levitsky and Roberts characterize the MAS as a movement left rather than a populist left, differentiating it from the Venezuelan and Ecuadoran cases; see Steven Levitsky and Kenneth M. Roberts, "Latin America's Left Turn: A Framework for Analysis," in *Resurgence*, ed. Levitsky and Roberts, 1–28.

Chapter 3

Populism in Democratic Times: Populism, Representative Democracy, and the Debate on Democratic Deepening

Enrique Peruzzotti

"Populism" is a polemical term that has generated and still generates heated academic and political debate in Latin America and elsewhere. Originally, the concept of populism was conceived as a useful tool to analyze the stage of development associated with the political and economic incorporation of the popular sector in the region. It is difficult, however, to pigeonhole the concept or narrow its analytical utility to the explanation of that specific historical experience. The term continues to be used to account for political experiences that take place in an institutional and socioeconomic context that is quite different from the conjuncture that gave rise to the national-popular regimes of the mid–twentieth century. Furthermore, the concept is employed in other regions of the world—

Earlier versions of this chapter were presented at the Woodrow Wilson International Center for Scholars, the University of Leicester, and at the Facolta di Scienze Politiche, Universita degli Studi di Cagliari. The author thanks the participants in those meetings for their comments. I am particularly grateful to Cynthia Arnson and Carlos de la Torre for their helpful suggestions on a previous draft of this chapter.

from the United States to Europe—to describe political movements that bear little resemblance to those that emerged in post–World War II Latin America. In Europe, for instance, populism largely refers to rightist politicians and xenophobic movements that, far from promoting political and social inclusion, seek to stigmatize specific sectors of society such as immigrant workers and ethnic and religious minorities.[1]

Populism expresses a particular way of envisioning politics and democracy, and thus it remains and will remain a constant presence in democratic societies. Consequently, any discussion of populism, and particularly of its current revival in regions like Latin America and Europe, inevitably forces one to address a series of tensions and ambiguities that are present in the notion of democracy itself. Such tensions and ambiguities help to explain the differing normative status that is attributed to populism: Although many consider it an obstacle to the development and consolidation of democratic institutions, others view it as the very expression of democracy and of politics itself. In Latin America, analysts early on recognized the ambiguous contribution of populism to the agenda of democratization. They acknowledged that populist movements were inclusionary, contributing to the political and socioeconomic incorporation of the popular sector; but at the same time they questioned the accompanying institutional forms and political styles that frequently undermined the rule of law and representative mediations. Classical populist regimes in Latin America simultaneously combined greater degrees of democracy and authoritarianism.

The Debate over the Role of Populism in Democratic Times

In recent years, however, there has been a conceptual and political shift in the evaluation of populism. The contemporary rendition has lost much of its ambiguity when evaluating populism's contribution to the process of democratization. Populism is no longer considered a threat to liberal democracy; rather, it is viewed as a necessary antidote to the ills of representative politics. According to this interpretation, populism acts

---

1. See Cass Mudde, *Populist Radical Right Parties in Europe* (Cambridge: Cambridge University Press, 2007); and H.-G. Betz, *Radical Right Wing Populism in Western Europe* (London: Macmillan, 1994).

as a healthy countervailing force against the elitist tendencies of representative government, helping to dissolve the oligarchic accumulation of political power that representative government can generate. More extreme arguments condemn representative government altogether and call for a return to "the political" as incarnated in populist leaders and movements. In this version of the argument, it is representative government, not populism, that—by replacing politics with administration and innocuous institutional games—blocks the possibility of a truly emancipating politics.

Are the previous arguments plausible? Is populism the best strategy for democratic deepening? Or does it represent a simplistic response to the shortcomings of existing democratic regimes? Are there alternative ways to democratize existing democracies other than through populist strategies? This chapter challenges the notion that populism can successfully reconstitute representative linkages in a democratic and sustainable way, calling for a move away from the contemporary celebration of populism to explore alternative responses that could address existing democratic deficits within a representative framework. Rather than searching for a direct form of democracy or unmediated politics, it is necessary to enhance and expand the mediating mechanisms of indirect democracy, for they are what make possible the practice of democratic representation. The ills of democratic representation should be cured through the development of more effective and inclusive representative structures rather than by making democracy simpler. Prioritizing unmediated processes of populist identification over the mediated politics of representative government, far from renewing or deepening existing Latin American democracies, could instead jeopardize the institutional accomplishments of past decades. The problem with populism is that because populist movements and leaders often see themselves as the very incarnation of the will of the people, they end up eliminating rather than bridging the representational gap that defines the political bond under indirect democracy, a development that can ultimately lead to the destruction of democratic representation. It is this latter possibility —the breaking with the limiting corset of representative politics—that some radical theorists of democracy value the most in their evaluation of populist phenomena.

Behind some of the contemporary theoretical defenses of populism is a tiresome vision of liberal or representative democracy as a regime that tends to neutralize the political and stabilize elitist rule. Undoubtedly, many contemporary liberal democracies—in particular minimalist and delegative versions—provide ample justification for such criticisms. However, it would be misleading to equate democratic representation with such degraded versions of democratic rule. The answer to the democratic deficits of minimalist or delegative democracies is not to be found in political immediacy but in re-creating, building, and adding complexity to the field of political mediations to ensure the political system's greater responsiveness to citizens' demands.

It is not the intention of this chapter to engage in a detailed analysis of current theories of populism or their alleged contribution to democratization. Instead, I focus on one specific aspect that present debates bring to the fore: the relationship between populism and representative politics. The next section presents an overview of current debates on the role of populism in a democracy. Then I outline the features that best characterize the classical populist model. The next section distinguishes between three democratic projects that are dominant in Latin America today: the minimalist, the delegative, and the populist models. The final section argues for the need to move beyond all these previous models through the development of a more complex model of democratic representation that could serve as a road map for a process of democratic deepening.

Populism and Representative Democracy

The current revival of the notion of populism has prompted debates about its internal connection to democratic ideals.[2] Populism is a form of

---

2. Margaret Canovan, "Trust the People! Populism and the Two Faces of Democracy, *Political Studies* 47 (1999): 2–16; Benjamin Arditi, "Populism as a Spectre of Democracy: A Response to Canovan," *Political Studies* 52 (2004); Gianfranco Pasquino, "Populism and Democracy," in *Twenty-First Century Populism and the Spectre of Western European Democracy*, edited by Daniele Albertazzi and Duncan McDonnell (London: Palgrave Macmillan, 2008); Nadia Urbinati, "Democracy and Populism," *Constellations: An International Journal of Critical and Democratic Theory* 5, no. 1 (1998): 110–24; Yves Mény and Yves Surel, *Democracy and the Populist Challenge* (New York: Palgrave, 2002); Francisco Panizza, ed., *Populism and the Mirror of Democracy* (London: Verso, 2005); Carlos de la Torre, "The Resurgence of Radical Populism in Latin America," *Constellations:. An International Journal of Critical and Democratic Theory* 14, no. 3 (2007); Kenneth Roberts, "Latin America's Populist Revival," *SAIS Review* 27, no. 1 (2007).

politics that hopes to redeem the promise of popular sovereignty, placing the people back at the center of politics and challenging the conservative forces of elitism. As a result, many rightly argue that the study of populism cannot be disassociated from that of democracy and should be valued as a potential strategy to democratize existing democracies.

The defense of populism as a democratizing strategy is argued in two ways. First, populism is seen as a force that periodically needs to come to the rescue of liberal democracy, resurrecting politics from the oligarchic tendencies of representative government. Second, populism is portrayed as a more radical variant of democracy, more attractive than representative democracy.

The first argument considers that contemporary democracies are inevitably torn by the countervailing forces of elitism and populism.[3] From this standpoint, populism provides an antidote to representative politics. With its appeals to the people against the status quo, populism offers a necessary check on the elitist logic that dominates contemporary representative regimes. Certainly, such a check might sometimes lead to questionable political practices and to assaults on the institutional system of representative democracy; yet overall, its role as an antidote to the ailments of representative democracy largely compensates for whatever side effects it might produce. Populism might be a disturbing presence in public life—polarizing politics, suspending representative mediations, eluding checks and balances—yet it brings a fresh political impulse that shakes off the ossified institutional structures of representative government. This is why Benjamin Arditi argues that it is wrong to conceive of populism as a marginal or pathological political phenomenon that bears no relation to democratic politics. There is, in his view, a relationship of interiority between populism and democracy, with the former representing a paradoxical presence that simultaneously disturbs and renews democratic practices. Populism, Arditi concludes, is a "specter" that both "accompanies democracy and haunts it."[4]

---

3. See, e.g., Arditi, "Populism as a Spectre"; Benjamin Arditi, "Populism and the Internal Periphery of Democratic Politics," in *Populism*, ed. Panizza; Philippe C. Schmitter, "A Balance Sheet on the Vices and Virtues of Populism," *Romanian Journal of Political Science*, 2006; and Jack Hayward, "The Populist Challenge to Elitist Democracy in Europe," in *Elitism, Populism, and European Politics*, edited by Jack Hayward (Oxford: Oxford University Press, 1996).

4. Arditi, "Populism as a Spectre," 141; Arditi, "Populism and the Internal Periphery," 9. Arditi actually refers to three possible modes of populism, "'the rougher edge

The second defense of populism instead sees it as the very manifestation of radical democratic politics.[5] From this perspective, populism is
not just an internal edge of representative government but also represents a political alternative to it that can bring to life a more radical form
of democracy. Proponents of this argument see an obstacle to true democratic politics in representative regimes, because their institutional webs
of mediating structures tend to privilege the logic of administration over
that of politics. For Ernesto Laclau, the only sine qua non of democracy
is the construction of the people.

Populism is the path to reconstructing the political by creating an ambiguous vision of the demos ("the people"), according to Laclau.[6] He
considers it ambiguous because the constituted unity of the group as
people does not say much about the ideological content of this construct.
The notion of populism, Laclau rightly argues, is not related to specific
ideological positions but instead expresses a social rationale of political
identity formation. Ideological and conceptual vagueness are intrinsic to
this form of identity building. Populism, in his view, requires ideological
simplicity and emptiness, drawing an antagonistic division around some
empty signifiers. What matters is its effectiveness in drawing such an antagonistic frontier and its ability to divide society into two irreconcilable

mode" being an intermediary one between a populism that is fully compatible with
liberal democracy and other more radical expressions of the phenomenon that
openly undermine and endanger democratic representation. I focus on this intermediary understanding of populism, which I think is the one that reflects a recent way
of conceptualizing the phenomenon of populism. One could argue that the third
mode is to be found in the classical formulations of the problem of populism (e.g., in
the work of Gino Germani on Peronism). I am uneasy about the first mode, for I
believe it leads to some stretching of the concept, which then becomes undistinguish-
able from other forms and/or trends that are the normal currency of democratic
politics. This is also why I am wary of some contemporary uses of the term neopopulism to label administrations that in my view bear little resemblance to populism. I return to some of these arguments in this chapter's second and third sections
when I respectively discuss the differences between current "audience" and "delegative" democracies and the classical populist experiences.

5. The most forceful argument of populism as a radical form of politics is presented by Ernesto Laclau, *On Populist Reason* (London: Verso, 2005). For a very
interesting analysis of the public role of Laclau, see Vicente Palermo, "Consejeros
del Príncipe: Intelectuales y populismo en la Argentina de hoy," *RECSO* 2 (2011).

6. Laclau, "Populism: What Is in a Name?" in *Populism*, ed. Panizza, 48. For the
distinction between "politics" and "the political" see Laclau, *On Populist Reason*, 67.
Also see Carl Schmitt, *The Concept of the Political* (Chicago: University of Chicago
Press, 2007).

camps. The specific ideological contents that are mobilized to construct the empty signifier of the people in each particular conjuncture are irrelevant to a formal theory of populism. What matters is not the content but the role that signifiers play in polarizing society into two antagonistic camps. Signifiers of an entirely opposite political orientation can serve the same purpose, argues Laclau: "This is why between left-wing and right-wing populism, there is a nebulous no-man's-land which can be crossed—and has been crossed—in many directions."[7]

Several conditions need to be present for such a strategy of populist identification to be successful. The first is the existence of a crisis of representation or incorporation; that is, the accumulation within society of social demands that cannot be properly addressed by existing institutional arrangements.[8] The second is the articulation of those unsatisfied social demands, or, in Laclau's terminology, the establishment of an "equivalential" relation between them. The third precondition is the unification of those various demands as a group—"the people"—that identifies itself with the whole of society. The people, Laclau argues, are a part of the community that views itself as the only legitimate totality.[9] This can only be accomplished by the political construction of an enemy; populism entails the rejection of the "absorbing" logic of democracy by postulating the radical exclusion of its enemies. If successful, this process of identification results in the drawing of an antagonistic frontier within society between two incompatible camps. Only such an antagonistic logic can put an end to a hegemonic formation.[10]

7. Laclau, *On Populist Reason*, 87.

8. The emergence of a gap between the institutional order and certain sectors of society is the basic prerequisite for the possibility of populism: "Without this initial breakdown of something in the social order, . . . there is no possibility of antagonism, frontier, or, ultimately, people." For Laclau, however, the presence of a gap is in itself insufficient. There has to be a thematization of such a gap, the building of a perception that the very presence of such a gap prevents the harmonious continuity of the social. This requires a conceptual shift from difference to equivalence. Laclau, *On Populist Reason*, 85.

9. Ibid., 81.

10. To undermine an existing hegemonic institutional configuration, populism needs to eliminate the logic of "differentiality" that helps to reproduce it and to replace it with one of radical antagonism. By posing a part that identifies itself with the whole—and which therefore radically excludes those groups that do not fall under such an understanding of the people—populism puts an end to the egalitarian and differentiating logic of a crystallized hegemonic order. We are confronted instead with the partition of society into two irreducible camps structured around two in-

The antagonistic logic of populism, Laclau argues, helps restore the political to its proper status. A world without populism is in his view a world without politics, a world where politics has been replaced by administration. His analysis blurs the lines between populism and the political. His concept of populism is not simply describing one particular form of politicization, but rather the political as such.[11] Populism is consequently reified as the only strategy to achieve democratization.[12]

Although with different emphases, both these arguments see in populism an attractive road to democratic deepening. Whether it is viewed as a "rougher edge" of representative democracy that brings new life to it or as an alternative to representative government tout court, populism is put forth as a strategy to promote the democratization of existing democracies. There is, however, an important difference in the way the two arguments conceive of populism. If populism is to remain a rougher edge of representative democracy—revitalizing politics without openly challenging representative institutions—it must necessarily assume a *soft* form. In contrast, the proponents of the second argument described above have in mind a *hard* and antagonistic manifestation of populism that aims to eliminate the mediating structures of representative government altogether. Several authors of chapters in this volume also subscribe to this distinction between soft and hard populism. For instance, in chapter 4 Francisco Panizza argues that populist interventions can assume different forms distinguishing "*populismo leve*" from more antagonistic expressions. In his view, an ample variety of populist interventions fall along a spectrum whose poles are, respectively, a soft form of populism that does not threaten democratic institutions and a hard form of antagonistic populism that aims to eliminate the mediating structures

compatible equivalent terms. Laclau rightly argues that the friend-foe distinction is the defining logic of populist identification and that such a mode of political unity represents a rather distinctive strategy that is at odds with the logic of representative institutions. Laclau, *On Populist Reason*, 83–84. His is perhaps the most sophisticated theoretical attempt to develop a formal conceptualization of the phenomenon of populism. His theory conceptually confines the notion of populism to a certain antagonist way of constructing "the people" that serves to distinguish this particular logic from other phenomena that might bear some resemblance to populism but that cannot be properly subsumed under its conceptual axis. I will return to his point when discussing the conceptual links between populism and "delegative" democracy.

11. Laclau, *On Populist Reason*, 67.

12. Alexandros Kioupkiolis, "Radicalizing Democracy," *Constellations: An International Journal of Critical and Democratic Theory* 17, no. 1 (2010): 142.

of representative government.[13] As they explain it in chapter 1, de la Torre and Arnson's notion of radical populism also aims to distinguish the political processes that take place in Bolivia, Ecuador, and Venezuela from milder expressions of such phenomena.[14]

In this chapter, I narrow my analysis to the stronger version of populism. I tend to agree with Ernesto Laclau and many others when they argue that populism is, by definition, a form of identity building organized around a friend/enemy axis. The very way in which the identity is constructed—if successful—opens up a process of political polarization that tends to divide society into two irreconcilable camps.[15] Populist leaders view themselves as the sole incarnation of the people and consequently deny any status to those who fall outside this definition.[16] Much of what falls under the category of soft populism lacks this antagonistic component. It is difficult to dissociate the confrontational element of the category without draining it of meaning, given that its effectiveness as a strategy of political identification lies precisely in its capacity to divide society around a single axis: the people versus their enemies. A "friendly enemy" or an "adversary" lacks such polarizing potential, and it is an unlikely concept for triggering an effective process of populist identification.[17] Charismatic politicians might be successful in mobilizing the sup-

13. See chapter 4 of the present volume, by Francisco Panizza.

14. See chapter 1 of this volume.

15. To defend a strong notion of populism does not mean that such processes of identification are inevitably successful at drawing such an antagonistic line or that they always result in the establishment of an alternative form of institutionalization. This phenomenon might be reduced to a populist intervention that does not radically alter the institutional environment or socioeconomic structure of the society in question. Yet on most occasions, those interventions are likely to affect the performance and legitimacy of representative institutions. In this sense, I agree with Francisco Panizza when he emphasizes the need to think of populism as specific interventions, although I prefer to narrow the concept to antagonistic forms.

16. This notion of the people is far from ambiguous, as Laclau claims. Instead, it eliminates the intrinsic ambiguity that characterizes the modern (empty) notion of the people. As Rosanvallon rightly notes, there is a gap between the clarity of the political principle of popular sovereignty and the problematic/ambiguous nature of the people as a social and political subject. Pierre Rosanvallon, "Reflections on Populism," http://www.booksandideas.net/A-Reflection-of-Populism-htm. Laclau confuses simplicity with ideological ambiguity. Populism is a simplistic (if ideologically ambiguous) response to such contradiction that results in the creation of an unambiguous notion that aims at filling out the "emptiness" of democratic power by postulating the "embodiment" of the people in a leader, party, or movement.

17. This might generate other forms of identification that are usual currency in

port of significant sectors of the electorate by generating forms of identification that do not generate the political divisions or ruptures that characterize populist interventions. The latter, however, is part of the routine of democratic politics that bears little resemblance to the redemptive character of populism.

I am skeptical about the analytical usefulness of stretching the concept to include nonantagonistic forms of populism. I am not sure to what extent such an exercise in conceptual stretching contributes to analytical clarification, for if one accepts a broader definition it becomes difficult to distinguish popular politicians like Tony Blair, José Mujica, Carlos Menem, and Barack Obama from leaders such as Umberto Bossi, Jean-Marie Le Pen, Juan Perón, and Hugo Chávez. The adjective "populism" is consequently used to pinpoint a wide variety of political developments. What one has in the end is conceptual confusion. As Margaret Canovan argues,

> One of the reasons for current confusion about the meaning of "populism" is that besides being used to describe the confrontational politics that mobilizes ordinary people against those inside the establishment, the term also refers to a classic tactic available to political insiders, a kind of "catchall" politics that sets out to appeal to the people as a whole.[18]

Canovan nevertheless stretches the concept, pointing to a rise in contemporary Western democracies of what she calls a "politicians' populism," which she distinguishes from more classical forms of the phenomenon. In her view, Jean-Marie Le Pen's Front Nationale in France, the Freedom Party of Jörg Haider in Austria, and Umberto Bossi's Northern League in Italy are the contemporary expressions of the adversarial politics of identification that characterizes classical populism.[19] Unlike classical populism, the contemporary brand of populism not only does not resort to polarizing strategies but avoids politicizing society altogether. The politician's populism that is becoming an ingrained feature of con-

---

democratic politics (Manin) but do not generate the political division and rupture that characterize populist interventions. As noted, charismatic politicians might be successful in mobilizing the support of significant sectors of the electorate. The latter, however, is part of the routine of democratic politics, not a moment of exception.

18. Canovan, *The People*, 77.
19. Ibid., 74.

temporary audience democracies presents itself as a "neutral" form of government that serves the interests of all. It does not challenge representative government but "is fully compatible with the institutional regime form of liberal-democratic politics."[20] In brief, in its current incarnation populism does not express the essence of the political but instead of antipolitics; it is a form of political intervention that—far from mobilizing and politicizing marginal groups—feeds the cynicism about democratic politics that permeates large sectors of society.[21]

Such an expanded definition of populism rests on an objectionable premise: that processes of identification are foreign to the practice of democratic representation. It assumes an image of representative politics whereby the variables of leadership, personality, and charisma are completely absent; thus, the practice of democratic representation is reduced to the narrow confines of rational deliberation and interest bargaining. Yet it would be unrealistic to negate the fact that the processes of identification whereby public officials try to establish some sort of emotional bond with the electorate are not an integral component of the political life of liberal democracies; identification, bargaining, and deliberation represent different venues for bridging the distance that representative government inevitably introduces between rulers and the ruled.[22] Even Carl Schmitt, the most conspicuous enemy of representative government, admits that these two principles can coexist under representative democracy.[23]

20. Arditi, "Populism and the Internal Periphery," 77.

21. Canovan, *The People,* 78.

22. Furthermore, one could argue that representative democracy is a type of regime that presupposes, if it is going to work properly, the presence of those multiple political logics (reasoning, bargaining, and identification). Where such plurality is suppressed by a one-sided pursuit of one of those logics at the expense of the others, the practice of democratic representation is negatively affected.

23. According to Carl Schmitt, representation is in open tension with the idea of democracy. He understands representative government as a system of mediations and democracy as a form of government that presupposes the unmediated identification of the ruled with the rulers. It is misleading, he argues, to treat the so-called representative democracy as a subtype of democracy since the very workings of representative government undermine the possibility of a democratic identity. The central institution of representative government—parliament—entails, in his view, the insertion of a mediating structure that stands as an obstacle to "true" democracy. The notion of "free representation" is predicated on the lack of identity between mediated and unmediated will: it supposes that the only legitimate popular will is the one that is generated through a complex system of constitutional and institutional

Here, I consequently restrict the term "populism" to a political strategy that promotes a process of antagonistic identification that, if successful, divides society into two irreconcilable camps. Such a strategy is predicated on a specific notion of the "people" that negates any legitimate political status to those not included within this term. The politics of populism is framed within a conception of politics and the political as war that is insensitive to issues such as constitutional restraints, divisions of power, and checks and balances. This is precisely what gives a radical impulse to this form of politicization, for it avoids falling prey to the trappings of the neutralizing logic of liberal-democratic regimes. To downplay this dimension of populism is to turn a blind eye to its most distinguishing feature.

The Rise of Classical Populism in Latin America

To understand the historical conditions that gave rise to classical populist regimes in Latin America, it is necessary to analyze the peculiar interaction that democracy and liberalism established on the continent. Liberalism and democracy have historically developed a tense and conflicting relationship in Latin America that has differentiated its experience from that of other regions. The genealogy of the conflict goes back to the very beginnings of the continent's political modernity. In contrast to other regions, in Latin America democratic ideals were already present at the genesis of the modern political order. As a result, democratic institutions were incorporated at a very early stage in several countries of the region.[24] As Tulio Halperin Donghi argues, democracy in Latin America was an unavoidable presence from the very creation of a new political order and thus presented a constant problem for state-building elites and for the constitutional experiments of the nineteenth century.[25]

mediations. For representative institutions to function properly, he argues, representatives have to be independent of the "immediate popular will." See Carl Schmitt, *Constitutional Theory* (Durham, N.C.: Duke University Press, 2008).

24. Françoise-Xavier Guerra, *Modernidad e Independencias: Ensayo sobre las revoluciones hispánicas* (Mexico City: Fondo de Cultura Económica, 2000); Hilda Sábato, *La Política en las Calles: Entre el voto y la movilización: Buenos Aires, 1862–1880* (Buenos Aires: Editorial Sudamericana, 1998).

25. Tulio Halperin Donghi, "Liberalismo argentino y mexicano: Dos destinos divergentes," in *El Espejo de la Historia: Problemas argentinos y perspectivas latinoamericanas*, by Tulio Halperin Donghi (Buenos Aires: Editorial Sudamericana, 1987).

The answer to such an early presence of democracy was the establishment of an institutional order that formally incorporated democratic institutions but at the same time distorted their performance through electoral fraud or other mechanisms oriented toward consolidating the social and political hegemony of dominant elites.[26] Therefore, though many oligarchic regimes combined elements of democracy and liberalism, their actual dynamics distorted democratic representation so that dominant elites could retain political power. Democratic rights and elections were formally recognized but were frequently violated by a variety of informal mechanisms. The classical experience of populism in Latin America is intrinsically related to the crisis of these oligarchic regimes. Classical populist regimes built their democratic credentials by denouncing the democratic flaws of the oligarchic order that had deprived large sectors of society of effective political representation.[27] Their promise was to replace such a democratic facade with real democracy by granting effective democratic rights to those sectors that had previously been excluded from political participation.

Populist regimes consequently emerge as a democratizing reaction against the shortcomings of the liberal, representative regimes of the oligarchic order.[28] Populist interventions are a response to a crisis of representation or, to use Gino Germani's language, to a crisis of political incorporation.[29] The promise of populism is the closing of such a repre-

The participation of the lower classes in the Wars of Independence was much more prominent in Latin America than the role they played in the creation of national states in Europe. See Gino Germani, "Middle-Class Authoritarianism and Fascism: Europe and Latin America," in *Authoritarianism, Fascism, and National Populism*, by Gino Germani (New Brunswick, N.J.: Transaction Books, 1978), 66.

26. Natalio Botana, *El Orden Conservador* (Buenos Aires: Editorial Sudamericana, 1979); Carlos de la Torre, *Populist Seduction in Latin America* (Athens: Ohio University Center for International Studies, 2000), 35; Sábato, *La Política en las Calles*.

27. De la Torre, *Populist Seduction*, 58.

28. See Gino Germani, *Política y Sociedad en una Época de Transición* (Buenos Aires: Editorial Paidos, 1979), 198–200.

29. In some cases, such a crisis was aggravated by authoritarian attempts to neutralize access to participation by establishing semiauthoritarian or openly authoritarian regimes. This in turn led to a double representative crisis involving those who had already been formally incorporated as well as sectors that were recently mobilized. For example, Germani argues that between 1943 and 1945 Argentina was experiencing a double crisis of incorporation and that consequently there were two mobilized masses: the new proletariat and the urban middle classes. The latter mobi-

sentational deficit through the installation of a "true" democracy. In a context where electoral competition is perceived to be distorted by fraud, the issue of clean elections emerges as the decisive yardstick for evaluating a regime's democratic character. The end of fraud and electoral manipulation is presented as the key to making elections a true verdict of popular aspirations. As Juan Domingo Perón proudly stated:

> In the political arena, . . . we have cured the illness that has affected the nation for more than a century, and we began by eliminating that which gave Argentinean democracy the sheen of invalidity: electoral fraud, fraud which made clear to any observer the true and terrible lie of democracy in Argentina.[30]

Free elections are the cornerstone upon which classical populist regimes build their democratic credentials. Electoral success in free elections is crucial for building the democratic legitimacy of the new regime, for winning the election is interpreted as the empirical confirmation that a leader embodies popular aspirations. Elections are the legitimate way to establish the democratic credentials of the regime.[31] Yet elections—as Carl Schmitt warned—can be at the service of very different goals depending on the particular political context in which they take place. Elections, Schmitt argued, can serve either the principle of representation or of antagonistic identification. Under populism, they clearly serve the latter; they are viewed as a decisive moment when the majority makes its pronouncement. Such a decision can neither be challenged nor be the subject of subsequent deliberation. The following interpretation by Juan Domingo Perón of his electoral triumph helps to illustrate the differences between this mode of will formation and a liberal-constitutional deliberative one:

lized to recover the political freedoms and democratic institutions suppressed by the military regime of 1943. Gino Germani, "Structural Change, Fascist Attempts, and the Rise of Lower Classes and National Populism," in *Authoritarianism*, 173.

30. Juan Domingo Perón, "Discurso del 25 de julio de 1949," 1949: "En la arena política, . . . hemos curado la enfermedad que ha afectado a la nación por más de un siglo, y empezamos por eliminar aquello que dio a la democracia argentina un viso de nulidad: el fraude electoral, fraude que hacia visible a los ojos de cualquier espectador la terrible mentira que realmente era la democracia en la Argentina."

31. This emphasis on elections is of course dictated by the historical context that gave birth to populist democracies in the region. The sociopolitical conditions thus mark an important difference between classical populist and current delegative democracies. I return to this distinction in the third section below.

When our firm and unshakeable will is confronted with that of our opponents, there remains only one problem to resolve: Who has the justification and who has the right to impose their will? We have given the people the opportunity to choose, in the cleanest election in the history of Argentina, between us and our opponents. The people have elected us, so the problem is resolved. What we want is now done in the Republic of Argentina.[32]

The electoral act is interpreted as a momentous decision point that forecloses any subsequent debate. The electoral triumph confers the "right to impose" the majority's will.[33] In this understanding of democracy, *elections become the decisive moment of the representative contract*: They are momentous, decisive acts that preclude any subsequent challenge or deliberation. Electoral delegation entails an act of political abdication on the part of the electorate, which must passively accept and conform to the leadership principle.[34]

The populist model of democracy is at odds with any idea of accountability. Elections are viewed exclusively as a process of popular authori-

32. Perón, "Discurso del 25 de Julio," 9: "Confrontada nuestra firme e inquebrantable voluntad con la de nuestros oponentes solo queda un problema a elucidar: Quien tiene la razón y quien tiene el derecho a imponer su voluntad? Le hemos dado al pueblo la oportunidad de elegir en la elección mas limpia de la historia argentina entre nosotros y nuestros oponentes. El pueblo nos eligió a nosotros, por lo tanto dicho problema está resuelto. En la República Argentina se hace lo que nosotros queremos."

33. Democratization is envisioned as a gradual process of homogenization of the political landscape whose final point of arrival is the untenable fiction of a unanimous will. The following quotation from a speech by Perón illustrates this conception of democracy as leading to the political homogenization of society: "Our doctrine . . . is a patriotic doctrine. Therefore, I see no inconvenience in introducing it everywhere. If it were a bad doctrine I would be the first one in challenging it; but being a good one, we should try to introduce it everywhere, in all men and women, so we can assure the triumph of a unified collective action." Perón, "Discurso del 25 de julio," 46.

34. I have developed these arguments in Enrique Peruzzotti, "Civil Society and the Modern Constitutional Complex: The Argentine Experience," *Constellations: An International Journal of Critical and Democratic Theory* 4, no. 1 (April 1997). On the features and perdurability of Latin American populism, see also de la Torre, *Populist Seduction*. Also the arguments developed by Guillermo O'Donnell about current delegative democracies, which, as argued above, extrapolate many of the features that are constitutive of the populist forms of democratic self-understanding into a postpopulist socioeconomic context. Guillermo O'Donnell, "Delegative Democracy," in *Counterpoints: Selected Essays on Authoritarianism and Democratization*, edited by Guillermo O'Donnell (Notre Dame, Ind.: Notre Dame University Press, 1999), 159–73.

zation that excludes any element of accountability. Furthermore, populism tends to ignore or bypass mechanisms of checks and balances and of the separation of powers. It considers that such an institutional structure of representative government ties up the popular will, making it politically impotent. Popular sovereignty is politically threatened by the excessive zeal exhibited by representative government to protect and give voice to minorities. It considers that constitutional guarantees and accountability mechanisms are tools at the service of minorities, which use them to weaken the majority's standing.

To execute popular aspirations, it is necessary to ignore or dismantle the institutional apparatus of representative democracy.[35] This obviously implies a reorientation of the democratic principle to the executive power; the popularly elected president appears as the institutional power that directly expresses the democratic will of the people, whereas the legislative and judicial powers represent constitutional constraints on the majority. To preserve its democratic substance, the president must always keep direct contact with the people, and this usually leads to the establishment of forms of communication that bypass representative channels of opinion formation and aggregation. Elections, the mass media, and mass mobilizations are the prominent mechanisms that a leader has at hand to stay in constant connection with the people, and they all play a central role in populist regimes.

In its condemnation of the vices of oligarchic rule, populism ends up drawing a drastic opposition between liberalism and democracy, without taking into consideration that certain elements of the liberal tradition cannot be eliminated without jeopardizing the very possibility of democratic representation. Populism strives to eliminate the tension that inevitably exists between democracy and liberalism without acknowledging that such tension is indispensable for the proper functioning of democracy. Although liberal constitutionalism imposes clear limits on popular aspirations, it simultaneously provides the cornerstone upon which the edifice of modern representative democracy is established.[36] The establishment of a constitutional state based on the idea of universal human rights—by divorcing right and might—made institutionally pos-

---

35. Paul A. Taggard, *Populism* (London: Open University Press, 2000), 116.

36. David Beetham, "Liberal Democracy and the Limits of Democratization," in *Democracy: Critical Concepts in Political Science*, vol. 1, edited by Michael Saward (London: Routledge, 2000), 91.

sible the idea of democracy as an empty place of power. The politics of rights that the latter inaugurates aims at maintaining the place of power as an empty one against authoritarian claims to fully embody the people.[37] To eliminate this dimension of democratic politics is equal to destroying the very foundations of the modern democratic project. This is not to say that a liberal democracy cannot be the target of further democratization; it can be one as long as the democratizing intervention does not eliminate the liberal components altogether and turn democracy into electoral authoritarianism. What liberal components are necessary to preserve the proper functioning of democratic representation? Those that limit and constitutionally constrain state power and guarantee the political autonomy of citizens in civil society: fundamental rights; the principle of the separation of powers; and the presence of representative mediations like parliament, parties, and the public sphere.[38] These institutions, though predating modern democracy, serve as institutional safeguards that prevent democracy from degenerating into whatever an elected government decides are the popular aspirations of the moment.[39]

What are these liberal components that should be questioned and removed? They are those elements that attempt to isolated the process of decisionmaking from the influence and control of citizens, attempting to suppress the creative dialectic between instituted and instituting power that the edifice of modern liberal democracy made possible. This is the problem with many of the contemporary democratic regimes that rest on a very thin understanding of democratic representation, undermining the conditions for continued contestation, and thus eliminating the creative dimension of democratic politics. Democracy is consequently reduced to elitist rule, because political representation is understood as an activity that largely falls on the shoulders of political elites. There are differences within the minimalist model, particularly in relation to the degree of accountability they are willing to tolerate. Yet their common denominator is the desire to reduce the political role of citizens in democratic representation to a minimum.[40] In Latin America, the concept of delegative de-

37. See Claude Leffort, "Politics and Human Rights," in *The Political Forms of Modern Society: Bureaucracy, Democracy, and Authoritarianism*, edited by John B. Thompson (Cambridge, Mass.: MIT Press, 1986), 239–72.

38. Beetham, "Liberal Democracy," 291–92.

39. Ibid., 293.

40. Enrique Peruzzotti, "Two Approaches to Representation," Working Paper, Departamento de Sociología, Pontificia Universidad Católica del Perú, 2006.

mocracy aims to describe a local variant of the minimalist model. What is behind such a concept? I next turn to a discussion of delegative democracy and its alleged similarities with populist forms of politics.

Are Current Democratic Regimes Populist?
A View of the Concept of Delegative Democracy

The concept of "delegative democracy," which was coined by Guillermo O'Donnell, was meant to distinguish a subtype of democracy that differs from the representative one by its notorious deficit in all forms of accountability except the electoral one. The concept was a call to attention regarding the shortcomings that the current process of democratization was experiencing in a selected number of national cases. According to O'Donnell, the pattern of democratization had bifurcated. On one hand, in those societies that already had a previous and successful history of liberal democracy—Chile and Uruguay—the process of democratic consolidation was framed within the institutional and cultural parameters of liberal democracy. On the other hand, those countries that had historically been characterized by institutional instability and populism—Argentina, Peru, and Brazil—were generating a particular form of democracy that bore little resemblance to its representative cousin.

The idea of delegative democracy was developed to describe a particular form of conceiving and exercising democratic power that leads to the establishment of a particular subtype of polyarchy. Delegative democracies, O'Donnell argues, represent a degraded version of "polyarchy" whereby citizens can regularly exercise their right to vote in relatively free elections but see their civic rights repeatedly curtailed by the authoritarian behavior of public authorities.[41] What distinguishes delegative regimes from other forms of polyarchy is the absence of an effective system of checks and balances and a notorious concentration of power in the executive.

O'Donnell focuses his attention on the behavior of executive leaders and how they understand and interpret their role. Delegative democracy presupposes a particular way of understanding democratic representa-

41. Guillermo O'Donnell, "On the State, Democratization and Some Conceptual Problems: A Latin American View with Glances at Some Post-Communist Countries," *World Development* 21, no. 8 (1993): 1361.

tion whereby the electoral victory is seen as an authorization to act without major institutional restrictions. Populist and delegative democracies share significant similarities. It is therefore no coincidence that delegative democracies emerge in countries with strong populist traditions.[42] In fact, many analysts view delegative democracies as the current incarnation of the populist ideal. To support their assertion, they draw attention to the features that both regimes have in common: concentration of power in the executive, disregard for the division of power and for mechanisms of checks and balances, interpretation of the electoral mandate as an authorization to act as the president sees fit, and so on. There is no doubt that there is some overlap between the ways in which delegative and populist leaders understand their role. However, can delegative democracy be blindly associated with past populist experiences?

Guillermo O'Donnell is reluctant to make such a claim. In his view, significant features of populism are missing from current delegative regimes, the most salient being the mobilization of the people that has characterized classical populist experiences like *peronismo* and *velasquismo*. Far from promoting the politicization and mobilization of popular sectors, O'Donnell argues that delegative regimes thrive in a political culture characterized by a significant degree of political apathy.[43] What seems to be missing in the delegative experience is something that earlier theories of populism emphasized: the presence of "an available mass." Classical populism emerged from the crisis of political inclusion that deprived ordinary citizens of effective representation. Populism presented itself as the vehicle that would end this representational deficit by fully incorporating into public life the sectors that oligarchic rule had previously ignored.[44] This is not the type of scenario that gave rise to delegative democracy. Except for the particular circumstances that gave rise to Fujimori—the combination of a crisis of representation together with the threat of the Shining Path—the rest of the classic examples of delegative democracy refer to societies that are recovering from a new form of military rule: bureaucratic authoritarianism.

The experience of state terrorism, with its traumatic legacy of human rights violations, makes the current historical conjuncture different from

42. O'Donnell, "Delegative Democracy."
43. O'Donnell, "On the State," 1367.
44. See Gino Germani, *Política y Sociedad en una Época de Transición* (Buenos Aires: Paidos Editorial, 1979); and chapters 1 and 4 in this volume.

that of classical populism, for two reasons. The first refers to a feature that was always highlighted by analysts of Latin American populism: newly mobilized social sectors that lack political representation. Given the repressive nature of bureaucratic-authoritarian regimes and their radical elimination of all forms of political intermediation between state and society, the transition to a regime of free elections was considered a collective accomplishment *by all sectors of society* (and not just by a particular sector of the population, as in the case of classical populism).[45] This is why in these cases one cannot talk about the presence of an "available mass," for the whole population had been silenced and politically excluded by bureaucratic authoritarianism. To find a similar scenario of struggles for the incorporation of politically excluded groups, we need to turn our attention to the political experiences of Bolivia and Ecuador and the activation of the indigenous movement.

A second element that differentiates the present scenario from that of classical populism is the popular perception of democracy and representation. The trauma of state terrorism gave rise to an active regional network of human rights organizations and to novel forms of politics organized partly around a liberal agenda: the politics of human rights and of social accountability that aimed to draw clear institutional boundaries between state and society while also strengthening the system of checks and balances and the division of power to ensure governmental accountability. Latin American civil societies have a more demanding attitude regarding democracy—particularly in relation to rights protections and checks on government—which generates a significant social pressure to move to a constitutional form of representative democracy. The politics of rights is a crucial antidote to the populist attempt to fill in the empty space of democratic power with a figure that claims to embody the people as one. It is precisely the role of rights-oriented groups to continuously challenge any attempt by a leader, movement, or party to occupy such an empty place.

In such a cultural context, it is difficult for political leaders to build their democratic credentials based solely on the existence of free elections, as was the case with classical populism. This is not to downplay the political significance of the consolidation of democracies stemming from regular, competitive, and free elections in a region like Latin America

45. Guillermo O'Donnell, *El Estado Burocrático-Autoritario: Triunfos, derrotas y crisis* (Buenos Aires: Editorial de Belgrano, 2002).

that has historically been characterized by institutional instability and recurrent authoritarianism. Yet this accomplishment is not enough in and of itself; there are now other claims that are considered just as relevant as free elections, such as the constitutional limitation of state power and the establishment of strong guarantees for the protection of human rights. The emergence of a politics of human rights and of social accountability signals the existence of a social and cultural environment that poses informal limits to the delegative executive and that challenges important aspects of the populist democratic tradition.[46] The aim of these new forms of civic politics is to channel democratic dynamics into the track of *a representative* form of democracy.[47] A strategy of polarizing identification would consequently encounter significant resistance.[48]

Is one to conclude that the specter of populism is gone? Definitely not. As argued above, the phenomenon of populism is likely to arise wherever there is a crisis of incorporation or a crisis of representation that is generated by the malfunctioning of mechanisms of political mediation. The shortcomings that delegative and minimalist models of democracy

46. Enrique Peruzzotti, "Towards a New Politics: Citizenship and Rights in Contemporary Argentina," *Citizenship Studies* 6, no. 1 (2000).

47. Enrique Peruzzotti, "Demanding Accountable Government: Citizens, Politicians and the Perils of Representative Democracy in Argentina," in *Argentine Democracy: The Politics of Institutional Weakness*, edited by Steven Levitsky and Maria Victoria Murillo (University Park: Pennsylvania State University Press, 2005). Even the phenomenon of *fujimorismo* in Peru had to confront those novel claims of human rights and accountability. See Catherine Conaghan, *Fujimori's Peru: Deception in the Public Sphere* (Pittsburgh: University of Pittsburgh Press, 2005); and Nicolás Lynch, "Los usos de los medios en el Perú de Fujimori," in *Controlando la Política: Ciudadanos y Medios en las Nuevas Democracias Latinoamericanas*, edited by Enrique Peruzzotti and Catalina Smulovitz (Buenos Aires: Termas Editorial, 2002).

48. Faced last year with vocal opposition from agricultural producers to the new export tax plan implemented by her administration, Cristina Fernández de Kirchner opted for a populist strategy that attempted to resuscitate the "people versus the oligarchy" discursive axis of the national-popular tradition. This discursive shift, however, found little receptivity in a postdictatorial Argentina, with its new sensibility regarding the issue of governmental accountability. Peruzzotti, "Demanding Accountable Government." We could judge the success of Cristina Fernández's strategy by its results; it not only failed to polarize Argentine society into two camps, but it also quickly depleted the political capital of *kirchnerismo*. The president's political support fell dramatically, from the 60 percent popularity she enjoyed in her first months in power to her current level of support in the low 20s. The draining in political support that she has suffered in the past two years has not created a strong nor unified oppositional camp. Instead, her former supporters have distributed themselves among an ideologically heterogeneous plurality of oppositional forces.

exhibit in many societies (models that are predicated on a very restrictive and elitist understanding of democratic representation) are likely to generate the conditions for the reappearance of populism. It is no coincidence that the clearest expressions of populist politics are to be found in countries like Ecuador and Venezuela, which had experienced the crisis of a liberal-representative political order and had no experience of bureaucratic authoritarianism.[49] As with classical populism, Chávez makes his claim to democracy by opposing the notorious shortcomings of the previous institutional order, which, in his view, was nothing but an oligarchic facade preventing the Venezuelan people from truly expressing their will. The inability of the representative regime established in 1958 to provide an adequate response to popular demands led to its solidification and the decay of all mediating institutions. The Caracazo palpably illustrates the gulf between the government and the people of Venezuela.[50] The inability of the Caldera administration to reverse course by implementing drastic measures to restore some degree of political trust in the institutional system paved the way for the emergence of Hugo Chávez.[51] In Ecuador, Rafael Correa's leadership stems from a similar set of circumstances and political environment.[52]

Conclusion: Strategies of Democratic Deepening and Democratic Representation

The future of populism in Latin America will depend on the ability of current regimes to pursue reforms that can recreate and strengthen democratic representation. It will require a process of democratic deepening that continually moves the region away from existing delegative and

49. Jennifer McCoy and David J. Myers, *The Unraveling of Representative Democracy in Venezuela* (Baltimore: Johns Hopkins University Press, 2006).
50. See chapter 9 of the present volume, by Margarita López Maya and Alexandra Panzarelli.
51. Ibid.
52. Carlos de la Torre, "The Resurgence of Radical Populism in Latin America," *Constellations: An International Journal of Critical and Democratic Theory* 14, no. 3 (2007); Flavia Freidenberg, "El Flautista de Hamelin: Liderzago y Populismo en la Democracia Ecuatoriana," in *El Retorno del Pueblo: Populismo y Nuevas Democracias en América Latina*, edited by Carlos de la Torre and Enrique Peruzzotti (Quito: FLACSO, 2008); César Montúfar, "El Populismo Intermitente de Gutiérrez," in *Retorno del Pueblo*, ed. de la Torre and Peruzzotti.

minimalist regimes and toward a form of representative democracy that institutionalizes a broad and pluralist set of mediated politics that dramatically improves the political system's receptiveness to citizen demands. The deepening of democracy in Latin America forces one to elaborate a stronger notion of political accountability than those that prevail nowadays in political and academic debate. Without negating either the relevance of horizontal and electoral mechanisms of accountability or the diverse informal expressions of social accountability, it is necessary to advance the development of a dense set of mediated politics that strengthen the channels of communication between state and society. Although the emergence of a politics of social accountability has provided a much-needed input in a region that has tended to disregard *legal* mechanisms of accountability, it is in itself insufficient for it cannot fully address the deficit of political representation that feeds the populist impulse.[53]

The politics of social accountability might help expose the horizontal deficit of accountability that has characterized delegative democracies and to denounce any attempt at eliminating the separation between law and power. However, the defense of a legal state and the efforts to strengthen horizontal accountability do not automatically result in better political responsiveness. In fact, several variants of the minimal model of democracy also advocate for the existence of strong horizontal controls.[54] The politics of social accountability can foster a transition from delegative to minimalist democracies, but it cannot properly advance an agenda that focuses on the problem of political receptiveness. It is necessary to envision another transition from minimal to a deepened form of representative democracy. The latter requires not limiting democratic struggles to the paradigm of human rights politics but making an effort to expand the existing political repertoire in new directions in a way that would creatively address the social and political deficits of existing democratic regimes.

There is a need to develop an agenda of political and institutional reform that could provide a viable alternative to the "populist seduction"

53. I have developed this argument at length; see Enrique Peruzzotti, "El Otro Déficit de la Democracia Delegativa: Retomando el debate acerca de la rendición de cuentas en las democracias contemporáneas de América Latina," *Journal of Democracy en Español* 2 (July 2010): 47–64.

54. See Adam Przeworksi, Susan C. Stokes, and Bernard Manin, eds., *Democracy, Accountability, and Representation* (Cambridge: Cambridge University Press, 1999).

of a simpler democracy. The latter supposes the expansion of the field of mediated politics by establishing new arenas for public deliberation that could improve the channels of communication of citizens with the political authorities.[55] The populist response—however attractive it might look in periods when formal institutions have lost their appeal—might provide only short-term relief to society at the expense of further widening the gaps in representation and accountability.

Democratic representation is an inherently intricate task that is realized through a complex system of institutional intermediations that need to be constantly re-created and reinvented to avoid the dangers of institutional ossification that might open the doors to a populist outcome. Instead of pursuing the unrealistic task of eliminating representative mediations in an impossible search for an authentic form of direct democracy, one should patiently engage in the creation and recreation of new spaces and arenas that can dramatically improve the political receptiveness of democratic institutions to popular demands. This is not an unrealistic project, and in fact many democracies in Latin America are already engaging in very interesting experiments in participatory innovation.

---

55. See Andrew Selee and Enrique Peruzzotti, eds., *Participatory Innovation and Representative Democracy* (Washington, D.C., and Baltimore: Woodrow Wilson Center Press and Johns Hopkins University Press, 2009); and Leonardo Avrtizer, *Participatory Institutions in Democratic Brazil* (Washington, D.C., and Baltimore: Woodrow Wilson Center Press and Johns Hopkins University Press, 2009).

Chapter 4

What Do We Mean When We
Talk About Populism?

Francisco Panizza

Francisco Panizza

"Más populista será tu abuela!"[1]

—José "Pepe" Mujica

The title of this chapter alludes to the seemingly never-ending debates about the definition of populism, while its epigraph alludes to the strong negative connotations associated with the term. As is well known, there is little agreement among scholars about the meaning of this term that has been associated with historical periods, sociological processes, economic policies, and styles of governance, among others. I am neither ignoring the myriad views on populism nor seeking to join the detailed debate about its ultimate meaning that is undertaken elsewhere in this book.

The debate about populism can be divided between those who propose a more expansive definition of populism and consider it a multi-

1. It is difficult to translate this idiomatic expression, which means, literally, "More populist would be your grandmother." An approximate translation that captures the meaning of the phrase would be, "Populist, my ass!"

faceted concept, and those who argue that empirical variations among different modalities of populism can only be accommodated by adopting a minimalist definition of the term. Suffice it to say that political concepts are not true or false, but more or less useful. There are good reasons (as indicated above in chapter 1, the introduction) to opt for a minimalist definition of populism, centered on its political-discursive core, and to use it to distinguish analytically among its different dimensions.

Of course, other definitions of populism and many questions are left unsettled by this minimalist definition, including whether populism refers to leaders, movements, or political regimes; about the links between leaders and followers; and above all, about its democratic or antidemocratic effects.[2] As mentioned above, however, a significant body of work argues that populism is primarily characterized by a distinctive discursive strategy aiming at the constitution of popular identities. As a mode of identification, a populist appeal operates by establishing a relation of political antagonism between "the people" (as the plebs or the underdogs) and some kind of oppressive power (e.g., the state, the political establishment, the economic oligarchy, an ethnic group, or the party system). Key to this definition is the notion, discussed in greater detail below, that the politically constructed identity of "the people" depends on a constitutive outside—a threatening heterogeneity against which other-

---

2. For definitions of populism that, while stressing its political nature, take into consideration other elements, see Flavia Freidenberg, "El flautista de Hammelin: Liderazgo y populismo en la democracia ecuatoriana," in *El Retorno del Pueblo: Populismo y nuevas democracia en América Latina*, edited by Carlos de la Torre and Enrique Peruzzotti (Quito: FLACSO–Ecuador and Ministerio de Cultura, 2008), 189–237; Alan Knight, "Populism and Neo-Populism in Latin America, Especially in Mexico," *Journal of Latin American Studies* 30 (1998): 223–48; Kenneth M. Roberts, "Neoliberalism and the Transformation of Populism in Latin America: The Peruvian Case," *World Politics* 48 (1995): 82–116; Kenneth M. Roberts, "Latin America's Populist Revival," *SAIS Review* 27, no. 1 (2007): 3–15; and Kurt Weyland, "Clarifying a Contested Concept: Populism in the Study of Latin American Politics," *Comparative Politics*, October 2001, 1–22. For a discussion of the relations between populism and democracy see Koen Abts and Stefan Rummens, "Populism and Democracy," *Political Studies* 55 (2007): 405–24; Benjamin Arditi, "Populism as a Spectre of Democracy: A Response to Canovan," *Political Studies* 52, no. 1 (2004): 135–43; Francisco Panizza, "Introduction," in *Populism and the Mirror of Democracy*, edited by Francisco Panizza (London: Verso, 2005), 1–31; and Francisco Panizza and Romina Miorelli, "Populism and Democracy in Latin America," *Ethics and International Affairs*, Spring 2009, 39–46.

wise heterogeneous social identities morph into a homogenous popular one.[3] Margaret Canovan emphasizes the systemic nature of the antagonistic relationship when she defines populism as "an appeal to 'the people' against both the established structure of power and the dominant ideas and values," whereas Carlos de la Torre highlights the mutually constitutive nature of the actors in conflict when he defines it as the construction of a Manichaean and moral discourse that positions the *pueblo* in antagonistic opposition to the "oligarchy."[4]

To claim that populism is about the discursive constitution of popular identities means that the identities of the people and of their oppressor are the result of a political operation rather than socioeconomic categories. Thus, in his book *The Populist Persuasion: An American History*, the historian Michael Kazin traces the history of populism throughout America's political life, as it changes the mutually constructed identities of the people and of their oppressors—from the financiers of Wall Street to the Washington elite—and changes its political colors to suit progressive radicals and right-wing conservatives at different points in time.[5]

This chapter takes the discursive notion of populism as a starting point and deconstructs it in order to argue five main points. First, an understanding of populism needs to take into account its symbolic, representational, political, and normative dimensions and the relations among them. Second, the emphasis on the formal, antagonistic nature of populism's political appeal underscores its normative element, or what Canovan calls its "redemptive" dimension. Third, as a mode of identification—or, as Kazin puts it, "a flexible mode of persuasion"—populist appeals are compatible with a variety of ideological formulations and institutional settings, but their political effects are constrained by the political institutions—or lack thereof—within which the appeal operates.

3. This concept of populism is strongly associated with the seminal works by Ernesto Laclau. See Ernesto Laclau, *Politics and Ideology in Marxist Theory* (London: Verso, 1977); Ernesto Laclau, "Populism: What's In a Name?" in *Populism*, ed. Panizza, 32–49; and Ernesto Laclau, *On Populist Reason* (London: Verso, 2005).

4. Margaret Canovan, "Trust the People! Populism and the Two Faces of Democracy," *Political Studies* 47 (1999): 2; Carlos de la Torre, "Populismo Radical y Democracia en los Andes," *Journal of Democracy en Español* 1 (2009): 24–38. See also Enrique Peruzzotti, "Populismo y Representación Democrática," in *Retorno del Pueblo*, ed. de la Torre and Peruzzotti, 97–124.

5. Michael Kazin, *The Populist Persuasion: An American History* (Ithaca, N.Y.: Cornell University Press, 1995).

In some cases, populist appeals can become dominant and populist identities can structure the political field for long historical periods, while in other circumstances they are more limited in their scope, efficacy, and durability.[6] Fourth, political actors use populist appeals in combination with other modes of political identification. Thus, it makes more sense to talk about *populist interventions* rather than about *populist actors* or *regimes* to signify that politics—particularly democratic politics—always carries within it the traces of populism and that populism is never an encompassing totality that completely defines a leader, a party, or a regime. Fifth, and finally, though normative judgments about populism are inevitable, the relationship between populism and democracy cannot be established in abstract terms, but should be assessed in relation to the political context where populism and democracy interact. The following sections explore each of these dimensions of populism, concluding with a suggestion that different varieties of populist intervention have context-dependent relations with democratic institutions, and that it is important to make explicit their normative implications.

"Más Populista Será Tu Abuela"

The following political story encapsulates many of the issues and ambiguities involved in studying populism. A full appreciation of the relevance of the story would require a long contextual explanation, but I will try to be concise. The story refers to José "Pepe" Mujica, the former Tupamaro guerrilla leader (quoted in the epigraph), who won the November 2009 presidential election in Uruguay to become the country's president in March 2010. In a well-argued article published early in the electoral campaign in May 2009, the free market economist Ernesto Talvi claimed that deep structural changes in Uruguayan society had set up the socioeconomic conditions for the emergence of what he called "populist tendencies" in the country. He argued that a decline in educational standards and the migration of hundreds of thousands of highly qualified citizens had led to the shrinking of the country's traditional middle classes and to the expansion of a poorly educated, poorly qualified social sector whose chances of social mobility were extremely limited and whose members had therefore become dependent on social assistance from the state. He further argued that given the increasing size of this social underclass,

---

6. Canovan, "Trust the People!" 9–14; Kazin, *Populist Persuasion*, 3.

one should not be surprised by the emergence and political success of what he described as "atypical candidates whose language, ways of dressing, and attitude are in contrast with the more formal 'suit and tie' candidates characteristic of the country's political class."[7]

In all but name, Talvi was referring to José Mujica, the presidential candidate of the left-of-center Frente Amplio (more on his language and way of dressing below). Mujica's answer, published in his blog, was as swift as it was peerless. It is worth quoting a rather lengthy excerpt from his reply to show its true flavor:[8]

> It seems that a new and terrible threat hovers over Uruguay: It is called José Mujica and he is the bearer of a deadly virus, the virus of populism. I am not exaggerating. Read the newspapers and you will find a summary of the theory formulated by the economist Talvi, from the CERES institute [a free market economic think tank]. You will learn that in our poor country there is a third of the population who, due to their lack of education, are useless and only aspire to state handouts and who, by definition, vote for those who look more likely to shower public money over their heads.
>
> If we go a little further with this theory, we find out that this bunch of good for nothings identify with their leaders because they dress badly, use coarse language and have no carpets in their homes.
>
> The newspapers didn't name anybody. Probably they were referring to Ignacio de Posadas or Pedro Bordaberry [two upper-class politicians].

7. Ernesto Talvi, "Tendencias Socioculturales y Cambio Político," *CERES: Resumen de Prensa* (Montevideo), May 2009.

8. The full quotation, in Spanish, reads: "Parece que una nueva y terrible amenaza se cierne sobre el Uruguay: Se llama José Mujica y es portador de un virus tenebroso, el populismo. No exagero; lean los diarios y se van a encontrar con el resumen de la teoría formulada por el economista Talvi, del instituto CERES. Se van a enterar de que en nuestro pobre país hay un tercio de la población que por falta de educación no sirve para nada, sólo aspira a que el Estado les dé todo y por definición votan a quien tiene pinta de ser bueno para hacer llover dinero público sobre sus cabezas. Un saltito más en la teoría y nos enteramos de que esa manga de inútiles reconocen a sus líderes por lo mal que se visten, lo toscos que son para hablar y la falta de alfombras en sus viviendas. No nombraron a nadie faltaba más. Probablemente se referían a Ignacio de Posadas o a Pedro Bordaberry. Pero como yo tengo manía de persecución y además me gusta hacerme la víctima, se me ha metido en la cabeza que se referían a mí. Por lo que me apuro a contestarle, al economista Talvi, que más populista será tu abuela."

But as I have a persecution complex, I imagine that they were referring to me. To which I hasten to reply to Mr. Talvi: *Más populista sera
tu abuela.*[9]

The colloquial and "unpolitical" tone of Mujica's reply appears to
give credence to Talvi's claim that, at least judging by his use of language,
Mujica is indeed a populist. However, wrapped in the everyday colloquial language that is part of his political trademark, Mujica's reply
shows a shrewd understanding not only of the political implications of
Talvi's claim but also of the arguments about populism.

Mujica acknowledges that the term "populism" has multiple meanings and that within certain contexts it can be taken as a compliment. He
is well aware, however, that this is not the sense in which Talvi has used
the term. Quoting Mujica again:[10]

I am aware that in the world of political analysis the word "populism"
is used in more than one sense, and that within a certain context, it
may even be considered a term of praise. This is not the meaning used
by Mr. Talvi and less so by the newspapers. They said "populism" in
its everyday sense, associated with cheap politicians that chase votes
by promising paradise on earth to the poor and that, once in office,
use state money to give them a false prosperity for a limited time until
everything bursts.[11]

I do not know if Mujica has ever read Dornbusch and Edwards's
economic definition of populism as the short-term pursuit of growth and
income distribution at the cost of higher inflation and large fiscal deficits,
but linguistic differences apart, the similarities between the two definitions are remarkable.[12] Mujica strongly denies being a populist in the eco-

9. José Mujica, "Más populista será tu abuela!" *Pepe tal cuál es* (blog), June 1,
2009, http://www.pepetalcuales.com.uy/articulo/14.
10. "Estoy enterado que en el mundo del análisis político se usa la palabra "populismo" en más de un sentido y que en algún contexto puede considerarse hasta un
elogio. No es esa la versión a la que se refirió Talvi ni menos los diarios. Dijeron
"populismo" en el sentido de todos los días el que está asociado a políticos más bien
baratos, que consiguen votos prometiéndole el paraíso a los pobres, y una vez en el
poder, usan al Estado par regalarles un tiempito de prosperidad mentirosa, hasta
que todo revienta."
11. Mujica, "Más populista."
12. Rudiger Dornbusch and Sebastian Edwards, eds., *The Macroeconomics of
Populism in Latin America* (Chicago: University of Chicago Press, 1991).

nomic sense of the term used by Dornbusch and Edwards, but also in the common political sense used by some political analysts, which makes it synonymous with demagogy and manipulating the lower sectors of the population. As he put it:[13]

> We don't use the poor. If we speak for them politically it is because they feel that they matter to us and that we are going to do everything within our means, in good faith, to improve their lot, just as happened with Lula in Brazil.[14]

Several points in this exchange are worth noting. Mujica is right in rejecting that he is a populist in Dornbusch and Edwards's economic meaning of the term or in the normatively charged political equivalent of the demagogue. As a politician of the left, he has been critical of neo-liberalism and advocates more state intervention in the economy, but he has never advocated the type of fiscally irresponsible policies commonly associated with economic populism. Politically, he establishes a distinction between manipulating the poor, an accusation often levied against populist politicians, and "speaking for them politically," which he seeks to vindicate. He compares himself with President Lula da Silva in a nod to ongoing arguments about "the radical populist" (bad) and the "social-democratic" (good) left in Latin America, and he aligns himself with the latter. And yet he bears some of the markers of identity traditionally associated with populist politicians.[15]

The Symbolic Markers of Populist Identity

In what ways can it be said that, in spite of his protestations to the contrary, Mujica is indeed a populist? The first is via the traditional markers of identity to which Talvi alluded. These include the use of a distinctive type of political rhetoric, style of dressing, and other symbolic elements

---

13. "Nosotros no usamos a los pobres. Si los expresamos políticamente, es porque sienten que nos importan y vamos a hacer todo lo posible, de buena fe para que mejoren. Tal como sucedió en Brasil con Lula."

14. Mujica, "Más populista."

15. For a normative distinction between varieties of the left, see Jorge Castañeda, "Latin America's Left Turn," *Foreign Affairs* 85, no. 3 (2006): 28–43; and Jorge Castañeda and Marco A. Morales, eds., *Leftovers: Tales of the Latin American Left* (New York: Routledge, 2008).

that set him apart from the political establishment and draw him closer to the popular sectors. Because of populism's personal and anti-institutional traits, symbols, rhetoric, and political style have always weighed heavily in analyses of populism. Populist identification is strengthened by the leader's adoption of cultural elements that are considered marks of inferiority by the dominant culture. It is not the purpose of this chapter to closely analyze Mujica's speeches, but his speech permanently transgresses the rhetorical rules of political discourse, particularly the highly conventional rules of public speaking followed by mainstream Uruguayan politicians. He uses vulgar language both in the sense of the plebeian language of the popular sectors (the plebs) and in his occasional use of coarse terms in public.[16] His attire is also an integral part of his political appeal. Famously, he had never worn a suit in public until late in the electoral campaign, when he had his first suit made in preparation for a visit to President Lula in Brazil. Tellingly, the suit, rather than the substance of Mujica's visit, made headlines. His personal appearance is rather unkempt. He leads a notably austere life on a small farm on the rural outskirts of Montevideo, where he often receives visitors in a barn.

There is an ethical element in Mujica's simple lifestyle. He is a strong critic of consumerism and, rare for a politician, he practices what he preaches.[17] But he is also a seasoned politician who is well aware that rhetoric and appearances are powerful drivers of political identification. I am not arguing here that rhetoric and clothes alone make a politician a populist. Historically, populist leaders have come from all social classes and have used language in various ways, but one cannot understand politics without being aware of the centrality of symbols in political life. Using nonpolitical rhetoric (i.e., rhetoric that does not fit with the rules of political discourse) brands the speaker as an outsider to the political establishment. Moreover, when this language incorporates expressions, forms of speech, musical styles, and clothing characteristic of the popular sectors, it does not just convey an antielitist message but also turns social hierarchies upside down by publicly featuring cultural elements that are considered characteristic of socially inferior or uneducated people. Examples abound in Latin America and elsewhere. In Ecuador,

16. Herbert Gatto, "Cultura villera y política," *El País Digital*, September 2, 2009, available at http://www.elpais.com.uy/Paginas.
17. Alejandro Nogueira, "El palo de la colmena," *El País Digital*, June 21, 2009.

Abdalá Bucaram's lack of manners and unorthodox use of profanities and verbal improprieties was presented by the media as an embarrassment to the country's civility and proof that he was unfit for high office. However, as Carlos de la Torre notes, by consciously embodying the dress, language, and mannerisms of the common people, who were despised by the elites and their middle-class imitators, Bucaram attracted the vote of those who saw in him a reflection of themselves and the elevation of their own culture to the public realm.[18]

In the United States, George Wallace purposely mispronounced words to foster an image of himself as an uneducated hillbilly, a trait that highlighted both his distance from the centers of power and his proximity to the people.[19] And of course Hugo Chávez has a masterful command of rhetorical codes that allows him to swiftly switch within the same speech from a statesmanlike quotation of economic figures to the colloquial and personal, and from the quasi-religious language of the visionary prophet to nationalist, anti-imperialist, rhetoric mixed with a coarse "*que se vaya al carajo*" injunction against the U.S. ambassador.[20]

An analysis of the politics of dress and appearance in populism, from Perón's celebration of the *descamisados* (the shirtless) to Evo Morales's iconic jumpers, would reinforce the argument that though symbols are important for any politician, they are particularly crucial in the populist mode of identification. Socioeconomic background, race, ethnic origins, and other markers of exclusion are important symbolic elements that have helped politicians such as Evo Morales and Lula da Silva be perceived by their followers as "one of them," as ordinary folks, instead of one of their countries' traditional political or economic elites. I am not arguing here that politicians who speak, dress, and look "like the people" are necessarily populists or that, conversely, all populist politicians speak, dress, and look "like the people." This is clearly not always the case. For instance, Ecuadorian president Rafael Correa, who is considered a populist by many scholars, is a highly educated member of the middle class,

18. Carlos de la Torre, *Populist Seduction in Latin America* (Athens: Ohio University Center for International Studies, 2000).

19. Kazin, *Populist Persuasion*; Joseph Lowndes, "From Founding Violence to Political Hegemony: The Conservative Populism of George Wallace," in *Populism*, ed. Panizza, 144–201.

20. José Pedro Zúquete, "The Missionary Politics of Hugo Chávez," *Latin American Politics and Society* 50 (2008): 91–121.

well accustomed to addressing university audiences.[21] What I am arguing is that if populism is a mode of identification, we need to be aware of
the full symbolic repertoire of markers of identity that connect politicians to social sectors whose members suffer discrimination and subordination. In a region such as Latin America, where cultural exclusion reinforces socioeconomic inequalities, being culturally at one with "the
plebs" carries a particularly potent political message: The leader does
not so much speak for the people or to the people but *converse with the
people* because he or she is one of them.

Representing the People

Here we need to move from talking *like* the people to speaking *for* the
people—that is, from rhetoric to representation. This distinction is of
course analytical, given that form and content can never be completely
separated in the analysis of discourse. But at the heart of populism is a
claim to speak *for* the people, a claim that needs to be further explored.
In an impromptu speech after he had won the primary election for the
presidency of the Frente Amplio, Mujica captured the combination of
the formal and substantive elements of political representation that I am
seeking to discuss here:[22]

> I know what I represent within the Frente Amplio and within this so-
> ciety that built archetypes. There is a black [president] in the United
> States, an Indian [president] in Bolivia and I said without hate, that the
> country should know that I represent those at the bottom of society.[23]

Most definitions of populism emphasize the populist leader's direct
appeal to the plebs or, as Mujica put it, to those "at the bottom of society." It is not easy, however, to establish whether a direct relationship
between the leader and the people actually exists or what it precisely en-

21. Carlos de la Torre, "El Tecnopopulismo de Rafael Correa," *Latin American
Research Review* 48, no. 1 (2013): 24–43.
22. "Sé lo que represento dentro del Frente Amplio y dentro de esta sociedad que
construyó arquetipos. Hay un negro en Estados Unidos, un indio en Bolivia y sin
odio lo digo, que el país sepa que represento a los que vienen bien de abajo."
23. José Mujica, "Represento a los de abajo," *Espectador.com*, June 28, 2009,
http://www.espectador.com/1v4_contenido_print.php?id=155498.

tails. A leader's direct appeal to the people is obviously more likely in weakly institutionalized political systems with few mediating political structures between politicians and their constituents. In other cases, however, populist leaders have been the heads of highly organized political movements. Moreover, even in countries with relatively strong and stable representative institutions, particularly those with presidential systems, citizens directly identify themselves with political leaders above and beyond the parties to which they belong. A case in point is Lula da Silva, who won almost 60 percent of the popular vote in the 2006 presidential election in Brazil, while his party, the Partido dos Trabalhadores polled only about 20 percent of the vote. And in Argentina, the Partido Justicialista (Peronista) has been a highly effective political machine that mediates relations between Peronist candidates and their followers.[24]

What is characteristic of populism is not so much the direct relationship between the leader and the people but the leader's ability to reach those who regard themselves as having no voice in the political system. Who are these voiceless underdogs? To put it in slightly simplistic terms, they are those who suffer from economic, social, or political exclusion, or at least those who regard themselves as such. I therefore suggest that speaking for the people combines both the politics of recognition and the politics of redistribution. As has already been argued, "the people" is a political construct that does not necessarily coincide with socioeconomic categories. But in a region like Latin America that has the highest levels of socioeconomic inequality in the world, any claim to represent the excluded is highly likely to appeal to the poor.

In many countries of Latin America, electoral preferences have become increasingly defined by socioeconomic cleavages, with the middle classes voting for established politicians and the poor voting for political outsiders. The trend toward electoral polarization along socioeconomic lines has been reinforced by the implementation of targeted social programs and other welfare benefits, from Chávez's *misiones* to Lula da Silva's Family Grant, that have consolidated the links between leaders (now as presidents) and disadvantaged sectors of society. In the case of Lula da Silva, social programs were an important contributing factor in the significant shift in his electoral base of support—from the urban pro-

---

24. Steven Levitsky and Maria Victoria Murillo, *Argentine Democracy: The Politics of Institutional Weakness* (University Park: Pennsylvania State University Press, 2005).

gressive middle classes and the organized working class of the State of São Paulo and other industrial areas that were his main constituency in the 2002 election, toward poor voters in the relatively less developed rural areas in the north and northeast of the country that gave him overwhelming support four years later.[25] In the case of Uruguay, where the Frente Amplio government implemented similar social programs during its first term (2005–10), the political implications of this shift were encapsulated in Talvi's argument about the new welfare-dependent populist constituency of the uneducated and the unemployable. In a more sophisticated way, the relation between populist representation and economic benefits is elaborated by Kurt Weyland's argument that redistributive struggles for the appropriation of rents from commodities are at the heart of the populist revival in Latin America, an argument iterated with a different normative charge by Joseph Stiglitz's rather throwaway remark that "if by populism one means worrying about how the bottom two-thirds of the population fares, then populism is not a bad thing."[26]

The identification of "the people" as the poor and its corollary, the importance of the politics of redistribution, are important aspects of populist representation in contemporary Latin America and raise a number of questions about the relations between politics and the economy in the appeal of populism. Economic benefits and appeals to the poor alone, however, do not account for populist representation. Representation is about giving voice and recognition to the politically excluded, as much as about giving economic benefits to those disadvantaged by the economic system. Throughout the history of Latin American populism, the politics of recognition has marked the incorporation into the political scene of hitherto-subordinated popular urban sectors. Carlos de la Torre captures early examples of the politics of recognition in Ecuador when he reminds us that José María Velasco Ibarra

25. Wendy Hunter and Timothy Power, "Rewarding Lula: Executive Power, Social Policy and the Brazilian Election of 2006," *Latin American Politics and Society* 49 (April 2007): 1–30; Cesar Zucco, "The President's 'New' Constituency: Lula and the Pragmatic Vote in Brazil's 2006 Presidential Elections," *Journal of Latin American Studies* 40 (2008): 29–49.

26. Kurt Weyland, "Politics and Policies of Latin America's Two Lefts: The Role of Party Systems vs. Resource Bonanzas," paper prepared for Twenty-Sixth Congress of Latin American Studies Association, Montreal, September 5–9, 2007; Joseph Stiglitz, "Is Populism Really So Bad for Latin America?" *New Politics Quarterly*, Spring 2006, 61–62.

introduced mass politics into Ecuador, partly incorporating previously excluded people into the political community. As he put it "[Velasco] democratized public spaces by bringing politics from the salons of the elites to the streets. His followers *who were for the first time addressed in the public plazas, asserted their right to occupy public sites*" (emphasis added).[27] A similar plebeian irruption still resonates in Argentina's political imagination with reference to the mythical occupation of the Plaza de Mayo by the workers of the periphery of Buenos Aires on October 17, 1945.

The politics of recognition and the politics of redistribution went hand in hand in Evo Morales's rise to the presidency of Bolivia. The importance of the redistribution of oil rents is seen in his Movimiento al Socialismo (MAS) party's campaign to increase the royalties that the oil and gas companies paid to the state, along with subsequent confrontations over the allocation of hydrocarbon rents between the central government and the eastern provinces of Santa Cruz, Beni, Pando, and Tarija that are rich in natural gas and mineral resources. However, although the politics of recognition and the politics of redistribution can seldom be completely separated, the campaign for the recognition of the cultural, political, and social equality of Bolivia's indigenous majority has been a dominant feature of Morales's political appeal. It is striking to note how Morales's speeches are dominated by moral and political universals—"dignity," "equality," "sovereignty," "justice," and "liberation" —rather than by strictly economic issues. The reason for this emphasis lies, according to Morales's inaugural speech, in the history of the cultural and racial discrimination, political exclusion, and economic exploitation of Bolivia's indigenous majority:[28]

The indigenous peoples are the majority of the Bolivian population. . . . These peoples, historically, we have been marginalized, humiliated, hated, despised, condemned to extinction. This is our history: these

27. Carlos de la Torre, "Velasco Ibarra and 'La Revolución Gloriosa': The Social Production of a Populist Leader in Ecuador in the 1940s," *Journal of Latin American Studies* 26 (1994): 689.

28. "Los pueblos indígenas—que son la mayoría de la población boliviana. . . . Estos pueblos, históricamente hemos sido marginalizados, humillados, odiados, despreciados, condenados a la extinción. Esta es nuestra historia; a estos pueblos jamás los reconocieron como seres humanos, siendo que estos pueblos son los dueños absolutos de esta noble tierra, de sus recursos naturales."

peoples were never recognized as human beings, [in spite of] being the
exclusive owners of this noble land, of its natural resources.[29]

In the case of Venezuela, there is no question of the importance of
high oil revenues in explaining Chávez's popularity.[30] What is important
to question, however, is the crude, economically based account whereby
popular support for Chávez is the exclusive result of social handouts that
bribe the poor into voting for him. If the political conflict in Venezuela
in the 1990s and 2000s had been defined only by struggles about the distribution of oil rents, it is unlikely that it would have led to such a radical
rupture of the political order as seen in the Bolivarian Revolution. A full
account of *chavismo* requires focusing on its political elements as much
as on its economic ones.[31] As Julia Buxton put it, "In 1998 Chávez was
not elected on a left-wing platform, promise of economic redistribution
or because he pledged to confront neoliberalism. Crucially, Chávez was
elected because he promised to create a completely new form of democracy, a qualitatively distinct model of institutional and constitutional
organization and a new type of political engagement for Venezuela's
citizens."[32] Thus, the initial definition of Chávez's foundational project
was Bolivarian rather than socialist. Chávez drew from the populist tradition the notion of a virtuous people rising from a long period of oppression in a never-ending struggle for social justice, and from the military tradition the notion of himself as a selfless patriot willing to sacrifice
his own self-interest and well-being for the people of his country. His
political discourse is aimed at making his followers feel that they are
participants in a long-running struggle for the liberation of the Vene-

29. Evo Morales, "Discurso de posesión del Presidente Constitucional de la
República, Evo Morales Aima pronunciado el 22 de enero de 2006," Portal de la
Presidencia de Bolivia, available at http://www.presidencia.gov.bo.
30. Fernando Coronil, "Chávez's Venezuela: A New Magical State?" *Harvard
Review of Latin America*, Fall 2008, 3–4; Manuel Hidalgo, "Hugo Chávez's Petro-
Socialism," *Journal of Democracy* 20, no. 2 (2009): 78–92; Matías Riutort, "La
Economía Venezolana en el 2007 y Perspectivas para el 2008," *Temas de Coyuntura*
56 (December 2007): 115–26; Weyland, "Politics and Policies."
31. For a review of *chavismo,* see Steve Ellner, "Hugo Chávez's First Decade in
Office: Breakthroughs and Shortcomings," *Latin American Perspectives* 37 (January
2010): 77–96.
32. Julia Buxton, "Venezuela: It's Not the Economy Stupid," paper submitted to
conference on Latin America and the Caribbean in the Global Financial Crisis, Institute for the Study of the Americas and Foreign and Commonwealth Office, London, April 21–22, 2009.

zuelan people in the same way that Miranda and Bolívar, together with the people of Venezuela, liberated Venezuela from the Spanish yoke two hundred years ago.[33]

Given these observations, we are now able to better conceptualize what is meant in populist discourse by "representing the people." In 2006, Colombia's 1,000-peso note had a drawing of Jorge Eliécer Gaitán against a background of people marching in the street. Variations of this emblematic drawing have been used on book covers, posters, pamphlets, and other publications to represent the relationship between the leader and the people in the iconography of populism. The drawing conveys the notion that populist representation is different from the liberal forms of political representation that typically take place in parliamentary chambers. It is not just the openness of the streets in contrast with the confined spaces of parliaments that distinguishes one from the other, or the physical immediacy between the representative and the represented illustrated in the drawing, in contrast to the institutional mediations that characterize liberal democratic representation. In the very process of representing the people, the populist leader constitutes them as a people. The combination of collective grievances and symbolic unity that is of the essence of popular identities is a political operation. It requires the homogenization of highly heterogeneous social groups with divergent interests and multiple identities. As Ernesto Laclau puts it, the imaginary unity of a heterogeneous people can be represented if the leader serves as a kind of blank canvas—a surface for the inscription of the desires, affections, and demands of diverse popular actors, The extreme form of singularity is an individuality, and singularity leads to the identification of the unity of the group with the name of the leader.[34] The same Colombian 1,000-peso note quotes Gaitán: "*Yo no soy un hombre, soy un pueblo*" (I am not a man, I am a people). In the populist imagination, the leader is at one with the people because by acting in his or her name, he or she is acting in the name of the people.[35]

33. Colette Capriles, "The Politics of Identity: Bolívar and Beyond," *Harvard Review of Latin America*, Fall 2008, 8–10; Zuquete, "Missionary Politics," 102.

34. Laclau, *On Populist Reason*, 99–100.

35. Paula Biglieri, "El Retorno del Pueblo Argentino: Entre la Autorización y la Asamblea. Argentina en la Era K," in *En el nombre del pueblo: La emergencia del populismo Kirchnerista*, edited by Paula Biglieri and Gloria Perelló (Buenos Aires: UNSAM Edita, 2007), 61–84.

The authoritarian overtones of this claim are easily apparent and have been expressed in the argument that relations between the leader and the people are necessarily top-down.[36] As Arditi notes, the centrality of the leaders and their direct rapport with the "common man" transform populist leaders into something akin to infallible sovereigns, in that their decisions are unquestionable because they are theirs.[37] And yet the identification between the leader and the people can never be complete or achieved through one directional, top-down appeals from the leader to the people. Identity, at both the personal and political levels, is only the name of what we desire but can never fully obtain.[38]

Populist Antagonisms and Populist Interventions

In this analysis of populism, we need to move now from political representation to political strategies. Enacting redistributive policies and giving political recognition to excluded citizens are important elements of the populist mode of identification but do not by themselves define populism. Populism is a political strategy as much as a mode of identification. At the heart of the populist claim to represent the people is the ambiguous meaning of "the people" as signifying both a section of the community (the plebs, the underdogs) and the demos (the citizens). By appealing to the people as the plebs, populist leaders make visible (i.e., politicize) the dividing line between an excluded section of the political community and the community as a whole. The leader's promise is to make those excluded from the existing order—indigenous groups, peasants, the urban poor, ethnic minorities, and other groups—full members of the political community. Having defeated their oppressors, the plebs will then become the demos (the legitimate holders of sovereignty) and will thereby be able to fully exercise their sovereign rights.[39]

Kazin's history of American populism shows how different political narratives about the conflict between the powerful and the powerless run

36. Roberts, "Neoliberalism."

37. Arditi, "Populism."

38. Y. Stavrakakis, "Identity, Political," in *Encyclopedia of Democratic Thought*, edited by P. A. B. Clarke and P. and J. Foweraker (New York: Routledge, 2001), 333–37.

39. Gerardo Aboy Carlés, "La Especificidad Regeneracionista del Populismo," paper presented at Eighth Chilean Congress of Political Science, Santiago, November 13–17, 2006.

through America's civil life. Who the powerful and the powerless are has been defined and redefined by progressive and conservative versions of populism at different points in time, drawing the political battle lines that have characterized and continue to characterize American politics.[40] Canovan also notes the political antagonism that is at the heart of populism when she defines it as "an appeal to 'the people' *against* both the established structure of power and the dominant ideas and values."[41] The existence of an external "other" is a condition for the unification of naturally fragmented popular identities and divergent interests; as Glenn Bowman put it, "in oppressing all of [these identities and interests], the oppressor simultaneously renders all of them 'the same.'"[42]

How is the political antagonism characteristic of populist strategies of identification discursively constructed? Ernesto Laclau's writings on populism offer an elegant theory of the formal construction of antagonisms through the analysis of what he calls relations of differences and relations of equivalences. Although no society is structured exclusively by relations of differences or relations of equivalences, relations of differences predominate in highly institutionalized political orders—such as liberal, pluralist democracies—whereas relations of equivalences predominate at times of crisis when institutions lose their power to structure social relations. Laclau argues that when institutional channels cannot differentially absorb a series of social demands, these become unsatisfied demands that enter into a chain of solidarity or *equivalence* with one another, as equally unmet grievances. Populist leaders politicize these grievances, creating a relation of antagonism in the form of a political frontier between the people and what they identify as those responsible for the denial of their demands, such as "neoliberalism" or "the *partidocracia*" (the partyocracy).[43]

We can give some substance to this rather abstract elaboration by referring to contemporary developments in Latin America. In a formulation that closely resembles Laclau's chain of equivalences, Kenneth Roberts draws parallels between the current wave of political incorporation and the previous one that took place around the middle of the twen-

40. Kazin, *Populist Persuasion.*
41. Canovan, "Trust the People!" 2.
42. Glenn Bowman, "Constitutive Violence and the Nationalist Imaginary: The Making of 'The People' in Palestine and 'Former Yugoslavia,'" in *Populism,* ed. Panizza.
43. Laclau, *On Populist Reason,* 36–38.

tieth century during the import-substitution industrialization period, which was also dominated by populist politics. Roberts notes the declining capacity of state institutions to respond to social citizenship claims in the midst of the debt crisis and market-oriented structural adjustment programs of the 1990s and early 2000s, and he argues that unmet social needs and heightened economic insecurities provided a basis for the collective articulation of political grievances against neoliberalism.[44]

One of the specific ways collective grievances were effectively articulated is analyzed by Moisés Arce and Roberta Rice in their of study of social protest in Bolivia in the first half of the 2000s. They show how protests were characterized by the formation of a new cross-class, cross-ethnic, cross-regional, cross-generational, and cross-sectoral collective identity defined in opposition to neoliberalism. Although protests were initially specific and localized, such as the demand for water rights in Cochabamba, they quickly spread to other parts of the country and developed into a generalized opposition to the government's economic policies and to the country's so-called traditional parties. What made the protests so effective was the ability of the movements' organizers to synthesize the claims of disparate groups into a powerful critique of the country's political and economic order—a critique with the appeal and power to mobilize thousands of people to take part in marches, roadblocks, and other forms of direct action. How was it possible to achieve such a heightened level of unity and mobilization, particularly given that the new coalitions lacked institutional channels of social representation and that mobilizations often occurred without a general coordinating body and with each civil society group pursuing its own agenda? Arce and Rice's answer is that "neoliberalism" became an organizing symbol (what Laclau would call an empty signifier) against which social movements agitated to build support for their mobilizations.[45]

A number of points in Roberts's and Arce and Rice's analyses of social protests merit further consideration. Arguably, Arce and Rice's account of social mobilization in Bolivia underestimates the role of key union and indigenous political leaders in coordinating the protests and does not properly deal with Evo Morales's ability to crystallize social

44. Kenneth M. Roberts, "The Mobilization of Opposition to Economic Liberalization," *Annual Review of Political Science* 11 (2008), 330.
45. Moisés Arce and Roberta Rice, "Social Protest in Post-Stabilization Bolivia," *Latin American Research Review* 44, no. 1 (2009): 98; Laclau, *On Populist Reason*, 69.

antagonisms at a higher political level. What is important for the purpose of this chapter, however, is to draw on the implications of their analyses for a better understanding of populist politics.

There are many examples in Latin America of political strategies of dichotomization of the social space. Hugo Chávez has systematically used political antagonisms to rally his supporters against the full range of "enemies of the people," from the traditional parties to the economic oligarchy and from former president Uribe of Colombia to the "devil Bush" and U.S. imperialism. The politics of antagonism, framed as the opposition between the people on the one hand and partyocracies and neoliberalism on the other, have also played a significant role in the political strategy of Rafael Correa in Ecuador.[46]

The populist strategy of creating political antagonisms makes it possible to draw a distinction between so-called populist leaders and popular ones. Political leaders such as José Mujica and Lula da Silva may speak and look like the people and legitimately claim to represent those at the bottom of society; but their strategy of political incorporation is that of bridge builders who seek social and political compromise, rather than of trench diggers who pursue disruption and rupture. Lula da Silva is surely one of the few political leaders in the world equally at ease at the World Economic Forum and at the World Social Forum. And in his inimitable language, Mujica has consistently made a strong argument for the politics of compromise over the politics of antagonism:[47]

> To govern is not to do whatever you would like to do. Governing with a progressive outlook is to darn everyday. It is to tirelessly weave political alliances and, above all, social alliances, to broaden your support base as much as possible. There will always be social contradictions, but if one allows one side to unmercifully bash the other with an iron bar, we end all being hurt and the pie gets smaller.[48]

46. Catherine M. Conaghan, "Ecuador: Correa's Plebiscitary Presidency," *Journal of Democracy* 19 (April 2008): 46–60.

47. "Gobernar no es hacer lo que se quiere. Gobernar con una visión progresista es zurcir todos los días. Es tejer incansablemente alianzas políticas y sobre todo alianzas sociales, para ensanchar todo lo posible la base de sustentación. Las contradicciones sociales van a seguir existiendo, pero si uno deja que una punta dé fierro a la otra, sin piedad, terminamos todos lastimados y achicando la torta."

48. José Mujica, "Gobernar no es hacer lo que se quiere: Es zurcir, bordar y tejer," *Pepe tal cuál es* (blog), April 1, 2009, http://www.pepetalcuales.com.uy/articulo/5/.

The Normative Dimension of Populism

The distinction between populist (i.e., the predominance of the politics of antagonism) and popular (the predominance of the politics of differences) strategies of political incorporation of the popular sectors is crucial for understanding contemporary Latin American politics, but it needs some probing. If political antagonism is the essence of populism, does this mean that all political strategies that dichotomize the political space are necessarily populist? Clearly not. In the nineteenth century, the urban political elite in Latin America framed their political discourse around the dichotomy of "*civilization or barbarism*" to justify their fight against the rural caudillos. Moreover, antagonism (the definition of the enemy) is, at least according to Carl Schmitt, constitutive not just of populism but also of politics itself, meaning that it cannot be an exclusive, distinctive feature of populism.[49]

Laclau solves this problem by arguing that populism is effectively the same as politics.[50] For reasons that I cannot elaborate here, I think that this is an unsatisfactory solution. One cannot have a purely formal (ontological) definition of populism based on the constitutive role of antagonism. A thorough understanding of populism must incorporate both the formal dimension of antagonism together with populism's normative dimension, in which those at the bottom of society are said to be excluded by the political order in violation of fundamental principles of political equity (representation) or socioeconomic equity (redistribution). In this approach, the promise to repair the injustice (the politics of incorporation) is at least as crucial for the understanding of populism as is the creation of antagonism between the people and their oppressors.[51] Whether the reparation of the injustice requires the destruction of the system (the foundational aspect of populism) or working within the system is largely context dependent, particularly on the strength of a country's political institutions. Recently, radical left-wing populist leaders have sought to restore the sovereignty of the people by changing constitutional orders and founding the Bolivarian Republic in Venezuela and a plurinational participative democracy in Bolivia. Historically,

49. Carl Schmitt, *The Crisis of Parliamentary Democracy* (Cambridge, Mass.: MIT Press, 1988).
50. Laclau, "Populism," 47.
51. Carlés, "Especificidad Regeneracionista."

however, many populist movements in Latin America have acted pragmatically to incorporate those at the bottom of society into the system through corporatist forms of political representation, social policies, and politically mediated handouts. It is worth recalling that, at the time, this was denounced by the left as evidence of populism's conservative nature.[52]

In practice, the two alternatives—working within the political order, or seeking to found a radically new one—are at the opposite end of a continuum that can be subject to a variety of populist interventions. In the context of a crisis of representation—such as occurred in Bolivia, Ecuador, and Venezuela in the late 1990s and early 2000s—the foundational aspects of populism became dominant, whereas in other more institutionalized contexts, populist antagonisms were mediated and constrained by the involvement of political institutions.

In Argentina, the governments of the late Néstor Kirchner (2003–7) and Cristina Fernández de Kirchner (2007–) illustrate how context defines the reach and limits of populist antagonism. For some scholars, the Kirchners have represented the return of populism in Argentina. They, particularly Néstor, centralized power in the presidency, ruled by decree, and used public funds to secure the allegiance of state governors and to grease the wheels of the Justicialista Party's patronage machine. They rallied against neoliberalism and the market democracy of the 1990s and adopted many of the nationalist politics and policies of the Peronist left of the 1970s. Néstor Kirchner became well known for his propensity to pick political fights with a wide variety of enemies, ranging from the International Monetary Fund to the military, and for his close alliance with President Hugo Chávez. Perhaps the best example of the politics of antagonism in the Kirchners' administrations was the confrontation between the farmers and President Cristina Kirchner in 2008 that followed the government's attempt to introduce a new sliding scale for export taxes on grains and oil seeds. The confrontation bisected and polarized Argentine society. It had a strong normative dimension, as Cristina Kirchner accused the (rich) farmers of selfishly refusing the government much-needed tax revenue to implement its ambitious social programs. For a moment, politics in Argentina resembled politics in the Andean countries. The confrontation spilled into the streets, with

52. Otavio Ianni, *O Colapso do populismo no Brasil* (Rio de Janeiro: Civilização Brasileira, 1968).

farmers blocking highways and supporters and opponents of the government marching in the streets of Buenos Aires. It also evoked past struggles between Perón and the so-called *oligarquía latifundista*. Yet the government lost the fight because Congress voted down the tax. The resolution of the conflict through institutional means recalls Levitsky and Murillo's argument that, whatever the superficial similarities between Kirchner and Chávez, Argentina is not Venezuela. That is, in spite of the Kirchners' populist interventions and the weakness of the country's party system, the institutional and societal foundations of democratic pluralism in Argentina are much stronger than they are in Venezuela, making the dividing line between the people and their enemies more difficult to sustain.[53]

Does it make sense to speak of populism in highly institutionalized political systems with checks and balances, a strong and active civil society, and well-functioning representative institutions? I think it does, as long as one does not refer to populism as a political regime or as a kind of encompassing totality but, as suggested above, as a set of interventions within a given institutional and political environment. To understand what is meant here by interventions, it is important to recall Kazin's observation that when tracing the history of populism in the United States, he does not contend that his subjects were populists in the same way that they were unionists or socialists, Protestants or Catholics, liberal Democrats or conservative Republicans. Rather, his premise is that all these people employed populism as a flexible mode of persuasion. As he put it, "Populism, of course, was not the sole element in their rhetoric; but its significance is, I think, impossible to deny."[54]

Though agreeing with Kazin, I would use the broader term *interventions* to encapsulate a wider range of material and symbolic practices associated with the populist mode of identification beyond just rhetoric. In some cases, symbolic practices refer to the leader's personal characteristics or political trajectory that cast him or her as an outsider to the established order. In the 2008 U.S. election, Sarah Palin used her status as an ordinary "hockey mom" from a distant state to appeal to "ordinary folks" and bash the Washington elite. However, the discursive effects of a leader's biography are not always under his or her control, and they

53. Steven Levitsky and María Victoria Murillo, "Argentina: From Kirchner to Kirchner," *Journal of Democracy* 19 (April 2008): 16–30.
54. Kazin, *Populist Persuasion*, 6.

can become a political battleground. Although Barack Obama had probably the most unlikely personal background of any past U.S. presidential candidate, he never sought to build political capital by distancing himself from the political elite as did Sarah Palin. Significantly, however, Obama's unconventional life story was taken by his supporters as embodying his promise of change, and was used by the extreme right to signify a threat to American values and patriotism by suggesting that he is a Muslim and may not even be a U.S. citizen. It is also worth remembering that in 2002 scholars emphasized Lula da Silva's personal biography as an indicator of the wider radical change thought to have been produced by his electoral victory.[55] And writing in the late 1990s, the Uruguayan scholar Jorge Lanzaro claimed that "Mujica has a populist profile, based on charisma, anti-establishment stances and an appeal to the poor, which was strengthened by his personal traits and his lineage as a member of the 1960s Tupamaros guerrilla movement, as well as his affinity for the ruling Kirchners in Argentina and the 'Bolivarian' left."[56]

The fear and mistrust created among the business and middle classes by Lula da Silva's and Mujica's personal and political biographies have been largely allayed by the two leaders' cautious reformist policies and consensual politics. And yet Lula da Silva's and Mujica's political roots and life trajectories, as well as their bonds with the popular sectors, still distinguish them from their countries' political elites. This symbolic distance can provide the raw material for populist interventions, often in conjunction with other forms of political rhetoric. The case of Lula da Silva illustrates this point. When he was confronted with allegations of corruption against his government during the 2006 electoral campaign, he used both the populist discourse of the outsider under attack from the political elite and the institutional discourse of differences to defend himself and his party against the accusations.

Thus, during a tour of the Northeast, where he had strong popular support among Brazil's poor, President Lula said:[57]

---

55. So, e.g., the British historian Perry Anderson argued that Lula da Silva embodied "a popular life experience and a 'bottom up' trajectory of social and political struggle without equal for any other contemporary head of government." Perry Anderson, "Balanço: FHC deixou saldo negativo, diz historiador," *Folha de São Paulo,* November 10, 2002.

56. Jorge Lanzaro, "Social Democracy Lives in Latin America," http://project-syndicate.org/commentary/lanzaro1.

57. "A mesma elite que levou Getúlio [Vargas] à morte, que levou Juscelino

The same elite that led Getúlio [Vargas] to his death, that submitted Juscelino [Kubitschek] to the biggest ever process of accusations and lies, [the same elite] that toppled João Gulart, that very same elite tried to bring me down. The only difference in my case is not that I was better [than them]. [The difference is] that they found out that I had an asset which they were not aware of, . . . [an asset] called the Brazilian people.[58]

However, the following day he argued that corruption was a structural element of Brazilian politics:[59]

Don't think that each individual's wrongs [i.e., corruption] is their personal fault or the fault of their parties. What is going on [i.e., corruption] is the result of an accumulation of deformities rooted in the political structure of our country.[60]

It is clear from these excerpts that Lula was presenting himself as part of "the people" who were under attack by an ever-present, dominant elite that had already brought down other popular leaders and, at the same time, was presenting corruption as an attribute of the political system, of which his party, the Partido dos Trabalhadores, was part. On the first argument, he was being accused of corruption because he was under attack from the system. On the second one, members of his party and the party itself had engaged in corrupt acts because they were part of the system. We can also recall Lula's much-quoted statement that the financial crisis of 2008–9 was caused by "white, blue-eyed people" and not by "blacks, poor, or indigenous peoples" to see why Lula has become, in the words of President Obama, "the most popular politician on Earth."[61]

[Kubitschek] ao major processo de acusação e de mentiras, que tirou João Goulart, essa mesma elite tentou me tirar. Só que a diferença básica no meu caso não é que eu fosse melhor. E que tinha um componente que eles não contavam e descobriram que exitstia, chamado povo brasileiro."

58. "Lula diz que, sem reforma, novos escândalos surgirao," *Folha de São Paulo*, July 24, 2006.

59. "Não pensem que o erro de cada um é individual ou partidário. O que acontece são os acúmulos de deformações que vêm da estrutura política do nosso país."

60. "Lula diz que, sem reforma."

61. See "Obama about Lula 'The Most Popular Politician on Earth,'" http://www.liveleak.com/view?i=37d_1238723472.

If the shadows of a life lived as an outsider or the occasional jabbing at the system from within were all that there is to populist interventions, the appeal of populism in highly institutionalized political systems would be real but limited, a kind of populism "lite." However, another characteristic of populism makes it a potentially powerful political force in any democratic environment. Canovan argues that modern democracy presents two faces—one redemptive, the other pragmatic. She further argues that although the two faces are opposed, they are also interdependent and that between them lies a gap in which populism is liable to appear. She establishes the distinction between redemptive and pragmatic policies by noting that while pragmatically democracy is a form of government and a way of coping peacefully with the conflicts of modern societies by means of a collection of rules and practices, it also has a redemptive aspect in which the people are the only source of legitimate authority and salvation is promised to them if and when they take charge of their own lives. She concludes that at least some degree of democracy's redemptive promise of salvation is necessary to lubricate the machinery of pragmatic democracy, and that if redemption is not present within the political system, it may well reassert itself in the form of a populist challenge.[62] There is a parallel formulation of the relation between populism's redemptive promise and everyday democratic practices in Kazin's claim that populism is "rooted in the gap between American ideals and those institutions and authorities whose performance betrays them." As he put it: "It is only when leftists and liberals themselves talked in populist ways—hopeful, expansive, even romantic—that they were able to lend their politics a majoritarian cast and help to markedly improve the common welfare."[63]

For certain versions of populism, the redemptive dimension of democracy cannot be realized within the system because there can be no shared common ground between the people and their oppressors. Thus, the gap between the two dimensions of democracy cannot be breached

---

62. Canovan, "Trust the People!" 110–11.

63. Kazin, *Populist Persuasion*, 289; also 6–7. It should be noted, however, that the "rhetorical optimism" that, according to Kazin, characterizes populism's redemptive message has in many cases turned out to be a discourse of fear and loathing, as is the case with racist, right-wing populist parties in Europe. For this variety of populist discourse the solution to the perceived injustice suffered by some underprivileged ethnic group can lead to ethnic cleansing or to demands for the expulsion of immigrants who are the ones that are truly "at the bottom of society."

under the existing institutional rules, and the system must be reconstituted on different bases. Redemptive rhetoric digs deep into the past to evoke Amerindian forms of collective organization and democratic deliberation in Bolivia or selective Bolivarian ideals in Venezuela in order to contrast them with the inequities of the present and inspire the people to strive for a better future.

However, rhetorical optimism can also be put to work in an attempt to close the gap between the redemptive and pragmatic dimensions of democracy without ever achieving total closure or, alternatively, tearing apart the political order. Lula da Silva was increasingly perceived, particularly within Brazil, as an ultrapragmatic politician who made pacts with his former right-wing critics and had largely embraced the so-called neoliberal legacy of his predecessor, Fernando Henrique Cardoso. Many analysts trace the public origins of Lula's pragmatic turn to his famous "Letter to the Brazilian People" published at the beginning of the 2002 electoral campaign, in which he promised that, if elected, his government would comply with the fiscal and monetary conditions imposed by the International Monetary Fund. However, it is worth recalling that the pragmatic promise to repay the IMF was not at the heart of Lula's 2002 campaign; rather, the campaign emphasized the redemptive promise of ending hunger in a country where millions of people still suffered from malnutrition. And though his style of government became increasingly pragmatic and less redemptive, and the Fome Zero (Hunger Zero) promise pragmatically morphed into the highly effective Bolsa Família social program, the redemptive dimension of Lula's rhetoric could still be found, perhaps too conveniently, in his speeches in the international arena, where he campaigned for a rebalancing of the world order in favor of those who are more in need. As he put it in an address to the 2009 World Social Forum:[64]

> What these people [the political and economic elites] did not perceive is that today the most humble people of Latin America—the Indians of Bolivia, the Indians of Ecuador, the Brazilian Indians, the rubber tappers, the workers of Venezuela and Paraguay, the people—have

64. "O que essa gente [the political and economic elites] não percebeu é que hoje o povo mais humilde da América Latina, os índios da Bolívia, os índios do Equador, os índios brasileiros, os seringueiros, os trabalhadores da Venezuela, do Paraguai, as pessoas aprenderam a não ter mais intermediário para escolher os seus dirigentes. As pessoas votam diretamente e escolhem en que elas confiam."

learned not to have intermediaries when choosing their leaders. The people vote directly and choose [leaders] whom they trust.[65]

There are times when an electoral slogan captures the redemptive message of democracy. In the 1989 electoral campaign, Carlos Menem told the Argentine people *"Síganme no los voy a desfraudar"* (Follow me, I will not let you down). His command can be interpreted in many different ways. It can be seen as evidence of the personalistic and top-down nature of populism and of the programmatic emptiness, if not duplicity, of his campaign promises. But at that time, when the Argentine people were suffering from terrible economic hardships, his slogan conveyed the promise of lifting people out of their hardship and of better times to come. Obama's politics is in many ways the antithesis of Menem's populism. His 2008 electoral campaign slogan "Yes, We Can" conveyed a very different message than Menem's "Follow Me." It was a convocation to a collective endeavor rather than a command to follow the leader. The slogan "Yes, We Can" brilliantly encapsulated the rhetorical optimism of redemptive democracy while giving hope and voice to millions of U.S. citizens who did not feel represented by traditional politicians.

Conclusion

Am I arguing that politicians such as Pepe Mujica and Lula da Silva are populists? If so, would not this claim stretch even further what is already a highly contested concept? And what about the political implications of calling such a group of politicians "populists?" In answering these questions, it is first important to heed Kazin's warning that debates about who is or is not a true populist are often an indirect way of announcing one's political opinions—or, better said, one's aversions.[66] Second, as I have argued above, populism is one among a variety of political discourses used by politicians to establish relations of identification with their audience. This is why I use the term *populist interventions* to signify that populism refers to a political strategy rather

65. "Discurso do Presidente da República, Luiz Inácio Lula da Silva, durante o encontro com participantes do Forúm Social Mundial 2009": panel "América Latina e o Desafio da Crise Internacional," January 29, 2009.
66. Kazin, *Populist Persuasion*, 6.

than to the persona of a leader. In practice, we still call some leaders "populists," although, with a few exceptions, who they are and why they are considered populists remain hotly contested. The combination of the negative connotations associated with branding a politician a populist (*Más populista será tu abuela!*) and the argument that politicians can and do use populist interventions as part of a broader set of political appeals helps to explain the otherwise confusing and seemingly intractable question of how to establish whether a certain leader is or is not a populist.

Notably, the same commentator can describe a certain politician as both an antipopulist and a populist, without being aware of the implications of his arguments. So, writing in *The Guardian* on January 19, 2012, the political analyst Jonathan Freedland chastised Obama for not being a populist:

> Above all, he tried to accommodate the Republicans for too long. He believed his own rhetoric, which promised an end to Washington partisanship. . . . *He should have drawn a clear dividing line between him and them, defining himself as the defender of the national interest and of the hard pressed and casting the Republicans as the enemy.* (emphasis added)[67]

However, just nine days later, Freedland noted that a new study had found that the conflict between the rich and everyone else has replaced race and immigration in the minds of U.S. voters as the key point of tension in American society. Freedland observed, "President Obama's populist State of the Union Address this week suggests he recognizes this shift and now believes that redressing the country's wild economic imbalance is a vote winner."[68]

To the extent—and only to the extent—that the populist mode of identification is central to the leader's appeal and political strategy can we say that leaders such as Chávez and Morales *are* populists. And to the extent that leaders such as Mujica, Lula, and Obama tend to use a

67. Jonathan Freedland, "Barack Obama's Presidency, Three Years On: Is It Time to Give Up Hope? He Promised Radical Change, a New Kind of Politics—Many One-Time Believers Now Say He Has No Stomach for a Fight," *The Guardian*, January 19, 2012.

68. Jonathan Freedland, "Bash the Poor, Wave the Flag—and Voters Forget Their Wallets," *The Guardian*, January 28, 2012.

more pluralist discourse that emphasizes differences rather than antagonisms, we can argue that they are not populist. However, though simplifications are unavoidable even in scholarly debate, to brand Chávez and Morales as populists nonetheless implies an element of oversimplification. Morales's appeal to the politics of antagonism in attacking his political enemies did not prevent him from negotiating with the opposition the final version of the new Constitution in order to end a conflict that was in danger of tearing the country apart. For all of Chávez's rhetorical bashing of the opposition, there is very little actual political violence in Venezuela; elections have been largely free of fraud, suggesting that, in spite of Venezuela's deep polarization, there is an unstated agreement about limits that includes an element of democratic pluralism. And though "twenty-first-century socialism" may express populism's redemptive promise, it also conveys the promises of other political discourses, such as participatory democracy, socialism, and nationalism, in a context where liberal democratic institutions have not been completely set aside.

A characterization of populism in terms of populist interventions also has the advantage of making it easier to understand that populism, or rather populist interventions, can also be a feature of highly institutionalized political systems. This should not be particularly controversial given the long history of populism in the United States and the more recent rise of right-wing populism in highly institutionalized democracies in Western Europe and elsewhere. It is clear, however, that the impact of populist interventions is usually very different in highly institutionalized political systems than in those whose institutions are weak or in crisis. Institutions place significant constraints on attempts to divide society into two antagonistic camps. President Lula da Silva may play the populist card when confronted with allegations of corruption, and his status as "father of the poor" may resemble that of his predecessor Getúlio Vargas, but his style of governance is framed by the country's political institutions, which makes it very different from that of President Chávez's Bolivarian Republic or even from that of Vargas. In Uruguay, President Mujica may be an outsider to the country's traditional political elite, but he is very much an insider to the party system, and his leadership is exercised within the constraints imposed by his own party, the Frente Amplio, and by the broader parliamentary forces.

The populist mode of identification has several dimensions, which I have referred to here as (1) "speaking like the people" (the symbolic irruption of a marker of exclusion into the public sphere); (2) "speaking for the people" (voicing the grievances of those who do not feel represented by the system); (3) a political strategy (the politics of antagonism); and (4) a normative element (the promise of redemption). Arguably, these distinctions are more analytical than substantive, but an understanding of populism should primarily focus on the discursive construction of the antagonism between the people and the established structure of power as its defining element. Other studies of populism have argued that top-down leadership and an unmediated relation between leader and followers are constitutive characteristics of populism. Although these features can be effectively found in many studies of populism, their presence and relevance are an empirical matter, and their absence does not per se indicate the absence of populism. The very different relations between Morales, Chávez, and Correa and their respective supporters is the best illustration of the contingent nature of these features. In populist discourse, however, the antagonism between the people and their oppressors is only part of a political journey of redemption leading to the full incorporation of those who regard themselves as being denied some fundamental economic or political right of the body politic.

Radical populism in contemporary Latin America can be understood as part of a broader process of social and political incorporation that has taken two different strategies. The populist one believes that the liberation of the people from injustice and oppression requires the refounding of the political order. As such it is antisystemic, majoritarian, polarizing, and based on the logic of an antagonism devoid of any mediating institutions or values. In contrast, the other strategy frames the conflict between the powerless and the powerful within a shared set of liberal democratic procedural rules and the recognition of common interests between different social classes and political actors. It consists of a mixture of pragmatic and redemptive politics that, while denouncing the failures of the socioeconomic order and the limitations of political institutions to define the true meaning of democracy, also strengthens democratic pluralism by giving recognition to the excluded and addressing their socioeconomic demands.

In describing the two strategies of political incorporation, it is important to be aware of their normative connotations. As highlighted by Mujica's colorful rejection of the populist label, populism is indeed a toxic brand. Arguably, by taking the "us-versus-them" confrontation to the limits, populist strategies could end up fracturing societies and creating new forms of exclusion on both sides of the political divide. The potentially exclusive nature of populism is even more evident in the cases of anti-immigrant discourse in Europe and right-wing populism in the United States. But no strategy of political incorporation can be subject to normative claims if it is completely divorced from the sociopolitical context in which it operates. It could be argued that it is difficult for a genuine process of social and political inclusion—one that seeks to advance the cause of those at the bottom of highly unequal societies—to take place without polarization and conflict, an argument that, as noted above, has been directed by left-wing critics against Obama's attempts at achieving compromises with the Republicans. On these grounds, some scholars have defended populist ruptures as necessary for the creation of a more just social order.[69] There are indications that some leaders commonly regarded as "bad (radical) populists" are increasingly aware of this argument, and may even embrace being regarded as populists. Intriguingly, it is perhaps this transformative power of populism that the "good leftie" (*más populista será tu abuela*) Mujica had in mind when he noted that, within certain contexts, populism could be regarded as a term of praise. Conversely, pragmatism, reconciliation, and compromise occasionally may not necessarily be good things. Think, for instance, of the failure of Lula da Silva's pragmatic political style to clean up the cesspool of Brazilian politics and of the alliances he set up with some of the country's most unsavory conservative politicians. It may be impossible to avoid normative judgments when we engage in political analysis, but it is important to make clear on what grounds we make them. This chapter has sought to highlight the gray areas and add shadows to a topic that has too often been presented in black and white.

69. Ernesto Laclau, "La Deriva Populista y la Centro Izquierda Latinoamericana," *Nueva Sociedad* 205 (September–October 2006): 56–61.

Chapter 5

Populism and Social Policy in Latin America

Kurt Weyland

Latin America holds the record for social inequality among the regions of this planet. As a result, even its middle-income countries are home to surprisingly large numbers of poor people. And its other social indicators, such as basic education and health levels, are also lower than its overall levels of economic prosperity and the resulting availability of resources would permit. This unfortunate disjuncture between economic and social development raises the question of the best political strategy for overcoming the pressing problems afflicting millions of people: What reform efforts are most promising for enhancing popular well-being and boosting health and education standards, especially among less well-off sectors?

Alternative Strategies for Social Policy Reform

In a global perspective, the best model for combining mass prosperity with generous welfare seems to be European social democracy. As many studies document, social-democratic labor movements and political parties in North-Central Europe have over the decades attained substantial and sustainable progress in significantly diminishing social inequality, guaranteeing enviable health and education levels, and virtually eliminating poverty.[1] But while there have been a few efforts to approximate social-democratic reformism in the developing world,[2] and while a number of Latin American parties have taken inspiration from European social democracy, such as the Party of the Brazilian Social Democracy (Partido da Social Democracia Brasileira, PSDB) of former president Fernando Henrique Cardoso (1995–2002), these emulation efforts have encountered tremendous obstacles and faced considerable criticism, for two main reasons.

First, European social democracy took decades to improve popular living standards. Such gradual reform appears painfully slow in a region suffering from urgent problems. Many common citizens and politicians lack the patience to embark on this "long march" of prudent change. Therefore, even successful advances do not necessarily guarantee the political rewards for which their initiators hope. For instance, although President Cardoso's education and health reforms in Brazil significantly improved policy outputs and outcomes, his self-defined social-democratic party lost the subsequent election—ironically to a socialist party that promised a more determined attack on social problems, but that has enacted fewer and less important education and health reforms than its ideologically more moderate predecessor. Thus, despite an objectively good track record, a patient reform strategy may not yield commensurate political payoffs: Therefore, it holds limited attraction for ambitious political leaders.

Second, the systematic, sustained pursuit of a social-democratic strategy depends on political-organizational preconditions that cannot easily be constructed. Gradual reformism rests on a solid political base provided by broad, well-organized, and programmatically oriented parties and interest associations, especially encompassing trade unions. This type of organization has always been uncommon in Latin America; the significant erosion of union density in many countries and the collapses

---

1. See, e.g., Evelyne Huber and John Stephens, *Development and Crisis of the Welfare State* (Chicago: University of Chicago Press, 2001).
2. Richard Sandbrook et al., *Social Democracy in the Global Periphery* (Cambridge: Cambridge University Press, 2007).

of several party systems have further diminished the chances for social democracy to emerge. Although a few nations—especially Chile, Costa Rica, and Uruguay—have managed to apply basic social-democratic principles, and although Brazil has taken modest steps in the same direction, elsewhere the chances for persistent gradual reformism along European lines are bleak.

The difficulties facing social democracy in Latin America raise the main question examined in this chapter: Does an alternative strategy for pursuing social change that does not rest on demanding organizational preconditions but on the will of political leaders offer greater promise? In other words, can political agency fill the vacuum left by unpropitious structures and institutions? In Latin America, the most willful leaders who have claimed to pursue social change have been populists; these personalistic, plebiscitarian leaders have deliberately tried to overcome structural and institutional constraints.[3] Latin American populism thus embodies unbounded agency. Can it push forward social progress under unpropitious circumstances?

Interestingly, the very absence of the preconditions for social democracy in the region has allowed for the frequent emergence of populism. The weaknesses of political parties and interest associations have opened up room for these personalistic, plebiscitarian leaders, who use antielite rhetoric and promises to benefit the long-neglected, poorer masses in order to win and retain government power. The erosion of parties and associations in recent decades, which has posed increasing obstacles to social democracy, has further facilitated the rise of populism. Therefore, it is important to investigate whether Latin American populism can fill the reform deficit left by the difficulties confronting social democracy and bring urgently needed social progress: Can populism improve social policies and enhance health and education standards in a sustainable way?

To address this important question, this chapter probes the relationship of populism and social policy. It argues that although social reform efforts are not a defining, "necessary" feature of populism, Latin American populist movements usually undertake such efforts. But due to the weak institutionalization of populism and the ample latitude that it leaves for personalistic leaders, these reform efforts tend to be haphazard, un-

---

3. To avoid repeating the term "populism," I interchangeably use "personalistic, plebiscitarian leadership," which captures the defining features of populism.

systematic, mistargeted, politicized, and not very sustainable in fiscal, political, and institutional terms. Specifically, populist leaders use their discretionary power to push for relatively fast and substantial social change, but these advances often suffer from inefficiency, problematic design, and deficient implementation and are subject to setbacks and reversals. Due to populism's inherent fickleness, its accomplishments do not tend to last. Whereas presidents inspired by social democracy construct their reformist edifices brick by brick, populist leaders build sandcastles that rise quickly but are just as quickly washed away by the waves of changing economic or political conjunctures.

The chapter develops these arguments through a conceptual and theoretical analysis of populism in the following section. The subsequent section demonstrates that these arguments apply both to the neoliberal populism of the 1990s, as exemplified by Alberto Fujimori in Peru, and the revival of more radical populism in contemporary Venezuela under Hugo Chávez; thus, the features of social policy highlighted here tend to be associated with different varieties of populism, not only its recently revived leftist variant.[4] Comparisons with the nonpopulist social policies enacted by presidents Fernando Henrique Cardoso and Luiz Inácio Lula da Silva in Brazil and by the Concertación administrations in Chile provide further support for this point.

Populism and Social Policy Reform: Theoretical Considerations

Before examining the social policy initiatives of populist governments in contemporary Latin America, it is useful to begin with some broader theoretical reflections. This section tries to shed light on the relationship of populist leadership and social reform efforts in general. From this discussion, I then derive conjectures about the likely advantages and disadvantages of the social policy efforts undertaken by populist administrations.

---

4. The administration of Evo Morales in Bolivia (2006–present) does not qualify under my definition of populism, which—as explained in the next section—highlights personalistic leadership and the organizational weakness of mass followers. The Bolivian Movimiento al Socialismo, by contrast, encompasses many social movements that arose from the bottom up, have autonomous capacity for demand making, and therefore leave much less room for personalistic leadership than Chávez has.

The Role of Social Policy in Populism

What is the relationship of populism and efforts to expand and improve social policies in Latin America? What can populism accomplish, and what does it intend to accomplish? These questions require some conceptual and theoretical discussion because the very notion of populism is far from clear. Over the decades, Latin American populism has been defined in diverse ways, which in turn have implications for its relationship to social policy. Traditionally, scholars adopted multidimensional concepts that defined populism via a bundle of socioeconomic, political, historical, and discourse characteristics.[5] Expansive, heavily distributive, or mildly redistributive social policies were a core element of this package. According to this conceptualization, populist movements and leaders by their very nature sought to bring social progress to large sectors of the population.

In recent decades, however, even some political leaders who did not pursue expansionary social policies but on the contrary imposed austerity and adjustment used typically populist political strategies and managed to attract and maintain plebiscitarian mass support through a person-centered, quasi-direct, largely unmediated and uninstitutionalized relationship with their popular followers. Peru's Alberto Fujimori (1990–2000), the prototype of this neoliberal populism, imposed a brutal shock program without any social cushion to control raging hyperinflation; yet because Peru was facing a severe crisis, he elicited strong popular support that sustained his government for a decade, despite the complete absence of an organizational base. This case and the similar experiences of Carlos Menem in Argentina (1989–99) and, for some time, Fernando Collor de Mello in Brazil (1990–92) showed that the political features of populism can flourish although the socioeconomic elements that an older generation of scholars saw as a core element of this concept are absent. Several scholars therefore untied the multidimensional definition of populism,[6] and some authors defined populism in purely political

5. See the extended discussion by Kurt Weyland, "Clarifying a Contested Concept: 'Populism' in the Study of Latin American Politics," *Comparative Politics* 34 (October 2001): 1–22.

6. Kenneth Roberts, "Neoliberalism and the Transformation of Populism in Latin America," *World Politics* 48 (October 1995): 82–116; Kurt Weyland, "Neopopulism and Neoliberalism in Latin America: Unexpected Affinities," *Studies in Comparative International Development* 31 (Fall 1996): 3–31.

terms via personalistic, plebiscitarian leadership, leaving its association with socioeconomic features as a topic for empirical analysis.[7]

This political conceptualization of populism, which has been adopted in the present book, refrains from stipulating a necessary connection between populism and expansionary social policies.[8] Populist leaders need not rely on the large-scale distribution of social benefits to capture and retain a mass following. In fact, not all of them do. Besides the tactics of neoliberal populists—who used a bold, determined attack on a severe crisis to demonstrate their charisma and boost their popular support—there are other options, such as the anti-immigrant slogans employed by contemporary right-wing populists in Europe. This xenophobic rhetoric appeals to some mass sectors as an effort to establish a market reserve for domestic labor, and to others as a symbolic defense of the purity of "the people," the main referent of populist discourse. Given this variety of options, populist leaders do not feel compelled to use social policy initiatives to attract support and boost their political influence.

However, although efforts at social policy reform are not a defining feature and necessary characteristic of populism, many personalistic, plebiscitarian leaders, especially in Latin America, seek to increase the distribution of social benefits when they command the requisite financial resources. Even neoliberal populists who emerged from the nadir of hyperinflationary crises and enjoyed an inflow of fiscal revenues due to renewed growth or determined privatization programs proceeded to in-

7. Alan Knight, "Populism and Neo-Populism in Latin America, Especially Mexico," *Journal of Latin American Studies* 30 (May 1998): 223–48; Weyland, "Clarifying a Contested Concept."

8. This political definition of populism via personalistic leadership that sustains itself through a quasi-direct, uninstitutionalized relationship to fairly unorganized mass actors captures the distinctive features of populism much better than discursive conceptualizations, e.g., Kirk Hawkins's definition of populism via a Manichaean discourse of good vs. evil. See Kirk Hawkins, *Venezuela's Chavismo and Populism in Comparative Perspective* (Cambridge: Cambridge University Press, 2010), 5–6, 33–36. But this reconceptualization, which yields a striking "false positive" with U.S. president George W. Bush (77, 81–82), misses the crucial role of personalistic leadership. Populism appeals to "the people," but it does not recognize them as actors in their own right (as participatory bottom-up approaches do); instead, the amorphous people can act only via their leader, to whom they cede a great deal of political autonomy and unaccountable power. Because Hawkins does not clarify the conceptual field in which populism is situated, he overlooks that populism embodies a top-down, not a bottom-up strategy. See Kurt Weyland, "Latin America's Four Political Models," *Journal of Democracy* 6 (October 1995): 128–31.

crease social spending and extend benefits to previously marginalized sectors. As soon as the Peruvian economy began to recover, for instance, Fujimori loosened his tightfisted austerity program and embarked on a social spending spree, timed opportunistically to facilitate his 1995 reelection. Thus, when financial constraints ease, Latin American populists tend to undertake social initiatives. The political purpose—namely, to ensure populists' main goal of retaining government power—is often blatantly obvious. Hugo Chávez, for instance, suddenly rolled out his wide-ranging *misiones* when he faced a serious opposition challenge in a recall election.

Thus, although expansionary social policies are not a definitional characteristic of populism, personalistic, plebiscitarian leaders like to undertake social reform efforts and usually do so when circumstances permit. The main question for this chapter therefore is how successful these initiatives are: Are the social programs of populist leaders a promising option, given the difficulties facing social democracy? Do populist policies attain substantial social progress and sustainably improve education and health standards?

The definitional characteristics of populism—that is, its central political features—suggest a negative answer. Populist leadership is personalistic and plebiscitarian, not institutionalized. Political initiative emanates from the will—and whims—of the leader, not the mass base. Populists deliberately seek autonomy and a wide room to maneuver; they avoid being hemmed in by political coalitions, alliances with interest associations, and institutional constraints. Instead, they try to bend or break the checks and balances that the established constitutional framework seeks to guarantee. When they manage to boost their latitude and concentrate political power, their initiatives are difficult to stop. Radical populists such as Chávez, for instance, promise to "refound" their country by thoroughly overhauling existing institutions and policy programs, replacing established political elites, and concentrating power that will permit them to pursue their initiatives without constraint.

But the power base of populist leaders is shady due to the lack of organizational intermediation and institutionalization. Although they cannot be hemmed in by the discredited opposition and although they dismantle mechanisms of accountability to boost their own leadership, that leadership itself stands on a precarious foundation. Because personalistic, plebiscitarian leaders do not build institutionalized parties, they cannot discipline their mass followers and therefore do not command reliable support. When their charisma fades, more and more supporters defect. Therefore, their political star can fall as quickly as it rose. Adored by the masses one year, they may be vilified the next. The Peruvian populist Alan García, for instance, commanded sky-high popularity ratings of about 90 percent in 1986 yet saw his approval plummet below 10 percent by 1988.

These political features of populism, which are inherent to its central strategy, have contradictory implications for the nature, quality, and sustainability of its social policies. Personalistic, plebiscitarian leaders seek to effect social change more quickly than social-democratic gradualism, but this speedy advance comes at the expense of good policy design, careful implementation, and fiscal and political consolidation. Populism can produce impressive results in the short run, but it often has a disappointing performance in the medium and long runs. The grandiose promises to refound the country often remain unfulfilled—because of incompetence, waste, and institutional and financial precariousness. Populists' capacity to act quickly and decisively inherently risks rashness, deficient planning, shoddy implementation, and weak sustainability. To use a metaphor inspired by Marx's famous comment about religion, populism is like opium: It triggers a quick "high"—but that is followed by a lengthy hangover and malaise.

Advantages of Populist Social Policies

On the positive side, populist leaders are willing and able to undertake ambitious social policy initiatives quickly. When they succeed in pushing aside institutional checks and balances, personalistic, plebiscitarian leaders govern the country at will and use all the fiscal and institutional instruments of the state as well as the political resources of their movement to push for the goals that they have autonomously set. Even before they attain this plenitude of power and independence, they have considerable room to maneuver in the social policy sphere. Many existing social programs can be changed, and new benefits can be created by executive decree, without parliamentary consent. Even if formal rules stipulate the need for congressional approval, populist leaders often disrespect these strictures and "get away with" such usurpation.

As a result, populist leaders can rapidly expand social programs, extend coverage, and improve benefits. When they have the requisite funds, there is little that can stop them. Therefore they can quickly boost indicators of social policy outputs. These bursts of activism can yield impressive short-term success as many people receive entitlements they had not enjoyed before.

Moreover, the new social programs often have a pronounced pro-poor orientation and thus favor particularly needy groupings. Personalistic, plebiscitarian leaders have a political incentive to target their policy initiatives at marginalized sectors that had long been neglected. Whereas under the classical populists of the 1930s to 1950s, formal-sector workers were the primary target, the neopopulists of recent decades have tended to bypass these by-now-included sectors and have concentrated on mobilizing support from the urban informal sector and the rural poor, who suffer from acute needs. These deprived groupings are likely to reward their benefactor with intense support, for material reasons and because a national government finally cares about them. The poor are opportune targets for populists because even limited expenditures can make a significant difference in their lives; focusing on the less well-off is therefore a politically efficient move, especially in terms of electoral payoffs.

Marginalized sectors also tend to be left out by national-level parties and interest associations; lacking supralocal organizational ties, they are particularly available for mobilization by a populist leader who shuns organizational intermediation. By contrast, parties that seek to emulate social democracy have connections to established interest associations, such as trade unions, that make up somewhat better-off sectors. Therefore, they often feel compelled to concede benefits to their core constituencies. But because the organized working class and lower middle class rank in the middle or upper half of Latin America's skewed income pyramids, these social policy reforms do not do much to diminish inequality and boost absolute equity by alleviating urgent social needs. Therefore, trade unions' strength is not associated with progressive policy outputs and social outcomes in developing countries.[9] By contrast, populist leaders have political incentives to make a preferential option for the poor and to be progressive in targeting their social policies.

In sum, populist social policies have several advantages and strengths. Populists try hard to extend benefits as much as possible, they move fast, and they put a priority on particularly needy sectors. Moreover, populist

---

9. James McGuire, "Labor Union Strength and Human Development in East Asia and Latin America," *Studies in Comparative International Development* 33 (December 1999): 3–34.

initiatives in the social sphere have some coherence, which is derived from the political core of populism. Although personalistic, plebiscitarian leaders are notorious for being headstrong and unpredictable, and although they make sudden twists and turns in response to changing opportunities and challenges, they do follow an underlying strategy. Anchored by the political goal of maintaining power, this strategy includes —as a crucial instrument—expansive social policies with a special effort to benefit the poor.

Disadvantages of Populist Social Policies

These advantages, however, which are particularly visible and impressive in the short run, come at the expense of several problems that undermine the effectiveness and sustainability of populist social policies in the medium and long runs. First, the very rush with which personalistic, plebiscitarian leaders proceed causes many of their policy programs to be ill prepared and poorly designed. Because populists often act to address an immediate political need, they tend not to base their policy reforms on a careful analysis of the problems to be addressed, a systematic evaluation of alternative options, and thorough program elaboration. Instead, they put action ahead of reflection and decree change without giving serious attention to high-quality policy design.

In fact, populist leaders put a priority on effectiveness over efficiency. They want to boost their following at all costs, and therefore they make little effort to husband limited funds. Instead, they tend to throw money at problems. As Max Weber pointed out in his analysis of charisma, which many populist leaders possess, their claim of extraordinary, "supernatural" capacities and their pursuit of messianic goals lead to the neglect of earthly pursuits such as economic planning and financial accounting.

As a result, the fiscal foundation of populist expenditure programs is often flimsy. Whereas social democrats base their gradual reforms on firm foundations, such as nondistortionary tax reforms, populists quickly seize on any funds that happen to become available. In particular, they take advantage of temporary windfalls, although these funding sources are likely to dry up soon. For instance, neoliberal populists such as Fujimori drew on revenues from the sale of public enterprises. Yet privatization creates a one-time inflow of funds and cannot sustain expenditure programs over the long run. Similarly, the "radical" populists of recent years, especially Hugo Chávez, have relied on the windfall rents provided by the international oil price boom of the mid-2000s; in fact, this torrent of exceptional revenues has not only allowed them to expand social programs but has also tempted them to proceed with boldness in their economic policies and their whole political strategy as well.[10] Yet the striking price increases that produce such windfall rents are followed sooner or later by busts, which undermine the financial foundation of the newly extended benefit programs—and of radical populism in general.

The autonomy and unconstrained power that many populist leaders enjoy also allow them to use social policy initiatives very directly to pursue their political self-interests. Therefore, they do not put a priority on resolving real social needs but seek the easiest political payoff. Although populists often concentrate their social policy initiatives on particularly disadvantaged sectors, they do not necessarily address those people's urgent needs but instead offer visible benefits that have a particularly high political payoff. Carlos Salinas de Gortari's "neopopulist" National Solidarity Program, for instance, was notorious for building basketball courts rather than combating infant mortality or improving basic education in Mexico.

Moreover, due to the predominance of personalistic leadership, populist social policies often lack institutionalization and are implemented and administered in a haphazard fashion. The failure to follow clear rules contributes to inefficiency, waste, and corruption. It also allows for discretion in the concession of benefits to individual people, which can be used to favor political supporters and exclude the opposition. Given the absence of guaranteed, enforceable rights, social programs morph into the provision of clientelistic favors that keep poor people dependent on the leader. Thus, populist social policies tend to turn into political patronage rather than guarantee citizenship.

The weak institutionalization of populist social programs, their instrumental usage for advancing the political self-interests of personalistic leaders, and the resulting performance problems all threaten the preservation of these benefit programs over time, especially across alternations in government. Because these initiatives are largely the brainchild of a populist leader, they have difficulty acquiring their own

10. Kurt Weyland, "The Rise of Latin America's Two Lefts," *Comparative Politics* 41 (January 2009): 145–64.

identity and legitimacy. If a populist president falls, these initiatives likely also fold.

In sum, the promise and performance of populism in the social policy arena are decidedly mixed. On one hand, personalistic, plebiscitarian leaders can expand social programs quickly and thus benefit large numbers of citizens, especially from long-"excluded" destitute sectors, in the short run. On the other hand, they act haphazardly, tailor social programs toward their political self-interests, and institute programs that suffer from improvisation, inefficiency, waste, and limited fiscal and political sustainability. Especially from a long-term perspective, populism therefore does not offer a promising social policy program.

Of course, what is a realistic standard of assessment? It would be problematic to apply an ideal yardstick, against which any real-world experience would by definition fall short. In fact, do the problems discussed here not characterize Latin American social policy in general? Are they really typical and distinctive of populism? To address these concerns, the following examination of populist experiences draws comparisons with nonpopulist social policies. The social policies instituted in contemporary Brazil and Chile are indeed of higher quality; they are better focused on priority problems, organized more systematically and executed more efficiently, and more sustainable in fiscal and institutional terms. Thus, the comparison shows that despite the obstacles facing social democracy in Latin America, it holds greater promise in the social policy arena than does populism. Moreover, the dysfunctionalities of populist social policies emanate from the very nature of this political strategy, especially the predominant position of a personalistic, plebiscitarian leader and the weak institutionalization of the mass base.

The Social Policy Performance of Contemporary Populism

To substantiate the points advanced so far, this section analyzes the features of social policy under populist governments of different ideological orientations and contrasts them with nonpopulist experiences. Given the tremendous attention that academics and other observers have paid to Hugo Chávez and his ambitious *misiones*, this interesting case certainly deserves scrutiny.[11] Yet in line with the political conceptualization

11. Overviews are given by Greg Wilpert, *Changing Venezuela by Taking Power*

of populism applied in this book, which does not include social policy orientation and overall ideological goals in the core definition, nonleftist experiences with populism also merit close attention. Indeed, it is particularly noteworthy that more centrist or right-wing populists, such as Alberto Fujimori in Peru, have also ended up boosting social expenditures and creating programs that shared the above-mentioned features with their ideologically distant counterparts; although the Peruvian autocrat recruited more *técnicos* in economic policy institutions, he used social policy largely for his political pursuits, exposing it to the dysfunctionalities discussed in the preceding section.

Brazil under Fernando Henrique Cardoso (1995–2002) and Luiz Inácio Lula da Silva (2003–present) and Chile under the Concertación coalition serve as contrasting cases here. The classification of Cardoso and the last four Chilean presidents as nonpopulists is uncontroversial. Lula da Silva, however, used to be subsumed under the rubric of populism—yet only by observers who applied a nonpolitical, policy-focused definition of this concept. Moreover, the rather orthodox economic policies that Lula da Silva has enacted as president have silenced even these voices. Therefore, recent Brazilian and Chilean governments can provide a useful foil for analyzing the particular characteristics of populist social policies.[12]

Advantages of Populism

Populist leaders expand social programs quickly as soon as the political need for securing support arises and fiscal resources permit it. Accordingly, in mid-2003 Chávez created a wide range of new benefit programs—his

---

(London: Verso, 2007), 120–44; and Steve Ellner, *Rethinking Venezuelan Politics* (Boulder, Colo.: Lynne Rienner, 2008), 120–23, 150–51, 168–69, 181–83, 191–92.

12. Interestingly, recent populist governments in Brazil and Chile, especially the administration of Fernando Collor de Mello (1990–92), displayed the same tendencies as Fujimori and Chávez. E.g., Collor impetuously enacted an ill-designed and badly implemented education program (Centros Integrados de Atendimento à Criança, CIACs), which withered away after his downfall, and other social policy initiatives, e.g., an emergency health program intended to combat a cholera epidemic, which was plagued by rampant corruption. Thus, the contrast with Fujimori and Chávez highlighted in this chapter did not emerge primarily from institutional characteristics of the Brazilian and Chilean states but from the political strategies pursued by presidents and their core allies. The social performance of Brazil's most recent populist leader was as problematic as that of his Peruvian and Venezuelan counterparts —not as good as that of his compatriots Cardoso and Lula da Silva.

misiones, "missions to save the people"—when he faced the challenge of a recall election yet was flush with oil rents. The *misiones*—which provide health care, educational services and scholarships, food subsidies, and a variety of other social transfers and which are funded with billions of dollars—soon came to cover millions of Venezuelans. Despite his different ideological orientation, Fujimori acted similarly in 1993, when Peru was beginning to recover from the severe crisis of the late 1980s and the brutal austerity measures that this neoliberal populist himself had imposed in the early 1990s. As soon as tax revenues began to rise again, and as privatization proceeds filled state coffers, Fujimori went on a school-building spree and breathed life—and cash—into a social investment fund to bolster support for his upcoming reelection drive.

Despite their transparent political motivations, both Chávez's and Fujimori's social policy initiatives rapidly and substantially improved the material well-being and life chances of large numbers of people. Although the official statistics produced by these nontransparent, autocratic governments need to be interpreted with caution, the available evidence suggests that both Chávez's and Fujimori's new social programs extended important benefits to large sectors of the citizenry that had been or felt "excluded."[13] Moreover, these programs sought to increase poor people's human capital through basic education and health care and to augment their productive capacities by supporting local investment projects or producer cooperatives. Thus, to the extent that these initiatives attained their goals, they held the potential of creating beneficial multiplier effects as well.

By contrast, nonpopulist governments expand social benefit programs more slowly. For instance, the Programa Saúde da Família, a national family health care effort that turned into a flagship initiative of the Cardoso administration in Brazil, was implemented quite slowly. This basic health program was designed in 1993–94 on the basis of initiatives that had started in the state of Ceará in 1987, and it came to cover a significant share of the population only starting in 1998.[14] Similarly, the Lula da Silva government gradually extended its high-profile condi-

13. See, e.g., World Bank, *Peru: Improving Health Care for the Poor* (Washington, D.C.: World Bank, 1999); Neritza Alvarado Chacín, "Misiones sociales, pobreza y exclusión: La experiencia de la Misión 'Barrio Adentro' en el Estado Zulia," *Fermentum* (Mérida) 18, no. 51 (January–April 2008): 231–33, 236–41.

14. Judith Tendler, *Good Government in the Tropics* (Baltimore: Johns Hopkins University Press, 1997).

tional cash transfer program Bolsa Família, which amalgamated four preexisting governmental programs, over the course of a couple of years. Interestingly, the groundwork for this program was actually laid by Lula's predecessor, Cardoso, who in turn had found inspiration in earlier local programs. Thus, rather than embarking on drastic departures, nonpopulist leaders proceed slowly and steadily and build on already-existing foundations. Similarly, the social investment fund instituted by the Chilean Concertación in 1990 started its operations cautiously and never reached nearly the size of its Peruvian counterpart. Having applied high standards for project design and implementation, it benefited only a small portion of the citizenry. In sum, nonpopulist governments do not address social needs as quickly and broadly as populist leaders.

As another important advantage of their populist approach to social policy, Chávez's and Fujimori's novel programs channeled a large volume of benefits preferentially to poorer sectors. The Bolivarian leader's *misiones* target especially long-excluded sectors that include what seems to be his most fervent mass base; Mercal stores, for instance, that offer low-priced food items, are located predominantly in the poor *barrios* of Caracas, not its middle-class *urbanizaciones.* Because the neoliberal principle of targeting the destitute coincided with his populist political strategy, Fujimori also gave his social policies a distinctly pro-poor orientation. Whereas the middle class and the organized working class were particularly affected by his austerity measures and structural adjustment policies, such as the fallout of privatization and trade liberalization, the poor in the *pueblos jóvenes* of Lima and the interior countryside benefited from new basic health and education programs and the antipoverty investments subsidized by a high-profile social fund.[15] Thus, as is typical of contemporary populism, which tends to bypass the formal-sector middle class and the organized working class, even this market reformer gave his social initiatives a socially progressive, redistributive bent.

The nonpopulist governments of Brazil and Chile have also targeted poorer sectors, for instance through Cardoso's family health program, Lula da Silva's conditional cash transfers, and the Concertación's social fund and other progressive benefit programs. But these administrations,

---

15. World Bank, *Peru: Improving Health Care for the Poor* (Washington, D.C.: World Bank, 1999), 3, 6, 11, 26, 29, 53; Christina Paxson and Norbert Schady, "The Allocation and Impact of Social Funds: Spending on School Infrastructure in Peru," *World Bank Economic Review* 16 (2002): 297–319.

which politically rest on stronger parties and their affiliated interest associations, are also responsive to demands from the organized working and middle classes. Therefore, they tend to spread the distribution of benefits more widely and face resource constraints that make it difficult to massively favor the poorest sectors. Accordingly, though Lula da Silva's Bolsa Família is a high-profile initiative that has attracted tremendous publicity, it receives only 0.5 percent of gross domestic product in funding and takes up a minuscule share of public expenditures; the program, which now covers approximately 45 million Brazilians, thus pales in comparison with the social security system, which channels approximately 5 percent of gross domestic product to 2 to 3 million former civil servants and government employees alone. Similarly, with the assumption of government power by the Concertación parties in 1990, targeting in Chile broadened; the center-left coalition, which had ties to professional associations and trade unions and their formal-sector constituencies, abandoned the virtually exclusive focus on the poorest sectors that had been imposed by the military regime and began to also include working-class and lower-middle-class groupings. Although sustained economic growth greatly diminished poverty in Chile, and although innovative social programs enacted by the Concertación contributed significantly to this achievement, governmental social expenditures under this antipopulist administration came to focus less exclusively on the poorest sectors than before.[16] And although the economic and social policy achievements of the center-left coalition have certainly had very positive effects on poorer sectors, the Chilean governments of the 1990s and 2000s seem to have had less of a pronounced pro-poor "bias" than the populist administrations of Fujimori in Peru and Chávez in Venezuela.

In sum, the social programs enacted by personalistic, plebiscitarian leaders in contemporary Latin America do have some advantages. Above all, these governments have extended new social benefits more quickly than have nonpopulist administrations, and they have made special, disproportionate efforts to reach the poorest sectors—which are most available for populist mobilization. Given the widespread poverty and stark inequality that continue to afflict many Latin American countries, the populist approach to social policy can thus boast strengths.

16. Mauricio Olavarría Gambi, *Pobreza, Crecimiento Económico y Políticas Sociales* (Santiago: Editorial Universitaria, 2005).

Disadvantages of Populism

On balance, however, the downsides of populist social policies outweigh their strengths, especially from a medium- and long-term perspective. Although personalistic, plebiscitarian leaders can rapidly extend benefits coverage, they have difficulty sustaining this accomplishment in fiscal terms and consolidating it institutionally. The success they attain is therefore often temporary; it rises and falls with the leader's political fortunes. Moreover, the very rush to expand social programs creates serious dysfunctionalities. In comparison with the social programs designed by nonpopulist administrations, which are also certainly far from perfect, populist benefit programs tend to be particularly ill prepared, mistargeted in design, flimsy in administration, and subject to corrosion in implementation. As is typical of populism, these programs promise much more than they end up fulfilling; through ambitious goal proclamations, they create high expectations among the citizenry but face significant, usually increasing, difficulties in living up to them. By contrast, nonpopulist social policies tend to attain steadier, more sustainable progress because they emerge from more systematic preparation and design, have a more solid fiscal base, and apply institutionalized mechanisms of administration and implementation. In the medium and long runs, this approach is therefore more sating than the attractive hors d'oeuvres served by personalistic, plebiscitarian leaders, which are not always followed by a full meal.

Design flaws and mistargeting. The very rush with which populist leaders enact and implement their social policy programs can lead to design flaws, and the immediate political-electoral motivations that drive these initiatives exacerbate these risks. For instance, Fujimori—flush with privatization revenues and intent upon securing his reelection in the upcoming 1995 contest—decreed two new health programs in 1994 that had opposite guiding principles. Whereas the Program of Basic Health for All followed a top-down targeting approach, the Local Committees for Health Administration embodied a bottom-up participatory approach. These divergent programs were never integrated into a coherent system; it remained unclear which locality would be covered by which one of these programs and how their divergent logics would coexist.[17]

17. Christina Ewig, "Piecemeal but Innovative: Health Sector Reform in Peru," in *Crucial Needs, Weak Incentives: Social Sector Reform, Democratization, and Glo-*

The populist approach to social policy can also lead to a serious mistargeting of programs. Although personalistic, plebiscitarian leaders tend to give priority to the poor and thus target their initiatives in social terms, they often do not focus on the most important needs of these poor people; instead, they enact programs that have particularly high visibility and therefore the maximum political payoff. In the period before his 1995 reelection, for instance, Fujimori went on a school-building spree, which allowed him to bask in glory by attending innumerable inauguration ceremonies. He paid much less attention to enabling these schools to actually function by paying teachers, providing textbooks, and ensuring maintenance—expenditures that are ongoing, do not receive much public attention, have little political payoff, and are therefore of limited attraction to a populist leader. These constant inputs, however, are at least as important for the sustainable operation of an education system as the provision of physical infrastructure.

Similarly, Fujimori surprised his own public health officials in mid-1997 by suddenly announcing the creation of a free health insurance program for public school children (Seguro Escolar Gratuito, SEG). While this new program had a social angle in that it excluded the better-off students attending private schools, it covered a population cohort that is of low priority from a public health standpoint; older children and adolescents are among the segments that are least at risk of suffering health problems and needing care. Domestic and international health experts wrung their hands at this mistargeting and pushed for redesigning this insurance program to focus it on infants and small children, who are highly vulnerable and therefore need coverage more urgently. But for Fujimori's populist strategy, this mistargeting was actually functional, because it allowed him to extend coverage to a large sector of the population while keeping effective fiscal outlays very limited.[18] Redirecting the program toward infants and small children would have been much more costly.[19] Thus, this substantive mistargeting constituted one of the calculated, politically motivated gestures that are so typical of populism. Although the SEG was suboptimal for public health, it maximized Fujimori's electoral interests.

---

balization in Latin America, edited by Robert Kaufman and Joan Nelson (Washington, D.C.: Woodrow Wilson Center Press, 2004), 231–38.

18. Ewig, "Piecemeal but Innovative," 240–41.

19. Kurt Weyland, *Bounded Rationality and Policy Diffusion: Social Sector Reform in Latin America* (Princeton, N.J.: Princeton University Press, 2007), 161–62.

Chávez's populist government has also mistargeted social programs for political reasons. To prepare for his renewed reelection in October 2012, for instance, the president has extended housing subsidies to the middle class.[20] From a social standpoint, these relatively better-off sectors are not a priority in a country that continues to suffer from a great deal of poverty, despite booming international oil prices; even the incumbent government had to admit that 2 million Venezuelans remain destitute. But because Chávez's electoral adversary threatened to make political inroads in the middle class, the president obviously decided to use his discretion over voluminous petroleum rents to "buy" support from these sectors. Clearly, populism puts political payoff ahead of social need.

Moreover, in the implementation phase, Chávez's social programs have been politicized in a more punitive fashion than the social programs enacted by his neoliberal counterpart in Peru. Whereas Fujimori extended social insurance coverage to nonpriority sectors, the Bolivarian Revolution seems to have excluded individuals who qualified on social grounds but who had offered political support to the opposition. In the most blatant instance of such electorally motivated filtering, politicians allied with Chávez published the list of people who had signed the proposal for holding a recall referendum on the populist leader; the available evidence suggests that these individuals suffered systematic discrimination, including a denial of social benefits.[21] This retaliatory use of

20. "Chávez anuncia ampliación de subsidios habitacionales para la clase media," *El Universal,* August 17, 2012.
21. Human Rights Watch, *A Decade under Chávez: Political Intolerance and Lost Opportunities for Advancing Human Rights in Venezuela* (New York: Human Rights Watch, 2008), 15–28, esp. 27–28. See also Chang-Tai Hsieh, Daniel Ortega, Edward Miguel, and Francisco Rodríguez, "The Price of Political Opposition: Evidence from Venezuela's *'Maisanta,'"* unpublished manuscript, Wesleyan University, Middletown, Conn., 2007; María Pilar García-Guadilla, "La praxis de los consejos comunales en Venezuela: ¿Poder popular o instancia clientelar?" *Revista Venezolana de Economía y Ciencias Sociales* 14, no. 1 (April 2008); Michael Penfold-Becerra, "Clientelism and Social Funds: Evidence from Chávez's *Misiones,*" *Latin American Politics and Society* 49 (Winter 2007): 63–84, 74–75; and Guillermo Rosas and Kirk Hawkins, "Turncoats, True Believers, and Turnout: Machine Politics in the Absence of Vote Monitoring," unpublished manuscript, Washington University, Saint Louis, 2008. For the clientelistic use of social policy under Fujimori, see, e.g., Pedro Francke, "Cambios Institucionales en los Programas Sociales (1980–2005)," in *Construir Instituciones: Democracia, Desarrollo y Desigualdad en el Perú desde 1980*, edited by John Crabtree (Lima: Pontificia Universidad Católica del Perú, 2006), 99–104; and Norbert Schady, "The Political Economy of Expenditures by the Peruvian

discretion undermined not only horizontal equity in social policy but also contradicted Chávez's proclaimed goal of empowering poorer sectors and stimulating their autonomous participation. If social benefit concession is effectively conditioned on support for the populist leader, dependency and sycophancy tend to prevail, participation turns into acclamation engineered from the top down, and social programs serve to establish and solidify clientelistic linkages—problems that are also highlighted in chapter 9 below, by Margarita López Maya and Alexandra Panzarelli.[22] Although it is unclear how widespread the active, punitive misuse of social programs has been, the strong association of the *misiones* with Chávez and his heavy usage of ideology and propaganda seem to skew benefit concession via self-selection: Followers of this plebiscitarian, populist leader are much more likely to seek benefits than people from unaligned sectors or opposition supporters, who are deterred by the open political usage of the *misiones*. As a result, equity goals suffer.

Although nonpopulist governments also hope to obtain political payoffs from their social policy initiatives, they do not resort to such channeling of benefits for electoral reasons. For instance, Lula da Silva's flagship program, the conditional family grant Bolsa Família, significantly helped his 2006 reelection as large numbers of poor people rewarded the president, who himself had emerged from desperate poverty, for using his position to give back to the destitute.[23] But there is little if any evidence that resource allocation has been targeted for political reasons. Instead, well-defined objective criteria guide the distribution of benefits, and where local authorities have misused the program for clientelistic purposes, institutional mechanisms of supervision and sanction have remedied the problem.[24] In Chile, the Concertación has also established

Social Fund (FONCODES), 1991–95," *American Political Science Review* 94 (September 2000): 289–304.

22. García-Guadilla, "La praxis de los consejos comunales"; Irey Gómez Sánchez and Luis Alarcón Flores, "Política social y construcción de ciudadanía en Venezuela," *Multiciencias* (Universidad del Zulia) 9, no. 2 (May–August 2009): 169–75; Mabel Mundó, "Las misiones educativas ¿Política pública para la inclusión o estrategia para el clientelismo político?" *Cuadernos del CENDES* (Centro de Estudios del Desarrollo, Universidad Central de Venezuela) 26, no. 71 (May–August 2009): 28–29, 37, 40–41.

23. Wendy Hunter and Timothy Power, "Rewarding Lula: The Brazilian Elections of 2006," *Latin American Politics and Society* 49 (Spring 2007): 1–30.

24. Wendy Hunter and Natasha Sugiyama, "Building Citizenship or Reinforcing

clear procedures that preclude the political targeting of social programs. A hypervigilant opposition and conservative press ensured that any distortions and deviations were quickly rectified. Thus, not only do non-populist governments undertake few efforts to politicize social programs, but vibrant pluralism and political competition also forestall any temptations. Public opinion and opposition parties would not let the government get away with an electorally motivated mistargeting of social benefit programs. The hegemonic tendencies of personalistic, plebiscitarian leaders and their systematic attacks on the opposition and the media emasculate these counterweights and open up ample room for manipulation.

Other forms of substantive mistargeting are also less likely under non-populist administrations. The systematic design and preparation of new social programs by experts, consultations with international organizations that command a wealth of technical knowledge, and the vetting of many initiatives before public opinion and Congress tend to filter out programs that put political payoffs far ahead of social needs. Although these administrations are no strangers to the lobbying of special interests, gimmicks that presidents announce with great fanfare but that do not address pressing substantive needs, such as Fujimori's SEG, are less common than under populism.

Implementation problems. The rush with which personalistic, plebiscitarian leaders enact social programs and the political goals that drive them also weaken the administration, effectiveness, and efficiency of these benefit programs. Often, these programs get off the ground as improvisational campaigns that lack regularized procedures and well-designed delivery mechanisms—and these problematic, improvised arrangements frequently end up persisting.[25] Usually, these initiatives are not implemented by established line ministries, which—despite problems of bureaucratic rigidity and inertia—have accumulated experience in providing social services and transfers. Instead, a new delivery apparatus is built

Clientelism? Contributions of the Bolsa Família in Brazil," paper for 105th Annual Meeting, American Political Science Association, Toronto, September 3–6, 2009.

25. Neritza Alvarado Chacín, "Las estrategias de inclusión social en Venezuela: Un acercamiento a la experiencia de las misiones," *Convergencia* (Universidad Autónoma del Estado de México) 51 (September–December 2009): 102–11; García-Guadilla, "La praxis de los consejos comunales"; Mundó, "Misiones educativas," 55, 61.

from scratch. Although the sense of mission instilled by the populist leader can initially motivate the new personnel to move mountains, the excess of voluntarism and lack of standard operating procedures over time tends to cause increasing dysfunctionalities, which come to predominate when the initial enthusiasm fades. The absence of organizational structures leads to an unclear division of responsibilities and a duplication of effort, gives rise to waste, and opens the door to corruption.[26]

Although nonpopulist governments are not immune to these problems and scandals, they tend to be more widespread and massive under personalistic, plebiscitarian leadership. In Fujimori's Peru, for instance, credible accusations of corruption in a social emergency program already surfaced in early 1992; and after the president's ignominious downfall in late 2000, an amazing web of corruption involving all sectors of his government came to light. Similarly, Chávez's first high-profile social program, Plan Bolívar 2000, was notorious for corruption, and similar accusations have plagued later policy programs.[27] Given the worsening lack of transparency, the billions of petrodollars sloshing around Bolivarian Venezuela, and the historical tradition of widespread corruption, it is highly likely that knowledgeable observers' claims of high levels of malfeasance are correct; indeed, the country's score on Transparency International's Corruption Perception Index fell from a low 2.3 in 1998 to a dismal 1.9 in 2008.[28] The absence of reliable information also creates enormous difficulties in guaranteeing efficient resource use; it seems that in *chavista* Venezuela, nobody knows where billions of petrodollars that were supposedly invested in social programs have actually ended up.

These implementation issues limit the actual accomplishments of important social programs. For instance, on the basis of the available data, scholars have raised doubts about the success of Chávez's literacy campaign.[29] Chávez himself had to admit in 2009 that his high-profile health

26. World Bank, *Peru: Improving Health Care*, 5–6, 45; World Bank, *Peru: Institutional and Governance Review* (Washington, D.C.: World Bank, 2001), chaps. 4–5; Chacín, "Misiones sociales," 195, 214, 217–21.

27. Boris Saavedra, "Democracy at Risk: President Chávez and the New Role of the Armed Forces," paper prepared for Twenty-Third International Congress, Latin American Studies Association, Washington, September 6–8, 2001, 18–19.

28. See www.transparency.org; and Gustavo Coronel, *Corruption, Mismanagement, and Abuse of Power in Hugo Chávez's Venezuela* (Washington, D.C.: Cato Institute, 2006).

29. See Daniel Ortega and Francisco Rodríguez, "Freed from Illiteracy? A

mission Barrio Adentro had failed to guarantee the reliable provision of health care; indeed, more than half the recently created health posts had already been abandoned.[30] The negative repercussions of other public policies have created additional implementation problems in social policy. Thus Chávez has sought to improve popular nutrition and shield poorer sectors from the rampant inflation caused by his distortionary economic policies; for this purpose, he has created a chain of stores where foodstuffs are sold at massively subsidized prices. But because this populist leader's revival of Venezuela's oil rentier model has further discouraged food production, the shelves are often empty; though the government guarantees low prices, it cannot guarantee a food supply at these prices.[31] The popular stores therefore have a mixed record in attaining their goals; and as economic distortions have accumulated over the years, this record seems to be deteriorating.

Implementation problems are certainly not unheard of in Chile and especially in Brazil. But they do not seem to be nearly as widespread under nonpopulist governments. Recent field research on the administration of Lula da Silva's family grant, for instance, suggests that even on the periphery of the urban metropolis and in the rural interior, the concession and provision of benefits runs smoothly and the criteria for eligibility are applied with considerable rigor; neither waste nor corruption seems to be significant.[32] The reasonably reliable administration of social programs arises from their gradual implementation, which allows for the buildup of institutional capacity. For instance, the innovative health insurance program enacted in Chile under Socialist president Ricardo Lagos (2000–2006), Plan AUGE (Acceso Universal con Garantías Explícitas en Salud), started with a modest coverage of health problems and added more treatments step by step over the course of several years. This gradual approach allows for administrative

Closer Look at Venezuela's *Misión Robinson* Literacy Campaign," *Economic Development and Cultural Change* 57 (2008): 1–30; Mundó, "Misiones educativas," 51–61; and Francisco Rodríguez, "An Empty Revolution: The Unfulfilled Promises of Hugo Chávez," *Foreign Affairs* 87 (March–April 2008): 54–56.

30. Hans-Jürgen Burchardt, "Zurück in die Zukunft? Venezuelas Sozialismus auf der Suche nach dem 21. Jahrhundert," in *Venezuela heute: Politik, Wirtschaft, Kultur*, edited by Andreas Boeckh, Friedrich Welsch, and Nikolaus Werz (Frankfurt: Vervuert, 2011), 434–35.

31. This problem is admitted even by observers who sympathize with the "Bolivarian Revolution," e.g., Wilpert, *Changing Venezuela*, 69, 72, 102–3, 192.

32. Hunter and Sugiyama, "Building Citizenship."

adjustments and corrections and tends to guarantee better functioning in the medium and long run than populism's high-speed social policy initiatives.

Problems of institutional and fiscal sustainability. The rash enactment and improvised organization of populist social programs also weaken the chances of their survival beyond the eventual end of the populist leader's control of the government. Because they are not run by the existing line ministries, these novel benefit programs are not integrated into the regular institutional framework; instead, they usually constitute appendixes of the presidency. As a result, they do not acquire the institutional solidity of regular state institutions, reinforced by the employment stability and tenure of their personnel. Instead, they are sustained by the political will of the leader and his underlings.[33] When a populist leader falls from power, these social programs are therefore threatened with contraction and involution. Although their formal structures may not disappear, they run the risk of turning into hollow shells. In Peru, for instance, the National Institute for Educational and Health Infrastructure, which President Fujimori had used for his school-building spree, ran into trouble soon after he had to resign in late 2000; a scandal about malfeasance further debilitated this weakly institutionalized fund. And because the Venezuelan *misiones* are even more closely associated with Chávez's populist leadership, their lack of firm institutionalization exposes them to even higher political risk.

The financial base of populist social programs is even more precarious, jeopardizing their continued operation. Especially during the time before his 1995 reelection, Peru's Fujimori seems to have financed a good deal of social expenditures in the new targeted and emergency programs directly or indirectly via privatization revenues, which by nature constitute a temporary influx of funds. Even more clearly, as chapter 9 below also highlights, Chávez has used the tremendous increase in oil rents provided by the recent international price boom to pump billions of dollars into his *misiones*, especially—for blatant political reasons—in preelectoral times, as he has done again in 2012.[34] The funds for these programs have not come out of the regular government budget but out

33. For Chávez's missions, see Thais Maingon, "Caracterización de las Estrategias de la Lucha contra la Pobreza: Venezuela 1999–2005," *Fermentum* (Mérida) 16 (January–April 2006): 94–96.

34. "24% creció gasto del Gobierno central en el primer semestre," *El Universal,* July 9, 2012.

of a special development fund fed largely by the state-owned oil company PDVSA (Petróleos de Venezuela). Thus, windfall revenues have sustained the tremendous expansion in social spending under the Bolivarian leader.[35] If these temporary revenues dry up, the fiscal sustenance of these programs is at risk. In fact, the decline in international petroleum prices in 2008–9 put strong pressure on public finances in Venezuela; the available evidence suggests that several *misiones* suffered severe resource cuts and contracted significantly during those years.[36]

By contrast, nonpopulist governments put new social programs on a more solid foundation by allocating regular budget revenues. Both Brazil's conditional family grant and Chile's new health insurance program, for instance, are funded in this sustainable way. Although this financial mechanism does not protect these social programs from all budget cuts, it makes such losses, which would need to be approved by Congress, less likely. More important, it guarantees a funding source that tends to have a much more reliable yield than one-time privatization proceeds or windfall rents. Indeed, Chile, which also benefited from the recent international commodity price boom as a copper exporter, successfully sterilized a large part of this temporary income via a stabilization fund; only a small share of this extraordinary influx of resources was used for immediate public spending. Therefore, the social benefit programs created by nonpopulist administrations have a fairly stable fiscal foundation. They are not exposed to a serious risk of contraction in case economic conjunctures change.

In particular, nonpopulist governments do not make the fundamental mistake of funding programs that are meant to be permanent with revenues that by nature tend to be temporary. Populist leaders, by contrast, give in to the temptation to use any available resources for extending new benefits; driven by the political need to fortify their inherently fickle mass base, they incur spending commitments despite the absence of a solid financial base. Their improvisational style of decisionmaking can bring quick progress but also risks equally rapid setbacks.

35. Mundó, "Misiones educativas," 43, 62; Weyland, "Rise of Latin America's Two Lefts."

36. Carlos Aponte Blank, "El gasto público social durante los períodos presidenciales de Hugo Chávez, 1999–2009," *Cuadernos del CENDES* 27, no. 73 (January–April 2010): 48–52, 60; "Socialism on the Never-Never," *Economist*, June 18, 2009; "Ajustes en Mercal demuestran insostenibilidad del subsidio," *El Universal*, May 20, 2009.

Conclusion

This examination of the social policies enacted by personalistic, plebiscitarian leaders and the comparison with nonpopulist programs demonstrates the advantages and disadvantages of fairly unbounded agency. As captured in the definition of populism as a political strategy that informs this chapter, populist leaders command considerable autonomy, zealously concentrate power, seek to escape from institutional checks and balances, and bend or break constraints. As a result, these leaders have the ability to effect change and enact reforms quickly, even when facing considerable opposition. Given the pressing social problems that plague many Latin American countries, this capacity to make a difference and to do so quickly constitutes a significant advantage. Moreover, personalistic, plebiscitarian leaders often emerge as relative outsiders and are not as beholden to established interest groups and better-off social constituencies as are many long-standing politicians. Therefore, they tend to use their autonomy and power to extend social benefits to previously neglected sectors, whose members are particularly likely to suffer from destitution. Populist leadership thus has the potential to alleviate Latin America's notorious equity problems.

Unbounded agency, however, also has serious downsides. Whereas personalistic, plebiscitarian leaders can successfully push for change, their voluntaristic approach and resort to imposition diminishes the quality of the programs they enact. Decreed without much debate and consultation and implemented in a rush, populist social programs tend to have design flaws, such as unclear assignment of tasks and responsibilities, a lack of regular procedures and institutionalization, and vulnerability to inefficiency, waste, and corruption. Moreover, the strong political motivations that drive populist social policy lead to the mistargeting of benefits, such as the provision of "visible" goods that—at least on their own—do not have the highest priority in terms of social needs. The punitive and deterrent political use of benefits in *chavista* Venezuela is particularly worrisome.

Last but not least, personalistic, plebiscitarian leaders are much better at creating new programs than at guaranteeing their fiscal and institutional sustainability. They often base their benefit programs on temporary revenue sources, which jeopardizes their long-term survival. And to run these programs in a discretionary fashion out of the presidency, they avoid building solid administrative institutions. As a result, these new social programs are exposed to the risk of cutbacks, if not elimination. Indeed, the explicit association of a new benefit program with a personalistic, plebiscitarian leader creates political vulnerabilities—the uncertain fates of these leaders, who can fall as quickly as they rose, can jeopardize the survival of "their" social programs as well.

As the comparative analysis of this chapter suggests, these sobering findings apply to populists of different political orientations, including left-wing leaders who espouse particularly ambitious rhetoric and grandiose promises such as Hugo Chávez. Claiming to refound Venezuelan politics, this charismatic president has pushed the political strategy of populism particularly far, completely revamping his country's institutional framework, eagerly concentrating power, and mobilizing millions of followers. Therefore, and due to the unprecedented oil revenue windfall from 2003 to 2008, Chávez has achieved greater short-term accomplishments than his neoliberal counterpart Fujimori. But they have also stood on especially precarious foundations, due to intense political polarization, weak planning, deficient implementation, and a highly volatile revenue base. Moreover, driven by top-down initiatives from the leader, the new social policy programs have done little to attain their proclaimed goal of empowering the masses and allowing for their autonomous action; instead, as in Fujimori's Peru, the available evidence suggests that clientelism has proliferated and that the politicization of benefit distribution has bred sycophancy and dependency.[37] Thus, even on the social front, the grand proclamations to build the "socialism of the twenty-first century" look more like a mere resurrection of the traditional strategies and patterns of the Latin American populism of the twentieth century.

By contrast to these risks, the social policies pursued by nonpopulist governments look more promising. Although much slower in expanding benefit coverage and thus in addressing urgent social needs, these admin-

37. García-Guadilla, "La praxis de los consejos comunales"; Gómez Sánchez and Alarcón Flores, "Política social y construcción de ciudadanía en Venezuela," 169–75; Mundó, "Misiones educativas," 28–41; Chacón, "Estrategias de inclusión social," 116–24. Pro-Chávez observers focus on the launching of missions, present data only up to 2005–6 (in 2011), and barely touch on these problems of implementation and sustainability. See, e.g., Carles Muntaner, Haejoo Chung, Qamar Mahmood, and Francisco Armada, "History Is Not Over: The Bolivarian Revolution, 'Barrio Adentro,' and Health Care in Venezuela," in *The Revolution in Venezuela*, edited by Thomas Ponniah and Jonathan Eastwood (Cambridge, Mass.: Harvard University Press, 2011), 232–53.

istrations guarantee greater sustainability. The social progress that is made is less likely to be eroded due to financial, political, and institutional setbacks. Although, given political limitations and resource constraints, the nonpopulist governments in Latin America are far from producing achievements similar to those of European social democracy, their inspiration in this model yields better results than their strong-willed populist counterparts end up attaining.

Chapter 6

From the Peróns to the Kirchners: "Populism" in Argentine Politics

Hector E. Schamis

Social scientists communicate through concepts, as Giovanni Sartori acknowledged a while ago.[1] Concepts are the basic unit of thinking in social science inquiry, and, as such, they determine the questions one asks and the places where one looks for answers. To the extent that concepts slice a complex, chaotic, and otherwise unintelligible reality, they play descriptive and explanatory functions simultaneously. Conceptual precision therefore is a key methodological and theoretical goal. Failure in this regard is often conducive to ambiguity, a lack of rigor in the connection between meaning and term, and undenotativeness, looseness in the linkage between meaning and empirical referent. When this happens, one is in the domain of conceptual stretching, that is, when existing concepts become vague, either because we alter the definition as we go along or because the term does not capture the world out there effectively.

1. Giovanni Sartori, "Concept Misformation in Comparative Politics," *American Political Science Review* 64 (1970).

Scholars of comparative politics have often spent intellectual energy correcting conceptual stretching. For example, Philippe Schmitter opened a whole new field of inquiry by rejecting the view of "corporatism" as ideology and by redefining the concept as a mechanism for interest intermediation.[2] Aware of the changing content of "democracy" over time, Robert Dahl proposed treating it as an ideal and coined the term "polyarchy," instead, to capture a political system whose defining attributes are extensive participation and full public contestation.[3] To the extent that democracy did not always mean what we mean today, Dahl's effort was not only semantic; it was also about the clarification of meaning and, mostly, historical specificity. Similarly, the discussion of neoconservative economics in the Southern Cone of Latin America suggested a reexamination of the notion of "bureaucratic-authoritarianism," its historical anchorage, and its decreasing capacity to grasp the new character of military rule in the 1970s.[4]

If any of these efforts at concept formation and refinement were successful, it is only to the extent that they were more or less capable of picturing the world accurately. If so, they have thus facilitated communication and eased the collective process of inquiry. Students of Latin America today confront another, increasingly common, case of conceptual stretching: populism, new populism, neopopulism, and other related formulations. My argument here is that the object to which the term refers to today is by no means the same as what the term referred to when originally formulated. "Populism," and those we identify as "populists," has changed so dramatically since the original meaning of the term that continuing to use it has become a source of theoretical ambiguity and empirical confusion. Due to the overuse of the concept, we are facing a case of homonymy—the same word for different meanings.

The overuse of populism has meant that we have traveled with it through space, comparing different more or less populist experiences,

2. Philippe Schmitter, "Still the Century of Corporatism?" *Journal of Politics* 36 (1974).

3. Robert Dahl, *Polyarchy* (New Haven, Conn.: Yale University Press, 1971).

4. Alejandro Foxley, *Latin American Experiments in Neoconservative Economics* (Berkeley: University of California Press, 1983); Joseph Ramos, *Neoconservative Economics in the Southern Cone of Latin America, 1973–86* (Baltimore: Johns Hopkins University Press, 1986); Hector E. Schamis, "Reconceptualizing Latin American Authoritarianism in the 1970s: From Bureaucratic-Authoritarianism to Neoconservatism," *Comparative Politics*, January 1991.

but we have also traveled through time, stretching the historical specificity with which all concepts—and not just those in the social sciences—must comply. As such, we have lost the historical anchorage of the term, falling into the trap of empirical vagueness. For concepts are also data containers. Their analytical power resides in common empirical understandings, namely, in that they tell us, in a simplified way, the type of otherwise complex phenomena that one should expect to find. If the historical anchorage of a concept is lost—that is, if there is uncertainty as to the facts to be found—one is forced to define and redefine the term each time one mentions it. Communication becomes difficult at best.

This is exactly what has been going on with populism. I first discuss recent scholarship on populism in Latin America, which for the most part approaches it as a political phenomenon only, leaving aside the economic components and ultimately depicting a different species. Next I reconstruct the "biography of the concept," which is necessary to capture its historical specificity.[5] I do so with reference to the ur-case of populism, the political economy of Argentina since 1945. I discuss how populism, in its historical meaning, became exhausted once the strategy of import-substitution industrialization was dismantled. I examine the process of democratization and the transformations of Peronism, a response to the exhaustion of its populist content, and a response to a rapidly democratizing society. I conclude with a reflection on the challenges posed by the legacies of populism—"postpopulism"—for the future of democracy in Argentina and in Latin America more generally.

The Study of Populism in Democratizing Latin America

Postauthoritarian Latin America sparked a renewal of interest in populism. The end of military rule brought old movements back to the street, and long-standing identities back to center stage. With the opening of democratic competition, populist political forces sought to capitalize on their vast organizational resources to appeal to their historical base of support. Once military rule ended in the face of popular mobilization, an important attribute of the 1980s was that the architecture of power of

5. I borrow this notion from Erik Olin Wright, *Classes* (London: Verso, 1985), chap. 2.

newly democratic Latin America could not ignore the centrality of old populist politics and their leaders. A second major characteristic was that the debt crisis was a long-term event, with repercussions to be felt well into the future. Indeed, the expression "the lost decade" was more than a metaphor, as the end of voluntary lending after 1982 had devastating effects for the region as a whole; in fact, they were worse than the Great Depression.

Latin America thus walked into the 1990s with a fragile democratic system and in debt, recession, and macroeconomic disequilibria. The debt crisis had precipitated the severe downturn of the 1980s but had also exposed the inherently vulnerable foundations of the region's economies: overly protected, plagued by price distortions, and structurally inflationary. These economies thus had to adjust in the absence of credit, and they had to reform to be able to return to international financial markets so as to resume growth. In this context, the great challenge was how to go through the "transformational recession"—the fact that in economic liberalization experiments, things have often gotten worse before they got better—while simultaneously upholding basic democratic rules and attending to the social agenda that had been postponed under military rule.

The road ahead seemed uphill, especially if, as some of the literature on the politics of economic adjustment had claimed, market reform experiments needed extraordinary levels of executive discretion and autonomy to be implemented.[6] Furthermore, dismantling the structure of protectionism and downsizing the state would disproportionately hurt import substituters and urban wage earners; thus, the transformational recession would provide incentives to oppose reform to the very traditional constituencies of populism.

Yet, paradoxically, only populist leaders could muster enough organizational and symbolic resources to implement reforms that were painful but inevitable, and which thus required the demobilization of those affected by economic change. "Neopopulism" thus became populism

---

6. Joan Nelson, ed., *Fragile Coalitions: The Politics of Economic Adjustment* (New Brunswick, N.J.: Transaction Books, 1989); Joan Nelson, ed., *Economic Crisis and Policy Choice: The Politics of Adjustment in the Third World* (Princeton, N.J.: Princeton University Press, 1990); Stephan Haggard and Robert Kaufman, eds., *The Politics of Economic Adjustment* (Princeton, N.J.: Princeton University Press, 1992); Stephan Haggard and Robert Kaufman, *The Political Economy of Democratic Transitions* (Princeton, N.J.: Princeton University Press, 1995).

plus neoliberalism. It appeared that without the military, as in Chile in the 1970s and 1980s, neoliberalism in a democratic regime could only move forward on a populist vehicle. In the late 1980s and early 1990s, therefore, scholarly work focused on the spectacle of populist leaders running for office on the typical rhetorical and programmatic stands of their predecessors, but sharply turning to liberal economic policies once elected.

Although for some this was somewhat of an unexpected event, "bait-and-switch populism," for others it was less surprising, if not obvious.[7] Arguably, to the extent that populist politics had historically been based on a charismatic leader in charge of a powerful presidency, low institutionalization of political parties, and a fragmented political system, populism appeared well suited to implement neoliberal economic policies. From Salinas's Mexico to Fujimori's Peru and Menem's Argentina, in this view neoliberalism appears well suited for neopopulism, both promoting an institutionally sparse state and a legislative process largely based on executive decree interventions.[8] Furthermore, given the asymmetrical regional implications of market reform, it appeared that only populist leaders could navigate the turbulent waters of territorial politics and arbitrate between urban and rural constituencies.[9]

By the end of the 1990s, however, Latin America seemed to be experiencing reform exhaustion. Sustained fiscal adjustment, trade opening, and privatization looked discredited in the face of sluggish growth and persistent inequality. Corruption in the conduct of these reforms—which occasionally coincided with, or led to, severe currency and banking crises—added to the general feeling of disappointment. Latin America apparently became disenchanted with the Washington Consensus, and so it turned to the left. Some of this left has emerged as institutionalized

7. Paul Drake, "Comment," in *The Macroeconomics of Populism in Latin America*, edited by Rudiger Dornbusch and Sebastian Edwards (Chicago: University of Chicago Press, 1991).

8. Kurt Weyland, "Neopopulism and Neoliberalism in Latin America: Unexpected Affinities," *Studies in Comparative International Development* 32 (Fall 1996): 3–31; Kurt Weyland, "Neopopulism and Neoliberalism in Latin America: How Much Affinity?" *Third World Quarterly* 24, no. 6 (2003); Kenneth Roberts, "Neoliberalism and the Transformation of Populism in Latin America: The Peruvian Case," *World Politics* 48, no. 1 (October 1995): 82–116.

9. Edward L. Gibson, "The Populist Road to Market Reform: Policy and Electoral Coalitions in Mexico and Argentina," *World Politics* 49, no. 3 (April 1997): 339–70.

)olitical parties, but much of it, in contrast, has displayed a
ilist character. Especially in the Andes and in Argentina
chners, even if more in discourse than in actual policy, the
st neoliberalism has resurrected some of the populist themes
of the past: redistributionism and anti-American nationalism, among
others.[10]

Through much of the democratization process, therefore, populism is
pictured as a malleable phenomenon, one that can conform to neoliberalism and display right-wing features, as much as reflect the tenets of
nationalism and even socialism, and exhibit left-wing attributes. Populism
is considered to arise under different economic policies; thus, it is treated
only as a form of politics but, it must be highlighted, a circumscribed
form of politics, one debased of any material and institutional foundations. Thus, populism is often seen as a set of rituals, a form of politics
that draws on passions rather than on institutions, arguably to advance
the redemptive nature of democratic participation. In sum, if populism
can be so many different things, its level of specificity needs to be reduced
to such an extent that it must be defined as no more than a "style" of
politics.[11]

This presents two problems. One is methodological, because a concept reduced to one defining characteristic expands its extension to the
point of fully dissolving its analytical power. In other words, the number
of cases the concept grasps will be so high that one will lose any capacity
to build middle-range theory, the core of comparative analysis. The second problem is historical, because by excluding the original economic
policies of populism, and by accepting that any economic policy can go
hand in hand with populism, we ignore the record of populists—that is,
what they have done when in office does not seem to matter as much.

10. See the special issue of *Journal of Democracy*, "A 'Left Turn' in Latin America?" 17, no. 4 (October 2006); Steve Ellner, "Revolutionary and Non-Revolution-
ary Paths of Radical Populism: Directions of the Chavista Movement in Venezuela,"
Science and Society 69, no. 2 (April 2005): 160–90; and Kirk Hawkins, "Populism in
Venezuela: The Rise of Chavismo," *Third World Quarterly* 24, no. 6 (December
2003): 1137–60.

11. For populism as rituals, see Carlos de la Torre, *Populist Seduction in Latin
America: The Ecuadorian Experience* (Athens: Ohio University Press, 2000); and
Carlos de la Torre, "Populist Redemption and the Unfinished Democratization of
Latin America," *Constellations* 5, no. 1 (March 1998): 85–95. For populism as style,
see Alan Knight, "Populism and Neopopulism in Latin America, Especially Mex-
ico," *Journal of Latin American Studies* 30, no. 2 (May 1998): 223–48.

Once we violate the biography of the concept, as we thus use it in a trans-historical fashion, we lose its empirical specificity altogether.

Defining and Historicizing the Concept: The Political Economy of Populism

The concept of populism is intended here to define a specific and historically determined political phenomenon that evolved in Latin America largely as a series of responses to the Great Depression and its aftermath. Typically, the emergence of populist forms coincided with the initiation and/or consolidation of the period of effective incorporation of subordinate groups into the political system in a context of rapid economic and social modernization. Its main defining characteristics are movement, proindustrialization, multiclass, urban, inclusionary, reformist and redistributive, corporatist, nationalist, and a charismatic leader.[12]

Movement

Populism is not a party, though it may be. It is not a union, though it is generally based on unions. Populism is fundamentally a national movement—a heterogeneous, fluctuating, and dynamic cluster of mass organizations brought together under the control of state policies and agencies. In the case of populism in Argentina, the Peronist movement was originally organized in sectoral terms: the political branch, which addressed political competition and controlled the territorial party struc-

---

12. My approach to the study of populism owes much to the works of Torcuato Di Tella, "Populism and Reform in Latin America," in *Obstacles to Change in Latin America*, edited by Claudio Veliz (New York: Oxford University Press, 1966); Fernando Henrique Cardoso and Enzo Faletto, *Dependency and Development in Latin America* (Berkeley: University of California Press, 1979); Ottavio Ianni, *A Formacao do Estado Populista na America Latina* (Rio de Janeiro: Editora Civilizacao Brasileira, 1975); Gino Germani, *Politica y Sociedad en una Epoca de Transición* (Buenos Aires: Paidos, 1962); Guillermo O'Donnell, *Modernization and Bureaucratic Authoritarianism* (Berkeley: Institute for International Studies, 1973); Ruth Berins Collier and David Collier, *Shaping the Political Arena* (Berkeley: University of California Press, 1991); Paul Drake, *Socialism and Populism in Chile* (Urbana: University of Illinois Press, 1978); Thomas Skidmore, "The Economic Dimensions of Populism in Argentina and Brazil: A Case Study in Comparative Public Policy," *New Scholar* 7, nos. 1–2 (1979): 129–66; Michael Conniff, *Populism in Latin America* (Tuscaloosa: University of Alabama Press, 1999).

ture; the labor branch, which was controlled by the state under corporatist mechanisms of intermediation; and the women's branch, where originally Eva Perón created a structure of patronage along with her charity foundation and fostered the enfranchisement of women.

Proindustrialization

Populism favors import-substitution industrialization (ISI). A legacy of the Depression, populism sought to either initiate or accelerate the process of domestic industrialization through a series of state policies that included tariffs, credit subsidies for local firms, import controls, real exchange rate appreciation, and heavy public spending and investment. Typically this process had a bias in favor of consumer goods—the "easy phase"—that supported both domestic production and consumption, expanding the internal market but simultaneously leading to recurrent balance-of-payments and macroeconomic crises.

These stylized facts fit well with the early Peronist experience of 1946–52 and later in 1973–76. Upon coming to office in 1946, the Perón government issued legislation to increase the interventionist role of the state in the economy, most notably, a five-year economic plan and the creation of the Instituto Argentino de Promoción del Intercambio (Argentine Institute for the Promotion of Trade), a new state agency that held a monopoly over the foreign exchange originated in the export of agricultural products. This institutional innovation secured the redistribution of the agrarian surplus toward industrialization and the expansion of the state-owned sector. The other key policy components were high tariffs and exchange rate management. The exchange rate regime was usually one of fixed (but adjustable) rates in order to maintain lower levels of inflation and encourage industrialization. High trade barriers allowed ISI to be pursued with fixed exchange rates, compensating for real exchange rate appreciation. A fixed parity was pursued to keep a steady price in industrial inputs and capital goods.

However, because Argentina's exports consisted mainly of food products (or wage goods), a devaluation would put pressure on industrial wages. Therefore, under ISI, a fixed exchange rate was the preferred alternative for industrialists and urban workers, in contrast to the export-oriented agricultural sector, which supported a competitive exchange rate. The periodic overvaluation of the real exchange rate caused by the fixed nominal parity and the general bias of economic policy toward the protection of industry were meant to provide important disincentives for agriculture.

The limits of ISI recurrently led to balance-of-payment crises and devaluations. The stop/go nature of ISI was accompanied by cycles of repression and loosening in the exchange rate. The acceleration of growth led to decreasing exports (because a larger percentage of the wage goods were consumed internally due to growing incomes) and increasing imports (especially inputs and capital goods to sustain the expansion of the manufacturing sector), generating balance-of-payment crises when official external reserves reached low levels.[13] At times, the constraints inherent to the development strategy were magnified by external shocks, and external crises occurred even if the economy was not necessarily expanding fast. Despite existing capital controls, exchange rate crises during most of this period resulted from the decline in reserves caused by the gradual deterioration of the trade balance, which also fueled inflation.[14]

Multiclass

Whether early or delayed, populism is a response to the breakdown of the hegemonic rule of the agroexport elite. As the Great Depression eroded the basis for the oligarchic mode of domination, a multiclass compromise emerged to foster governability by trying to reconstruct hegemonic domination. To talk about a multiclass coalition entails far more than saying that populist leaders came into office through a very heterogeneous vote—a trait that applies to all political parties, given that the goal of winning elections in modern democracies forces them to become catchalls. The core dimension of populism as a multiclass coalition is, instead, that its members obtain material rewards from it. This multiclass coalition—formed by domestic-oriented industry, organized labor, and the new urban middle classes associated with the expansion of the state apparatus—was inherently unstable, however. It was capable of

13. O. Braun and L. Joy, "A Model of Economic Stagnation: A Case Study of the Argentine Economy," *Economic Journal*, 1967, 868–87; Carlos Diaz-Alejandro, "A Note on the Impact of Devaluation and the Redistributive Effect," *Journal of Political Economy* 71 (1963).

14. Guido Di Tella, "Argentina's Most Recent Inflationary Cycle, 1975–85," in *Latin American Debt and the Adjustment Crisis*, edited by Rosemary Thorp and Laurence Whitehead (Pittsburgh: University of Pittsburgh Press, 1987).

articulating demands effectively during periods of growth but prone to political crisis during economic slowdowns.

As in Argentina's "impossible game," the political limits of this unstable alliance were set by the nature of the distributional conflict under ISI.[15] Rapid industrialization had helped produce autonomous forms of mobilization that surpassed the organizational forms designed from above to control the popular sector. During democratic periods, labor's influence tended to increase, generally leading to higher wages. Frequently, this happened in the context of accommodating monetary policies that fueled inflation. When the macroeconomic constraint intrinsic to the development strategy converged with growing wage pressures, important industrial groups and parts of the middle classes tended to abandon the original ISI coalition. The convergence of balance-of-payment and inflationary crises recurrently aggravated the three fundamental cleavages of populism—class, labor/capital; sector, industry/agriculture; and region, urban/rural. The resulting political crises created the conditions for a coup, which was often the outcome. Thus, high levels of inflation, international currency reserves insufficient to sustain normal levels of imports and service the external debt, and growing social unrest were the reasons often invoked by the military to justify a political intervention that would "reestablish order and clean up public finances."

A paradigmatic illustration of these cycles can be seen in the 1973–76 Peronist government. Its economic program represented the culmination of the ISI strategy of development: It established a fixed exchange rate, and at the same time it instituted price controls, increased wages and salaries, and implemented active fiscal and monetary policies to foster industrial activity and employment. This imbalanced mix was helped initially by an important improvement in the terms of trade, which were at an all-time high. During this period, the industrial sector reached its largest share of contribution to the gross domestic product (GDP), real wages climbed to the highest level for the whole half century, and unemployment stood below 4 percent.

By mid-1974, however, political and economic conditions had begun to deteriorate rapidly. The exchange rate peg continued during the third quarter of 1974, but by 1975 the terms of trade had declined significantly and the economy had entered a recession. The government tried stimulative fiscal and monetary policy, but this only fueled inflation, making the

15. O'Donnell, *Modernization*.

real exchange rate decline even further. The deterioration of the external accounts forced sharp adjustments of the exchange rate in the last quarter of 1974 and in the second quarter of 1975, this last one becoming the first of a series of "maxidevaluations." In a setting marked by deteriorating economic conditions, political uncertainty, and escalating violence, the Peronist government was toppled by a coup in March 1976. From then onward, there was a steady decline in industry's share of GDP, real wages fell, and the entire ISI experience was terminated.

Urban

Populism in Latin America is an urban phenomenon. This does not mean that populism does not enjoy the support of groups in rural areas—in fact, it does. Fundamentally, however, it means that the movement's center of gravity is in the city, among organized wage earners, industrialists, and the state. As the engine of growth shifted from agriculture to industry, there were accompanying comprehensive demographic, sociological, and cultural changes. In a nutshell, populism is the political vehicle for internal migration and rapid urbanization, and it expressed the exploitative and exclusionary nature of that process. Peronism's *"aluvión zoológico"* (zoological landslide) is exactly that.

Inclusionary

Populism promotes the incorporation of subordinate groups into the political process. It does so with three complementary mechanisms. First, consumer-oriented industrialization expands the domestic market, incorporating a vast number of new groups into the economic process. Second, populism legitimizes and institutionalizes labor organizations—with populism, labor unrest is for the first time a policy problem, not only a police problem. And third, populism promotes participation by excluded groups and their enfranchisement—for instance, in the first Perón government, women were granted political rights and voter turnout grew from 18 to 50 percent of the population. As such, populism completes the process of democratization.

Reformist and Redistributive

Populism is not a revolutionary movement, but its emphasis on inclusion and social justice makes it a potent agent of social reform and redistribution. As with the Peronist programs and incomes policies, which expanded the welfare state and promoted a larger proportional contribution by wage earners to the GDP—up to 50 percent in 1952 and in 1974—this is one of the most distinctive attributes of the populist experience.

Corporatist

The organization of groups on the basis of their occupational categories—corporatism—is populism's favored form of political representation. As an institutional space sanctioned, created, and controlled by the state, corporatism pursued economic policy coordination—which was crucial for accelerated, state-led industrialization—and tripartite negotiations among labor, capital, and the state—a fitting vehicle for the incorporation of labor. Thus corporatism played a role in meeting the redistributive goals and in the reproduction of the multiclass coalition of support. Peronism's elective affinity with corporatism, however, reveals its rather ambiguous approach to political democracy. Its "social contract," in fact, was based on a strong sphere of social rights; redistribution; an instrumentalist approach to the democratic process, whereby political rights were little more than a tool for gaining power; and a historical mistrust of civil rights—to the extent that the liberal component of citizenship does include the right to private property, it is often seen as an instrument for maintaining the privileges of the elite and for reproducing existing inequalities.

Nationalist

As Juan Linz has noted, populism does not possess an ideology in the strict sense of the term. At best, it holds a series of amorphous mentalities, generally defensive and reactive views of the world.[16] Nationalism in populist movements should be seen in this light, though emphasizing that it is an economic form of nationalism more than a representation of identity. The "who are we" of populism is determined by the conflicts associated with the perennial impossibility of accomplishing national control of economic resources. In this sense, populism can afford to be

16. Juan Linz, "An Authoritarian Regime: Spain," in *Cleavages, Ideologies, and Party Systems,* edited by Erik Allard and Yrjo Littunen (Helsinki: Transactions of the Westermarck Society, 1964).

more or less progressive, as much as it can be more or less reactionary—and it has been both. It can also be more or less democratic, as much as more or less authoritarian—and it has also been both of these. What populism cannot afford, however, is to be cosmopolitan and internationalist. Populism is anti-imperialist, reactive against neocolonialism, and defensive vis-à-vis the international status quo. Populism pursues autarchic national development, which, as in Perón's narrative, is about declaring "economic independence."

A Charismatic Leader

Populist movements are generally led by charismatic figures who use their special qualities to avoid and circumvent institutionalized decision-making. At a time of internal migration and rapid urbanization, these leaders constitute themselves as heirs of the old caudillos of the countryside. As such, this style of leadership also corresponds to a specific developmental phase of Latin America—the early stages of industrialization.

Populism and its central ingredients could not outlive the 1970s. The indebtedness process and growing financial integration, crowned by the debt crisis of the 1980s, would signal the end of ISI as a dominant strategy of development. In this inflation-prone, politically unstable decade, growth was based on a strict view of efficiency and a static notion of comparative advantage. As a result, the state would move from serving as the locus for class compromise to being an instrument of structural transformation. The military abandoned its concern with state-led development and adopted policies based on the free interplay of market forces and a monetary approach to the balance of payments. Social fragmentation thus accelerated, and collective representation suffered. This outcome undermined the base of populism at its root—there were fewer workers in industry, there were lower rates of unionization, public enterprise was under attack, and there were more concentrated units of capital. A new chapter in the country's economic history was in the making after 1976.

Dismantling Import Substitution: Decomposing the Material Bases of Populism

At the outset, the March 1976 coup did not seem very different from the previous authoritarian experiments that had marked Argentina's turbulent political history. As time went by, however, this new regime revealed its exceptionally coercive nature: Political activity was banned, strike rights were withdrawn, and the military forced the disappearance of thousands of dissenters.

What appeared as indiscriminate repression, however, was not irrational—it turned out to be a tool for economic liberalization. At the time, in orthodox economic circles, the political crisis that led to the military takeover was seen as a straightforward consequence of protracted ISI. Allegedly, protectionism in the manufacturing sector had swollen domestic industry, artificially increasing its market power, and thus it had also strengthened unions, artificially increasing their political power. In the process, while firms became more and more inefficient, unions became more and more radical. Protectionism and expansive welfare state policies delivered by populists had encouraged ever-increasing demands on state resources. The minister of the economy, José Martínez de Hoz, a prominent member of the agroexport and financial elite, thus spent about a third of his time traveling from barrack to barrack, explaining the rationale for his economic program and trying to convince the armed forces of the need to abandon their long-term concern with state-led industrialization.[17] In the end, tariff reduction was appealing; it would seek not just to allocate resources more efficiently but also to discipline hypermobilized organized groups, decompose the social base of Peronism, and restore order.[18]

Accordingly, by April 1976, the authorities had devalued the currency, liberalized prices, frozen wages, and reduced export taxes and import tariffs. In June 1977, additional measures deregulated the banking industry by easing the entry of new financial institutions, reducing reserve requirements, freeing interest rates, and redirecting public-sector borrowing toward private credit markets. As a result, real interest rates became positive, leading to a considerable slowdown in 1978. Despite the recession, inflation had remained stuck at about 150 percent, prompting the economic authorities to deepen stabilization policies and accelerate the course of liberalization. The government thus launched the "20th of December 1978 Program," the cornerstone of which was an exchange

17. David Pion Berlin, "The Fall of Military Rule in Argentina, 1976–1983," *Journal of Interamerican Studies and World Affairs*, Summer 1985.

18. Adolfo Canitrot, "La Disciplina como Objetivo de la Política Económica: Un ensayo sobre el Programa Económico del Gobierno Argentino desde 1976," *Estudios CEDES* 2, no. 6 (1979).

rate policy based on an active crawling peg.[19] The *tablita*, as this program came to be known, consisted of a series of preannounced devaluations based on a declining rate of inflation. With the *tablita* came the elimination of restrictions on trade and capital accounts. Through these measures, the government expected to bring the economy more in line with international prices and induce a process of reallocation according to Argentina's comparative advantages.[20]

The preannounced exchange rate, set at levels below the rate of inflation so as to reduce inflationary expectations, increased real exchange rate appreciation. With trade and financial liberalization, this new competitive environment put pressure on manufacturing firms, especially those in the consumer-oriented ISI sector. Domestic real interest rates higher than international ones and the exchange rate risk offset by the *tablita* generated massive inflows of capital and drove firms into dollar-denominated debt, either to keep their operations afloat or to engage in arbitrage. As is characteristic of exchange rate–based stabilization programs, real exchange rate appreciation and the oversupply of foreign credit financed a consumption boom in imports, which was instrumental in gathering support among the otherwise castigated middle sectors, precisely during the most coercive phase of the military regime. As a result, private external debt increased from $4 billion in 1978 to $9 billion in 1979, leading to a threefold increase in total (private and public) debt between 1978 and 1981. Most private debt was concentrated in large firms and banks; one-third of it among ten banks and ten industrial firms.[21] Argentines thus made up the term *patria financiera* (financial motherland) to refer to the main beneficiary of the liberalization process.[22]

19. Carlos Rodríguez, "El Plan Argentino de Estabilización del 20 de Diciembre," *CEMA Documento de Trabajo* 5 (1979).

20. Exchange rate–based stabilization was pioneered by Argentina, Chile, and Uruguay in the 1970s. In the early 1980s, these countries also experienced similar balance-of-payment crises associated with real appreciation and current account balances unsustainable in the medium term, which produced runs on the currency and drainage of Central Bank reserves. This issue became a highly debated one in the 1990s, as across-the-board capital account liberalization contributed to analogous crises in Mexico in 1994, Asia in 1997, Russia in 1998, and Brazil in 1999.

21. A. Humberto Petrei and James Tybout, "Microeconomic Adjustments in Argentina during 1976–1981: The Importance of Changing Levels of Financial Subsidies," *World Development* 13, no. 8 (August 1985): 949–67.

22. In the early 1970s, disputes within the Peronist movement developed between

The term *patria financiera* also captured the reality that industrialization had ceased to be the engine of the economy. Financial intermediation and the service sector more generally had become the cornerstone of the new strategy for development. As in similar programs in the Southern Cone as a whole, the liberalization of cross-border capital flows opened an entirely new chapter in Argentina's political economy. While under ISI, real exchange rate appreciation generally led to foreign exchange crises due to the accumulation of trade deficits over time; from 1978 on, attacks on the currency through transactions on the capital account could suddenly deplete international reserves. This occurred after 1979, in fact, when the deterioration of the balance of payments conveyed the limits of the predetermined exchange rate, leading to massive outflows of capital in anticipation of a future devaluation.[23]

This inherently vulnerable macroeconomic context was further compounded by changes in the nature of the country's distributional conflict. Under ISI, income struggles among sectors had been based on the distribution of the agrarian surplus, but as commodity prices began to decline in the second half of the 1970s (eventually collapsing in the mid-1980s), economic groups increasingly began to direct demands toward the state. The military government responded to these pressures in three ways. First, it revitalized an existing program of sectoral incentives called "regime of industrial promotion," and combined this with tax exemptions for firms relocating to frontier provinces (due to the military's security concerns). Second, it increased public investment in infrastructure, petrochemicals, and the military-industrial complex, generating opportunities for contractors and suppliers of the state, which took advantage of old legislation that gave priority to domestic firms in public auctions. And third, in 1981–82, the Central Bank enacted a program whereby private debtors could transfer their foreign obligations to the state. These multiple subsidies generated larger deficits—peaking at 16 percent of GDP

factions that advocated either a *"patria socialista"* or a *"patria peronista."* Later on, and as a consequence of the influence accumulated by labor leaders during the 1973–76 Peronist government, the public made references to the *"patria sindical."* In the late 1970s and early 1980s, allusions to the *"patria financiera"* conveyed that power was now located in the financial sector.

23. The ensuing banking crisis prompted the government to take over fifty-nine financial institutions between March 1980 and December 1981 alone. See Luis Giorgio and Silvia Sagari, "Argentina's Financial Crises and Restructuring in the 1980s," in *Bank Restructuring: Lessons from the 1980s*, edited by Andrew Sheng (Washington, D.C.: World Bank, 1996), 161–73.

in 1983—which, when monetized in the context of an open capital account with a fixed exchange rate, also contributed to rapidly wiping out foreign exchange reserves, leading to sharp devaluations and explosive cycles of ever-increasing inflation.

Paradoxically, a military-sponsored liberalization experiment institutionalized Argentina's secular distributional conflict at the level of the fiscal sector. More than ever before, influence over the destination of state resources was the main way to resolve intersector and intrasector rivalries and, thus, the way alliances among economic groups were built. By the turn of the decade, severe fiscal constraints limited the government's largesse in the overall distribution of subsidies, forcing firms to pursue economies of scale in rent seeking, and increased the selectivity of the process, generating incentives for favoritism, overinvoicing, and misappropriation, among other practices. Thus, by the early 1980s a few private groups had accumulated vast amounts of wealth while the economy as a whole was verging on the brink of collapse. In the manufacturing sector, for example, firms able to access industrial promotion and public contracts expanded significantly during the 1976–83 period, while the sector as a whole declined from 27.5 to 22 percent of a negative-on-aggregate GDP. These beneficiaries, in turn, were virtually the same ones that were responsible for 79 percent of the total private external debt that was transferred to the state, but that represented only 5 percent of all private debtors.[24] At this point, a new distributional coalition was formed, one not based on the rents of protectionism but on the perks of state contracts. The success of this group—which was nicknamed *patria contratista* (contractor motherland) by the public, but which self-identified as "the captains of industry"—was based on its members' capacity to access the wielders of political power and their effective control of

24. These data are from Jorge Schvarzer, "Estrategia Industrial y Grandes Empresas: El Caso Argentino," *Desarrollo Económico* 18, no. 71 (October–December 1978): 307–51; Jorge Schvarzer, "Cambios en el liderazgo Industrial Argentino en el período de Martínez de Hoz," *Desarrollo Económico* 23, no. 91 (October–December 1983): 395–422; Mario Damill and José María Fanelli, "Decisiones de Cartera y Transferencias de Riqueza en un Periodo de Inestabilidad Macroeconómica," *Documento CEDES* 12 (1988); Daniel Aspiazu, Eduardo Basualdo, and Miguel Khavisse, *El Nuevo Poder Económico en la Argentina de los Años Ochenta* (Buenos Aires; Legasa, 1986); Eduardo Basualdo, *Deuda Externa y Poder Económico en la Argentina* (Buenos Aires: Nueva América, 1987); and Eduardo Basualdo and Daniel Aspiazu, *Cara y Contracara de los Grupos Económicos: Estado y Promoción Industrial en la Argentina* (Buenos Aires: Cántaro, 1991).

mostly family-owned diversified economic conglomerates through highly centralized decisionmaking structures.[25]

In the 1980s, therefore, fiscal crisis, indebtedness, and deindustrialization led to the deepest recession since the 1930s—and eventually to the "lost decade." In the process, these events also changed Argentina's social structure in a dramatic way, as morphological studies at the time showed. For example, the proportion of industrial workers among all wage earners declined from 23 percent in 1954 to 13 percent in 1985. The industrial labor force diminished by 33 percent between 1976 and 1983. Between 1947 and 1960, the manufacturing sector absorbed 41 percent of all new entrants into the labor market, but between 1970 and 1980 that proportion dropped to 7 percent, while finance and the service sector grew from 33 to 86 percent. Additionally, census data confirm that the fastest-growing occupational category in the city of Buenos Aires was the self-employed, which rose from 11 percent in 1960 to 18 percent in 1980.[26]

These developments would have crucial consequences for the future of populism and for the political process more generally. The class-based political socialization forged by the unions in the workplace was challenged by an increasingly atomized and individualizing occupational structure. As the social changes shaped by deindustrialization eroded class-based bonds of political solidarity, so too did the structural power of the labor movement, Peronism's main social base. In a nutshell, if the children of blue-collar, unionized Peronist workers became cab drivers, it is conceivable that their political choices would vary accordingly. Equally dramatic changes took place among the other main partner in the populist coalition, the import substituters. Although bankruptcies increased steadily, driven by simultaneous trade liberalization and real exchange rate appreciation, those who managed to survive the new competitive environment did so mainly by becoming diversified and inte-

25. For detailed studies, see Pierre Ostiguy, *Los Capitanes de la Industria: Grandes Empresarios, Política y Economía en la Argentina de los Años 80* (Buenos Aires: Legasa, 1990); and Luis Majul, *Los Dueños de la Argentina* (Buenos Aires: Sudamericana, 1992).

26. These data are from UN International Labor Organization, *Yearbook of Labour Statistics* (Geneva: International Labor Organization, 1983); and Héctor Palomino, *Cambios Ocupacionales y Sociales en Argentina, 1947–1985* (Buenos Aires: CISEA, 1987). For an analysis of how these structural changes were favorable for the emergence of conservative electoral agendas and coalitions, see Edward Gibson, *Class and Conservative Parties: Argentina in Comparative Perspective* (Baltimore: Johns Hopkins University Press, 1996).

grated financial-contracting conglomerates, a pattern that also signals a clear change of policy preferences, and thus of political allegiances. The old national bourgeoisie thus became extinct, and so its main organizations were dismantled and its leaders were sent into exile. As it turned out, for the military government, decomposing populism was as multiclass a phenomenon as populism itself.

By 1982, the military had been cornered by domestic discontent and was internationally isolated after the Falklands/Malvinas war, so it had to execute a quick withdrawal from office, leaving behind a truncated liberalization experiment with monumental foreign debt, a high concentration of economic power, and a vacuum of political power. Argentina walked into a democratic transition in the most adverse economic context imaginable.

Democratization and Postpopulism

In October 1983, for the first time since its emergence as a political force in 1945, Peronism lost a national election in a free and fair contest. Although there were some indications of this shift in a few public opinion polls, the outcome of the election nonetheless took the entire country by surprise, ultimately shocking the Peronist leaders in disbelief. Seen in retrospect, however, this was to be expected. The structural changes spelled out above highlight that the material bases of populism had eroded, and consequently so had Peronism's traditional organizational capabilities. Wage earners' share of national income, which had been about 50 percent under the Peronist administrations in 1952 and 1974, shrank to an abysmal 23 percent in 1982. The promise of social justice and redistribution, the core normative dimension of populism, thus became more utopian than ever. Society's values and attitudes also appeared to have shifted in the direction of a revalorization of the procedures and institutions of liberal democracy—that is, a normative context supportive of full political rights but also of individual rights and constitutional guarantees. As a result, in a society victimized by gross human rights violations, the illiberal "social contract" of populism—full political rights and expansive social rights, but often at the expense of civil rights—lost meaning and traction.

With a historical identity forged as "the party of civil liberties" and a candidate who was a founding member of human rights organizations, the Unión Cívica Radical (Radical Civic Union) and Raúl Alfonsín entered office in December 1983. Argentina rediscovered democracy—liberal democracy, that is—and Alfonsín changed the vocabulary of politics. In this, he was a revolutionary. The problem was that, after defeating Peronism, he soon gave in to the hegemonic temptation and tried to create a "third historic movement"; namely, his strategy was to absorb the labor movement (largely Peronist) into a new permanent electoral majority.[27] An extensive de-Peronization of the working class, however, depended on prolonging the initial success of the Austral Plan, the stabilization program launched in mid-1985, but also on the availability of resources to distribute material rewards and divide the labor leadership. Given these coalition-building priorities, the Radical Civic Union government sought to retain discretionary control over key macroeconomic variables, thus avoiding the structural reforms deemed necessary to make disinflation durable.

Conflicting objectives also characterized the approach vis-à-vis business. On the one hand, the government emphasized the need to increase the economy's overall competitiveness (via deregulation, export promotion, etc.) in order to put a definitive end to inflation. On the other hand, the capacity of the leading financial and industrial firms to set key prices compelled the authorities to involve the captains of industry more formally in the policymaking process.[28] This political alliance translated into more orthodox macroeconomic management (e.g., money supply reductions, spending cuts, interest rate increases) but was combined with a microeconomic approach that maintained a rather closed trade regime and selective subsidies for firms in the manufacturing sector. The micro soon affected the macro. By 1987–88, outlays for public contracts and the regime of industrial promotion represented 2 percent of GDP and more than half of the nonfinancial fiscal deficit.[29] With a fiscal position already compromised by debt service payments and the collapse of commodity prices, inflation resumed in earnest.

27. See Luis Aznar et al., *Alfonsín: Discursos sobre el Discurso* (Buenos Aires: EUDEBA/FUCADE, 1986).

28. See Ostiguy, *Los Capitanes de la Industria*, 328–38; and William Smith, "Democracy, Distributional Conflict, and Macroeconomic Policymaking in Argentina, 1983–89," *Journal of Interamerican Studies and World Affairs* 32, no. 2 (Summer 1990): 1–42.

29. World Bank, "Argentina: Public Finance Review, from Insolvency to Growth," Report 10827-Ar, February 11, 1993.

During this period, especially from 1980 and throughout the democratic transition, the exhaustion of ISI and the subsequent weakening of its material basis of support were paralleled by the erosion of the movement as the main organizational form of Peronist identity. The movement, which had been organized in a corporatist fashion by sectors, though dominated by labor, was not the best tool for electoral competition, and it was also prone to authoritarian tendencies, particularly in the way candidates were selected. The 1983 and 1985 defeats were humiliating, but they buttressed the approach of those who fostered the idea of a proper political party with democratic mechanisms of participation. The ensuing internal debate and conflict led to the creation of the Renovación Peronista, an attempt to democratize Peronism and make it a viable option again.[30]

Consequently, led by the *"renovadores"* in the main districts, the Peronists—now, more properly, the Partido Justicialista (Justicialista Party)—won by a landslide in the September 1987 congressional and gubernatorial elections. This outcome further impaired the Alfonsín administration's capacity for economic management. The government thus made a last attempt to recover stability in August 1988 through yet another package, the Plan Primavera (Spring Plan).[31] This program was based on a series of price agreements with the peak associations of industry and commerce, on tighter monetary and fiscal policies, and on the adoption of a fixed exchange rate. Yet Argentina's political and macroeconomic context at the time was overly precarious, preventing the government from enforcing compliance across society. In fact, agricultural interests exhibited zero tolerance for exchange rate appreciation and labor rejected wage restraint.

By the end of 1988, the credibility deficit of the Plan Primavera was widespread. As long as the government was determined to maintain the nominal anchor and the capital account remained open, the Central Bank was forced to intervene in currency markets, eroding its reserves. This process accelerated as of January 1989, when the realization that the macroeconomic imbalances were unsustainable led to runs against the currency, flight from money, and other forms of financial adaptation.

30. For these debates over the years, see the magazine *Unidos* from May 1983 to August 1991.

31. For an article by the Central Bank president during most of this period, José Luis Machinea, see "Stabilization under Alfonsín's Government: A Frustrated Attempt," *Documento CEDES* 42 (1990).

In early February, the situation deteriorated dramatically. The Central Bank authorities suspended foreign exchange auctions, unexpectedly ending their commitment to exchange rate stability. The largest corporations reacted to this unforeseen decision with a concerted run to the dollar that virtually collapsed the price system in domestic currency. At that point, the attack on the currency had become a political gesture, to the extent that the financial media described it as a "market coup."[32]

The Peronist Comeback and the Making of a New Alliance

The alleged market coup in February 1989 signaled a new chapter in Argentina's historical political economy. This coup, which was delivered against the Alfonsín government, was also a warning to the Peronist candidate, Carlos Menem, the front-runner in the May 1989 election. Menem acknowledged the message. The populist rhetoric of his campaign—"productive revolution" and massive wage increases (*salariazo*)—was abandoned as soon as he was elected, and he embraced an agenda defined as "popular liberalism." Menem's sudden conversion, it was said, was a hyperrealist and hyperpragmatic response to hyperinflation. He reportedly had no option but to strike a deal with the captains of industry. In fact, when he was inaugurated in July, the Central Bank's reserves equaled $500 million and the monthly inflation rate was 190 percent. The new government needed to prioritize the reconstruction of the fiscal base. The distribution of rents through subsidies and public contracts could not continue, but at the time no government could afford the opposition of the large economic conglomerates, whose corporate culture had been forged more in the political arena than in the marketplace.

Accordingly, Menem delivered an unambiguous political signal by filling the key economic policymaking positions with top executives of Bunge y Born (Argentina's oldest conglomerate and a staunch adversary of Peronism) and leaders of the Ucede political party (the earliest and most articulate advocate of economic liberalization). With this support, Menem pursued the centralization of authority in his office, a task he deemed essential for overcoming the economic crisis and launching a

32. *Ambito Financiero*, December 15, 1989, 1–2.

reform program. On the president's initiative, in August Congress approved the State Reform Law, which made virtually all public companies eligible for privatization, and the Economic Emergency Law a month later, which gave extraordinary powers to the executive to expedite the divestiture process. This legal framework set the stage for the elimination of industrial subsidies, the reduction of import restrictions (with some significant sectoral exceptions), cuts in public expenditures and employment, and increases in tax collection.

The announcement of the privatization of politically sensitive state-owned enterprises—such as the telephone and airline companies, television channels and radio stations, and some railroads—signaled the initiation of Menem's privatization experiment. This way, the government reinforced its free market commitment in order to convince business elites that the Peronist ideological conversion was neither temporary nor instrumental. Aside from a handful of cases, and beyond explicit political effects, the pace of the divestiture process was slow, largely due to persistent inflation, which even produced two more hyperinflationary episodes, in August 1990 and February 1991.

The appointment of Domingo Cavallo as minister of the economy in March 1991 signaled a qualitative change in the overall program of reform, and gave a decisive impetus to the privatization process. Cavallo's first task was to launch a new anti-inflation strategy, the Convertibility Program, which was discussed and approved in Congress. This program, which was in effect for more than a decade, pegged the peso one-to-one to the dollar, determined the full convertibility of domestic currency, and transformed the monetary and exchange rate functions of the Central Bank into a quasi–Currency Board, whereby the monetary base had to equal liquid international reserves. The program had immediate positive effects, bringing inflation down to one digit in just three months.

Price and exchange rate stability, and what appeared as a commitment to rules rather than discretion, were considered necessary conditions for full-fledged privatization, especially given the increase in private-sector demand for credit to finance the purchases of state-owned firms. After 1991, divestiture operations involved the state's power, gas, water and sewerage, steel, and petroleum firms, among others; and by 1994, the privatization program extended to the social security area, following a Chilean-style reform program in combination with a public pillar. Because, in general, the divestiture process entailed a payment method that included foreign debt paper, purchasing consortia often included a creditor bank, an international firm operating in the area to be privatized, and a large domestic firm belonging to one of the main economic groups. The case of the telephone system is illustrative: The public monopoly was privatized as a duopoly, which included Citibank, Telefónica de España, and the local Techint group as one half, and Morgan Bank, France Telecom, and the Pérez Companc group as the other.[33]

Because the government maximized speed and fiscal proceeds, companies were generally tendered undivided and with monopoly rights, and with less-than-optimal regulation in place.[34] As a consequence, contractors and suppliers specializing in certain areas took advantage of their information, experience, and effective access to these organizations, and took over energy, water, petroleum, railroads, and highway firms, for the most part in association with foreign banks and international operators.[35] The result was a pattern of concentration of ownership and of capital markets, along with horizontal diversification whereby domestic firms participated in the ownership of various privatized companies. This context was conducive to rapid gains in the productive efficiency of the privatized firms, the result of rate increases, the preservation of protected markets, and regulatory flaws.[36] This occurred not just in the public utility sector, where monopolies tend to prevail due to economies of

---

33. See Claudia Herrera, "The Privatization of the Argentine Telephone System," *CEPAL Review* 47 (August 1992): 149–61.

34. This was especially the case in the telephone industry. On the multiple problems of regulation, see Andrea López et al., "Nuevas relaciones entre el Estado y los usuarios de servicios públicos en la post-privatización," INAP, Dirección Nacional de Estudios y Documentación, 1997; Alice Hill and Manuel Abdala, "Argentina: The Sequencing of Privatization and Regulation," in *Regulations, Institutions and Commitment: Comparative Studies in Telecommunications*, edited by Brian Levy and Pablo Spiller (Cambridge: Cambridge University Press, 1996); and Ben Alfa Petrazzini, "Telephone Privatization in a Hurry: Argentina," in *Privatizing Monopolies*, edited by Ravi Ramamurti (Baltimore: Johns Hopkins University Press, 1996).

35. For a detailed account on the active participation of future beneficiaries in various stages of the legal design of the divestiture process, see Ana Margheritis, "Implementing Structural Adjustment in Argentina: The Politics of Privatization," Ph.D. diss., University of Toronto, 1997.

36. See Pablo Gerchunoff and Guillermo Cánovas, "Privatización en un Contexto de Emergencia Económica," *Desarrollo Económico* 34, no. 136 (January–March 1995): 483–512; and Pablo Gerchunoff and Guillermo Cánovas, "Privatization: The Argentine Experience," in *Bigger Economies, Smaller Governments*, edited by William Glade (Boulder, Colo: Westview Press, 1996), 191–218.

scale and high barriers of entry, but also in tradables and areas subject to competition, such as oil refineries, air transportation, and international telecommunications.

For the Menem government, reversing the traditional economic policy tenets of Peronism and building unprecedented ties with economic elites entailed refashioning power relations between the Peronist Partido Justicialista and organized labor—the so-called backbone of the Peronist movement, its traditional, though increasingly alienated and fragmented, societal basis of support. To this end, the government adopted two distinctive approaches. One was the classic divide-and-conquer strategy, in order to propel proreform union leaders into positions of power. At the very least, proprivatization leaders generally counted on the explicit support of the presidency in their union careers. In other cases, such leaders were rewarded with greater political payoffs, as in the case of the leader of the telephone union, who was appointed undersecretary of telecommunications, and in the case of the top leaders of the powerful oil union, who were appointed to the board of directors of the privatized oil company.

The second strategy involved the distribution of material payoffs. Similarly to different varieties of employee-share ownership programs implemented in Chile, Britain, and Hungary, among others, the Menem privatization effort adopted the so-called Participatory Property Program. This program consisted of keeping a percentage of the privatized assets in order to distribute stock among workers, but under administration of the union. In contrast to other versions of people's capitalism, in Argentina this program was extremely selective; unions had to secure and mobilize political support in order to have access to the shares. And even more selectivity, in fact, was displayed in the privatization of social security, as friendly unions were allowed to open their privately owned pension funds, as in the cases of commerce, electricity, automobile, and restaurant unions.[37]

Seen in retrospect, therefore, privatization constituted the very political instrument of Menem's reform program. Although it allowed the government to navigate the turbulent waters of internal party politics

---

37. For a detailed account, see María Victoria Murillo, "Union Politics, Market-Oriented Reforms, and the Reshaping of Argentine Corporatism," in *The New Politics of Inequality in Latin America*, edited by Douglas Chalmers et al. (New York: Oxford University Press, 1997).

and reshuffle organized labor's politics, it was also conducive to finally securing a lasting deal with the captains of industry. The Central Bank replenished state coffers, and the contractors made up for lost rents. In fact, the domestic groups involved in the largest privatization operations —Macri, Techint, Bridas, Pérez Companc, Astra, Soldati, and Roggio, among others—were also the main beneficiaries of public contracts and the regime of industrial promotion in the 1970s and 1980s, and also among the largest private debtors that transferred their foreign obligations to the state through the subsidy implemented in 1981–82.[38] In sum, throughout the 1990s the captains of industry consolidated their economic leadership and, by constituting themselves in the dominant distributional coalition, thus reaffirmed a political centrality that no government could afford to ignore. As a result, it is no exaggeration to say that, if the military sought to eradicate populism in the 1970s, it was Menem, a Peronist, who signed its death certificate in the 1990s.

Economic Collapse and Democratic Crisis: Justicialismo to the Rescue

In 1999, Menem transferred power to Fernando de la Rúa of the Radical Party, who had campaigned in favor of the continuation of the Currency Board despite its clear signs of exhaustion as a viable economic strategy. This was not a mistaken reading of Argentine society, however. The country had changed dramatically during the Menem decade. After years of high and at times out-of-control inflation, along with an ongoing "dollarization from below," Argentine voters were demanding stability and at the ballot box were rewarding those politicians capable of delivering it. Moreover, the electorate's preferences between full employment and low inflation began to shift decidedly in favor of the latter, therefore conveying a higher tolerance for recession.

Thus, by 2000 the Currency Board appeared to be in place to stay, just as it began to show the predictable problems of stabilization based on the use of the nominal exchange rate as anchor. Typically, these programs lead to an appreciation of the real exchange rate and a falling real

---

38. These data are from Instituto Nacional de Estadística y Censos, *Anuario Estadístico de la República Argentina* (Buenos Aires: Ministerio de Economía y Obras y Servicios Públicos, 1997), 480–98.

interest rate, initially feeding a consumption boom of imports, a burst of investment, and a gradual deterioration of the current account. Under an open capital account, inflows of capital can finance the trade deficit in the short term. However, this current account deficit, in becoming unsustainable in the medium term, often induces inconsistent fiscal policies, affecting the credibility of the peg. At this point the sustainability of the regime itself comes into question; runs on the currency become widespread, usually with important losses in foreign exchange reserves (as the government tries to defend the parity), and inevitably there is a departure from the fixed exchange rate arrangement with a subsequent devaluation.

Thus, the boom phase of the cycle had begun to dwindle, and the bust was taking shape already by the turn of the decade. Despite the ongoing recession, in the context of the Currency Board, the government could not intervene with stimulative policies, thus weakening its fiscal position even further. Throughout 2001, this dynamic steadily increased Argentina's country risk index, which translated into exorbitant interest rate increases and worse debt repayment problems. By December of that year, determined to continue making debt payments, the government did so by using Central Bank reserves, which flew in the face of the very foundation of the Currency Board, and rolled over obligations with the private pension funds, which constituted a de facto expropriation. The rules that had governed the economy since 1991 were thus broken; but to make things even worse, the government also froze bank deposits to prevent a massive run to the dollar—imposing yet another loss of wealth on millions of citizens.

At that point the economy became ungovernable, but it was a long-simmering political crisis that put the finishing touches to both the Currency Board and the de la Rúa administration. The first symptoms came early, in October 2000, when the vice president resigned. As of that moment, the coalition in power broke down, but the president also turned his back to his own party and began to surround himself with a clique of unelected, nonpartisan advisers. Among them was Domingo Cavallo, once Menem's economic czar and the architect of the Currency Board who, coming back into office, demanded broad autonomy over the conduct of economic policy, just as he had done in the 1990s. His autocratic style reinforced a policymaking process that was already based on executive decrees, further marginalized Congress, and devalued the overall process of representation. By the time unrest broke out in the streets toward the end of 2001 and with a government that had alienated itself from political society and the party system, the ensuing power vacuum forced the president to resign. Menem-style politics—that is, discretionary rule—had backfired.

After the collapse of the de la Rúa government, the authorities devalued the currency and defaulted on the country's foreign debt, plunging Argentina into the worst recession in its history. After a series of interim presidents, a joint session of Congress appointed the Peronist senator Eduardo Duhalde as president to weather the crisis. Accordingly, he defined his priorities in terms of trying to regain stability and address widespread poverty through across-the-aisle collaboration. He pictured himself as a "transition president," whose ultimate goal was to complete de la Rúa's period and transfer power to a popularly elected president.

In a country that had been governed by presidential decrees for more than a decade, Duhalde's objectives were valuable, as they sought to overhaul the institutional procedures of democracy. Yet he faced too many obstacles to fully accomplish these goals, most notably the erosion of the party system. In fact, though the Radical Party was widely discredited after the de la Rúa debacle, Duhalde's own Peronist party, now suddenly again in power, was deeply fragmented along territorial lines, thanks to a structure of regional bosses in control of provincial political systems. As a result, three Peronist candidates competed for the presidency in the April 2003 election, and Duhalde's hand-picked candidate, the left-of-center governor of Santa Cruz Province, Néstor Kirchner, emerged victorious. Democracy, however bruised, had survived.

A "Left Turn": They Look Populist, They Sound Populist, They Must be Populist—but They Are Not

A good degree of continuity marked the transition from the Duhalde to the Kirchner administrations. The incoming president retained several of Duhalde's people in key parliamentary seats and in the Cabinet, most notably Roberto Lavagna, the economy minister. The transition was thus characterized by a good degree of programmatic coherence: to reinvigorate the economy on the basis of a competitive exchange rate, to negotiate rates and fresh investment with the privatized public utility sector, and to restructure the debt in default under conditions that did not affect long-term growth and poverty alleviation. This was an atypical political scenario. There was not only continuity of names and ideas, but there was also a tacit political pact between a sitting president and a former president who retained significant levels of influence. It seemed more like French cohabitation than anything Argentina had ever seen before.

This new arrangement reinforced stability, and Kirchner found more auspicious domestic and international economic conditions. Argentina restructured its foreign debt, obtaining an unprecedented reduction of 70 percent, and improved its fiscal condition. At the same time, prices for its major exports began to rise again. With a competitive exchange rate, it acquired a large trade surplus that fostered rapid growth and mounting foreign exchange since 2003. Yet this was exactly when the politics began to change, and not necessarily for the better. Riding on the boom, Kirchner sought to cut ties with Duhalde, and the opportunity to do so was the October 2005 midterm election. After emerging victorious from this contest, Kirchner sacked all the independent-minded members of his Cabinet (including Roberto Lavagna, who had been responsible for the economic recovery), exploited his weakened opposition by co-opting leaders from other parties, played on regional and factional divisions, and blatantly employed the government's fiscal resources to grease the wheels of Peronist party politics. Moreover, he permanently flirted with unconstitutionality by continuously extracting from Congress extraordinary powers to make unilateral decisions regarding such critical matters as foreign debt negotiations and the budgetary process.

After the 2005 election, it was clear that a Kirchner was going to run for the presidency in 2007—it just remained to be seen whether this was going to be Néstor or his wife, Senator Cristina Kirchner. Until this decision was made, the Kirchners' task was to build up their own electoral instrument, the Front for Victory. To this end, the Kirchners sought, first, to take over the structure of the Peronist party in the Buenos Aires province, so as to decompose the once-powerful Duhalde machine. Second, they sought to further divide the Peronist party, so that now weaker, smaller factions would be subordinated to the presidency. Third, they worked to co-opt the opposition parties, so they could gain support in districts with little or no organization of their own. With the president's strategy fully deployed, the nomination of the candidate would take place in due time, once the public opinion polls revealed which of the two Kirchners was more likable. Not that this was the first case of nepotism in Argentina's political practices, but never had it been so easy to carry it out at such a high level.

As it turned out, Cristina Kirchner got the nomination and won the election in October 2007 with 45 percent of the vote. Argentina regained stability, and its economy recovered from the deep crisis of 2001. Yet, paradoxically, the issues that were at stake in 2002 have not been fully and satisfactorily addressed. The recovery, in fact, has not been based on a program designed to attract investment and, thus, it is not an upturn that could sustain growth over time. On the contrary, the strong economic performance since 2002 has been driven by a deliberately high exchange rate and favorable international prices.[39] As such, this recovery began to show signs of exhaustion even before the international financial crisis of 2008. Once both variables began to change, as evinced by the real estate bubble and a gradual shrinking of the trade surplus, the less-than-spectacular performance began to affect the fiscal base. On this issue, the Kirchners only exacerbated the perennial weakness of Argentina's development—the secular inability, in an open and in a closed economy alike, to design economic policies that moderate, rather than magnify, the effects of the economic cycle.

The political system, in turn, seems to have encountered even more difficulties in recovering from the critical days of 2001–2. In a political setting marked by fragile institutions, fragmented political parties, and a development strategy unable to smooth out the effects of the economic cycle, the Kirchners found incentives to continue ruling by decree and, whenever possible, to reduce Congress to a mere appendix of the executive branch. As in the area of foreign policy, always loud and provocative, the government's approach was also confrontational at home—its rhetoric was and is generally bellicose and nationalistic, and its preferred political space is the street. In this sense, the Kirchners look populist and certainly sound populist. Yet in the absence of a strategy of industrialization, without any solid redistributive program to reduce poverty, and unable to organize and institutionalize a multiclass coalition of support, these traits can be explained by the legacies of populism that the Kirchners want to embody, but they are not enough for such a characterization.

39. Neal Richardson, "Export-Oriented Populism: Commodities and Coalitions in Argentina," *Studies in Comparative International Development* 44 (2009): 228–55.

Widowhood, Reelection, and Radicalization

On October 27, 2010, Cristina Kirchner's vote intention polls were at 19 percent. Her husband was performing slightly better, at 26 percent, yet he confronted a complex scenario inside the Peronist party. It was no secret at the time that several labor leaders and party bosses, those who control the buses for the rallies and the territory on election day, had expressed their rejection of Néstor's candidacy for 2011. After eight years in office, with those meager numbers and a complicated internal political juncture, the future of Kirchnerismo seemed in doubt, if not completely over.

On that day, however, everything changed. Tragedy hit the Kirchner family when the former president suffered a heart attack that morning and died in a hospital in the southern province of Santa Cruz, the district where their political careers had started. As of that moment the tears and the mourning attire gave back to the president a center stage she had lost. Constant references to "him," avoiding his name, attempted to construct her deceased husband as a deity—"Él," and his sacrifices, his legacy, and his light on our road became recurrent formulations. Cristina's grief combined with Néstor's political canonization seemed to give the Kirchner government the narrative it had never found, the utopia it had lacked—in sum, the liturgy with which they tried to build a long-lasting political movement.

Cristina Kirchner thus was reelected in October 2011 with 54 percent of the vote. Her campaign highlighted the prosperity of previous years, her redistributive social policy, and the human rights agenda that both Kirchners had kept alive, but she also benefited from a fragmented opposition. Once in office, however, she would drastically turn to the left. She would open the doors of her government to the youth activists of La Cámpora, the organization led by her son Máximo, would adopt a more belligerent discourse, and would depart even further from the classical tenets of Peronism, most notably by vindicating the leftist youth and the violent organizations of the 1970s.

The radicalization of her government certainly peaked in April 2012 with the expropriation of YPF-Repsol, the historically state-owned oil company that had been privatized in the 1990s. This nationalization, however, seemed more Chávez-like than anything else. For one, it was technically a confiscation, as compensation has not been paid and, by October 2012, there was no offer by the government. Still unable to return to credit markets, the nationalization has been basically a kitty, just as the takeover of the pension funds and the central bank reserves before. In 2012, growth slowed sharply and inflation rose. Discontent took to the streets in several cities, through several rounds of *cacerolazos* (pots and pans), the preferred form of protest. Nationalization of YPF is meant to cope with the energy sector's effect on the trade balance, in addition to restricting imports of a large number of products and imposing controls on currency markets.

As her approval rating of 70 percent in December 2011 halved by September 2012, the president faces increasing levels of uncertainty.[40] A constitutional reform to seek a third term that, not long ago, seemed secured began to disappear from the official discourse. Her political capital of 54 percent of only a year ago appears depleted in light of corruption, insecurity, and inflation. Populist or not, the Kirchners' politics is better characterized by patronage and concentrated executive authority in a setting marked by political fragmentation.[41] It is a form of politics depleted of institutionalized mediations (of which populism has had several) and, as such, it can only be a mere reflection of the economic cycle. When the economy grows, whoever is in power stays longer—Menem and the Kirchners—and when the economy slows down and becomes ungovernable, whoever is in power must leave early—Alfonsín, de la Rúa, and to some extent Duhalde himself. This is Argentina's Achilles' heel. In fat years and with favorable public opinion polls, this system can be sustainable. But if history since the return of democracy in 1983 is any guide, in lean years and with societal dissatisfaction, this system only contributes to more instability.

The Kirchners' decade is approaching this point of the cycle. To a great extent, their approach is a reflection of "Menem's mirror"—what is right appears left and vice versa, but otherwise the picture is identical. Whether democratic procedures are circumvented, twisted, and violated "to quickly achieve market efficiency and enter the first world," as in Menem's narrative, or in pursuit of "independence from the United States and the International Monetary Fund," as the Kirchners put it, makes

40. "Cae la confianza en el Gobierno," *La Nación*, September 30, 2012, http://www.lanacion.com.ar/1513035-cae-la-confianza-en-el-gobierno.

41. A comprehensive account of the transformation of Peronism from a labor-based to essentially patron-client party is given by Steven Levitsky, *Transforming Labor-Based Parties in Latin America: Argentine Peronism in Comparative Perspective* (New York: Cambridge University Press, 2003).

little difference. In terms of the quality of the democratic process and the prospects for democratic stability, Argentina remains under the long shadow of the 1990s.

The Populist Conundrum and the Future
of Democracy in Latin America

In Argentina and elsewhere in Latin America, populism as a political actor is history—and thus we should perhaps only use the concept for historical analysis. Once classic ISI ceased to be a feasible strategy—a result of increasing market integration and financial openness since the mid-1970s—the economic incentives of the multiclass, urban coalitions that had sustained populism disappeared. Without material bases of support, populism's structural foundations vanished. Such strains of "populism" as have come to power since the transitions of the 1980s have been crude imitations of the original, capable of re-creating its rhetoric and rituals but unable to reproduce its substance. The words "new" and "neo," or any other adjective one may choose to add to the concept to capture this observable difference, do not help analytically either, for naming is important. The African elephant's DNA is 98.5 percent identical to the woolly mammoth's, yet it is a separate species, not a neomammoth.

As students of Latin American politics, we still need to come to terms with "postpopulism," which is not any more unrelated to populism than "postcommunism" is to communism in Central and Eastern Europe. That is to say, though the species is extinct, its legacies are not. The essential progressive concerns of populism are as alive as ever. Decades after the end of military rule, long-standing goals such as a welfare state, social justice and political inclusion, substantive equality and dignity for working people, and rights for disadvantaged groups remain unfulfilled and continue to spark mobilization. Political vehicles from the past, however, are no longer viable in their original form. The issues remain the same, but new strategies are needed to address and resolve them.

Populist politicians, however, have been unable, or unwilling, to turn their mass movements into viable political parties. For the most part, these leaders have had difficulty finding a narrative that can consistently contribute to democratic stability. As such, several of them, like the Kirchners, are stuck in a postpopulist framework, where the specter of old-fashioned populism keeps coming back, perhaps as a witness to how incomplete the political incorporation of Latin America's poor remains, and as a painful reminder that the region is still the world's most unequal. The populist conundrum confronts Latin America with the familiar yet complex challenge of how to promote substantive democratization while reinforcing the procedures that make up democracy itself. The need to accomplish both tasks continues to present thorny issues in a region where the very word "institution" has long been taken to mean little more than a bag of tricks that ruling elites use to preserve their privileges and to deceive, exclude, and impoverish the people. Frequently, leaders who have come to power in pursuit of socially just ends have not felt compelled to do so following established rules and procedures. In a sad irony, these leaders have ended up weakening the very rights and institutions that the poor and destitute so desperately needed, especially when the economy has slowed down. As a result, the inequalities that they were supposed to correct worsened.

Righteousness does not make a good recipe for a democratic society either. If the right-wing Carlos Menem deserves criticism for packing his country's highest court, so too does the left-wing Hugo Chávez, regardless of their quite dissimilar goals. In a democracy, means are substantive and not merely formal, because rules are the only thing upon which contenders can always agree. Procedures are thus the glue that holds the polity together. This is the ultimate challenge for progressive thinking and practice in Latin America today: to reconcile the substantive goals of inclusion and equality with the goals—the equally substantive goals, I emphasize—of robust procedures and institutions.

Chapter 7

Populism, Neopopulism, and the Left in Brazil: From Getúlio to Lula

Leslie Bethell

In Latin America, in the study of both political history and contemporary politics, populism has been and continues to be an elusive concept that is notoriously difficult to define and is highly contested. It is perhaps best and most simply understood as a political phenomenon encompassing those movements and parties—and, above all, their charismatic leaders—that reach power (usually, though not always, through elections), exercise power, and retain power through some kind of direct or quasi-direct, unmediated relationship and identification (through personal history, personality, appearance, and, above all, language, rhetoric, and discourse) with previously unorganized and excluded sections of the population that are mobilized for the first time—*from above.*

Ideologically, populism has always been eclectic, vague, confused—and not to be taken too seriously. Populist discourse or rhetoric is built, simplistically, around a fundamental antagonism between the "people," loosely defined, and the established structures of power in the hands of an "elite" or "oligarchy," equally loosely defined, and more often than not around nationalist hostility to "imperialist" domination—by Great Britain, especially in the case of Argentina, and, more frequently, the United States.

Elected or otherwise, populist leaders have been invariably authoritarian and at best ambivalent toward such liberal democratic institutions as existed. At the same time, they fostered political inclusion, though not empowerment, and they delivered some measure of social justice through a mostly limited distribution of wealth and welfare provision to their social base, even if this invariably proved irresponsible from a strictly macroeconomic point of view. (Dornbusch and Edwards in 1991 famously defined economic populism as "the short-term pursuit of growth and income distribution at the cost of inflation and large fiscal deficits.")

For the so-called classical populists, or first-generation populists— who were active from the 1930s to the 1960s, a period that witnessed rapid economic and social change and the beginnings of mass politics in Latin America—it was the new and newly enfranchised urban working class and public-sector, white-collar urban lower middle class that were available for political mobilization. (The mass of the rural poor was largely ignored because they had no vote—often a consequence of illiteracy—or their votes were delivered to local landowners and political bosses.)

For some historians, the populist leaders and regimes of Latin America in this period were sufficiently reformist and nationalist to be considered part of the left, broadly defined. The socialist and communist parties were for the most part failures. Only Chile and Argentina (before World War II) had significant socialist parties that achieved a measure of electoral success. The communist parties, except for one brief period between the end of World War II and the beginning of the Cold War, were small, isolated, illegal—and heavily repressed; they had little success in either promoting revolution (though the Cuban Communist Party was able to capture the Revolution of 1959) or attracting electoral support. Thus, it is to a large extent true that the political space occupied in Europe by parties of the Communist and socialist/social-democratic left—and in the United States by New Deal Democrats—was occupied in Latin America by populists. Populist politicians and regimes, however, were generally in favor of maintaining the status quo, at best modestly reformist, rather than committed to social, much less socialist, transformation. They were mostly hostile to the left, and the left—the noncommunist left at least (Latin American communist parties were often ambivalent toward populism)—was hostile to them. They had more in common, it could be argued, with the European leaders and regimes of the fascist right.

In the historical literature on "classical" populism in Latin America, Getúlio Vargas, who was president of Brazil during the years 1930–45 and 1951–54, is always given a prominent place (usually, and unhelpfully, alongside Lázaro Cárdenas in Mexico and Juan Perón in Argentina). But was Vargas a populist? And, if so, when? And were there not other Brazilian politicians, at both the national and the subnational levels, who are equally or even more deserving of the epithet "populist"?

The so-called neopopulists emerged starting in the late 1980s, after many political scientists and sociologists had announced the end of populism in Latin America. Taking advantage of the persistence of extreme poverty and inequality—indeed, their worsening during the 1980s and 1990s—and the "third wave" of democratization, they were able to mobilize the previously politically unorganized and excluded low-income and ill-educated marginal sectors of the population. These sectors were made up of both the new urban poor, resulting from unprecedented rural-urban migration since the 1950s, and the rural poor, including in many countries the indigenous populations, which in most cases had been only recently enfranchised, thus significantly extending the social base of "classical" populism. Bypassing the established political parties, which had proved ineffective in articulating or responding to the economic and social demands of the poor, they created new social and political movements and successfully contested democratic elections.

In power, the neopopulists, like the classical populists, for the most part have been authoritarian and impatient with existing democratic institutions, the judiciary, the media, and so on—all of which they regard as fundamentally hostile to the interests of the "people." At the same time, they have in some cases fostered radical experiments in direct, participatory forms of democracy—but at the cost, it could be argued, of weakening or even destroying representative democracy. The "neopopulists of the right," or neoliberal populists—for example, Carlos Menem in Argentina, Alberto Fujimori in Peru, and Fernando Collor de Mello, president of Brazil from 1990 to 1992—implemented "neoliberal" agendas that did little to improve the condition of the people who had elected them. The "neopopulists of the left," however, adopted radical antipoverty programs and distributive social policies. Although for the most part, like the "classical" populists, these leftist neopopulists were generally opposed to and opposed by the traditional parties of the left, which were even weaker now than in the middle decades of the twentieth century, some, like Hugo Chávez in Venezuela and Evo Morales in Bolivia, have described themselves as "twenty-first-century socialists." The extent to which Luiz Inácio Lula da Silva, president of Brazil from 2003 to 2010, can be regarded as a neopopulist of the left is the final question to be addressed in this chapter.

The Years 1930–64

Getúlio Vargas first came to power in Brazil in 1930.[1] He was a landowner, lawyer, and governor of Rio Grande do Sul at the age of forty-eight. In the March presidential elections, in which only 10 percent of the adult population voted, he was the defeated candidate of the opposition. An armed rebellion six months later, led by dissident members of the political oligarchy and disaffected junior army officers, triggered a *golpe* (military coup) by senior army generals and the transfer of power to Vargas in November. Although there was a certain amount of popular discontent at the time, particularly as the first effects of the Great Depression began to be felt, and there was some enthusiasm for regime change in the Federal District (Rio de Janeiro) at least, popular forces played only a minor role in the "Revolution" of 1930. What Louis Couty, a French resident of Rio de Janeiro, had famously written almost fifty years earlier remained essentially true: "*O Brasil não tem povo*" (Brazil has no people)—that is to say, it has no popular forces that could be effectively mobilized for significant political, economic, and social change. At this stage in his career, Vargas saw little potential in popular political mobilization. *O povo* (the people) were political spectators, not political actors.

Vargas was head of a provisional government until July 1934. Under a new Constitution, he was then elected president by Congress for a fixed four-year term—although from November 1935 he governed under a state of siege. During this period, he first advanced and then destroyed

---

1. This section draws on my chapters in *The Cambridge History of Latin America*. See Leslie Bethell, "Politics in Brazil under Vargas, 1930–1945," and Leslie Bethell, "Politics in Brazil under the Liberal Republic, 1945–1964," in *The Cambridge History of Latin America, Volume IX: Brazil since 1930*, edited by Leslie Bethell (Cambridge: Cambridge University Press, 2008), 3–86, 87–164.

the political careers of the first two politicians in Brazil who might be called "populist."

The first was Pedro Ernesto Baptista, a distinguished medical doctor and political protégé of Vargas, who became *prefeito* (mayor) of the Federal District by indirect election in April 1935. He immediately began to appeal directly to the urban poor with populist rhetoric and a program of poverty alleviation, health care, education reform, and state ownership of basic utilities. Sympathetic to the communist-supported Aliança Nacional Libertadora, he became a victim of the repression that followed an attempted communist putsch in November 1935. In April 1936, he was removed from office and sentenced to three years in jail. He was released in September 1937, but was then in poor health. He died of cancer at the age of fifty-eight in August 1942. Huge crowds filled the streets for his funeral.[2]

The second populist politician was José Américo de Almeida, a well-known writer—the author of the classic 1928 social novel of the Northeast, *A bagaçeira*, and one of the leaders of the "Revolution" of 1930. In 1937, he became the "official candidate" in the presidential elections scheduled for January 1938. During the election campaign, he attacked the opposition candidate, Armando Sales, as a conservative elitist who was the representative of the *paulista* (São Paulo) plutocracy and foreign capital. José Américo presented himself as the candidate of the poor and forgotten, denouncing the conditions under which most Brazilians lived and promising to break up the large landed estates, extend social welfare provision, and redistribute wealth. Like Pedro Ernesto, José Américo was eventually accused of having communist sympathies, and he had already been forced to withdraw his candidacy when the elections were in any case aborted by the *golpe* of November 1937, which established Vargas as dictator under the Estado Novo (1937–45).[3]

An important feature of the Estado Novo was the creation of a new relationship between the state and organized labor—both workers in manufacturing industry and white-collar public employees, heavily concentrated in Rio de Janeiro and São Paulo. (By 1945, a quarter of Brazil's

2. Michael L. Conniff, *Urban Politics in Brazil: The Rise of Populism 1925–1945* (Pittsburgh: University of Pittsburgh Press, 1981) is, above all, a study of the political career of Dr. Pedro Ernesto.

3. There is no scholarly study of José Américo de Almeida. But see Aspásia Camargo et al., *O golpe silencioso: As orígens da república corporativa* (Rio de Janeiro: Rio Fundo Editora, 1989).

urban labor force—half a million workers—was unionized.) Repression was replaced by co-optation. On one hand, unions lacked autonomy and were subordinate to the state; workers were not permitted to engage in political activity, nor to strike. On the other hand, unions were legally recognized, union leaders had some (limited) political influence, and wage increases and social welfare benefits (pensions, medical care, etc.) were extended to increasing numbers of industrial workers, civil servants, and their dependents. As pressure for political "democratization" increased toward the end of World War II, the Estado Novo moved from co-optation to mobilization. *Trabalhismo* was invented by a regime that had begun to recognize the future *political* potential of organized labor. State propaganda increasingly emphasized the economic and social gains made by workers under the Estado Novo and promoted Vargas as "*o pai dos pobres*" (the father of the poor).[4] There was nothing in Vargas's past, or indeed in his personality, to suggest that he could become a charismatic populist political leader, but the ground was being prepared for a dramatic change of direction in 1945.

In the presidential and congressional elections finally scheduled for the end of 1945, all literate men and women over eighteen would have the right to vote; the vote would be obligatory; and though voter registration was generally by individual initiative, complete lists of employees in both the public and the private sectors (including many who were in fact illiterate) could be registered. All this was designed to expand significantly the political participation of the urban lower middle class and working class while maintaining the severe restrictions on the participation of the (mostly illiterate) rural population. The electorate was thus expanded from 10 percent to 35 percent of the adult population. For the first time in Brazilian politics, the urban working-class vote would be decisive in an election.

It is not clear whether Vargas, who had been president continuously since 1930 but had never been directly elected, intended or hoped to offer himself for election in 1945. He controlled the state apparatus. He could count on considerable political support from the non-export-oriented sectors of the rural oligarchy and industrialists, but also, he now believed with justifiable confidence, from the urban lower middle class, especially in the public sector, and organized labor. He founded

4. See the classic work by Angela de Castro Gomes, *A invencão do trabalhismo* (São Paulo: Edições Vértice/IUPERJ, 1988).

the Partido Trabalhista Brasileiro (PTB) and urged Brazilian workers to join it. But whereas the two "conservative" parties established in 1945 nominated candidates for the presidency—the Partido Social Democrático (PSD) nominated an army general, and the União Democrática Nacional (UDN) nominated an air force brigadier—the PTB did not. Vargas, however, encouraged public debate of the idea of a third candidate, a "civilian candidate of the people." João Batista Luzardo, who had reason to know, later argued that "Vargas had only one third candidate in mind: himself."

The six months from May to October 1945 witnessed an unprecedented level of political mobilization in Brazil's major cities. This activity was orchestrated in part by the Communist Party (Partido Comunista Brasileiro, PCB), which had been illegal, apart from a few months, since its foundation in 1922. But more particularly the mobilization was spurred by a new political movement, Queremismo, named for the slogan "Queremos Getúlio" (We want Getúlio). Behind Queremismo were the propaganda machine of the Estado Novo, government ministers, leading officials of the Ministry of Labor and the social welfare institutions, government approved union leaders (the so-called *pelegos*), national and state leaders of the PTB, and some "progressive" businessmen—the "fascist gang," as the British Embassy liked to call them. Mass demonstrations on a scale never seen before in Brazil were organized in Rio de Janeiro during August, September, and October.[5] It is scarcely credible, as is sometimes claimed, that Vargas knew nothing of Queremismo. Did he actually promote or merely tolerate it? Certainly he did nothing to stop it. Was his nomination as presidential candidate—and subsequent electoral victory—the aim? Or were they (was he) preparing the ground for a populist coup?

In the end, Vargas did not become a candidate, whatever the temptation. And to ensure that the elections scheduled for December were not aborted, as in 1937, the military removed him from power in October 1945. In the presidential elections, the late and somewhat reluctant support offered by Vargas was crucial for the victory of his former minister

5. See Leslie Bethell, "Brazil," in *Latin America between the Second World War and the Cold War, 1944–1948*, edited by Leslie Bethell and Ian Roxborough (Cambridge: Cambridge University Press, 1992), 33–65; and John French, "The Populist Gamble of Getúlio Vargas in 1945: Political and Ideological Transitions in Brazil," in *Latin America in the 1940s: War and Post-War Transitions*, edited by David Rock (Berkeley: University of California Press, 1994).

of war, General Eurico Gaspar Dutra, the candidate of the PSD *and* the PTB. (The PCB was for the first time allowed to contest an election, and its presidential candidate secured almost 10 percent of the vote.) In the congressional elections (in which candidates were allowed to run in more than one state), Vargas was elected senator in both Rio Grande do Sul and São Paulo and federal deputy in the Federal District and six other states, accumulating a total of 1.3 million votes. More than one-fifth of the Brazilian electorate voted for him. He chose to serve as senator for his home state, Rio Grande do Sul.

Under the postwar Liberal Republic (1945–64), there were regular elections for president, Congress, state governor and state assembly, and mayor and municipal council. And as a result of the growth of Brazil's population (from 40 million in 1940 to 70 million in 1960), urbanization (35 percent of the population was officially classified as urban in 1940, and 45 percent in 1960), some modest improvement in literacy rates, and higher levels of voter registration, the electorate grew from 7.5 million in 1945 to 18.5 million, more than a half of the adult population, in 1962. And because voting continued to be obligatory, the turnout was high. Given that the PCB——the principal, and virtually the only, party of the left—was once again illegal starting in May 1947, new possibilities were opened up for populist politicians.

In February 1949, in an interview with the journalist Samuel Wainer in *O Jornal*, Vargas was reported as saying, looking ahead to the presidential election of October 1950: "Yes, I will return, but not as a political leader, as leader of the masses." The PTB had electoral strength in Rio de Janeiro and Rio Grande do Sul, but this was not enough to win the presidency. Together with Governor Ademar de Barros, who had, as we shall see, built up a powerful political machine in the State of São Paulo (which accounted for 20 percent of the electorate), Vargas formed a Frente Popular against the PSD and UND and the "elite" and won the election with 48 percent of the vote in a three-way contest, with no less than a quarter of his votes coming from São Paulo. But he had in the end campaigned for the most part above parties, and he owed his victory to his direct, personal appeal to unionized workers and the people in general (at least those who had the vote) based on his record as president/ dictator under the Estado Novo and his project for further economic development and social reform.

The Vargas administration (1951–54) was made up of all party members and essentially was conservative. The decision to create a state-owned company, Petrobras, with a monopoly over oil reserves and their extraction, however, and the nationalist campaign launched under the slogan "*O petroleo é nosso*" (The oil is ours) to guarantee its passage through Congress, generated possibly the greatest level of urban popular mobilization seen thus far in Brazil. And in the second half of his mandate, Vargas attempted to strengthen his links to organized labor with the appointment of João (Jango) Goulart as minister of labor. Goulart, a young (thirty-four-year-old) rancher and politician from Rio Grande do Sul who was personally close to Vargas, had been national president of the PTB since 1952. He had the reputation, largely unwarranted, of being a radical *trabalhista*, an admirer of Perón in Argentina, and in favor of establishing a *república sindicalista* in Brazil.

In February 1954, Vargas implemented a 100 percent increase in the minimum wage, together with improvements in social welfare provision and pensions, and announced that he would extend existing labor legislation to rural workers, ending his speech with this provocative statement: "You [the workers of Brazil] constitute a majority. Today you are with the government. Tomorrow you will be the government." The pressure mounted, however, for his resignation. It was alleged by his enemies that he had dictatorial ambitions. Under the Constitution of 1946, he could not be reelected in 1955, but they recalled the political events of November 1937 and October 1945. To avoid being removed from office by the military a second time, Vargas committed suicide on August 24, and by this act ensured that *getulismo* would remain a powerful force in Brazilian politics long after his death.

Whatever the element of personal tragedy, Vargas's suicide was, and was intended to be, a political bombshell. Vargas left a *carta-testamento*, one of the most famous documents in Brazilian history. He had always been, he said, "a slave of the people." He had returned to power in 1950–51 "*nos braços do povo*" (in the arms of the people) and had sought to defend the people and particularly the very poor against the powerful interests, both domestic and foreign, that were impeding his efforts to govern the country in the national interest and the interests of the people. Now, old and tired, he was "serenely" taking the first step on the road to eternity, "leaving life to enter History."[6] If ever there was a populist document, this was it. His letter, whose transcript was immediately broad-

6. See José Murilo de Carvalho, "As duas mortes de Getúlio Vargas," in *Pontos e bordados* (Belo Horizonte: Editora UFMG, 1998). For a recent biography of Ge-

cast on national radio and published in all the newspapers, had an enormous popular impact. Hundreds of thousands of Brazilians went onto the streets of Rio de Janeiro, Porto Alegre, Belo Horizonte, Recife, and other cities. There were scenes of extreme emotion (and some violence). In Rio huge crowds accompanied Vargas's body to Santos Dumont Airport for transportation to Rio Grande do Sul and burial in São Borja.

At the subnational level, both state and municipal, there are several examples of populist politicians in Brazil during the Liberal Republic. For example, Leonel Brizola was elected mayor of Porto Alegre in 1958, governor of Rio Grande do Sul in 1958, and, with a huge popular vote, federal deputy for Guanabara (the city of Rio de Janeiro) in 1962. Miguel Arrães was elected governor of Pernambuco in 1963. And in São Paulo, Brazil's most populous and economically developed state, were Ademar de Barros and Jânio Quadros.

Ademar de Barros, a coffee *fazendeiro* and industrialist, who had governed São Paulo during the Estado Novo, in July 1946 formed the Partido Social Progressista as a political vehicle for himself in a state where interestingly (and significantly) all three major parties—the PSD, UDN, and PTB—were relatively weak. Projecting a "man of the people" populist image, with a powerful antielite message to a mass lower-class following, and spending on a massive scale, Ademar became São Paulo's first popularly elected governor in January 1947. *Ademarismo* was born.[7] Once in office, he made liberal use of public funds to maintain his popular political base and was not ashamed to use the slogan "*ele rouba, mas faz*" (he steals, but he gets things done). He helped elect Getúlio president in 1950, as we have seen. But in 1954, in a second attempt to become governor, Ademar lost narrowly to another populist, Jânio Quadros. In 1955 he ran for president, coming in third with 26 percent of the vote, but winning in both São Paulo and the Federal District. In 1957, he was elected *prefeito* of São Paulo city and, after failing in a second attempt to become president in 1960, was elected state governor again in 1962. Two years later, however, now with the overwhelming support of the *paulista* middle class, Ademar de Barros provided civilian backing for the 1964 antipopulist *golpe*.

túlio by a leading Brazilian historian, see Boris Fausto, *Getúlio Vargas* (São Paulo: Companhia das Letras, 2006).

7. See John D. French, "Workers and the Rise of Adhemarista Populism in São Paulo, Brazil 1945–47," *Hispanic American Historical Review* 68 (1988): 2–43; and Regina Sampaio, *Adhemar de Barros e o PSP* (São Paulo: Global Editora, 1982).

Jânio Quadros, who was born in the state of Mato Grosso, began a meteoric political career when he was elected to the municipal council of São Paulo at the age of thirty in 1947. In 1950, he became a state deputy, with the most votes of any candidate. In March 1953, he won a famous victory against the candidate backed by all three major parties to become *prefeito* of São Paulo, the first state capital to elect a mayor by direct popular vote—after eight nominated mayors since 1945. Finally, in October 1954, after only eight years in politics and eighteen months as mayor, Quadros was elected governor of the state, again without the formal support of any of the three major parties, narrowly defeating Ademar de Barros, his main rival for the popular vote. In these two elections Quadros, who never had the full support of organized urban labor, successfully mobilized the poor on the peripheries of the city of São Paulo and other major cities in the State of São Paulo. *Janismo* was Brazil's first taste of mass populism based on the support of the urban poor for a charismatic politician with a strong ethical (anticorruption) as well as antielite message.

In the presidential election of October 1960, Jânio Quadros became the candidate of a center-right coalition of five parties led by the conservative UDN, his earlier radical populism having apparently been abandoned. His campaign for president was remarkable, even by his own standards, for its ideological confusion. A contradictory and enigmatic personality, he was supported by many *empresários*, especially those linked to foreign capital, and the urban middle class, but also the 160 *sindicatos* affiliated to the Movimento Renovação Sindical and the "people" more generally, to whom he offered (e.g., in his speech to a crowd of 100,000 in Recife in September) nationalist-populist *reformas de base*, including the extension of social legislation to rural workers. He won the election with 5.6 million votes (48.3 percent of the vote, slightly better than Vargas in 1950), more than half provided by the State of São Paulo.

Jânio Quadros had built a political career, which had taken him from municipal councilman in São Paulo to president of the republic in fourteen years, on the margins of the party system, without an ideology or program or even much of an organization. He had a mandate for change, although apart from cleaning up politics and administration it was not clear what kind of change. He had raised great hopes for the future, but it was not clear what kind of future. As president, he was arrogant and authoritarian. He largely ignored the rules of the political game. He believed he could govern without Congress because "the people are with me." He did not negotiate with, nor try to co-opt, his opponents. Even his allies were uncomfortable with his more "populist" or "progressive" policies, which included antitrust legislation, controls on the remittances of profits abroad, agrarian reform, political reform to give illiterates the vote, and an independent, anti-imperialist foreign policy that included restoring diplomatic relations with the Soviet Union, establishing commercial relations with East Germany and the Eastern Bloc, and, above all, securing closer relations with postrevolutionary Cuba.

In August 1961, after only seven months in power, Jânio astonished the country by resigning, apparently believing that he would return, like Getúlio in January 1951 or De Gaulle in France in December 1958, "*nos braços do povo.*" The military and Congress moved quickly to appoint an interim successor. And no popular support materialized. The *povo* were apparently in shock, perplexed, and, to Jânio's disappointment, "very passive." "The people, where are the people?" he is said to have exclaimed forlornly when he arrived from Brasília at Cumbica Airport in São Paulo, prepared for exile.[8]

Whether João Goulart should be regarded as a populist politician is debatable.[9] He was a former minister of labor, president of the PTB, and Vargas's chosen heir. He was twice elected vice president during the Liberal Republic (when presidents and vice presidents were elected separately), in 1955 with Juscelino Kubitschek, and in 1960 with Jânio

8. For an excellent recent account of Quadros's political career, though more journalistic than academic, see Ricardo Arnt, *Jânio Quadros: O prometeu de Vila Maria* (Rio de Janeiro: Ediouro Publicações, 2004); and Vera Chaia, *A liderança política de Jânio Quadros (1947–1990)* (São Paulo: Editora Humanidades, 1991).

9. Guita Grin Debert, *Ideologia e populism* (São Paulo: T. A. Queiroz Editora, 1979), is a study of four Brazilian "populists": Ademar de Barros, Miguel Arrães, Leonel Brizola, and Carlos Lacerda. Michael L. Conniff, "Brazil's Populist Republic and Beyond," in *Populism in Latin America*, edited by Michael L. Conniff (Tuscaloosa: University of Alabama Press, 1999), examines the politics of eight populists: Getúlio Vargas, Pedro Ernesto, Ademar de Barros, Jânio Quadros, Juscelino Kubitschek, Brizola, Arrães, and Fernando Collor de Mello. João Goulart appears in neither list. Carlos Lacerda, the governor of Guanabara from 1960 to 1965, might be described as a right-wing populist, and Collor de Mello, president 1990–92, a neo-populist of the right. But if Juscelino Kubitschek, the president of Brazil from 1956 to 1961, is treated as a populist, we are in danger of further devaluing an already slippery concept. A recent biography of Goulart based on extensive research is by Jorge Ferreira, *João Goulart: Uma biografia* (Rio de Janeiro: Civilização Brasileira, 2011).

Quadros. And he became president in September 1961 by the accident of *renúncia*. So widespread was the concern on the right, both military and civil, about Goulart's supposed radical *trabalhismo* that before being allowed to take office he was forced to accept a parliamentary system of government under which his powers were severely reduced. After winning a plebiscite in January 1963 to restore the presidential system, Goulart pursued his agenda for what he himself regarded as moderate political and social reform, including the extension of the right to vote to illiterates, the legalization of the Brazilian Communist Party, improvements in the standard of living of urban workers (nonunionized as well as unionized), the extension of labor and social welfare legislation to rural workers, and agrarian reform. Despite being constantly rebuffed by the conservative forces entrenched there—and aware of a civil and military conspiracy, backed by the United States, against him—he persisted for more than a year with a strategy of conciliation and reform via Congress.

In an atmosphere of ideological radicalization, Goulart resisted mounting pressure from the more radical elements within the PTB, from both the PCB and the breakaway, pro-Chinese Partido Comunista do Brasil (both illegal), and from the smaller parties and movements on both the Castroist left and Catholic left, to mobilize urban and rural workers in favor of reform and take the struggle outside Congress, which was seen as full of reactionaries and no longer in tune with the aspirations of the people. His brother-in-law, Leonel Brizola, regarded him as weak and indecisive, with a *"horror de poder"* (horror of power). When in March 1964, disastrously miscalculating the relative strength of political forces in Brazil at the time, Goulart did finally make an opening to the left by proposing to implement his basic reforms by decree and transfer power "to the people," he was accused of attempting to turn Brazil into a communist dictatorship—another Cuba, even another China—and he was removed from power by a military coup whose declared purpose was to eliminate not only communism but also populism (i.e., *getulismo* and *trabalhismo*) from Brazilian politics.[10]

---

10. Octavio Ianni's well-known study of the 1964 *golpe* was titled *O colapso do populism no Brasil* (Rio de Janeiro: Civilização Brasileira, 1968); English translation, *Crisis in Brazil* (New York: Columbia University Press, 1970). An early, influential study of populist politics in the period 1945–64, especially the role of the PTB (and the illegal PCB), as manipulative of the workers, corrupt and authoritarian, was by Francisco Weffort, *O populismo no Brasil* (São Paulo: Paz e Terra, 1978). Daniel Aarão Reis Filho, "O colapso do colapso do populismo ou a propósito de uma her-

All in all, politicians to whom the label "populist" has been attached did not meet with much success in Brazil in the period 1930–64—at the national level at least. Getúlio Vargas, who only adopted a populist strategy after he had already been in power for almost fifteen years, was forced by the military within a few months to leave office in October 1945 and, after his reelection in 1950, was driven to suicide in August 1954. Ademar de Barros lost as many elections as he won in São Paulo and never reached the presidency. His nemesis, Jânio Quadros, was elected president but resigned after only seven months in power in August 1961. Finally, João Goulart survived as president for two and a half years but was overthrown by the military immediately after adopting a populist discourse and strategy in March 1964.

The Years 1985–2010

The beginning of the process of democratization in Brazil in the early 1980s and the transition to civilian rule in 1985, after twenty-one years of military dictatorship, brought the return to state and municipal politics of many of the old "populists"; for example, Leonel Brizola was elected governor of the State of Rio de Janeiro in 1982 (and again in 1990), and Jânio Quadros was elected mayor of São Paulo in 1985.[11] And the first direct presidential election since 1960, the first ever based on universal suffrage (Brazil's illiterates were finally given the vote in 1985), brought to power a politician usually bracketed with Latin America's neopopulists of the right: Fernando Collor de Mello.[12]

ança maldita," in *O populismo e sua história: Debate e crítica*, edited by Jorge Ferreira (Rio de Janeiro: Civilização Brasileira, 2001), provides a critique of both Ianni and Weffort and a defense of the social reformism of the PTB and the PCB and the economic and political benefits delivered to Brazilian workers by "populist" politicians. There is a rich literature on the PTB and populism. See, in particular, Castro Gomes, *A invenção do trabalhismo*; Lucília de Almeida Neves, *PTB: Do getulismo ao reformismo (1945–1964)* (São Paulo: Marco Zero, 1983); Maria Celina D'Araújo, *Sindicatos, carisma e poder: O PTB de 1945–1965* (Rio de Janeiro: Editora FGV, 1996); and Jorge Ferreira, *O imaginário trabalhista: Getulismo, PTB e cultura política popular 1945–1964* (Rio de Janeiro: Civilização Brasileira, 2005).

11. The first part of this section draws on the chapter by Leslie Bethell and Jairo Nicolau, "Politics in Brazil, 1985–2002," in *Cambridge History of Latin America, Volume IX*, ed. Bethell, 231–79.

12. We still await the first scholarly study of the Collor de Mello phenomenon.

Collor de Mello, the grandson of Lindolfo Collor, Vargas's first labor minister, was the thirty-seven-year-old governor of the northeastern state of Alagoas, the second-smallest and second-poorest state in Brazil. A member of a traditional oligarchic family with interests in the media, he was virtually unknown outside Alagoas. And he had no significant political party behind him. The Partido da Reconstrução Nacional (PRN) was created only months before the election. His program was rudimentary to say the least, but at hundreds of rallies throughout Brazil and on television, he made populist speeches denouncing corruption in both public and private life (which is ironic, in view of what was to come) and attacking the "traditional" politicians representing the Brazilian "elite." This was the case even though the political and economic elite, with no credible candidate of its own and fearing a victory for the left—especially its bête noir on the populist-nationalist left, Leonel Brizola—in general supported Collor de Mello.

The Brazilian electorate now numbered 82 million (out of a total population of almost 150 million)—compared with only 15 million in 1960. Voting for those over eighteen and under seventy was mandatory. A total of 72.3 million people voted, of whom 70 percent were voting for a president for the first time. Collor de Mello won the first round of the election with 30.5 percent of the valid vote (20.6 million votes), and he won the second-round runoff—against Luiz Inácio Lula da Silva of the Partido dos Trabalhadores (PT; Workers' Party), Brizola having lost to Lula in the first round by less than half a million votes—with 53 percent (35.1 million votes). It was Collor de Mello, not Lula, who received the strong support of the population with the lowest income and education; that is, 49 percent of voters with a family income of up to one monthly minimum salary, 55 percent of voters with a low level of education, and 49 percent of the inhabitants of small towns (up to 20,000 inhabitants) voted for him.[13]

Collor de Mello's base in Congress, however, was weak. Even after the November 1990 elections, the PRN, together with some allies on the right, had only 30 percent of the seats in the Chamber of Deputies and 40 percent in the Senate. Collor de Mello introduced a series of "neo-

---

But see Mario Sérgio Conti, *Notícias do Planalto: A imprensa e Fernando Collor* (São Paulo: Companhia das Letras, 1999).

13. Scott P. Mainwaring, *Sistemas partidários em novas democracias: O caso do Brasil* (Rio de Janeiro: Editora FGV, 2001), 44.

liberal" economic reforms, but two stabilization plans failed miserably. Menem was elected in Argentina in 1989 and Fujimori was elected in Peru in 1990 and each governed for ten years. Collor lasted only two and a half years. In 1992, he was engulfed in a corruption scandal involving extortion, kickbacks for favors, bribery, electoral fraud, and tax evasion. The popular demonstrations in the big cities demanding his removal from office represented the most significant mass political mobilization in Brazil since the movement for direct presidential elections (*diretas já*) in 1983–84 at the end of the military dictatorship. Collor de Mello was successfully impeached by Congress under the Constitution of 1988 and was removed from office in September 1992.

If Collor de Mello was a "neopopulist of the right," to what extent was (is?) the candidate he defeated in 1989, Luiz Inácio Lula da Silva, a "neopopulist of the left"? Lula, the seventh of the eight surviving children of a poverty-stricken rural family in the interior of Pernambuco in the Northeast, Brazil's poorest region, former metal worker and leader of the metalworkers' union of São Bernardo do Campo in the metropolitan region of São Paulo, with only four years of primary school education, was the leader of the PT. The PT had been founded in February 1980 by Lula and other "authentic" union leaders, together with progressive Catholic activists from the *comunidades eclesiais de base*, former urban and rural guerrillas, left-wing intellectuals, and members of small (illegal at the time) Trotskyist parties—but not the PCB. The PT was an avowedly socialist party, created toward the end of the military dictatorship and, uniquely in Brazilian political history, built *from below*.[14] As the military initiated a process of liberalization and finally withdrew to the barracks, the PT worked within the existing rules and institutions. It elected its first eight federal deputies in 1982, six of them in São Paulo, which provided 72 percent of its national vote. And in 1986, in the first congressional elections after the end of military rule, it elected sixteen deputies, including Lula himself in São Paulo. In 1988, it elected the mayors of São Paulo and several other *municípios* in Greater São Paulo and São Paulo State, Porto Alegre (Rio Grande do Sul), and Vitória (Espírito Santo).

As the candidate of the PT in the presidential election of 1989, Lula had the support of organized labor, sections of the urban middle class,

14. On the formation of the Partido dos Trabalhadores, see Rachel Meneguello, *PT: A formação de um partido, 1979–1982* (São Paulo: Paz e Terra, 1989); and Margaret E. Keck, *The Workers Party and Democratization in Brazil* (New Haven, Conn.: Yale University Press, 1992).

and the progressive wing of the Catholic Church. He polled 17.2 percent of the valid votes, totaling 11.6 million votes (and then 47 percent, 31.1 million votes, in the second-round runoff). He was, however, unable to attract the poorest and least-educated voters, who in the main, as we have seen, voted for Collor de Mello. In the elections of 1994 and 1998 (in 1998 with the support of the smaller parties of socialists and communists and Brizola's Partido Democrático Trabalhista, PDT, successor to the PTB), Lula lost to Fernando Henrique Cardoso of the center/center-left Partido da Social Democracia Brasileira (PSDB), backed by the parties of the center-right/right. Cardoso won a majority among *all* social groups, including the poorest, whether measured by education or income. The PT, with its solid social base in the industrial working class of São Paulo, never really bid for the votes of the very poor and underprivileged, who were heavily concentrated in the North and Northeast. Neither Lula nor the PT could be accused of populism in this period.

In light of Brazil's political history, political culture, and political system (and the defeat of the socialist left almost everywhere in the world in this period), the growth of the PT since 1980 had been a remarkable story. Not only had its candidate for president increased his vote in three successive elections—from 17 percent in 1989 (in the first round) to 27 percent in 1994 and 32 percent in 1998—but the party had increased its number of seats in both the Senate and the Chamber of Deputies in every congressional election. The PT had also won control of the Federal District (in 1994) and of Rio Grande do Sul (in 1998), as well as major cities like São Paulo and Porto Alegre. After the October 2000 municipal elections, the PT governed half the sixty cities with populations of more than 200,000 and six state capitals, including São Paulo for the second time and Porto Alegre for the fourth time.

And finally, in October 2002, at the fourth attempt, Lula won the presidential election. A number of factors explain why he was able to secure the support of voters who traditionally had not voted for him, both sections of the urban middle class and, especially, the poor (most of whom had previously preferred to vote for Collor de Mello and Cardoso)—apart from the weakness and division of the opposition. In the first place, the PT itself had changed. It had moved to the center ground. During the 1990s, the so-called Articulação (later Campo Majoritário) came to have a majority in the party and to adopt more moderate policies. After the expulsion of the Convergência Socialista in 1992, the other groups on the Marxist, Trotskyist, and socialist left wing of the party were increasingly outmaneuvered and, at least in decisionmaking at the top, somewhat marginalized. Lula's Carta ao Povo Brasileiro (June 2002), though emphasizing the need for social policies to reduce poverty and inequality, committed a future PT government to the market economy, macroeconomic stability, the control of inflation, and fiscal equilibrium—that is to say, to a continuation of the economic policies of the Cardoso administration.[15] Second, political alliances were broadened. For the first time, besides the parties of the left, Lula received the support of a party of the center/right, the Partido Liberal. Third, the PT for the first time developed a public relations and media campaign based on the personal history and personality of Lula with a strong emotional appeal: "*Lula, paz, e amor*" (Lula, peace, and love). Even so, it would be difficult to argue that it was overall a "populist" electoral strategy and campaign.

In 2002, Lula polled 39.4 million votes (46.4 percent of the valid votes), but he could not quite achieve what Cardoso had achieved in 1994 and 1998: outright victory in the first round. In the second round, however, he was comfortably elected with 52.8 million votes (61.3 percent of the valid vote). The election and transfer of power to a candidate of the left (although Lula had never been a man of the left, ideologically at least, and the PT had abandoned the label "socialist" before the elections) represented an important landmark in the consolidation of democracy in Brazil.

In the government, Lula maintained the "responsible" economic policies of the previous Cardoso administrations (1995–2002), but he was more committed to poverty reduction and modest redistribution of income through compensatory social policies. At the same time, though encouraging some early experiments with participatory democracy in states and *municípios* controlled by the PT, most famously in Porto Alegre, Lula appeared committed to the further strengthening of Brazil's existing democratic institutions. As a result of the compromises made to win power and the less-than-radical policies pursued in power, the left wing of the PT broke away in 2004 to form the Partido Socialismo e Liberdade (PSOL).

After courting disaster in 2005—as a series of corruption scandals undermined the PT's credibility as an "ethical" party, rocked Lula's gov-

15. See, e.g., David Samuels, "From Socialism to Social Democracy: Party Organization and the Transformation of the Workers' Party in Brazil," *Comparative Political Studies* 37, no. 9 (2004).

ernment, and severely dented his own popularity—Lula rescued himself from political death and went on comfortably to win reelection in October 2006. His social and political base had been dramatically transformed since 2002, however. Research on the 2006 elections clearly shows that Lula was elected overwhelmingly by the poor, mainly in the North and Northeast.[16] In the less-developed 50 percent of Brazil's 5,500 *municípios* (the so-called *grotões*), Lula secured 66 percent of the vote in the first round (and 74 percent in the second round). In the more-developed *municípios* of the South and Southeast, where the middle class, certainly the professional middle class, had turned against him largely because of corruption and his association with some of the worst elements in the old political oligarchy, he actually lost the election (with only 41 percent of the vote).

Lula's success with the poor and uneducated, *o povão*, was not, however, the result of a typically polarizing antielite, antiglobalization, anti-American populist discourse. Personal identification was, of course, an important factor—Lula as "one of us," Brazil's first president, unlike Getúlio Vargas and João Goulart, from a desperately poor background in both the Northeast and São Paulo. But Lula's success can be largely explained as the political dividend from four years of improved economic growth; higher levels of employment in the formal sector; low inflation; regular increases in the minimum wage above the rate of inflation; easier access to credit; and, above all, a significant reduction of poverty resulting from the comprehensive, but modest and relatively cheap, conditional cash transfer program, Bolsa Família. A total of 4.1 million households were already benefiting from Bolsa Família in June 2004; by July 2006, 11.4 million households were benefiting (thus totaling 35 million individual Brazilians, mostly in the Northeast and North).

The first three years of Lula's second administration (2007–9) were notable for a continuation of the moderate, "progressive" social policies pursued during his first administration within a framework of "respon-

16. See Jairo Nicolau and Vitor Peixoto, "As bases municipais da votação de Lula em 2006," 2007, http://www.forumnacional.org.br/forum/pforum6 2a.asp; Cesar Zucco, "The President's 'New' Constituency: Lula and the Pragmatic Vote in Brazil's 2006 Presidential Elections," *Journal of Latin American Studies* 40 (2008): 29–49; and Wendy Hunter and Timothy Power, "Rewarding Lula: Executive Power, Social Policy and the Brazilian Elections of 2006," *Latin American Politics and Society* 49 (2007): 1–30.

sible," orthodox macroeconomic policies and consolidated democratic institutions. Therefore, it remained difficult to describe Lula as a neo-populist of the left—although he was remarkably tolerant toward those politicians and governments in South America for whom this description was more appropriate.

Why, with its high levels of poverty and social inequality, its low levels of education, and therefore the continued existence of second-class and even third-class citizens, has Brazil been generally more resistant to the neopopulism of the left than many other Latin American countries? The country's size and complexity, and in particular its federal system, have been offered by way of explanation. Also, the conservative nature of the Brazilian people, especially the poor, their tolerance of social injustice, their limited demands, and their historical resistance to political mobilization have been mentioned as possible reasons. More immediately relevant is the fact that, despite the need for political reform, especially electoral and party reform, in the interests of more effective governability, greater accountability, and a reduction in the disturbing level of political corruption, Brazil has had since the late 1980s, for the first time in its history, a reasonably well-functioning representative democracy—with regular, free, and fair elections based on universal suffrage; a multi-party system; an independent Congress; an independent judiciary; an independent media; and, not least, a relatively strong and active civil society. Since 1994, Brazil has also had a generally stable economy, and since 2004 (except in 2008–9) improved levels of economic growth.

Furthermore, the dominant political parties of the left/center-left, the PT and the PSDB, which have been the principal contestants in every presidential election since 1994, are well-established social-democratic parties, though the strength of the PT's commitment to democratic practice is questioned by some. The biggest party in Brazil (in number of federal deputies, senators, governors, state deputies, mayors, and local councilors) is the solidly centrist and clientalistic Partido do Movimento Democrático Brasileiro (PMDB). It has not fielded a candidate for the presidency since 1994, but it plays a decisive role in elections—and in government. There are parties of the center-right, like the Partido da Frente Liberal / Democratas, but no strong parties of the right that clearly represent the "elite," the "oligarchy," and therefore provide an easy target for politicians with populist tendencies. And U.S. imperialism is not in Brazil the target for populists that, for historical reasons, it is in many Spanish American republics.

Epilogue

A word of caution is in order before one pronounces populism in Brazil dead. With his popularity at an all-time high (70–75 percent approval), especially among the poorest sections of Brazilian society and the rapidly expanding lower middle class (which now makes up almost 50 percent of the population), his principal political base, and at the same time growing international recognition and admiration ("the most popular politician on Earth," President Obama called him), and with Brazil having survived the financial crisis of 2008–9 better than most countries, in the second half of 2009 there was increasing evidence of Lula's populist inclinations—which, if they had existed in the past, had been successfully constrained or repressed. Former president Fernando Henrique Cardoso articulated the concerns of many Brazilians when in November 2009, in his monthly newspaper column, which is widely syndicated throughout Brazil, he referred to Lula's increasingly undemocratic behavior, lack of respect for the Constitution and the law, and populist authoritarianism, which was in his view heading in the direction of what he called "*subperonismo-lulismo.*"[17]

Social scientists had already begun to identify this new political phenomenon: *lulismo*. Lula was regarded by many as having come to terms with the political and social realities of Brazil and with the constraints imposed by international financial capitalism in his second administration and as thus having abandoned what was left of the original PT project—the radical social transformation of Brazil with the support of the popular social movements and the antipopulist, socialist left—in favor of an essentially conservative modernization of Brazilian society directed by the state (now in the hands of the PT and its allies), for which he was able to mobilize not only the mass of the poor and poorly educated but also the remnants of the traditional political oligarchy and Brazil's new economic elite based on finance, agribusiness, construction, oil and gas, and so on. The economist Delfim Netto, minister of finance and minister of planning during the military dictatorship, argued in an interview in September 2009, not entirely mischievously, that Lula had saved capitalism in Brazil.[18]

17. Fernando Henrique Cardoso, "Para onde vamos?" *O Estado de São Paulo*, November 1, 2009.
18. For preliminary analyses of *lulismo*, see André Singer, "Raízes sociais e ideo-

The year 2010 was an election year—with elections for president, both houses of Congress, state governors, and state assemblies in October. There had been considerable discussion throughout 2009 about whether the Constitution could and would be changed to allow Lula to run for a third term. Although almost certain to win if he ran, and despite indicating in a number of subtle ways that he might run, and some popular demonstrations in favor of *"mais quatro"* (four more years)—sometimes using the slogan "Queremos" (We want Lula), with its echoes of Getúlio in 1945—Lula finally resisted the temptation, thus reinforcing the view that he was no populist. *"Eu não brinco com a democracia"* (I don't play around with democracy), he had declared in June 2009. He believed firmly, he insisted, in Brazil's democratic institutions (even though, disturbingly, according to Latinobarómetro, 40 to 45 percent of Brazilians still do not), and particularly in the alternation of power. He was popular, he liked to say, but not populist.[19]

The presidential election of 2010 was therefore the first since the transfer from military to civilian rule twenty-five years earlier in which Luiz Inácio Lula da Silva was not a candidate. Lula, however, went to extraordinary, unprecedented lengths actively to promote, often in breach of the electoral law, his personally chosen successor, Dilma Rousseff, whom the PT, with some reluctance and some dissent, had finally accepted as its candidate in February 2010. (More than one commentator compared Lula's imposition of Dilma with the famous *dedazo* of Mexican presidents during the period of domination by the Partido Revolucionário Institucional.) For Dilma, it has to be said, was a very problematic candidate. An ex–urban guerrilla during the military dictatorship, she was not a historic *petista*; for twenty years she had been an active member of Brizola's populist PDT and had only joined the PT in 2000. A sixty-two-

lógicas do lulismo," *Novos Estudos CEBRAP*, November 2009, 82–103; and Rudá Ricci, *Lulismo: Da era dos movimentos sociais à ascensão da nova classe média brasileira* (Brasília: Fundação Astrojildo Pereira and Contraponto, 2010). Recent studies of the changing nature of the Workers' Party include Wendy Hunter, "The Partido dos Trabalhadores: Still a Party of the Left?" in *Democratic Brazil Revisited*, edited by Peter R. Kingstone and Timothy J. Power (Pittsburgh: University of Pittsburgh Press, 2008), 15–32; Wendy Hunter, *The Transformation of the Workers' Party in Brazil, 1989–2009* (Cambridge: Cambridge University Press, 2010); and Lincoln Secco, *História do PT* (Cotia, S.P.: Atelie Editorial, 2011). The Delfim Netto interview is in *O Globo*, September 20, 2009.
    19. E.g., see the speeches reported in *O Globo*, June 3 and 6, 2009.

year-old technocrat, lacking charisma and abrasively authoritarian in manner, Dilma Rousseff had served as secretary of energy in the state government of Rio Grande do Sul, as minister of mines and energy in the first Lula administration, and as head of the Casa Civil (i.e., the president's chief of staff) in the second, but she had never before contested an election. Moreover, she had recently suffered from lymphatic cancer and there were doubts as to whether she was fit enough to undertake the rigors of a presidential campaign and, potentially, assume the presidency in January 2011.

The big question, of course, was whether Lula could transfer to Dilma his immense popularity, based on the economic and social advances made by Brazil under his administration and, even more, on his personal history and charisma. He certainly worked hard to do so, and as it began to become more difficult than expected, his strategy and discourse turned increasingly populist. Government expenditures were significantly increased (to the level of fiscal irresponsibility, in the view of some economists) and, with full media exposure, Dilma was linked on every possible occasion to the Programa de Aceleração do Crescimento (PAC; Program of Accelerated Economic Growth) for massive public investment, mainly in infrastructure; to the government's social programs, especially Bolsa Família, which was to be extended from 11 to 13 million households (totaling 40–45 million people), and the "*Minha casa, minha vida*" housing policy; to the nationalist sentiments surrounding the discovery of offshore *pré-sal* oil (Brazil's "passport to the future")—and most of all to the president himself. Lula did everything in his power to make the 2010 election a plebiscitary election: for or against him (and his chosen candidate); for or against his record compared with that of his predecessor Fernando Henrique Cardoso; for or against "*nosso projeto*" (our project); and ultimately, for or against the people (*o povo*). The election was not essentially about Dilma, nor the PT; it was about Lula and his extraordinary empathy with the mass of the Brazilian people, especially the poor in the North and Northeast.

In a speech in Porto Alegre at the end of July 2010 that could hardly have been more "populist," Lula declared, to great applause, that *a direita* (the right) had devoted itself twenty-four hours a day to trying to hold back *as forças democráticas* in Brazil. He had suffered eight years of *ataques, provocações e infâmies*. But he had made it clear to the *elite*, whom he claimed had driven Getúlio Vargas to suicide and forced Jânio

Quadros and João Goulart to resign, that if they wanted to confront him, they would find him on the streets with *o povo brasileiro*. In Joinville, Santa Catarina, in September he argued that *a direita* had failed in its attempt to drive him out of power in 2005 (a reference to the *mensalão* crisis) because he had the one *ingrediente* his predecessors did not have—*vocês* (you, the people). In October, he boasted that he would always win in the street because he had established *uma relação real e direto com o povo*. When things get *feia* (ugly), he advised "Dilminha," in November, *vai para perto do povo*; when you do not know what to do, *pergunte ao povo*; in doubt, *o povo é a solução; o povo* will never disappoint you.[20]

With the help of the somewhat lackluster campaign of the candidate of the PSDB/Democratas opposition, José Serra, and with the strong support of the PMDB and the many other parties in the government coalition, Dilma Rousseff, who had been entirely invented by Lula, won the election in October with 47 percent of the vote in the first round and 56 percent in the second round—broadly, the support Lula had in 2006 —to become Brazil's first female president. A Dilma presidency had been frequently referred to as "*um terceiro mandato de Lula*" (Lula's third mandate). Hugo Chávez was not alone in comparing—in his case, favorably—Lula and Dilma to the Kirchners in Argentina. There remained (and remains) the strong suspicion that Lula was planning to contest the 2014 presidential election or, if Dilma's administration proved successful, her health was good, and she insisted on standing for reelection, perhaps even the 2018 election (when he would be seventy-three years old) and return to power, as Getúlio Vargas had done in 1950, "*nos braços do povo*."[21]

---

20. *O Globo*, July 30, September 14, October 4, and November 26, 2010.

21. In October 2011, Lula was diagnosed with cancer of the larynx. Five months later, he declared himself "cured." It remains uncertain what effect this illness will have on his health in the long term and therefore on his political ambitions. At the end of 2012, the Federal Supreme Court condemned and sentenced to imprisonment several leading figures in the PT, including Lula's chief of staff, José Dirceu, for their involvement in the *mensalão* corruption scandal during Lula's first administration. There followed an attempt to link Lula himself directly to the scandal. His response was to declare that *o povo* (the people) would be his judge. *O Globo*, December 12, 2012.

Chapter 8

Populism in Peru: From APRA to Ollanta Humala

Cynthia McClintock

In this chapter, following the emphases of the volume's coeditors, populism is defined by its political dimensions, among them (1) a divisive, confrontational discourse that pits "the people" against a domestic and/or foreign elite; and (2) charismatic, top-down leadership that concentrates power in the executive and disparages the rule of law and political institutions.[1] Further, emerging amid political and economic failures ("critical junctures") that deeply alienated citizens, populists are outsiders who rally their followers with emotional and moral appeals against the

---

1. The definition of populism is discussed by Carlos de la Torre and Cynthia J. Arnson in chapter 1 of this volume. Additional excellent discussions of the definition of populism include those by Kenneth M. Roberts, "Latin America's Populist Revival," *SAIS Review of International Affairs* 27 (Winter–Spring 2007): 3–15; Kenneth M. Roberts, "Neoliberalism and the Transformation of Populism in Latin America: The Peruvian Case," *World Politics* 48 (1995): 84–89; and Kurt Weyland, "Clarifying a Contested Concept: Populism in the Study of Latin American Politics," *Comparative Politics* 34 (2001): 1-22.

powers that be.[2] By this definition, populism has been not only recurrent in Peru since the 1920s, but almost constant.[3] As in other Latin American nations, however, the forms of populism in Peru have varied.

Three Peruvian political leaders are regularly cited as archetypes of the three most salient forms of populism specified in chapters 1 and 2 of this volume. Peru's Víctor Raúl Haya de la Torre is cited as an archetype of classical populism, emerging in the 1920s and 1930s amid the critical juncture of the Great Depression and subsequent adoption of import-substitution industrialization (ISI) policies in many Latin American countries.[4] Alberto Fujimori is considered an archetype of neoliberal populism, emerging amid the critical juncture of the post-1982 Latin American debt crisis and the introduction of free market policies.[5] A third Peruvian leader, Ollanta Humala, vis-à-vis his 2006 presidential campaign, is mentioned as an example of the radical populism that emerged in Latin America in the first decade of the twenty-first century amid dissatisfaction with neoliberalism.[6] This chapter explores these three leaders' political tendencies and agrees that they fit these three forms of populism, but it also points to distinctions between them and the conventional conceptual classifications.

Not only have archetypal populist leaders emerged in Peru, but also governments that have been populist in some respects but not in others. The 1968–75 military government of General Juan Velasco Alvarado was

2. See chapter 2 of this volume, by Kenneth M. Roberts; and Kirk A. Hawkins, "Is Chávez Populist? Measuring Populist Discourse in Comparative Perspective," *Comparative Political Studies* 42 (2009): 1040–67.

3. Kenneth Roberts also noted Peru's "serial populism"; see Roberts, "Latin America's Populist Revival," 12.

4. On the importance of critical junctures to the emergence of populist leaders, see chapter 2 in this volume. On Haya de la Torre as an archetypal populist leader, see Roberts, "Latin America's Populist Revival," 6; and Michael Reid, *Forgotten Continent: The Battle for Latin America's Soul* (New Haven, Conn.: Yale University Press, 2007), 75–80.

5. Roberts, "Neoliberalism," 92–112; Roberts, "Latin America's Populist Revival," 11; Kurt Weyland, "Neoliberal Populism in Latin America and Eastern Europe," *Comparative Politics* 31 (1999): 381.

6. On the nature of radical populism, see Carlos de la Torre, "Populismo Radical y Democracia en los Andes," *Journal of Democracy en Español* (2009): 24–37. On Humala as a radical populist, see Roberts, "Latin America's Populist Revival," 12-13; and Jorge G. Castañeda, "Where Do We Go from Here?" in *Leftovers: Tales of the Latin American Left*, edited by Jorge G. Castañeda and Marco A. Morales (New York: Taylor and Francis, 2008), 232.

quintessentially populist in its divisive discourse and repudiation of liberal democratic institutions; but, in contrast to other populist governments, it was not elected. It was a military government and was rarely classified as populist at the time. A second Peruvian president, Alan García, was regularly described as a populist during his 1985–90 government.[7] He was charismatic and sought a direct bond with Peruvians during constant speeches from his palace balcony. Also, he pursued expansionary economic policies, and if our definition of populism included economic dimensions, he would classify as a populist. However, as will be discussed below, with the exception of García's charisma, he did not meet the political dimensions of our definition of populism.

In the pages that follow, these five political leaders and their fit with populism and its three key variants—classical, neoliberal, and radical populism—are explored. To underscore the constancy of populism in Peru, the chapter proceeds chronologically. Also, given the military backgrounds of two of the five Peruvian populist leaders, the Peruvian experience suggests that the question of the relationship between the military and populism is worthy of greater scholarly consideration.

Classical Populism and Haya de la Torre

In all key respects, Haya de la Torre was a populist. He was charismatic and used divisive discourse to mobilize Peru's emerging middle and working classes, in particular on the country's North Coast, against both its oligarchy and imperialism. His emphasis was on the antagonism between imperialism and the oppressed peoples of Latin America (although, over time, this emphasis moderated). Also, his commitment to liberal democracy was tenuous at best—in part because democracy was inchoate and his electoral victory was unlikely to have been tolerated by Peru's elites.

Moreover, Haya was true to the classical populism variant that emerged in Latin America in the late 1920s and 1930s. As chapters 1 and 2 above indicated, in the wake of the Great Depression, foreign-oriented, liberal elites whose economic base was in agricultural, mining, and oil exports

---

7. García's 1985–90 government is classified as populist by Roberts, "Latin America's Populist Revival," 12, and as "neopopulist" by Weyland, "Clarifying a Contested Concept," 7, 11.

were discredited; populist movements called for the inclusion of broader sectors of the population and for ISI economic policies. This was indeed the case in Peru.[8]

Between 1895 and 1919, under what was called the "Aristocratic Republic," and between 1919 and 1930, under the authoritarian government of Augusto Leguía, export-led growth was robust in Peru. Leguía in particular enjoyed close ties with the United States, and U.S. capital flowed into Peru. Foreign companies often disrupted local operations but brought little benefit to Peru; for example, from 1916 to 1934 the United States–owned International Petroleum Company (IPC) had apparently no local suppliers and only 16 percent of the value of its total sales (primarily exports) stayed in Peru in the form of wages, taxes, or other payments.[9]

With up-to-date technology, sugar and cotton haciendas on Peru's coast and silver and copper mines in the highlands expanded at the expense of traditional landowners, smallholders, and peasant communities. "Forty families" were widely believed to control these exports and constitute Peru's "oligarchy."[10] From 1890 to 1920, sugar was Peru's most valuable export and Peru's sugar *hacendados* were considered the country's wealthiest oligarchs.[11] At this time, most of Peru's population was in the highlands, and the *hacendados* brought in large numbers of laborers from the highlands, often under false pretenses, as well as from China and Africa.[12] Wages were low, hours were long, and abuses were common.

This socioeconomic context—which was often called "dualistic" due to the coexistence of a modern, growing export sector beside traditional

8. Peter F. Klarén, *Modernization, Dislocation, and Aprismo: Origins of the Peruvian Aprista Party, 1870–1932* (Austin: Institute of Latin American Studies at the University of Texas Press, 1973).

9. Reid, *Forgotten Continent*, 39.

10. The concept of "the oligarchy" was used by Peruvians and scholars alike. One excellent study is by Dennis L. Gilbert, *The Oligarchy and the Old Regime in Peru*, Latin American Studies Program Dissertation Series (Ithaca, N.Y.: Cornell University, 1977).

11. On the value of Peru's exports during this period, see Rosemary Thorp and Geoffrey Bertram, *Peru 1890–1977: Growth and Policy in an Open Economy* (New York: Columbia University Press, 1978), 40.

12. In 1940, the populations of Cusco, Junín, and Puno were slightly more than 50 percent of the population of Lima; see Magali Sarfatti Larson and Arlene Eisen Bergman, *Social Stratification in Peru*, Politics of Modernization Series 5 (Berkeley: University of California, Institute of International Studies, 1969), 299.

economic sectors that were stagnant or even ravaged—shaped Haya's ideology, which was similar to that of other "classical populists."[13] Haya's views evolved in part through debates with José Carlos Mariátegui, Peru's first prominent Marxist, who argued that international capitalism had co-opted Peru's middle classes and accordingly that national transformation could come about only through the actions of the working class. By contrast, for Haya, Peru remained a feudal country where the working class was small and weak. Haya believed that if foreign investment were regulated by the state and the power of the oligarchy were eliminated, Peru's domestic bourgeoisie would thrive and the country would achieve growth with equity. The national transformation would be achieved not through class conflict but through the construction of a joint front among not only the peasantry and the proletariat but also the middle classes, which together would build a strong state and combat imperialism. ISI policies were implicit. Haya's ideas were circulated in newspapers, magazine articles, and pamphlets, and in 1936 they were published as a book, *El antimperialismo y el APRA*.

Haya fit the model of classical populism not only in terms of the socioeconomic context and his concomitant ideology but also in terms of his political strategy. He was not merely charismatic; he was also a preacher who promised redemption and formed an extremely close bond with his followers.[14] A spellbinding orator and prolific writer, he tapped many Peruvians' religious and emotional chords. His proclamation "Sólo el APRA [Alianza Popular Revolucionaria Americana, or American Popular Revolutionary Alliance—his party], salvará al Perú" ("Only APRA will save Peru"), which captured both Peruvians' frustration and hope for their nation in a religious metaphor, is the most famous in the country's history.

Further, like other classical populists, Haya was a dedicated and effective architect of political institutions that included the poor. In 1924, he founded APRA, which became the only institutionalized political

13. Excellent analyses of APRA's ideology include Klarén, *Modernization*, 132–35; Julio Cotler, *Clases, Estado, y Nación en el Perú* (Lima: Instituto de Estudios Peruanos, 1978), 211–36; and Steve Stein, *Populism in Peru: The Emergence of the Masses and the Politics of Social Control* (Madison: University of Wisconsin Press, 1980), 162–65.

14. On these characteristics of classical populism, see, in particular, Weyland, "Clarifying a Contested Concept," 16; and Reid, *Forgotten Continent*, 292.

party in Peru's history and endures to this day.[15] He worked with intellectuals, student militants, and union leaders to build party organs that were compared to extended families, churches, and (by critics) to "sects." In particular, on the North Coast and in Lima, workers and lower-middle-class Apristas (members of APRA) met two or three times a week at the party's Casas del Pueblo (Houses of the People). At these meetings, speeches were made, political strategy was discussed, and the party anthem, the "Marsellesa Aprista," was sung (see chapter 1). Moral discipline and austerity were encouraged; alcohol, for example, was prohibited. At the same time, the party offered material benefits, including medical and dental clinics, legal services, "popular restaurants," and sporting activities.[16] APRA was a disciplined party, and as such could be considered a top-down institution; conversely, virtually by definition political parties are hierarchical to some degree.

There was a major distinction, however, between Haya de la Torre and his populist counterparts in Argentina, Brazil, and elsewhere: Haya did not become his country's president. At first, he had appeared likely to gain power. He had been only in his twenties when he had become the foremost leader of the political opposition to the dictator Augusto Leguía. As a university student, he had been a key negotiator for the 1919 student-worker front that successfully demanded an eight-hour day. Subsequently, he had organized a network of "popular universities" for workers, and then, in May 1923, he had galvanized this network to successfully oppose a key Leguía project. As a result, he had been jailed in October 1923; he was deported and lived abroad, in Mexico and elsewhere, until 1931.

However, after the ousting of Leguía in 1931, Haya was defeated at the ballot box by former lieutenant colonel Luis Sánchez Cerro, who had led the overthrow of Leguía. Although a mestizo, Sánchez Cerro enjoyed the support of the oligarchy; at the same time, his modest, provincial background and darker skin appealed to popular groups. By contrast, Haya was fair-skinned, tall, and of upper-middle-class origins; his father

15. APRA was intended to be a regionwide movement. The Partido Aprista Peruano (PAP) was founded in 1930 to be the movement's party in Peru. However, the party is most commonly called APRA. Excellent analyses include Cotler, *Clases, estado, y nación*, 233–36; Klarén, *Modernization*, xi, 113–36; and Stein, *Populism*, 134–36, 150–61.

16. Thomas M. Davies Jr., "Victor Raúl Haya de la Torre and the APRA: The Politics of Ideology," unpublished paper, San Diego State University, 1985, 13.

had been the editor of a North Coast newspaper, and Haya had attended private school. Sánchez Cerro denounced APRA as anti-Catholic, anti-military, and closet-communist.

It was not surprising that Haya was defeated.[17] First, there were political factors. Sánchez Cerro was famous for his overthrowing of Leguía, and he enjoyed an ethnicity advantage. In addition, Haya had lived in exile for eight years and had been back in Peru for only a few months at the time of the election. Second, the working class was very small in Peru at the time. In 1930, fewer than 10 percent of Peru's population was estimated to live in cities larger than 20,000 people, versus 38 percent in Argentina, 32 percent in Chile, 19 percent in Venezuela, 16 percent in Mexico, and 14 percent in Brazil.[18] In 1940, only about 13 percent of Peru's population lived in the Department of Lima; the Southern Highlands Department of Puno was the second-most populated in the nation.[19] Peru's labor force was concentrated on Peru's North Coast, where the sugar industry was located, and in this area Haya's appeal was strong. In 1931, more than one-quarter of APRA's total vote came from the two North Coast departments of Lambayeque and La Libertad; in key coastal valleys, he won 90 percent of the vote.[20] Neither Haya nor any other political leader sought to build a social base in Peru's highlands because illiterates were not allowed to vote until 1980 and most highlanders were illiterate. For example, in 1940, 85 percent of the population over fifteen years of age in the Southern Highlands provinces of Apurímac, Ayacucho, Cusco, Huancavelica, and Puno was illiterate.[21]

Yet, despite this set of logical explanations for Haya's loss and despite a lack of evidence, APRA repudiated the 1931 electoral result as fraudulent and quickly became obstructionist in the legislature. In retaliation, Sánchez Cerro deported APRA's entire congressional representation. In 1932 in Trujillo, Apristas rebelled, executing roughly 60 members of the army; in reprisal, the military killed 1,000 to 2,000 Apristas. In 1933, Sánchez Cerro was assassinated by an Aprista. Under Sánchez Cerro's

17. Klarén, *Modernization*, 136.
18. James W. Wilkie and Peter Reich, *Statistical Abstract of Latin America*, vol. 20 (Los Angeles: UCLA Latin American Center Publications, 1980), 78.
19. Richard Webb and Graciela Fernández Baca, *Perú en Números 2005* (Lima: Cuánto, 2005), 212–14.
20. Klarén, *Modernization*, 136.
21. Larson and Bergman, *Social Stratification*, 363.

successor, repression of APRA intensified and Aprista militants continued to resort to violence.

The tragic events of the early 1930s were the start of a vicious circle in
Peruvian politics, something that was not uncommon in the era of classical populism. First, it was at a minimum not clear that Peru's elites
would tolerate a government that threatened their interests; second,
APRA did not accept the rules of the democratic game; and, completing
the vicious circle, Aprista militants' resort to violence deeply alienated
both Peruvian elites and the military. Between 1936 and 1968, when elections were held, APRA was proscribed to one degree or another, and at
various times Apristas were imprisoned and Haya was exiled.

As of the early 1960s, no government committed to ISI or other economic reform policies had been in power for any length of time in Peru,
and partly as a result, the country's economic structure was very traditional.[22] It was estimated that, in Peru in 1960, only 16 percent of gross
domestic product (GDP) was in manufacturing, versus 22 percent in
Brazil, 24 percent in Mexico, and 30 percent in Argentina.[23] Peru's Gini
index of land distribution was the most skewed among fifty-four nations
for which data were reported; a mere 280 families—fewer than 0.1 percent of all farm families—owned approximately 30 percent of the land,
and more than 50 percent of the best land.[24] Concomitantly, Peru's income distribution was among the most unequal in the region; in 1961,
the wealthiest 1 percent of the economically active population received a
staggering 30 percent of the national income.[25] The disparity in living
standards between the capital and the hinterlands was egregious.[26] Two
poles endured in Peru: At one pole were "the oligarchy" and perhaps
another 10 percent of the population, who were Caucasian, Catholic,

22. An outstanding analysis is by Thorp and Bertram, *Peru*, 145–300.
23. World Bank, *World Tables 1976* (Baltimore: Johns Hopkins University Press,
1976), 420.
24. Charles L. Taylor and Michael C. Hudson, *World Handbook of Political and
Social Indicators*, vol. 2 (New Haven, Conn.: Yale University Press, 1972), 267; Daniel Martínez and Armando Tealdo, *El Agro Peruano, 1970–1980* (Lima: CEDEP,
1982), 15–16.
25. Richard Webb, *Government Policy and the Distribution of Income in Peru,
1963–1973* (Cambridge, Mass.: Harvard University Press, 1977), 6–7.
26. Comparisons for inequality between regions are given for Peru, El Salvador,
and Ecuador by Cynthia McClintock, *Revolutionary Movements in Latin America:
El Salvador's FMLN and Peru's Shining Path* (Washington, D.C.: U.S. Institute of
Peace Press, 1998), 167–73.

Spanish-speaking, wealthy, and based in Lima; at the other pole were some 40 percent of the population, called "Indians," who were dark-skinned, at most nominally Catholic, Quechua-speaking, impoverished, and based in Peru's Southern Highlands. On numerous measures of political participation, too, Peru was "behind" its neighbors.[27]

At the same time, in the early 1960s Fidel Castro had come to power in Cuba and Marxist influences were growing in Latin America; in Peru, the need for reform appeared especially urgent. However, reform did not happen. Elections were held in 1962 and were won by APRA, but without the one-third of the vote legally required for election. The military intervened, elections were held again in 1963, and they were won by the military's preferred candidate, Fernando Belaúnde Terry, an architect. A democrat in the liberal political tradition, Belaúnde promised social reform without Aprismo (i.e., the doctrine of APRA), but he was unable to deliver—ironically, in part because of legislative obstruction by an alliance between APRA and a conservative party that had been APRA's archrival. The Belaúnde government did not deliver either on its promise of agrarian reform or its promise of nationalization of the IPC, a company that was widely resented in Peru.

Military Populism and the Government
of General Juan Velasco Alvarado

In 1968, led by General Juan Velasco Alvarado, Peru's military ousted the Belaúnde government. Although the 1968–75 Velasco government was most frequently described as "revolutionary" or "corporatist," in fact in key respects it fit the populist model.[28] Like classical populists,

---

27. David Scott Palmer, *"Revolution from Above": Military Government and Popular Participation in Peru, 1968–1972*, Latin American Studies Program Dissertation Series (Ithaca, N.Y.: Cornell University, 1972), 5–10.

28. The government commonly described itself as the "revolutionary government of the armed forces." Probably the most frequently cited description of the government was Abraham F. Lowenthal's "ambiguous revolution." See Abraham F. Lowenthal, "Peru's Ambiguous Revolution," in *The Peruvian Experiment: Continuity and Change under Military Rule*, edited by Abraham F. Lowenthal (Princeton, N.J.: Princeton University Press, 1975), 3–43. But the government was also classified as "corporatist," especially by its critics; definitions of corporatism varied considerably, however. For discussions of these debates, see Cynthia McClintock, *Peasant Cooperatives and Political Change in Peru* (Princeton, N.J.: Princeton University

Velasco divided Peruvians between the people and the oligarchy, and he favored ISI policies. Also, like recent populists, he repudiated Peru's traditional political parties and proclaimed an alternative "fully participatory social democracy." To a certain extent, like the government of Hugo Chávez, the tone of the Velasco government was that, with military support, it would finally carry out what APRA and subsequent liberal-democratic political parties had promised but not achieved. In other respects, however, Velasco did not fit the populist model. Most saliently, his government was a military one; it was not elected, and at no time did it promise national elections. Nor was Velasco charismatic.

Like APRA and other classical-populist movements, Velasco and his colleagues considered Peru's oligarchy a curse, condemning their country to social injustice and underdevelopment.[29] In Velasco's speeches, "the oligarchy" was one of the most frequently mentioned concepts; only "socioeconomic development," "social justice," "revolution," and "structural transformation" were mentioned more frequently.[30]

It was emphasized that the country's oligarchy had blocked Peru's national development and that the military government would bring about social justice for the country's people:

Today we are one, People and Government, People and Armed Forces. Today Peru is living the grand experience of its transformation. History will say that in these years an entire nation and its Armed Forces embarked upon the road to its definitive liberation, established the bases of genuine development, forced the power of the egoist and colonial oligarchy to yield, recuperated authentic sovereignty before foreign pressures and began the great task to realize social justice in Peru.[31]

Press, 1981), 39–47; Julio Cotler, "Democracy and National Integration in Peru," in *The Peruvian Experiment Reconsidered*, edited by Cynthia McClintock and Abraham F. Lowenthal (Princeton, N.J.: Princeton University Press, 1983), 3–38; and Abraham F. Lowenthal, "The Peruvian Experiment Reconsidered," in *Peruvian Experiment Reconsidered*, 415–30.

29. Velasco's principal speechwriter, the sociologist Carlos Delgado, was closely tied to Haya de la Torre; see Carlos Contreras and Marcos Cueto, *Historia del Perú Contemporáneo* (Lima: Instituto de Estudios Peruanos, 2004), 328.

30. Juan Velasco Alvarado, *Velasco: La Voz de la Revolución* (Lima: SINAMOS, 1972), vol. 1, xiii–xxvii, and vol. 2, xiii–xxviii (thematic indexes to the volumes).

31. Ibid., 1:57. The words were from Velasco's speech for independence day, July 28, 1969.

Ultimately, the consensus is broad that, indeed, the oligarchy was eclipsed by the Velasco government's reforms. Its agrarian reform was the most sweeping in Latin America save that of Cuba; almost all landholdings of more than 50 hectares were expropriated and transformed into various kinds of cooperatives, benefiting to different degrees approximately 25 percent of Peru's farm families.[32] The government also expropriated a broad spectrum of other enterprises that were largely owned by oligarchic families—from fishing, mining, and banking companies to daily newspapers.

In contrast to the youthful Haya, Velasco rarely used the word "imperialism," and his government regularly declared its desire for foreign investment, particularly in industry, which respected Peru's need for development.[33] However, the government did seek to regulate foreign capital and to distance Peru from the United States. Although at the time the government said that IPC was a unique case because it had violated Peru's laws, IPC was nationalized within a matter of days.[34] In subsequent years, additional United States–based companies were nationalized, including the Cerro de Pasco Company, Marcona Mining, and many fishmeal enterprises.

Overall, key tenets of ISI were adopted and the structure of power and wealth changed considerably in Peru.[35] Between 1968 and 1977, the state's percentage of Peru's gross national product increased from 25 to 50 percent; tariffs were raised and industry expanded from about 22 percent of GDP in 1964 to more than 26 percent in 1975.[36] Peru's income distribution improved, and the middle classes grew. However, the reforms did little to alleviate the lot of the country's poorest people—its highland peasants. There was not enough good-quality land to redistribute in these areas to make a major improvement in peasants' living standards, and public expenditures were not shifted toward highland agriculture. The government did, however, continue to expand educational opportunities, and it encouraged respect for the culture of indigenous peoples, in particular by recognizing Quechua as the second national language.

32. Cynthia McClintock, "Why Peasants Rebel," *World Politics* 37 (1984): 64–67.
33. Velasco, *Velasco*, 1:xiii–xxvii, 2:81, xiii-xxviii (thematic indexes to the volumes).
34. Ibid., 1:29.
35. An excellent summary is given by Lowenthal, "Peruvian Experiment Reconsidered."
36. Ibid., 427–28.

Although the Velasco government preceded both neopopulism and radical populism, it similarly repudiated liberal-democratic institutions. When Velasco was asked if he had any affinity for a political party, he replied that "I had some sympathy for the Christian Democrats, at the beginning. . . . The rest were pure blah-blah-blah."[37] The traditional political parties' leaders were considered to have been co-opted by Peru's elites and thus unable to undertake reforms; political parties were proscribed, and a "no-party" model was proclaimed.[38] Rather than a political party, the government created a political agency, the Sistema Nacional de Apoyo a la Movilización Social (National System for the Support of Social Mobilization)—or SINAMOS, an acronym that means "Without Masters." SINAMOS was supposed to build political participation and lead to the government's proclaimed "fully participatory social democracy," which was described as a leftist utopia:

We must build in our nation a fully participatory social democracy, that is to say, a system based in a moral order of solidarity, not of individualism; in an economy fundamentally self-managed, in which the means of production are predominantly social property, under the direct control of those whose work generates the wealth; and in a political order where the power of decisions, rather than being the monopoly of political and economic oligarchies, is widespread and rooted in social, economic and political institutions directed, with little or no mediation, by the men and women who form them.[39]

However, the government's claim to be building a "fully participatory social democracy" was not persuasive.[40] The contradiction between "a fully participatory social democracy" and a military government was impossible to resolve. For most Peruvians, the concept of democracy included freedom of speech and national elections.[41] Although the Velasco government was not severely repressive by the standards of Latin Ameri-

37. *Caretas*, February 3, 1977.
38. Carlos Delgado Olivera, *Testimonio de Lucha* (Lima: PEISA, 1973), 170–71.
39. Velasco, *Velasco*, 2: 271.
40. On these concepts, see Velasco, *Velasco*, 1:9, 2:271.
41. McClintock, *Peasant Cooperatives*, 299–301; Cynthia McClintock, "Post-Revolutionary Agrarian Politics in Peru," in *Post-Revolutionary Peru: The Politics of Transformation*, edited by Stephen M. Gorman (Boulder, Colo.: Westview Press, 1982), 145.

can military regimes of the time, approximately a score of dissidents were deported and Peru's major newspapers were expropriated and gradually became mouthpieces for the regime. Further, at no time did the Velasco government endorse the principle of elections or even referenda. The issue was especially salient with respect to SINAMOS officials; why were they appointed by the government rather than chosen by citizens? It was charged by some analysts that the actual purpose of SINAMOS was to mobilize support for the regime and that the government's goal was to control citizens in a hierarchical "corporatist" regime.[42] It seems unlikely that this was Velasco's goal; ultimately, worker and peasant organizations expanded dramatically, largely under the banner of the Marxist left.[43]

The military government's difficulties in the establishment of a political base were exacerbated by the fact that Velasco was not charismatic. Velasco had become president because he was the commander of the army at the time of the coup; he had no special achievements to his credit, but rather had climbed steadily up the bureaucratic ladder. He was not particularly handsome: "The face of General Juan Velasco Alvarado is the face of thousands of men who sit behind small, linoleum-covered desks at army barracks throughout Latin America."[44] Nor was he a gifted orator: "He sweats and fidgets profusely during his televised speeches, making them a droning agony both for the speaker and his audience."[45] Especially after he fell seriously ill in 1973, he did not travel around the country or even speak at rallies.

The government's problems were compounded by its significant ideological divisions; it was rarely clear what the government would do.[46] The reform process was uncertain and dynamic and depended a great deal on Velasco himself. Although in 1968 Velasco was thought to be a "conservative nationalist," he was caught up in the whirlwind of his own

42. See, in particular, Julio Cotler, "The New Mode of Political Domination in Peru," in *Peruvian Experiment*, 44–78. As mentioned above, definitions of corporatism vary.

43. McClintock, *Peasant Cooperatives*, 296–313; Henry A. Dietz, "Mobilization, Austerity, and Voting: The Legacy of the Revolution for Lima's Poor," in *Post-Revolutionary Peru*, ed. Gorman, 76–77.

44. Norman Gall, "Peru: The Master Is Dead," *Dissent*, June 1971, 306.

45. Gall, "Peru," 307.

46. An excellent discussion of factions, the military institution, and Velasco's leadership is given by Carlos Franco, "En relación con 'El Ocaso del Poder Oligarquico,'" *Socialismo y Participación* 4 (September 1978): 107–28.

reforms and, perhaps driven by personal resentments from his origins in a poor family in the coastal town of Piura, took the process further than most military officers wanted.[47] He was overthrown in a palace coup in August 1975 by his premier and finance minister, the considerably more conservative General Francisco Morales Bermúdez—who, less than two years later, in July 1977, announced a return to democracy.

Populism and the 1985–90 Government of Alan García

Whereas at the time the Velasco government was rarely classified as populist despite its fit in various key respects with the definition of the concept in this book, at the time the 1985–90 García government was often classified as populist despite its lack of fit with our definition.[48] García was considered a populist first because of his charisma and second because of his unsustainable, expansionary economic policies. However, his discourse was not divisive, and he respected liberal-democratic institutions. His administration was the first for APRA, and he was clearly eager to remain the party's leader for many years; but at the end of his administration, APRA remained Peru's only institutionalized party.

In 1980, the prospects for democracy in Peru were more favorable than ever before. No longer was an oligarchy looking out first and foremost for its own interests, and no longer was APRA proscribed. A new political left was expected to push for greater social justice; for the first time in the 1979 Constitution, illiterates were enfranchised. Peru's democratic transition was coinciding with a rhetorical U.S. commitment to democracy and human rights and also with a return to democracy in much of the region.

However, the return to democracy in Peru coincided as well with Latin America's debt crisis and its "lost decade," provoking tremendous challenges for democratic governance. Further, amid the economic cri-

47. Velasco was dubbed a "conservative nationalist" in Peru's newsmagazine *Caretas* in 1968; on this point and policymaking under Velasco, see Cynthia Mc-Clintock, "Velasco, Officers, and Citizens: The Politics of Stealth," in *Peruvian Experiment Reconsidered*, 275–308.

48. Among the many excellent analyses of the 1985–90 García government, see John Crabtree, *Peru under García: An Opportunity Lost* (Pittsburgh: University of Pittsburgh Press, 1992); and Carlos Reyna, *La anunciación de Fujimori: Alan García 1985–1990* (Lima: DESCO, 2000).

sis, the brutal, virulently Maoist Shining Path insurgency emerged in the country's Southern Highlands and expanded into many regions, including Lima. These challenges proved overwhelming for the government of Fernando Belaúnde, who was reelected in 1980. Ultimately, Belaúnde was perceived as impervious to the suffering of the Peruvian people; in cartoons, he was portrayed as sitting in the clouds. On economic policy, he spoke as a neoliberal, but in fact he initiated minimal free market reform and was at odds with the International Monetary Fund. With respect to the Shining Path, at first he belittled the threat but then endorsed wholesale repressive military action, which resulted in thousands of civilian deaths and more support for the insurgency.

In 1985, the young, gifted Alan García was elected in a landslide. García had been Haya's protégé and had succeeded Haya as the leader of APRA after Haya's death in 1979. In the campaign, García worked assiduously to change the image of APRA as divisive, sectarian, and gangsterish. Under Haya, the party's symbol had been a lone star; under García, a dove was added. The party's traditional slogan, "Only APRA can save Peru," was dropped; García's new slogans were "My commitment is to all Peruvians" and "A government for everyone." In his inaugural address, as in his other writings and speeches, García criticized the international financial community and the United States as imperialistic, but called on all Peruvians to work together "to form a nationalistic, democratic, and popular government, which will . . . be laying the framework for an autonomous and free society from which injustice, exploitation and misery are eliminated."[49]

García reveled in power and the limelight. His impromptu speeches from his palace balcony were so common that they were named the *balconazos*. Given his youth, energy, eloquence, and ability to bond with the Peruvian people, the odds that he would be making his mark in Peruvian politics for decades to come appeared very good. At no time, however, did he reject liberal democratic principles. Again in his inaugural address, for example, his first words were about democracy and the vote, and he extolled Belaúnde's respect for democracy.[50] A long-standing concern in Peru was the extreme centralization of power in Lima, and

49. See "President Alan García's Inaugural Address to Congress, July 28, 1985," *Andean Report*, August 1985, 3. See also Alan García, *El Futuro Diferente: La Tarea Histórica del APRA* (Lima: Editorial Imprenta DESA, 1982); and *Alan García: Three Speeches for History* (Lima: Editora Perú, 1985).

50. "President Alan García's Inaugural Address," 3.

García achieved the establishment of regions that elected their own governments. Although García was very popular during his first two years in office, there was no attempt to change the Constitution to allow for his immediate reelection. And because he enjoyed a majority in both houses of the legislature, he was rarely obstructed by it; however, in what was arguably his most notorious initiative, a bid in 1987 to nationalize ten private banks, he was indeed blocked.

Like the relationship between most presidents and their parties, the relationship between García and APRA was often tense.[51] García was criticized as imperious and tempestuous by the Apristas. His preference for decisionmaking with a close circle of non-Aprista friends, many of whom had ties to the 1968–80 military government, was also criticized. For his part, at times García lambasted the Apristas as cowardly and corrupt. Still, APRA stalwarts—such as the first vice president, Luis Alberto Sánchez, and the 1980 presidential candidate Armando Villanueva—remained very powerful. Luis Alva Castro, who had also been a Haya protégé, was García's first prime minister and economics minister; despite García's objections, Castro became APRA's 1990 presidential candidate.[52] Virtually throughout García's administration, twelve out of fourteen civilian Cabinet ministers were Apristas, and, with the exception of the vote on the nationalization of the banks, the party's traditional legislative discipline was maintained. Of course, the party has endured.

However, García's economic policies were clearly populist. In his inaugural address, he blamed Latin America's debt crisis on imperialism and the United States and said that Peru would pay no more than 10 percent of its export earnings to service its debt. His position outraged the international financial community and the Ronald Reagan administration. Following ISI, García introduced expansionary fiscal policies in the hope that domestic industrialists would seize the day; but, in 1987, as Peru's international reserves were running out, he concluded that they

51. On the relationship between García and APRA, see Cynthia McClintock, "Peru," in *Latin America and Caribbean Contemporary Record, Volume VII, 1987–1988*, edited by James M. Malloy and Eduardo Gamarra (New York: Holmes and Meier, 1990), B165–66.

52. Katrina Burgess and Steven Levitsky, "Explaining Populist Party Adaptation in Latin America: Environmental and Organizational Determinants of Party Change in Argentina, Mexico, Peru, and Venezuela," *Comparative Political Studies* 36 (2003): 904.

had failed to do so and made the rash decision to try to nationalize Peru's banks. At that point, not only foreign capital but also domestic capital was dismayed. In 1988, GDP plummeted by more than 8 percent, and in 1989 by almost 12 percent; during the two-year period, annual inflation was above 2,000 percent.[53] In 1989, the real minimum wage was a mere 23 percent of its 1980 level.[54] By 1990, Peru's per capita income had plummeted to the level of 1960–62.[55] The country's decline in per capita GDP during the 1970s and 1980s was the most severe in the region, except for Guyana and Nicaragua.[56]

Not coincidentally, the Shining Path expanded—seemingly inexorably. García saw the Shining Path as a serious problem that was the result of the destitution of the Southern Highlands and rejected an exclusively military approach to the problem; in 1985–87, he sought to provide economic aid to the area and to raise the military's respect for human rights. However, for various reasons (including perceptions of hypocrisy after a 1986 government massacre of Shining Path prison inmates), these efforts failed. By 1989, the Shining Path guerrillas numbered approximately 10,000 combatants, had the support of roughly 15 percent of the nation's citizens, and controlled about 28 percent of its municipalities.[57]

Neoliberal Populism and the
Fujimori Government

The government of Alberto Fujimori (1990–2000) was populist in its use of confrontational discourse and its concentration of power in the executive. As Kenneth Roberts first elaborated, however, Fujimori, Mexico's Carlos Salinas de Gortari, and Argentina's Carlos Menem represented neoliberal populism, which was quite different from classical populism.[58] These neoliberal leaders emerged at a critical juncture—in the late 1980s and early 1990s, quite a few years after the onset of Latin America's debt crisis—and responded to the particular problems and opportunities of

53. Kenneth M. Roberts, "Economic Crisis and the Demise of the Legal Left in Peru," *Comparative Politics* 29 (1996): 79.
54. McClintock, *Revolutionary Movements*, 165.
55. "A Ritmo de Rambo," *Caretas*, October 28, 2010, 56–57.
56. McClintock, *Revolutionary Movements*, 162.
57. Ibid., 73.
58. Roberts, "Neoliberalism," 108–16.

this era.[59] In particular, when they adopted free market reforms, they were able to use the resources from privatization to provide clientelistic benefits for the poor and gain support. In contrast to classical populists, their bête noire was not the oligarchy but "the political class," and they were not institution builders. In all these respects, Fujimori was a neo-liberal populist; however, it is important to point out that, relative to such neoliberal populists as Salinas and Menem, Fujimori not only did not build democratic institutions but actually destroyed them. Arguably, Fujimori's leadership was not personalistic (he governed closely with his country's military and intelligence services, in particular his spymaster, Vladimiro Montesinos). Arguably, too, Fujimori was not charismatic (Peruvians' support for him was based primarily on their perception that his government had succeeded rather than on any particular attraction to him).

Like Menem and various other neoliberal populists, Fujimori succeeded a president who had resisted the adoption of neoliberal policies, battled the International Monetary Fund, and ended his term in disgrace, with his country's economies in shambles. As indicated above, in the late 1980s Peru's economy was in free fall. Further, unlike Mexico and Argentina, Peru was also wracked by the violence of the Shining Path insurgency, which was expanding throughout the country and threatening Lima. All of Peru's political parties were discredited. Acción Popular was tarnished by the 1980–85 Belaúnde government, and APRA was discredited by the 1985–90 García government. For its part, the Marxist left had been robust in Peru and might have been expected to benefit from the crisis, but in fact it suffered. In Peru's legislature and local governments, the left was perceived to have failed to make a significant difference; class-based organizations, in particular labor unions, were eroding; and the left was severely factionalized.[60] Factionalism was exacerbated amid the challenge of the Shining Path and the demise of the Soviet Union.

At first, the 1990 elections were expected to be won by the renowned novelist Mario Vargas Llosa. But many Peruvians were worried by his alliance with discredited rightist parties and—despite the economy's dire straits—by his call for a neoliberal economic "shock." In the final months of the campaign, Fujimori won Peruvians' support. A former mathemat-

59. Ibid., 82–116.
60. Roberts, "Economic Crisis," 69–92.

ics professor and university head who had no political experience and no real political party, Fujimori was the quintessential outsider. Fujimori campaigned against Vargas Llosa's "shock" and sought to appeal to Peru's center and center-left voters, but also emphasized his ethnicity and background. The son of lower-middle-class Japanese immigrants, Fujimori looked more like the majority of Peruvians than the country's white-skinned presidents; also, persons of Asian origin were widely perceived as honest, hard-working, and smart. Fujimori's slogans included "A president like you" and "Work, honesty, and technology."

Immediately after Fujimori's election, he traveled to Washington and met with the heads of the International Monetary Fund, the World Bank, and the Inter-American Development Bank. At this time the George H. W. Bush administration was facilitating a more accommodating position at international financial institutions toward the plights of Latin American countries.[61] In particular, the Bush administration was providing more funds for Latin American debt reduction. Not beholden to a political party, with its concomitant political agenda, Fujimori abruptly reversed his campaign promises and implemented a policy package dubbed "Fujishock." State expenditures were slashed, foreign investment laws were eased, tariffs were reduced, and privatization was initiated. During the years 1990–93, Peru renegotiated its foreign debt and returned to the good graces of the international financial community.

Gradually, Peru's economy recovered. After two difficult years in 1991 and 1992, the economy grew by 4.8 percent in 1993 and by 12.8 percent in 1994.[62] In 1994, the telecommunications network became the first large state-owned enterprise to be privatized; the winning bid, from Spain's Telefónica, was for more than $2 billion—a sum equivalent to more than half of Peru's annual export earnings at the time.[63] Ultimately, between 1990 and 1998, more than 180 state holdings were privatized, for a total sale value of about $6.6 billion.[64] Of the government's privatization revenue, approximately $900 million was spent on social programs, schools,

61. Riordan Roett, "The Debt Crisis and Economic Development," in *Neighborly Adversaries: Readings in U.S.–Latin American Relations*, vol. 2, edited by Michael L. Rosa and Frank O. Mora (Lanham, Md.: Rowman & Littlefield, 2007), 205–18.

62. Cynthia McClintock and Fabián Vallas, *The United States and Peru: Cooperation at a Cost* (New York: Routledge, 2003), 99.

63. Ibid., 98; Roberts, "Neoliberalism," 104.

64. McClintock and Vallas, *United States and Peru*, 98.

and roads and other infrastructure for poor communities, primarily by the Ministry of the Presidency, which was directly controlled by Fujimori.[65] The ministry, which accounted for almost 10 percent of the national government's budget in 1992–93, ran its programs with clear political purposes; communities that had not supported Fujimori during a constitutional referendum in 1993 were directly targeted.[66]

One of the factors in both Peru's economic recovery and the capacity to channel economic aid to remote communities was the decimation of the Shining Path. In September 1992, a small, elite squad within Peru's antiterrorist police captured the leader of the Shining Path, Abimael Guzmán. Within the next few weeks, using information found in Guzmán's hideout, police arrested more than 1,000 suspected guerrillas. Although many Peruvians deserved credit for the eclipse of the insurgency (e.g., García established the elite antiterrorist police squad), Fujimori was the primary beneficiary. In 2000, 56 percent of Peruvians said that Fujimori's "defeat of terrorism" would be "what we will remember twenty years from now when we talk about Fujimori."[67] Indeed, during the 2011 elections, the greatest asset of the Fujimori name appeared to be its association with the defeat of terrorism.

Given Peru's economic recovery, its successful counterinsurgency program, and considerable government spending, Fujimori won Peru's 1995 elections in a landslide.[68] Support for Fujimori was quite even across Peru's departments and social classes.[69] However, even in Fujimori's heyday in the mid-1990s, his political project was not an important factor in Peruvians' support of his government. As the political scientist Catherine Conaghan explained:

Average Peruvians were not cheerleaders for authoritarianism, nor were they naive enough to believe Fujimori's claim that his was a pris-

65. Roberts, "Neoliberalism," 104.

66. Ibid., 104–5; Catherine M. Conaghan, *Fujimori's Peru: Deception in the Public Sphere* (Pittsburgh: University of Pittsburgh Press, 2005), 79.

67. Julio F. Carrión, "Public Opinion, Market Reforms, and Democracy," in *The Fujimori Legacy: The Rise of Electoral Authoritarianism in Peru*, edited by Julio F. Carrión (University Park: Pennsylvania State University Press, 2006), 133.

68. These three variables are demonstrated to have been key by Kenneth M. Roberts and Moises Arce, "Neoliberalism and Lower-Class Voting Behavior in Peru," *Comparative Political Studies* 31 (1998): 217–46.

69. Fernando Tuesta Soldevilla, *Perú Político en cifras 1821–2001* (Lima: Fundación Friedrich Ebert, 2001), 445, 497.

tine model of good government. For most of the duration of the regime, Peruvians were apathetic and cynical and understandably so. After years of war and economic stress, Peruvians were weary of politics.[70]

At the critical juncture of the late 1980s and early 1990s, in Peru and numerous other Latin American countries, it is not surprising that popular anger was directed at the elected civilian politicians who had failed to resolve their countries' crises. As indicated in chapters 1 and 2 of this volume, for Fujimori and other neoliberal populists, "the people" were pitted not against the oligarchy, which by this time had been largely eclipsed in these countries, but against "the political class."

Almost immediately after Fujimori's inauguration, he began to attack Peru's liberal-democratic institutions. He denounced members of Congress as "unproductive charlatans," Congress as a "large, heavy, thick-skinned pachyderm," and judges as "jackals."[71] He constantly hurled charges of corruption. Just like Velasco, Fujimori belittled not only existing political parties but also the concept of parties; they were *palabrería* (all talk and no action).[72] These accusations resonated among Peruvians and paved the way for the 1992 *autogolpe* (self-coup), when Peru's Constitution was suspended, its Congress was dissolved, its media outlets were closed, and a number of journalists and politicians were arrested.

In contrast to radical populists or Velasco, Fujimori did not propose a more participatory regime. He did not use the word "democracy" very much, but when he did the concept was vague.[73] Most frequently, he implied that a democratic government was one that was approved in opinion polls.[74] He justified the *autogolpe* on the basis of popular support for it.[75] Throughout the 1990s, Fujimori and Montesinos assiduously manipulated the media, in particular television, to bolster their approval ratings. Fujimori did not want a political party; vehicles—

70. Conaghan, *Fujimori's Peru*, 251.

71. Ibid., 30, 46.

72. Ibid., 4; Philip Mauceri, "An Authoritarian Presidency: How and Why Did Presidential Power Run Amok in Fujimori's Peru?" in *Fujimori Legacy*, ed. Carrión, 53.

73. See, e.g., the discussion of a "model of 'sui generis democracy'" in *Resumen Semanal*, June 7–13, 1995, 1.

74. Conaghan, *Fujimori's Peru*, 32–36, 251.

75. Ibid., 32–36.

Cambio 90 (Change 90), Nueva Mayoría (New Majority), Perú 2000, and Vamos Vecino (Let's Go, Neighbor)—were created for elections but quickly abandoned thereafter.

In contrast to most Peruvian presidents (and most conspicuously in contrast to García), Fujimori was not a compelling speaker and did not appear to enjoy working a crowd. However, in the context of the failure of García's 1985–90 government, Fujimori was able to turn these deficiencies into an advantage. One of his most frequent statements was "My deeds are my words."[76] He cultivated an image as an honest, efficient, austere technocrat who got things done.[77] His campaign slogans were not about his leadership but about the progress that Peru had achieved: in the 1995 campaign, they were "Peru can't stop" and "Peru has its chance."[78] Fujimori did make many visits to remote communities, and in the highlands he would dress in a poncho and Andean-style hat, but the emphasis was on the inauguration of public works.

Although the Fujimori government eschewed political parties, it did have an institutional base: the intelligence services and the military. During the 1990 presidential campaign, Fujimori was pleased with the help that Montesinos, a former army captain and lawyer for drug-traffickers, provided on a legal problem, and Montesinos became the de facto head of the National Intelligence Service (Servicio de Inteligencia Nacional). Immediately after his election, Fujimori moved to a military residence and signaled his interest in a close relationship with the military.[79] Fujimori, Montesinos, and the head of the joint military command, General Nicolás de Bari Hermoza Ríos, plotted and executed the *autogolpe*; on two occasions in 1992–93 when the government was threatened, Hermoza ordered his troops into the streets. For more than six years, Fujimori, Montesinos, and Hermoza were considered a "governing troika."[80] Rivalries intensified, however, and in 1998 Hermoza was forced into retirement.

76. Maxwell C. Cameron, "Endogenous Regime Breakdown: The Vladivideo and the Fall of Fujimori's Peru," in *Fujimori Legacy*, ed. Carrión, 282.

77. Conaghan, *Fujimori's Peru*, 96.

78. Ibid., 82.

79. Ibid., 25.

80. Ibid., 44; Carlos Iván Degregori, "Peru: The Vanishing of a Regime and the Challenge of Democratic Rebuilding," in *Constructing Democratic Governance in Latin America*, vol. 2, edited by Jorge I. Domínguez and Michael Shifter (Baltimore: Johns Hopkins University Press, 2003), 230–33; Sally Bowen, *The Fujimori File: Peru and its President 1990–2000* (Lima: Peru Monitor, 2000), 51–72.

In the late 1990s, Fujimori decided to pursue a third consecutive term. But Peruvians were skeptical. As Kurt Weyland has emphasized, Fujimori faced "a paradox of success": although Peruvians accepted Fujimori's authoritarianism when it appeared to help resolve Peru's crises, they were warier after the crises had been resolved.[81] Further, Peru's economy was slowing, and one of the various reasons was the Fujimori government's malfeasance; privatization processes were corrupt, economic agencies were politicized, and major negotiations were handled erratically.[82] It seemed very likely that, if Fujimori were to continue in power, the 2000 elections would have to be rigged. In this context, Montesinos's capacity to divert public funds for the campaign, to control electoral and judicial authorities, and to manipulate the media (especially to smear rival candidates) was ever more important.[83] Although Montesinos succeeded in rigging the election and Fujimori was inaugurated for the third consecutive time in July 2000, in September a leaked videotape showed Montesinos bribing an opposition member of Congress. The in-your-face evidence of corruption doomed the Fujimori regime.

Radical Populism and Ollanta Humala

In Peru's 2006 presidential election, Humala won the first round and came within five points of winning the runoff against Alan García. As mentioned at the start of this chapter, during this election Humala represented radical populism in key respects.[84] He is not Caucasian, and he had not held any previous political office; in 2006, he ran as an outsider aggressively confronting Peru's traditional political class. His nationalism and his calls for a larger state role in the economy and greater social inclusion were characteristic of radical populism. He was an ally of Hugo Chávez.[85] However, Humala did not entirely fit the criteria for radical

81. Kurt Weyland, "The Rise and Decline of Fujimori's Neopopulist Leadership," in *Fujimori Legacy*, ed. Carrión, 13–38.
82. Ibid., 27–33. Examples of erratic economic policymaking are provided by McClintock and Vallas, *United States and Peru*, 101–9.
83. Conaghan, *Fujimori's Peru*, 167.
84. See footnote 6 above.
85. Humala himself spoke of the alliance. See "Humala: Gobierno de Hugo Chávez será un aliado estratégico del Perú," *La República*, February 16, 2006. On the relationship, see Cynthia McClintock, "An Unlikely Comeback in Peru," *Journal of Democracy*, October 2006, 104–6.

populism. In particular, his career was in Peru's military, and his ideology appeared militaristic and intolerant; his conceptualization of democracy was inchoate. However, after the 2006 election, he moderated his stance dramatically, and in his winning 2011 campaign he was not a populist.

Like various classical populists, Humala emerged in a context of robust economic growth, but growth that was catalyzed by neoliberal economic policies under the governments of Alejandro Toledo (2001–6) and Alan García (2006–11), based on a commodity boom, and accordingly criticized as "neodualist."[86] Between 2001 and 2010, the value of Peru's trade more than quadrupled.[87] The annual average inflow of foreign direct investment to Peru during the period 2008–10 more than quintupled the annual average during 1998–2001.[88] Largely as a result, from 2002 through 2010 annual GDP growth in Peru averaged about 6.7 percent (vs. roughly 4.1 percent in Latin America overall); in total, over the nine years, real per capita GDP increased by roughly 50 percent.[89] Panama was the only Latin American country with GDP growth superior to Peru's during this period.[90]

However, debate about the benefits from Peru's growth to Peru's poor and middle classes has been intense.[91] On one hand, even as of the 2006 presidential election, numerous indicators were positive. According to official figures, the proportion of the population living in poverty fell about 10 percentage points—from 55 percent in 2001 to 44 percent in

---

86. Martín Tanaka and Sofía Vera Rojas, "La Dinámica 'Neodualista' de una Democracia sin Sistema de Partidos: La Situación de la Democracia en el Perú," *Revista de Ciencia Política* 30 (2010): 87–114.

87. These figures are from Richard Webb and Graciela Fernández Baca, *Perú en Números 2011* (Lima: Cuánto), 901.

88. Economic Commission for Latin America and the Caribbean, *Statistical Yearbook 2005*, cited by Corporación Andina de Fomento X Annual Conference: Trade and Investment in the Americas, "Statistical Appendix," 4, and "Foreign Investment Flows to Latin America and the Caribbean Remain Strong in 2010," *CEPAL News*, May 2011, 3.

89. The figures are from the April 2010 edition of the International Monetary Fund's World Economic Outlook Database, www.imf.org/external/pubs/ft/weo/2010/01/weodata/index.aspx. The percentage change from 2001 to 2010 is calculated from Webb and Fernández Baca, *Perú en Números 2011*, 453.

90. These figures are from the April 2010 edition of the International Monetary Fund's World Economic Outlook Database.

91. See the debate between Richard Webb and Michael Porter, who both earned their Ph.D.s in economics at Harvard University, in *Caretas*, December 10, 2009, 25.

2006.[92] The infant mortality rate, which in 1990 had been about 25 percent higher than in Colombia or Ecuador, was slashed, and as of 2006 was at a rate comparable to those countries', a higher percentage of the relevant age group was enrolled in secondary school in Peru than in Colombia or Ecuador.[93] Peru's Gini index of inequality was at 49.6 in 2006, a slight improvement from 2003 and a better figure than its neighbors'.[94]

But most Peruvians were not feeling the benefits of economic growth in their wallets. In 2006, real salaries for white-collar workers in Lima were no higher than in 2001, and the real minimum wage nationwide increased a scant 4 percent.[95] Nor was economic growth significantly alleviating Peru's long-standing regional inequality, and poverty remained severe in Peru's rural highlands. Between 2001 and 2006, poverty declined more steeply in urban than rural areas; as of 2006, approximately 30 percent of Peru's urban population was classified as "poor" compared with 69 percent of its rural population.[96] In 2006, less than 1 percent of Lima's population was classified as "extremely poor" versus 47 percent of the rural highlands population.[97] As international mining, energy, and logging companies gained large swathes of land in Peru's mountains and jungles, Peruvians in these areas often doubted that they were getting their fair share from the companies' operations. Many nearby communities feared damage to the environment.

Like other radical populists described in chapter 1, Humala subscribed to what scholars call dependency theory: Due to the co-optation and corruption of Latin America's political elites, transnational corporations make exorbitant profits in Latin American countries without suf-

92. Richard Webb and Fernández Baca, *Perú en Números 2008* (Lima: Cuánto), 599; Richard Webb and Fernández Baca, "La pobreza hizo click," *Caretas*, May 21, 2009, 34–36. The methodology for poverty calculation changed in 2001, and accordingly these figures are not comparable with those from earlier periods. For criticisms of these figures, see Richard Webb, "Quizás, Quizás, Quizás," *El Comercio*, June 2, 2008. The poverty line has been set to a low dollar figure.

93. World Bank, *World Development Indicators 2008* (Washington D.C.: World Bank, 2008), 118–19; World Bank, *World Development Indicators 2009* (Washington, D.C.: World Bank, 2009), 84–86.

94. World Bank, *World Development Indicators 2008*, 68–69; World Bank, *World Development Indicators 2009*, 72–3.

95. Webb and Fernández Baca, *Perú en Números 2007*, 629.

96. Ibid., 559.

97. Ibid.

ficient benefits for these countries' majorities. Charged Humala, "Peru's politicians sell the country out [*son unos vendepatrias*]; they have betrayed our country and handed it over to foreign interests."[98] Indeed, when commodity prices had been low, Fujimori had provided favorable terms for transnational corporations, including provisions that the terms would not be changed for long periods of time; so, as prices rose, Peru's revenue often did not.

Accordingly, Humala called for a greater role for the state in Peru's economy. He said that "strategic sectors" (oil, gas, electricity, and water) should be "nationalized"; that large companies should pay more taxes and be subject to windfall profit taxes; that foreign investment should be conditioned upon technology transfer, job creation, and community welfare; that the Peru–United States free trade agreement should be revised; that gas prices should be reduced by 25 percent; that almost $2 billion should be allocated annually for agricultural credit; and that the labor minister should be designated by Peru's major labor confederation.[99] In Humala's words, "We believe that Peru's economic model must be redefined so that the country becomes part of a regional bloc and enters into the process of neoliberal globalization as a country on the path to industrialization and with solid national industries."[100]

Like other radical populists, Humala is not from Peru's white upper class and has highlighted the importance of a Peruvian nation that is inclusive of nonwhite and indigenous peoples and, accordingly, becomes stronger, realizing the promises of its past. "Ollanta" is an Incan name, and the symbol of his party was an Inca-style pot with the colors of the Peruvian flag. At campaign rallies in 2006, Humala played the Peruvian national anthem and, again after the colors of the Peruvian flag, wore a red T-shirt with the words "Amor por el Perú" (Love for Peru) in white.

Humala was raised amid a quasi-fascist ideology called the "Ethnic-Cáceres Movement" (Movimiento Etnocacerista), which exalted the su-

98. "Humala arremtió contra neoliberalismo y clase política," *El Comercio*, December 16, 2005.

99. See "Estado debe administrar petróleo, el gas, los puertos, aeropuertos, etc.," *Expreso*, November 28, 2005; "Humala plantea impuesto a las 'sobreganancias' de las empresas," *Gestión*, January 6, 2006; "Ollanta Humala ofrece a CGTP conducir Ministerio de Trabajo," *El Comercio*, May 5, 2006; "Ollanta Humala lanza lluvia de promesas en mitin partidario," *La República*, May 11, 2006; and "Humala propone control de precios de combustibles," *Gestión*, May 16, 2006.

100. Abelardo Sánchez León and Martín Paredes, "Una Entrevista con Ollanta Humala," *QueHacer*, April–June 2008, 7.

periority of "the copper-skinned race."[101] Its founder was Humala's father, Isaac, who hailed from Ayacucho and spoke Quechua. The movement was named after General Andrés Cáceres, a Quechua-speaking, mestizo general during the War of the Pacific (1879–83). At the outset of the war, as Chile scored naval victories, the civilian president, Mariano Ignacio Prado, left Peru; the Chileans occupied Lima, and Peru's national government fell. Based in Peru's highlands, Cáceres organized and armed peasant groups against the oncoming Chilean army. Cáceres's peasant forces won several battles against the Chileans but also attacked some large landowners (many of whom hoped for an end to the war at any cost and collaborated with the Chileans). Ultimately, Peru made territorial concessions and signed a peace treaty in 1883. In 1886, Cáceres was elected president and was a key political leader for almost a decade. In short, the evocation of Cáceres connotes an interpretation of Peru's history in which the country is betrayed by white, civilian elites but defended by darker-skinned military leaders.

Especially in the early months of the campaign, Humala appeared to share the ideology of the Ethnic-Cáceres Movement. In August 2005, Ollanta presented himself at Peru's National Electoral Commission as the representative of the movement; but in 2006, his brother Ulises was also a presidential candidate and said he was the movement's standard-bearer.[102] During the campaign, Humala's family made incendiary comments that, in the view of most Peruvians, Ollanta did not repudiate. His mother spoke of shooting homosexuals, and his brother Antauro called for executing not only Toledo but also his wife.[103] In general, Humala appeared close to his family.

Although the implication of the ideology of the Ethnic-Cáceres movement was that the Humala family's circumstances were relatively humble—and indeed, in early 2006 almost half (47 percent) of Peruvians believed that Ollanta's social class was "low"—in fact this was not the case.[104] Despite Isaac's ideology, he was a well-educated lawyer.[105] Ollanta was

101. On the ideology, see Jorge Serrano Torres, "Los hermanos Humala y el etnocacerismo en el Perú," www.redvoltaire.net, uploaded February 21, 2005; and Carlos Basombrío, "The Elections in Peru," *Noticias* (Woodrow Wilson International Center for Scholars), Fall 2006, 24–25.

102. "El doble juego de Ollanta Humala," *La República*, November 6, 2005.

103. "Sanchochado Humalista," *Caretas*, March 23, 2006, 15.

104. *La República*, January 15, 2006. The poll was in January 2006.

105. Serrano Torres, "Los hermanos Humala," 5.

born in Lima and raised in a prosperous area of the capital; he studied at private schools and at the Sorbonne in Paris.[106] In 1995, when Ollanta was merely an army captain, he bought an apartment in one of Lima's wealthiest areas.[107] Ollanta's wife, Nadine, is from Ayacucho but looks Caucasian and completed her undergraduate studies at an expensive private university in Lima.[108]

Despite the reality of Humala's upper-middle-class Lima upbringing, the image of humble origins remained and his support was concentrated among poor, indigenous peoples. In a February 2006 poll, Humala enjoyed the support of 32 percent of Peru's poorest stratum but only 6 percent of its wealthiest stratum.[109] In the 2006 runoff, Humala won fifteen of Peru's seventeen departments in the interior but lost all eight departments on its more prosperous coast. Humala won by landslides in the poorest, most indigenous departments of the Southern Highlands: a stunning 83 percent of the vote in Ayacucho, and 70 percent or more in Huancavelica, Apurímac, Cusco, and Puno.[110] By contrast, he got only 38 percent of the vote in Lima.[111] The correlation between ethnicity and the vote for Humala was stronger than for any other political candidate since the calculation was first made in 1980.[112]

Like Chávez but unlike other radical populists, Humala was militaristic. Both Chávez and Humala had been lieutenant colonels and both were often called "*comandante*" (commander). Humala's identity was closely tied to the military institution; he emphasized, "I am proud that I commanded troops to defend Peru."[113] As mentioned above, Humala's family's Ethnic-Cáceres Movement was named after a Peruvian general who led the resistance against Chile during the War of the Pacific. In the movement's ideology, the army is the backbone of the state; after two sons have been born to a family, the third is to be incorporated into the military.

Humala promised a strong military and took confrontational postures toward Peru's neighbors. He said that he "would do everything

106. Ángel Páez and María Hidalgo, "Caudillo a la francesa," *La República*, December 4, 2005.

107. Ibid.

108. "¿Auténtico o imposter?" *El Comercio,* January 21, 2006.

109. *El Comercio*, February 12, 2006.

110. These figures are from Oficina Nacional de Procesos Electorales, www.onpe .hob.pe.

111. Ibid.

112. Tanaka and Vera Rojas, "Dinámica 'Neodualista,'" 108.

113. "Sanchochado Humalista," *Caretas*, March 23, 2006, 19, among other sources.

necessary to rebuild the armed forces," including the establishment of military industries.[114] Whereas since the late 1980s the commander of the armed forces has been appointed by the president, Humala said that this appointment should be made by the military institution.[115] Humala deplored key peace agreements between Peru and its neighbors: "In a secret treaty we gave Leticia away to the Colombians [in an agreement in the mid-1930s]; and in 1998, the Congress gave away Tiwinza [to Ecuador]."[116] Humala was particularly hostile toward Chile; he suggested an alliance with Bolivia to regain territories that the two countries had lost to Chile in the War of the Pacific: "We contemplate a Tahuantinsuyo Motherland, which will comprise Peru, Bolivia, Ecuador, the north of Chile, and the Argentine northwest."[117] Humala called for the suspension of the sale of natural gas to Chile, restrictions against Chilean investment in Peru's ports and agriculture, and an end to the monopoly of the Chilean airline Lan in Peru.[118]

As chapter 1 has stipulated, an important component of radical populism is an emphasis on direct democracy, in which "the people" are sovereign through such measures as plebiscites. However, Humala's beliefs about democracy were very unclear. He was an outsider, opposing the traditional political class—but in Peru that was the case also for Velasco and Fujimori. Indeed, Humala praised key dimensions of the Velasco government and, like Fujimori, used the term "*partidocracia*" (dictatorship of the political parties).[119] Humala called for a "democracy of the national majority" and "a new, more participatory, more representative political system"—but he did not elaborate.[120] He promised

114. "Ollanta: Debe existir revocatoria presidencial," *Gestión*, March 20, 2006.

115. Ibid.

116. "Humala manda 'al diablo' a los empresarios que pidan favores," *La República*, January 8, 2006; "Ollanta: Debe existir revocatoria presidencial," *Gestión*, March 20, 2006.

117. Carlos Monge, "Ollanta Humala, apoyado por su hermano Antauro, no oculta sus ambiciosos planes políticos," May 23, 2003, available at www.libreopinion.com. Also cited by Michael Radu, "Andean Storm Troopers," Foreign Policy Research Institute, May 4, 2005, available at www.fpri.org.

118. "Humala plantea eliminar la immunidad presidencial," *La República*, December 31, 2005; "Humala amenaza con rescindir contratos a empresas chilenas," *Gestión*, March 2, 2006.

119. "Confío en ganar con los votos de las organizaciones sociales," *La República*, May 7, 2006; "Vivimos en la campaña del miedo," *La República*, March 22, 2006.

120. Sánchez León and Paredes, "Entrevista a Ollanta Humala."

a new Constitution, largely replacing the 1993 Constitution established under Fujimori with the previous 1979 Constitution, and a "Second Republic"; but again specifics were scant.[121] It appeared that, without much thought, Humala was taking a page from the radical populists' playbook.

Humala's past actions provoked grave doubts about his commitment to democracy. In the early 1990s, during the Shining Path insurgency, when Humala commanded a military base in the Upper Huallaga Valley (a major coca-producing area), he was accused of serious human rights violations.[122] (He was subsequently exonerated.) He burst into Peru's political arena on October 29, 2000; at his military base in the Department of Tacna, Humala led what he said was a coup attempt against the Fujimori government. However, Humala's account was doubted; some journalists charged that the failed coup attempt had been a smokescreen to distract attention from Montesinos's escape from Peru, which had occurred the same day.[123] Further, in 2005 Humala's brother Antauro tried to overthrow the Toledo government. On New Year's Day, leading approximately 150 army reservists, Antauro seized the police headquarters in Andahuaylas and demanded Toledo's resignation. Amid the failed uprising, four police officers and two rebels were killed; Antauro was arrested. At the time Ollanta was a military attaché in South Korea and reportedly commented: "The *etnocaceristas* are people who are carrying out a daring action by asking for the resignation of a president who has lost legitimacy."[124]

Humala appeared to have little interest in political parties. He registered his party, the Peruvian Nationalist Party (Partido Nacionalista Peruano, PNP), only in November 2005—too late to meet the legal requirements for registration for the elections. To compete, Humala identified a registered party that would make him its presidential candidate: the Union for Peru (Unión por el Perú), which had been founded by former United Nations secretary-general Javier Pérez de

121. "Humala quiere nueva Carta Magna y 'Segunda República,'" *El Comercio*, December 14, 2005; "Humala reafirma su discurso en el Cusco y en Madre de Dios," *Perú 21*, April 6, 2006.

122. "Auténtico o imposter?" *El Comercio*.

123. Ibid.; Páez and Hidalgo, "Caudillo a la francesa," 27.

124. Alex Sánchez, "COHA's Report on Peru's Upcoming Presidential Elections," Council on Hemispheric Affairs, January 4, 2006, 3, available at www.coha .org/New_Press_Releases.

Cuéllar in the mid 1990s but had subsequently drifted. After Humala lost the presidency, the PNP and the Unión por el Perú split apart almost immediately.

Humala regularly signaled that he was not afraid to break the rules of the democratic game. Before the first round of the elections, he repeated frequently that if Lourdes Flores won, it would be by fraud, and he would destabilize her government. For a presidential debate, he arrived more than fifteen minutes late; he then placed a Peruvian flag on his podium and would not remove it at the request of the moderator (who finally removed it himself).

Given the nature of the Ethnic-Cáceres Movement, Humala's militarism, and the plethora of questions about his past, Peru's traditional political left was warier of Humala than the left in other Andean countries was of their radical populists; Humala was feared to be not a leftist but a rightist or even a fascist.[125] Indeed, he rejected the label "leftist," preferring the label "nationalist."[126] For example, top investigative journalist Gustavo Gorriti feared that Humala was "an enemy of democracy" under whom democracy would be "destroyed."[127]

However, after 2006, Humala underwent a stunning metamorphosis. Observed Steven Levitsky, for example: "[Humala] refrain[ed] from waging an antisystem campaign in 2011."[128] The transformation—and the questions it raised—was captured on the cover of a March 2011 issue of Peru's weekly newsmagazine *Caretas*.[129] On the cover, half of the image was Humala as a presidential candidate in 2006: wearing a red polo shirt, grimacing, and raising his arm in a threatening manner. The other half of the image was Humala as a presidential candidate in 2011: wearing a suit and tie, smiling, and holding a rosary in his relaxed hand. "Which is he?" (Cuál es?) was the question on the cover.

125. See, e.g., Gustavo Gorriti, cited in *Resumen Semanal*, March 15–21, 2006, 20. The point is also made by Kenneth Roberts, Leslie Bethell, and René Antonio Mayorga, "Conceptual and Historical Perspectives," in *The 'New Left' and Democratic Governance in Latin America*, edited by Cynthia J. Arnson with José Raúl Perales (Washington, D.C.: Latin American Program, Woodrow Wilson International Center for Scholars, 2007), 11.

126. "El fraude electoral ya empezó," *La República*, March 29, 2009.

127. Gustavo Gorriti, cited in *Resumen Semanal*, March 8–14, 2006, 18, 20.

128. Steven Levitsky, "Peru's 2011 Elections: A Surprising Left Turn," *Journal of Democracy* 22 (2011): 91. A similar analysis is made by Martín Tanaka, "Peru's 2011 Elections: A Vote for Moderate Change," *Journal of Democracy* 22 (2011): 81.

129. *Caretas*, March 24, 2010, cover.

Humala's metamorphosis began soon after the 2006 elections. Despite his threats during the campaign, he accepted his defeat and did not try to destabilize García's government. Rather, he simply pointed out the numerous campaign promises that García had made but was not keeping. He kept his distance from Chávez and emphasized, by contrast, his admiration for Brazil's former president, Luiz Inácio Lula da Silva ("Lula"); among his closest advisers were Brazilians who had worked on Lula's campaigns, and this fact was frequently mentioned in the media. He also kept his distance from his parents and brothers, and by contrast appeared frequently with his attractive wife and their children. (Of the five major candidates, Humala was the only one with a Peruvian spouse.) Concomitantly, he gained the support of various groups on Peru's traditional left. In 2010, he traveled for the first time to the United States; he had a cordial meeting with the U.S. assistant secretary of state for Western Hemisphere affairs, Arturo Valenzuela, and struck a moderate tone in his presentations to Washington audiences.

Humala's shift in part reflected Peru's very robust economic growth and the extension of the benefits of growth to larger numbers of Peruvians. Although between 2001 and 2005 real economic growth had been good, at about 4.2 percent annually, between 2006 and 2010 it was even better, at approximately 7.2 percent annually.[130] Between 2006 and 2010, Peru's poverty rate fell from 44.5 to 31.3 percent; this reduction was the best in the region.[131] In 2010, unemployment was estimated at less than 7 percent.[132] Various economists reported dramatic improvements in living conditions in Peru's countryside. On the basis of intensive research in a swathe of Peru's rural sector, in April 2011 Richard Webb calculated that "five years ago, less than half of rural households had electricity; now it is almost 80 percent. More than half of Peru's farmers now have a cell phone. The network of rural roads has . . . increased 63 percent over 10 years and the roads are substantially better, too. The average budget of Peru's rural family has improved 28 percent in five years."[133]

Still, discontent endured. Many—even most—Peruvians continued to report that they had not benefited from the country's growth.[134] In 2010,

130. Webb and Fernández Baca, *Perú en Números 2011*, 453.
131. Tanaka, "Peru's 2011 Elections," 79.
132. Economist Intelligence Unit, "Peru: Country Report," October 2010, 33.
133. Richard Webb, "Orden y justicia," *El Comercio*, April 11, 2011.
134. ConsultAndes, "Monthly Political Analysis," June 2009, 7.

white-collar workers' salaries in Lima remained stagnant, and the real minimum wage nationwide was still less than 4 percent higher than in 2006.[135] Peru's minimum wage, at about $190 month in 2009, was reported to be among the lowest in Latin America.[136] Conflict between indigenous communities and extractive companies was also escalating. In particular, in June 2009 in the northern jungle town of Bagua, indigenous groups blocked roads and waterways for fifty-five days to protest government decrees that they feared would facilitate the takeover of their lands. The police were sent to retake the area by force. In the ensuing clash, twenty-four police officers and at least ten protesters were killed; the indigenous association put the toll at more than forty protesters.[137] For most Peruvians, the violent conflict signaled a need for improved dialogue between the government, rural communities, and extractive companies.

In 2011, Humala was ready for the campaign and was willing to acknowledge the importance of economic growth. His new electoral vehicle, the Win Peru Alliance (Alianza Gana Perú), was duly registered; its new symbol was simply an "O," for both the candidate's name and "opportunity." As the campaign got under way, Humala emphasized his commitment to combating poverty and inequality, but did not impugn elites. For example, in the debate among Peru's presidential candidates before the first round of the elections, Humala's first reference was to Peru's renowned historian Jorge Basadre, who had called Peru both "sweet" and "cruel." Humala said that Peru is "sweet" because of the enormous capacity and potential of its people, but "cruel" because their work is not sufficiently rewarded. But blame was assigned only obliquely. "Recent governments did little against poverty and inequality; development has to reach everyone," concluded Humala.[138]

Given Humala's 2006 presidential campaign, he was no longer an unknown "outsider." Still, he was clearly not the candidate of Peru's political establishment, and he often pointed out that the other major presidential candidates—former president Alejandro Toledo; the former premier and economics minister, Pedro Pablo Kuczynski; former Lima

135. Webb and Fernández Baca, *Perú en Números 2011*, 381–82.
136. ConsultAndes, "Peru Key Indicators," January 18, 2010, 7.
137. "Commission to Probe Amazon Violence," *Latin American Andean Group Report*, September 2009, 11.
138. The first presidential debate was broadcast on Peru's news program *Cuarto Poder*, March 13, 2011.

mayor Luis Castañeda Lossio; and Fujimori's daughter, Keiko—had all been in positions of power previously and had not achieved significant change. This message resonated with voters; the number one reason given by his supporters for their intention to vote for him was that "he represents a change."[139] Also, his key slogan during the first round of the elections was "Honesty is the difference," and he was widely perceived as the candidate with the best plans to combat corruption, delinquency, and drug-trafficking.[140]

For the runoff against Keiko Fujimori, Humala moderated his positions yet further. Explicitly repudiating his positions during the 2006 campaign and also his party's 2010 platform, he reiterated that he would not upend the economic policies that had facilitated Peru's growth.[141] His key slogan became "Economic growth with social inclusion." Like most victorious Peruvian presidential candidates, first and foremost were his promises: dialogue for the amelioration of social conflict; a significant increase in the minimum wage; a reduction in the price of cooking gas; an expansion of Peru's conditional cash transfer program; day care for preschool children; university scholarships for deserving students; pensions for needy seniors; a restriction in gas exports so that Peru's supply would be sufficient; and, of course, the frontal combat of corruption and delinquency.[142] Humala did continue to endorse a windfall profit tax and said that his new programs would be paid for through this tax. Further, Humala was emphatic that he was committed to liberal democracy. He swore an "Oath for Democracy," promising to respect the Constitution, the separation of powers, human rights, freedom of speech, and term limits. With these economic and political shifts, Humala was able to gain the support of key establishment leaders, including Mario Vargas Llosa and Alejandro Toledo.

At the same time, not surprisingly, Humala's shifts raised questions about his true principles. In one of the most frequently repeated comments before the runoff, it was said that "there were doubts" about Humala—but that "there was proof" that Keiko would follow in the foot-

139. "Voto rural determina el primer lugar de Toledo," *El Comercio*, January 16, 2011.

140. "Aprobación del presidente García baja cuatro puntos," *El Comercio*, February 27, 2011.

141. E.g., see his interview on CNN en Español, June 3, 2011.

142. "Ollanta asegura que luchará contra la corrupción," *El Comercio*, June 3, 2011.

steps of her father. Still, it was clear that in 2011 Humala had not run as a populist; nor in his first eighteen months did he govern as a populist, and it appears very unlikely that he will revert to populism.

Conclusion

From Haya in the 1930s through the 1960s to Velasco in the late 1960s and early 1970s, Fujimori in the 1990s, and Humala in 2006, populism in Peru has been constant. The forms, however, have varied—including classical, neoliberal, and radical populism. Yet the fit between Peru's populists and the various populist forms has not been exact. In particular, for three of the four Peruvian populists, the military was an important component of the populist movement. Velasco was a general presiding over a military government, Fujimori's government was based in part on the military, and Humala was a lieutenant colonel whose original support base was the military. Although the Peruvian experience is unusual, other prominent populists, including Juan Perón and Hugo Chávez, had military careers, and comparative analysis of military populism could be fruitful.

The persistence of populism in Peru is not surprising. First, due in part to Peru's geography and colonial history, socioeconomic divides have been very deep. Second, to date liberal democracy has been widely perceived as insufficiently successful in bridging these divides. Although the failures of Peru's 1980–90 liberal-democratic governments are the best-known, there is a long history of elected governments that were perceived to be insufficiently committed to social reform.[143] As a result, popular frustrations and resentments were galvanized by populist leaders. In a vicious cycle, liberal-democratic institutions were weakened by populism; when liberal-democratic institutions were reattempted, they were less likely to achieve growth with equity and more vulnerable to populist challenges.

However, it now appears likely that liberal democracy will be sustained from 2001 at least through the next presidential election in 2016, and that its substantive record has been, albeit far from perfect, much better than in the past. The vicious cycle may finally have been broken.

143. Among these were the 1895–1914 "Aristocratic Republic," the 1939–45 and 1956–62 governments of Manuel Prado, and the 1963–68 government of Fernando Belaúnde.

Chapter 9

Populism, Rentierism, and Socialism in the Twenty-First Century: The Case of Venezuela

Margarita López Maya
and Alexandra Panzarelli

The electoral victory of Hugo Chávez Frías and his Bolivarian forces in December 1998 was a turning point in the Venezuelan sociopolitical process. Venezuelan society had been mired in an unresolved and deep crisis that had already lasted two decades, and thus it had seen many of the modernizing achievements of the twentieth century fall by the wayside. The dominant political parties, once populist in orientation, had ended up embracing neoliberal discourse and policies. President Rafael Caldera had promised to reverse this course when he took office for the second time in 1993, and he had also promised to reform the Constitution. Neither of those promises was kept, however, creating the material and emotional conditions for voters to take a stand in favor of a radical change in leaders and approach. Chávez and his movement triumphed at the ballot box, expressing politically what seemed at the time to be the aspirations of the majority: to build a participatory democracy, eschew neoliberal policies, and remove corrupt and out-of-touch political parties from power. More than a dozen years later, the *presidente coman-*

dante had turned his initial political platform into something he called twenty-first-century socialism, an undertaking marked by increasingly authoritarian tendencies. After sixteen elections—all of which he won—Chávez remained firmly rooted in power, becoming one of the most emblematic figures of Latin American populism. In 2011 and 2012, Chávez's diagnosis of and treatment for cancer infused the country's political life with great uncertainty. Amid his deteriorating physical health, presidential elections scheduled for December 2012 were moved up to October and opened as never before the question of eventual succession.

This chapter explores some of the aspects of *chavismo* that allow it to be characterized as a populist phenomenon. We view populism as a universal form of politics that promotes social inclusion and is characterized by a divisive discourse with a strong capacity to mobilize people. This discourse sets up two groups as irreconcilable and antagonistic forces: *the people*—the poor and/or powerless—versus *the oligarchy*, the power bloc.[1] We recognize populism as a form of direct democracy that privileges the connection between the leader and his base and rejects more mediated forms of democracy. Although it is essentially democratic, it tends to have little use for institutions of representation, instead prioritizing mobilization behind the leader as the political instrument par excellence, a characteristic that can eventually produce profound deficits of democracy.[2]

This chapter has four sections. The first emphasizes characteristics of the Venezuelan sociohistorical process that set the stage for the *moment of populist rupture* in 1998. The second looks at the concepts and images of *chavista* discourse that antagonize the adversary and recreate *el pueblo* (the people) as a political actor with a transcendent mission, the seductive idea that seals the connection between the leader and his base. In the third section, we explore the primary channels of communication between Chávez and his *pueblo*; and in the fourth, we review data on the social composition of the *chavista* base and the *chavista* elite. The final reflections attempt to assess the likelihood that this political phenomenon will continue.

1. Carlos de la Torre, *Populist Seduction in Latin America* (Athens: Ohio University Press, 2000), 13.

2. Enrique Peruzzotti, "Populismo y representación democrática," in *El retorno del pueblo: Populismo y nuevas democracias en Latinoamérica*, edited by Carlos de la Torre and Enrique Peruzzotti (Quito: FLACSO, 2009), 97–123.

Conditions That Motivated the Populist Rupture

The Chávez victory in 1998 was evidence of a resurgence of populism in Venezuela, a deeply rooted tradition that included radical versions in the twentieth century—like that of the *trienio adeco*, the three-year period of rule by the Acción Democrática (AD; Democratic Action) party, between 1945 and 1948—as well as more moderate versions that emerged in the post-1958 period of democracy, such as the first presidency of Carlos Andrés Pérez (1974–79).[3]

The oil economy has certainly contributed to the persistence of populist politics in Venezuela, though the oil issue must be considered along with other, deeper historical factors. In the nineteenth-century oligarchic republic, the charismatic caudillo (strongman) played a central role in controlling the social order after independence from Spain.[4] The petro-state of the twentieth century is distinguished by its significant fiscal income from the world market rather than from taxes paid by internal economic actors. This enables those who gain access to the state to gain significant power to act arbitrarily or without deference or accountability to the demands and pressures of civil society. The petro-state is also characterized by an exaggerated political rationality that predominates over economic and other rationales, making it highly susceptible to administrative inefficiency and corruption.[5]

In Venezuela, the oil industry has also engendered a very particular and strong form of nationalism, both among military, political, and bureaucratic elites and among the general population. This nationalism is based on the idea that all Venezuelans are owners of this national resource and that the role of the state, as the nation's representative, is to administer and defend it, both from external interests that seek to take control of the resource and from internal interests that may want to ap-

---

3. Steve Ellner, "El apogeo del populismo radical en Venezuela y sus consecuencias," *Revista Venezolana de Economía y Ciencias Sociales* 1 (January–March 1997): 77–100; Luís Gómez Calcaño and Nelly Arenas, *Populismo autoritario: Venezuela 1999–2005* (Caracas: CDCH-Cendes, 2006).

4. John Lombardi, *Venezuela: The Search for Order, The Dream of Progress* (New York: Oxford University Press, 1982), 227.

5. Terry Lynn Karl, "The Venezuelan Petro-State and the Crisis of Its 'Democracy,'" in *Venezuelan Democracy under Stress*, edited by Jennifer McCoy, Andrés Serbín, William C. Smith, and Andrés Stambouli (New Brunswick, N.J.: Transaction Books, 1994), 43–48.

propriate it for private benefit.[6] Those who gain power in Venezuela tend to legitimize themselves by employing a nationalist discourse featuring themes of equality and social justice as well as a certain level of mistrust of foreign corporations and powers. In the political culture of the twentieth century, the nation-state held the task of promoting modernity and progress, in the name of the people, through the administration of oil income.[7]

The Economic Crisis and the Arrival of the Neoliberal Paradigm

Venezuela's various democratic governments after 1958 constructed an official discourse in which democracy meant civil and political rights but also implied an economic model that would include everyone in the benefits of development.[8] Equally important is the fact that democracy in Venezuela was built upon the distribution of oil income by the state to the various social sectors, actors, and power groups in society, allowing a political game that was not zero-sum; in other words, no one lost except the national treasury. The arrangement led to the consolidation of one of the most stable democracies in Latin America for more than twenty years. However, after the oil bonanza years during Carlos Andrés Pérez's first administration (1974–79)—when this rentierist pattern was intensified—the economy experienced a downturn in the 1980s and, in response, governments adopted neoliberal practices, alternately applying heterodox and orthodox adjustment programs according to the dictates of the International Monetary Fund. These measures led to increased poverty and misery and also to greater inequality in the distribution of resources. At that point, a prolonged questioning began of the state, of political parties, and of the historic political agreements that had been the underpinnings of the democratic regime, the most emblematic of which was the Punto Fijo Pact of 1958. "Black Friday," in February

6. Fernando Coronil, *El Estado mágico: Naturaleza, dinero y modernidad en Venezuela* (Caracas: Nueva Sociedad, 2002), 410.
7. Fernando Coronil and Julie Skurski, "Dismembering and Remembering the Nation: The Semantics of Political Violence in Venezuela," *Comparative Studies in Society and History* 33, no. 2 (April 1991): 288–335.
8. Brian F. Crisp, Daniel H. Levine, and Juan C. Rey, "The Legitimacy Problem," in *Venezuelan Democracy*, ed. McCoy et al.

1983, the day when the economy's severe imbalances forced the Luis Herrera Campins government (1979–84) to close down the currency exchange and devalue the bolívar, was a first symbolic awakening for Venezuelans to the crisis in the oil economy. Responsibility for this crisis was attributed primarily to the two dominant parties of the political system: AD (Acción Democrática) and the Comité de Organización Política Electoral Independiente (COPEI; Social Christian Party).

The economic crisis continued, as did neoliberal policies (e.g., removing price controls and reducing current account spending), which meant that the non-zero-sum game in the relationships between political actors and power groups was no longer viable. This produced a growing sense of discontent, a rejection of the policies, and social protests. Society was splitting into two social poles as the rich became richer and the poor became poorer. The middle classes shrank as more and more of their members joined the ranks of the poor. The elites were increasingly questioned and political parties were rejected. Reports of corruption multiplied. The political parties, unions, and guilds of the two-party system stopped functioning as efficient channels for mediation and distribution of favors when the clientelistic networks fell apart as a result of the reduction in fiscal spending.[9] The weakening of all these representative institutions prompted increasingly combative, sometimes violent, popular protests led by public employees who had become independent from political parties, as well as by students, the unemployed, retirees, and members of the informal sector. According to the nongovernmental Program of Education/Action for Human Rights (known as PROVEA), in the nine years from October 1989 to September 1998 there was an average of 720 protests a year—about two a day. By 1998, when Chávez won the presidential elections, levels of poverty and extreme poverty were almost triple what they had been in 1983. Although the income of the richest 5 percent of Venezuelans was 41.59 times greater than that of the poorest 5 percent in 1979, by 1997 the top 5 percent was earning 53.11 times as much. These figures make it easy to imagine the discontent and resentment that began to poison the atmosphere, eventually leading to a rupture in the prevailing political order.

9. Kenneth Roberts, "La descomposición del sistema de partidos en Venezuela vista desde un análisis comparativo," *Revista Venezolana de Economía y Ciencias Sociales* 7, no. 2 (2001): 183–200.

"El Caracazo": The Poor and the Middle Class Abandon the Two-Party System

The still-unresolved economic crisis led to a decomposition of the social structure, which, as mentioned above, led to increasing confrontations between society and the state.[10] Many actors, lacking institutional channels for mediation, opted to play out the conflict through street protests.[11] On February 27, 1989, the second emblematic moment of collective awareness of the deepening crisis took place. This popular uprising, known as the "Caracazo," broke out in almost all the largest cities of the country and lasted for an entire week in the capital. Many cities were paralyzed by the multitudes who blocked roads and looted thousands of commercial establishments. The Caracazo subsided only after a belated attempt on the part of the Carlos Andrés Pérez government to control the situation. In an improvised and irresponsible action, the army violently repressed the poor and unarmed population, leaving hundreds dead.

The Caracazo was an unprecedented experience for Venezuelan democracy and drove a permanent wedge between the poor and President Carlos Andrés Pérez, the charismatic leader from the ranks of the AD, who in his first administration (1974–79) had presided over an extraordinary increase in oil prices and launched a political project that he called "The Great Venezuela." El Caracazo occurred sixteen days after the inauguration of his second term, when the government announced it would undertake a shock-style orthodox neoliberal economic adjustment program. The announcement left the poor and working classes feeling betrayed by the president, whose election promises and insinuations had generated expectations of a return to the golden years. It is highly symbolic that collective transportation fares were going up on the very Monday that the Caracazo began. The price hike was the result of rising gas prices, which, according to the new official discourse, had to be paid by the riders at prices that were closer to those of the international market. Oil had stopped being a resource that belonged to everyone.

10. Supporting documents and bibliography for this section can be reviewed in Margarita López Maya, *Del viernes negro al referendo revocatorio* (Caracas: Editorial Alfa, 2005), chaps. 2 and 3.

11. Margarita López Maya, "Movilización, institucionalidad y legitimidad en Venezuela," *Revista Venezolana de Economía y Ciencias Sociales* (2003): 211–27.

Pérez was never able to recover his popularity after ordering the repression of the protests, and neither his government nor democracy itself was able to regain legitimacy. One result of the Caracazo was a coup attempt three years later, when a group of army men, led by mid-level officers including Hugo Chávez, attempted to overthrow the president. Although the coup failed, it plunged the government into a political crisis from which it never recovered. In May 1993, Pérez was removed from office by the National Congress after the Supreme Court ruled that he could be tried for misappropriating funds from the presidential discretionary fund, or *partida secreta*.

The Political Crisis and the
Second Caldera Government

After Pérez's departure, Congress designated historian Ramón J. Velásquez as interim president and charged him with the difficult task of organizing elections in December 1993 in the midst of profound democratic instability.[12] During the election campaign, two candidates emerged from among the favorites, and both were nominated by groups outside the Venezuelan two-party system: former president Rafael Caldera; and a union leader, Andrés Velásquez. The latter was a candidate of La Causa Radical, a small leftist party with an anti-institutional image that had become attractive to the disenchanted electorate. The election results were close, and questions were raised about their integrity, but in the end the AD and COPEI lost for the first time since 1958. Caldera, the founder of COPEI and one of the main actors in forging the foundational agreements of Venezuelan democracy, won the election—but without the support of his party. At the time, Caldera represented a middle way between the radical break symbolized by La Causa Radical and the traditional response, represented by the candidates of AD and COPEI. One factor that worked in Caldera's favor was his social justice discourse, in which he promised to create an economic alternative to neoliberalism. He also promised to reform the Constitution in order to incorporate demands for decentralization, direct forms of democracy, and the personalization

12. Further references are given by López Maya, *Del viernes negro al referendo revocatorio*, chap. 11.

of the vote—aspirations that had been discussed in Venezuelan political and civil society since the 1980s.[13]

Caldera did not keep his promises. Although he initially appeared to have ended the political crisis and calmed the anxieties of the military, his government found itself sunk in a profound banking and financial crisis and responded by making alliances with the AD in Congress and pushing a second neoliberal package of structural adjustments. This alliance kept the constitutional reform from being passed, because the AD had always been the main obstacle to changing power relations in the country.

Public institutions continued their decline during the Caldera administration, as was visible in the growing inefficiency of government agencies and public services. Like Pérez, Caldera continued to develop targeted social policies with a neoliberal bent. He also furthered Pérez's neoliberal oil policy, which had ceded oil control to the high-level management of Petróleos de Venezuela (PDVSA). PDVSA then began a policy of internationalizing the company, which decreased its contributions to the public coffers and aggravated the fiscal deficit during those years. The so-called policy of Apertura Petrolera (Oil Opening) also increased the volume of production, to the detriment of the price per barrel on the international market. This policy ran contrary to those of the Organization of the Petroleum Exporting Countries, of which Venezuela was a founding member.[14] Contrary to the nationalist discourse of the democratic regime, the trend was toward a gradual reprivatization of the oil business. When the bottom fell out of oil prices on the world market in 1998—dragging down the Venezuelan economy once again and sparking another increase in poverty, inequality, and unemployment—the poor and the middle classes decided they were ready to turn to an outsider.

A survey published in 1995 by Latinobarómetro provides some clues as to what Venezuelans were seeking. Although 60 percent of those surveyed believed that democracy was the best system of government, they expressed little or no confidence in the legal system (70 percent), in Congress (78 percent), or in political parties (84 percent). Only one-fifth of the urban population believed that the election results had been clean,

13. Luis Gómez Calcaño and Margarita López Maya, *El tejido de Penélope: La reforma del Estado en Venezuela* (Caracas: CENDES-APUCV-IPP, 1990).

14. The purpose of the policy was to increase the involvement of the private sector, both national and international, in the operation, exploration, and refinement of petroleum and natural gas.

and almost half said that there was little difference between the candidates. When asked whether an "iron-handed" government would be good or bad for the country, 78 percent of Venezuelans responded that it could be good.[15]

The Populist Seduction: The Traits, Origins, and Symbolic References of Chávez

Since the failed coup attempt jump-started Chávez's political career in 1992, many factors have converged to give him an irresistible aura for the majority of the poor and recently impoverished.[16] His physical appearance and family origin are one factor: "A tall man, with a strong but not thick build, he is of the type of Venezuelan that hasn't received any new racial mixtures in the last 100 years. Curly black hair, Asian eyes, thick lips, a Grecian nose."[17] Chávez was born in a small town in the state of Barinas, far away from the parts of the country that were the most dynamic during the process of modernization. Barinas is located in the western high plains area, which allowed Chávez to benefit from the popular culture image of the *llanero:* a heroic character from the plains, indomitable but also undisciplined and irreverent, whose origin goes back to the independence period.

Chávez constructed a political discourse in which symbols and images —created from reinterpreted historical, military, religious, and cultural references—play a role of utmost importance. Every political event staged by Chávez or his party employs national symbols in an attempt to develop and strengthen his position. In the early stages of his first political movement—the Bolivarian Revolutionary Movement 200 (Movimiento Bolivariano Revolucionario 200; MBR 200)—his ideology was represented by the image of "the tree with three roots," with one root signifying the thinking of, respectively, Simón Bolívar, Simón Rodríguez, and Ezequiel Zamora. Rodríguez was Bolívar's teacher, and Zamora was a caudillo in the "Federal War," to which Chávez and the other movement

15. Friedrich Welsh, "The Political Impact of Public Opinion Studies in Venezuela," paper presented at twenty-first meeting of Latin American Studies Association, Washington, 1995.

16. This section updates a previous analysis by López Maya, *Del viernes negro al referendo revocatorio*, chap. 10.

17. Angela Zago, *La rebelión de los ángeles* (Caracas: Fuentes Editores, 1992), 14.

founders have attributed a profoundly democratic conviction for so-cial causes.[18] The reference to Bolívar, the most transcendent symbol of Venezuelan nationality, was made even stronger by incorporating into the name of MBR 200 not only the word "Bolivariano" but also the number "200," to represent the 200 years since the Liberator's birth. The first grassroots organizations were called Bolivarian circles, and in 1999 the name of the country itself was changed to the Bolivarian Republic of Venezuela. Nationalism is the first and the strongest element at the core of *chavista* symbology; however, because of the turn toward a socialist model, it was subsequently complemented with growing references to symbols and ideas that are important to the Latin American political left. Examples include constant anti-imperialist rhetoric against the United States and the highlighting of emblematic figures of the left, such as Che Guevara, Fidel Castro, and Salvador Allende.

Political polarization is a key ingredient. The aggressive tone that char-acterized many of Chávez's speeches was not common in the presidential discourse during the country's recent history. From the time of his first election campaign, Chávez was confrontational, using direct, aggressive, often insulting, and even lewd language against political parties, people, traditional power groups, and institutions. He was especially aggressive against the former political elite, tossing threats and insults that ranged from offering to "fry their heads" to calling them imbeciles, *escuálidos* (squalid ones), traitors, or *pitiyanquis* (little Yankees).[19] For a time, he called the owners of the largest private communications media in the country the "four horsemen of the Apocalypse."[20] He referred to one journalist, who had written what he considered an objectionable essay on his 2007 defeat in the referendum on constitutional reform, a *periodista de mierda*—roughly the equivalent of "a shitty journalist." Chávez also butted heads with the hierarchy of the Catholic Church on several occa-sions, saying at one point that some bishops were possessed by the devil. His confrontations with national and international journalists and intel-lectuals were ongoing and protracted. He called the historian and National

18. Ibid.

19. This term comes from a marriage of the French word *petit* (little) with *yanqui*, a pejorative term for someone who imitates and supports Americans.

20. "Discurso del Presidente de la República Bolivariana de Venezuela con mo-tivo del acto de entrega de la presidencia del grupo de los 77," United Nations, New York, March 16, 2003, http://www.presidencia.gob.ve/doc/publicaciones/discursos/Discursos_2003.pdf.

Academy of History member Elías Pino Iturrieta an "illiterate." He associated then–U.S. president George W. Bush with the devil and called him "Mr. Danger." On one occasion in Montevideo, he said before cameras to the delight of the journalists: "You are a donkey, Mr. Bush!"[21]

In addition to his aggressive and polarizing rhetoric, Chávez was profuse in his use of military and warlike language. The political struggles in which he and his followers were involved constituted epic "battles" against powerful enemies who are full of evil; he called on people to "put on their boots"; and at various moments he wore his military uniform. Since his movement had first begun in the barracks, military themes had played a central role in his symbology, though it had always been presented as a civilian-military alliance. As the first decade of the new century wore on, the military references began to prevail over the civilian. Chávez had people call him the *comandante presidente*, a title used by Cubans to address Fidel Castro, whom Chávez fervently admired. In 2004, Chávez created "electoral battle units" to organize his bases in the August presidential recall referendum. The central command, or "commando," of his reelection campaign in 2006 was organized by *batallones* (battalions), *pelotones* (squads), and *escuadras* (squadrons). In 2007, when he founded the Partido Socialista Unido de Venezuela (United Socialist Party of Venezuela), he called the organizing units of his new party *batallones socialistas*, which were made up of *patrullas* (patrols). The military references further polarize the context in which he places the transformation that he advocates and emphasize the transcendent and heroic nature of his struggles against political opponents who are identified as enemies.

Chávez's discourse also drew from a wide range of religious symbols that contribute to molding a totalitarian and salvationist vision of his political project and leadership. In his speeches, he constructed an all-inclusive view of the world with answers for everything and a final goal of creating a society of *new men*.[22]

The clear intention of Chávez's polarizing, heroic, and salvationist discourse and symbology was to confront and exclude a power structure and an elite group—internal and external—that he and his movement

21. Hugo Chávez, "Chávez 'You Are a Donkey' for Bush!" http://www.youtube.com/watch?v=v0RgGwrP4T8.

22. José Zuquete, "The Missionary Politics of Hugo Chávez," *Latin American Politics and Society* 50, no. 1 (Spring 2008): 91–121.

consider to be imperialistic, oligarchic, and corrupt. At the same time, he also created an effective discourse to include the poor. This discourse was centered on the idea that *the people* are the protagonists of history and the agents of transformations. He said "only the people can save the people, and I will be your instrument . . . but if blood must be spilled, Christ has given the example."[23] On occasions he, Chávez, was just "a piece of straw in the wind," a disposable element. He constantly used expressions aimed at increasing the people's self-esteem and at linking them to great nineteenth-century movements, especially the independence struggle and the Federal War. His many repeated laudatory phrases included references to the *bravo pueblo*, to the noble and brave people.

These same elements—to greater or lesser degrees—cause rejection, disdain, and, on many occasions, angry reactions from his adversaries. The insulting and exclusionary discourse is the most disliked. The names he used—like oligarchs, *negativos*, *puntofijistas*, *golpistas*, *pitiyanquis*, and counterrevolutionaries—ended up lumping very diverse political positions and public service careers into the same group. By so doing, he painted all his opponents with the same brush and continuously fanned the flames of polarization that have given him repeated victories at the ballot box. Other elements of his discourse, though not meant to be aggressive, were still not well received by his adversaries. Talk of "the people" as the center of the process was seen by the middle and upper classes as evidence of populist demagoguery. His informality was seen as improvisation. Allusions to baseball, for example, which he used frequently in his weekly *Aló Presidente* program, were seen as lacking seriousness and as improper for a statesman. His humor was considered to be in poor taste.

As has occurred with other populist leaders, notably the Colombian Jorge Eliécer Gaitán, Chávez's colloquial language, full of anecdotes and family references, democratized politics and humanized it, bringing it closer to the common people. The constant repetition of this discourse, as well as the almost daily presence of the president in the media, also led his followers to feel as if they are part of the decisions that affect their lives, and in this way they are once again beginning to feel included. The polarization between *chavistas*, on one hand, and the *escuálidos*, on the

23. See http://www.gobiernoenlinea.ve/docMgr/sharedfiles/Chavez_visita_Centro _Manantial_de_los_senos24122005.pdf.

other hand, served to create an adversary (as Gaitán did with his *convivialistas*) that his followers can clearly identify, erasing uncertainties in a world that has diverse and distant leaders and political elites.[24]

Channels of Communication between Chávez and His People

Consistent with the concept of populist leadership, President Chávez increasingly leaned toward weakening all forms of political mediation and opted for methods that are closer to an approach of "direct democracy." Three of these methods are at the heart of understanding both the enormous attraction he had for his followers and the strong legitimacy he has enjoyed among the majority of people in the country.

The Permanent Campaign

Between 1999 and 2012, Chávez presided over sixteen electoral processes that had little to do with the usual meaning of elections in traditional representative democracies. For one thing, Chávez was the main figure in all the elections, whether national, regional, local, or referenda. This was either because they relegitimized his position of power—like his 2000 election and 2006 reelection—or because his leadership provided coattails for the members of his political elite who cannot seriously compete with him. In the case of the referenda, the operating logic was always that of voting for or against Chávez. In this way, the leader was continuously relegitimized in a context where political parties play just a small role in mobilizing the base. For Chávez's reelection in 2006, for example, his campaign's central command was made up of leaders of the Movimiento V (Quinta) República (MVR; Fifth Republic Movement) and social organizations, while the other parties in the alliance functioned simply as advisers.[25] After 2006, this tendency toward personalization was driven by the use of plebiscites. And following the regional and local elections of November 2008, the president addressed his party:

24. Herbert Braun, *The Assassination of Gaitán: Public life and Urban Violence in Colombia* (Madison: University of Wisconsin Press, 1985), 25.
25. *El Nacional*, July 29, 2006.

"I have heard some say that this victory was due to this or that party. They are wrong; this victory belongs to Chávez and to no one else."[26]

In general, all the elections followed a plebiscitarian logic. In the regional and local elections, Chávez with some frequency named candidates who have little political support in the area, turning the elections into a "plebiscite of confirmation" for himself and his government.[27] The *kino*, a template used in the 1999 elections for Constituent Assembly representatives, was a case in point.[28] Chávez supporters were expected to vote precisely according to the indications of the *kino*. This situation became even more extreme in 2008, when Chávez named candidates for mayoral and gubernatorial elections who had little political support in their territories. Although the results as a whole were very positive for *chavismo*, there were some notable exceptions. In cities like Caracas and Maracaibo, and in states like Zulia, Miranda, and Carabobo, the strategy did not work and the official government candidates lost. Chávez was always on the campaign trail, taking part in a campaign where political parties and other mediating groups play a secondary role. The plebiscite-laden presidency, shaped by this ongoing campaign, made it harder for society to exercise any watchdog role over the state and threatened the continuity of democratic institutions in Venezuela. A similar tendency can be seen in other countries of the Andean region, such as Ecuador and Bolivia.[29]

The Communicator-State

The media has been a privileged channel for communication between the leader and the masses and is intrinsically linked to the plebiscite strategy. From the beginning of the first Chávez administration, either because there was no clear or coherent government communications strategy or

26. Hugo Chávez, "Discurso en la sede del Partido Socialista Unido de Venezuela," December 2008.

27. Pierre Rosanvallon, *La democracia inconclusa* (Bogotá: Aguilar, Altea, Taurus, Alfaguara, 2006).

28. The *kino* template got its name from a popular lottery game in the country. It explained in detail the columns and the positions that a voter should mark in order to "vote for" President Chávez, in spite of the fact that the president was not up for election.

29. Catherine Conaghan and Carlos de la Torre, "The Permanent Campaign of Rafael Correa: Making Ecuador's Plebiscitary Presidency," *International Journal of Press/Politics* 13, no. 3 (April 2008): 267–84.

because Chávez decided it should be that way, Chávez himself became the center of the strategy.[30] By 2004, when a complex state policy had taken shape, this centrality was reinforced, and the entire communications strategy revolved around two primary resources: nationwide government broadcasts on television and radio, and the Sunday *Aló Presidente* program. In the first eleven years of government, the nationwide broadcasts— which interrupt other programming to bring a government message— transmitted the equivalent of 1,038 hours, or approximately forty-three days, of official messaging. The weekly average for *Aló Presidente* through June 2008 was 4 hours and 21 minutes, but after January 2009 it increased to 6.22 hours.[31] By comparison, U.S. president Franklin D. Roosevelt, another leader who used the media to communicate with the nation during World War II, used 499 hours of official broadcasting time—twenty-one days in his twelve years in government—or just half the time that Chávez used in ten years. In addition, Venezolana de Televisión (VTV), the main state-owned television channel, was used almost exclusively for direct communication between the leader and the people and to indoctrinate people in the values of so-called socialism. Three out of four hours of programming were official propaganda and reproductions of clips from the national broadcasts and from *Aló Presidente*.[32]

After the 2002 coup, the government initiated what some have called a "communicator-state" strategy, building an entire communications infrastructure to confront the enemy—both internal and external—and spread the political-ideological program by influencing mass culture.[33] This infrastructure included not only the television station VTV—which has modernized and expanded its signal to the point where it covers the entire national territory—but also Vive TV, Ávila TV, and Telesur. Telesur was conceived in 2005 as a channel for various Latin American governments (Argentina, Cuba, and Uruguay), but it has ended up being largely another channel for the Venezuelan government to use to position Chávez's leadership in the region, given that it was funded almost entirely with Venezuelan petrodollars. In addition to these televi-

---

30. Marelis Morales and Javier Pereira, "La política informativa del Gobierno de Chávez," *Comunicación* 121 (August–September 2003).

31. Ángel Oropeza, "Comunicación como política de Gobierno versus comunicación como política de revolución," in *Hegemonía y Control Comunicacional*, edited by Marcelino Bisbal (Caracas: Editorial Alfa, 2009), 67.

32. Ibid.

33. Ibid.

sion stations, there was a growing state network of radio stations, in which National Radio of Venezuela (RNV) functioned as the center of a conglomerate of stations that transmitted the *Aló Presidente* program, along with other information and official propaganda to all the country's urban and rural areas. After 2004, RNV also had an international shortwave signal. The Bolivarian News Agency (ABN) was converted into the Venezuelan News Agency (AVN), with correspondents in Brazil, Argentina, the United States, Spain, and Colombia, as well as several newspapers. A satellite to transmit Telesur programming all over the continent was under construction.[34] This whole platform has been reinforced by the support and financing the government has given to numerous community radio stations, many of which support the president's policies and mobilize during election campaigns.[35]

Thanks to this strategy, the president became a daily figure in the lives of his followers. They saw him constantly, felt as if they were in contact with him, and felt as if they were participating in his administration. His overwhelming presence in audiovisual media and on the radio waves, not to mention newspapers, billboards, and graffiti, was one way of exercising top-down direct democracy. Chávez used the media to promote his agenda and to stigmatize and counter any initiative directed against him.

The construction of the political adversary and the struggle against that adversary played out in a significant way in this media space. Chávez had the support of Venezuela's largest media corporations early on, but this relationship was brief and turned quickly into a head-on confrontation. Some media owners became important actors in the political opposition to *chavismo*. The president stigmatized them, and they stigmatized him. Some private media groups acted within that same polarizing frame, weakening more complex and subtle expressions and ways of seeing the president, his administration, and the Bolivarian political project. The struggle between the two poles has been an ongoing obstacle for the development of politics and politicians; this is another reason that efforts to create mediating bodies tended to be weak. Various climactic moments have occurred in the struggle between the two poles, such as

34. Marcelino Bisbal, "Las comunicaciones del régimen," *El Nacional*, November 26, 2006.
35. Sujatha Fernandes, "Radio Bemba in an Age of Electronic Media," paper presented at Conference on Globalization and the Rise of the Left in Latin America, Princeton, N.J., December 6–8, 2007.

the television blackout during the April 11, 2002, coup and the closing of Radio Caracas Television on May 27, 2007.

Because this is such a strategic area, the Chávez government increasingly looked for ways to further reduce the influence of the private media. In December 2002, faced with a *paro cívico* (general strike) called by opposition forces backed by the private media, Chávez reacted by threatening to pass a law in Congress to regulate the media.[36] In 2005, with the new communications policy (Nuevo Orden Comunicacional), the strategy became more complex and also included a set of legal instruments—the Law for Social Responsibility in the Communications Media and the Telecommunications Law, among others—that gave the government tools it can use in case it needs to weaken media outlets it considers contrary to its interests. These laws contain important contributions for regulating this "fourth power," but they also include some ambiguities that can be subject to interpretation depending on the moment. As the branches of government—particularly the judicial branch—lost autonomy, the laws served to control or punish any media owner or journalist the president believed to be an adversary. The government also used other means of intimidation, including tax penalties, equipment confiscation, withdrawal of government advertising, abusive use of national broadcasting that results in huge losses for private media, and so on.[37] One emblematic case of the use of legal procedures for political retaliation and to reduce the influence of private media with opposing editorial lines occurred in 2007 with Radio Caracas Television, a network that had participated in actions that led to the 2002 coup. In December 2006, when Chávez was newly strengthened by his reelection, he dressed in his military uniform and announced to the owners from a military barracks that he would close their station. A few months later, the government used legal provisions to deny the company's application for the renewal of its radio waves concession.[38]

36. *El Nacional*, December 24, 2001.
37. Bisbal, *Hegemonía y Control Comunicacional.*
38. The state owns the radio waves and therefore authorizes concessions. Radio Caracas Television's concession was expiring in May 2007, and the state did not renew it. In 2009, citing the expiration of concessions, or that the people to whom the concession had been given were dead and that they were not inheritable, thirty-four private radio stations were taken off the air; see http://www.ifex.org/venezuela/2009/08/04/broadcasters_ordered_closed/es/.

People's Networks for Organization, Participation, Resource Distribution, and Mobilization around Elections

The construction of a vast social and political organizing network, driven by the government and centered on the figure of Chávez, constituted a third central communications strategy that the president used to reach his bases. An organizing strategy for effective and frequent mobilization was a central concern for the Venezuelan political regime, whose discourse rejected the conventional forms of representation of the liberal model. There were at least three stages in the evolution of Chávez's practices.

The first stage, before he came to power, was the formation of the Bolivarian movement as a vast popular national movement that was contained within and oriented by a political party: the Movimiento Bolivariano Revolucionario 200. Aside from its civilian-military composition and certain rituals—such as the Bolivarian pledge—MBR 200 was similar to other mass political parties in Venezuela. However, it was never able to embrace all those who sympathized with the leader, because they came from very diverse social and ideological paths. Even before 1998, therefore, the Bolivarian movement included—in addition to MBR 200 —various popular organizations, sympathizer groups, parties on the left, and prominent people who shared common views, especially on the emerging leadership of Chávez. The MVR was formed to bring all these groups together in a presidential campaign that year. The MVR was initially conceived as an electoral structure parallel to the party that would be tightly centralized and controlled by Chávez. When the MVR won that election and the following ones until 2006, it ended up replacing MBR 200, weakening the concept of the political party as a collective enterprise, and strengthening the more personalized, centralized, and pragmatic tendencies at play in the electoral process.

The second stage includes the first Chávez administration, between 1999 and 2007. The goal in this stage was for the MVR to gel as a political instrument of the movement, but the efforts were intermittent and not very successful. Sociopolitical organizations created outside the MVR and linked more directly with defending the president were more successful, as were groups with election-related goals such as the Bolivarian Circles, the Election Battle Units, and the Electoral Battalions. These organizations reinforced the vertical power structure and the political personalism around Chávez. On a parallel track, social organizations were created in poor urban neighborhoods and in the countryside to work with the government to manage public services in the communities. Community water committees, rural or urban land committees, health committees, neighborhood mothers' organizations, and other groups formed the basis of a new social fabric with different levels of autonomy and with the goal of putting into practice the constitutional right to participate in the direction of public policy. These groups experimented to find more efficient ways of promoting inclusion and self-development and to resolve very serious problems related to access to public services. They drove a significant "bottom-up" dynamic that generated a great deal of popular enthusiasm and helped explain the legitimacy that the president acquired among low-income sectors during those years. This dynamic coexisted with the "top-down" dynamics also being driven by the president and public officials, particularly military men in charge of some of the social programs, or "missions." For some time, this tension sparked a significant process of mobilization and politicization.

A third stage, still in progress, began during the second Chávez administration, with the displacement of participatory democracy by a model that Chávez called socialist. Under this new orientation, the president called for the dissolution of all political parties, including the MVR, in order to form the Partido Socialista Unido de Venezuela (PSUV; United Socialist Party of Venezuela) as the only party of the revolution. Community councils (CCs) were also created as primary hubs for a new model of society. They were directly under the orders of the president and received their resources from the presidency. With President Chávez at the top, they were fundamentally top-down structures that weakened democratizing practices, though tensions and contradictions that surfaced from bottom-up mobilization did persist. Both the PSUV and the CCs were supported with public resources, which strengthened political clientelism as a strategy of linkage with the leader. In January 2009, when the campaign for the constitutional amendment referendum was gearing up, the minister of popular power for participation, in a clear recognition of the status of the CCs as arms of the government and of the PSUV, ordered the CCs to cease their projects in order to work full time on finding the votes necessary to ensure the victory of the Chávez-backed proposal that would allow reelection in all positions.[39] Subsequently, government officials pressured, with varying degrees of intensity, for the CC spokespeople to be members of the party. The PSUV acts in a top-down

39. *El Nacional*, January 8, 2009.

fashion in which the president defines the party line, thus altering the balance of power between government officials, organizations for social mobilization, and legislators. In this way, these organizational modalities, which at first seemed to have the goal of empowering an emerging civil society, increasingly appear to have adapted to serve as a conduit for transmitting public resources to the organized communities so they can co-manage public services and mobilize Chávez voters when there are elections. Co-opting grassroots organizations was not the government's only strategy to advance its goals. Presidential takeover of the functions of various branches of government was another of the most defining characteristics of this period. It got to the point at which it became common to see the president giving orders to judges and congressmen from his *Aló Presidente* program. Once, he even said: "I am the law; I am the state."[40] This phrase, which was historically linked to King Louis XIV of France, did not seem far from Venezuela's current reality. The dismantling of institutions has gone hand in hand with making changes in the country's legal framework and passing successive laws that have enabled Chávez to govern by decree on various occasions. The opposition's boycott of the 2005 parliamentary elections gave Chávez the opportunity to issue direct instructions to the National Assembly for five years, in turn enabling the final dilution of institutionalism's last remains.

The Social Composition of *Chavismo*

Election results provide one way of identifying the social composition of the Chávez base in that they show the close relationship between social and political polarization in Venezuela. Most people from the middle and upper social classes tended to vote for any option in opposition to Chávez, while the poorest sectors voted for him. A polarization between the city and the countryside also became evident. Venezuela is a highly urban culture, but people in smaller cities, towns, and hamlets tended to turn out in large numbers for Chávez. This tendency was not so pronounced in large cities. Table 9.1 illustrates these trends, comparing the

40. Hugo Chávez Frías, August 28, 2008. See Gustavo Coronel, "Las Armas de Coronel," October 15, 2008, http://lasarmasdecoronel.blogspot.com/2008/10/yo-soy-la-leyyo-soy-el-estado.html.

Table 9.1. Percentage of Votes for Chávez in the 2004 Recall Referendum, in the 2006 Elections, and in the 2009 Constitutional Amendment Referendum— Examples of Polarization in Elections

Constituency	"No" Vote on 2004 Referendum	Votes for Chávez in 2006 Elections	"Yes" Votes on 2009 Constitutional Amendment
National	59.1	62.9	54.9
Metro area of Caracas	48.7	54.8	45.2
Municipality of Libertador	56.0	62.6	52.0
Antímano Parish	76.7	81.9	72.3
San Pedro Parish	28.0	32.3	25.4
Municipality of Baruta	20.6	24.2	18.6
El Cafetal Parish	9.3	10.9	8.1
Municipality of Chacao	20.0	23.3	17.4
Municipality of El Hatillo	17.9	20.3	16.9
Centro Club La Lagunita	5.7	7.8	4.5
Municipality of Sucre	47.1	53.1	43.8
La Dolorita Parish	73.1	78.4	68.5
Leoncio Martínez Parish	21.8	26.4	20.1
State of Zulia	53.1	51.4	47.3
Municipality of Maracaibo (Maracaibo)	47.9	46.9	40.6
Idelfonso Vásquez Parish	67.4	57.8	53.2
Olegario Villalobos Parish	26.3	26.9	21.9
State of Carabobo	56.8	61.7	52.4
Municipality of Valencia (Valencia)	47.6	52.4	45.1
Santa Rosa Parish	62.0	65.5	55.7
San José Parish	14.1	17.6	13.2
State of Lara	64.8	66.5	55.5
Municipality of Irribarren (Barquisimeto)	60.9	64.8	51.4
Unión Parish	72.5	74.7	61.5
Santa Rosa Parish	40.5	45.4	34.9

Source: República Bolivariana de Venezuela (www.cne.gob.ve).

results of the 2004 recall referendum, the 2006 elections, and the 2009 constitutional amendment referendum. The polarized nature of these elections has been a consistent characteristic since 1998.

Table 9.1 shows an illustrative sample of voter behavior from different cities and various income levels. In Caracas, three small municipalities with higher income levels—Baruta, Chacao, and El Hatillo—voted consistently against Chávez, while the larger municipalities—Libertador and Sucre, which include most of the poor neighborhoods in the city—consistently voted for Chávez. Within the various municipalities of Caracas, the table shows parishes with different social compositions that clearly illustrate the same trend. For example, Antímano Parish in the municipality of Libertador is one of the poorest parishes in the city, and it voted solidly in favor of Chávez. By contrast, the San Pedro Parish, made up primarily of middle-class voters, was more pro-opposition. One extreme example was that of the Centro Club La Lagunita, an upper-class residential sector, where the opposition got more than 90 percent of the votes.

The table also presents data from three states that are home to three of the largest and most populated cities. There, it is possible to see that the percentage of pro-Chávez voting throughout the state is higher than the percentage of pro-Chávez votes in the state capital alone. Chávez was more popular in rural, less developed areas. The table also compares the richest and poorest parishes in each of the cities. Chávez consistently lost in the wealthy parishes and won in the poorest.

In terms of the social composition of the leaders who have been part of the *chavista* elite over the years, the results are more diverse. Few studies have been done on the topic, but some data do make it possible to identify particular characteristics. One study of the composition of the 2000 National Assembly, for example, showed that the majority of the *diputados*, or congressmen, from the Chávez alliance (MVR and Movimento al Socialismo) identified their salaries as "sufficient" or "more than sufficient" (84.5 percent and 66.7 percent, respectively), while most congressmen from the Proyecto Venezuela considered their salary to be "insufficient" (75 percent). Fifty percent of the AD representatives also considered their salary to be "insufficient."[41] This information would appear to indicate that the income level of the *chavistas* then was the highest they had ever had, meaning that they came from lower-income social classes as compared with the other elites. In terms of education levels, 72.4 percent of the MVR members of Congress in the 2000 National Assembly were professionals (with university or graduate degrees), which was very similar to the education levels of the AD representatives, 75 per-

41. Elena Martínez Barahona, "Ante un nuevo parlamento en la V república bolivariana?" in *Venezuela: Rupturas y continuidades del sistema político 1999–2001*, edited by Marisa Ramos Rollón (Salamanca: Ediciones Universidad de Salamanca, 2002), 230–31.

cent of whom said they had a university or a graduate degree. It would seem, then, that *chavista* leaders form part of the professional elite even though they come from the lower and middle classes.

The military elite, another significant group within the *chavista* elite, shared similar characteristics. They also tended to have come from middle-class, lower-class, and even poor families, but they had reached a professional level of education. Jorge García Carneiro, Francisco Arias Cárdenas, and Chávez himself are good examples. General García Carneiro, who was minister of defense during the first Chávez government and later served as governor of the state of Vargas, was born and raised in a poor neighborhood of El Valle de Caracas Parish.[42] Chávez comes from a poor family with six children whose parents were schoolteachers in a town in the remote state of Barinas.[43] Arias Cárdenas comes from a humble Andean family with twelve children whose father made a living as a public bus driver.[44] Arias Cárdenas first attended seminary and then went into the army as a way of supporting himself and getting an education. These men were able to reach university levels of study in the armed forces.

Various studies have found that many of the middle-aged politicians and civilian public officials who got their start in deliberating bodies and public administration with *chavismo* tend to have significant levels of education, experience, and political commitment to counterhegemonic values that date back long before Chávez's rise to power. Some come from traditional parties like the AD and COPEI, but most belonged to parties on the Venezuelan left or were influenced by the process of social activism that played out in the country beginning in the 1960s.[45] For example, leaders of the La Causa Radical, which grew out of a 1970 division in the Partido Comunista de Venezuela and then split again in 1997 to form the Patria Para Todos party, have been key players in both Chávez administrations. These include Alí Rodriguez, Aristóbulo Istúriz, María Cristina Iglesias, Julio Montes, Bernardo Álvarez, and Francisco Sesto. All are university-educated professionals; they come from a history of social and political activism that began at least two or three decades ago;

42. Marta Harnecker, *Militares junto al pueblo* (Caracas: Vadell Hermanos, 2003).
43. Cristina Marcano and Alberto Barrera Tyszka, *Hugo Chávez sin uniforme* (Caracas: Editorial Debate, 2004).
44. Zago, *La rebelión,* 17.
45. Cristóbal Valencia Ramírez, "Venezuela's Bolivarian Revolution: Who Are the Chavistas?" *Latin American Perspectives* 32 (2005): 95.

and they have occupied various high positions in the government. All of them were ministers at some point.[46] Many social activists between the ages of forty and fifty years who worked in the various forms of community participation implemented by the Chávez government began their life of activism after being steeped in the social doctrine of the Catholic Church. From there, they went on to join leftist political parties or organizations within the urban popular movement.[47] Others came from popular organizations linked to the armed struggle of the 1960s, which later moved toward urban struggles as part of the popular movement.[48]

Final Reflections

Hugo Chávez's spectacular rise to power in Venezuela at the end of the twentieth century was the result of a number of crises in Venezuelan social life that had been simmering for decades. These crises led to a populist rupture as an instrument for change and social transformation to benefit those who were not satisfied with, or were excluded from, the established order. Chávez not only had a highly favorable social and economic scenario to work with; he also had a series of personal attributes that made him attractive to the masses.

When Chávez took charge of administering the government in 1999 and tried to stabilize the new power relationships represented by Bolivarianism, the task became more complicated. The multiple unsatisfied demands that Chávez articulated as an "empty signifier" needed to be met. Chávez was able to fulfill some of the most important expectations, not only of the poor but also of the middle class and intellectuals. The Constituent Assembly, which drafted the Constitución de la República

46. One outstanding example is that of Alí Rodríguez Araque, Partido Comunista de Venezuela commander of the armed struggle in the 1960s and then a member of the Partido de la Revolución Venezolana, whose leader was Douglas Bravo. He graduated from the Universidad Central de Venezuela with a degree in law, entered La Causa Radical in the 1980s, left in 1997, and—together with Istúriz, Iglesias, Alberto Muller Rojas, Sesto and others—founded the Patria Para Todos party. He has been the minister of hydrocarbons, minister of finance, foreign minister, president of PDVSA, ambassador of Venezuela in Cuba, and, since January 2010, minister of electric energy.

47. Margarita López Maya, "Orígenes de la democracia participativa en Venezuela," unpublished manuscript, Washington.

48. Ibid.

Bolivariana de Venezuela (CRBV; Constitution of the Bolivarian Republic of Venezuela) in 1999, institutionalized mechanisms for direct democracy both in the political arena—with referendums, citizen assemblies, recall elections, and so on—and in the administration of public services, fulfilling the aspirations of the poor and middle classes. He gave the military the vote and reaffirmed the centrality of the state, the universality of social rights, the obligation of the state to guarantee those rights, and state ownership of oil—all this in clear opposition to neoliberal paradigms. In his first years, the government seemed to be embarking on a path toward a state that, according to the debates and struggles of previous decades, would be a substantive democracy that did not sacrifice the institutions of liberal democracy.

In spite of the fact that Chávez was fulfilling long-delayed demands, the institutional changes he proposed clashed with powerful organized interests. Between 2001 and 2004, the business sector, the media, the management of the oil industry, union leaders, and the hierarchy of the Catholic Church, among other groups, assiduously and at times violently resisted changes in the relationships of power. The political confrontations reached their highest points with the coup, the oil strike, and the *guarimbas* (violent opposition-led street blockades). The fact that the president and his government survived these attacks—with the support of the armed forces and the mobilization of his followers in scenarios where political parties carried very little weight—consolidated populism as a way of conducting politics. It deepened the polarizing discourse and the centrality of the personal leadership of President Chávez, and it severely weakened the already diminished reputation that the representational institutions had among the poor. It was in this conflictive, polarized, and violent context that the more personalized and authoritarian tendencies of the new constitution project began to predominate.

Since the 2004 recall referendum, the explicit orientation of the state was to establish direct links between the leader and his people. As part of this orientation, the Nuevo Orden Comunicacional was launched as a government policy in 2005, and Community Councils were established by law in 2006. Parties shrunk in importance in comparison with the social organizations promoted by the presidency, which served to administer public services, defend the president, and/or mobilize the *chavista* bases at election times. The process of political-administrative decentralization was weakened in favor of a recentralization of the state. Power was concentrated in the presidency, Chávez legislated by decree, and the other government branches continued to lose their autonomy. In the name of the revolutionary process aimed at creating twenty-first-century socialism, liberal institutions of mediation like the National Assembly became weaker in favor of mechanisms like *parliamentarismo de la calle* ("street parliaments"), a participatory structure used occasionally since 2006 that called people to the plazas less for deliberation than for dissemination of information and defense of particular laws and rules. Deliberation and decisionmaking gradually became a process dominated by and exclusive to the president.

The reelection of Chávez in 2006 to a second six-year term, with absolute numbers and vote percentages not seen in Venezuela since 1958, appeared to corroborate Venezuelans' acceptance of the political regime that Chávez and *chavismo* were building. Although initially vague when it was put forth as an alternative model to capitalism and representative democracy, twenty-first-century socialism has become clearer. Although the president's constitutional reform proposal presented for approval in the 2007 referendum was rejected by the majority, much of its content has since been enacted through laws and regulations after the February 2009 approval of the constitutional amendment permitting the indefinite reelection of the president and all elected officials. These laws include the Partial Reform of the Organic Law for Decentralization[49] and the Special Law on the Organization of the Capital District.[50] The first transferred the control of airports and ports from regional authorities to the national executive branch and the second created the figure of "chief" of the Capital District, who, unlike elected governors and mayors, is freely named and removed by the president of the republic. Both laws violate the guidelines of the 1999 Constitution and support the recentralization of the state that was proposed and rejected at the ballot box. The Law of Partial Reform of Decree No. 6.239 with Rank, Value and Force of the Organic Law of the Bolivarian National Armed Forces, which officially changed the name of the army from the National Armed Forces to the Bolivarian Armed Forces, was another element of the defeated 2007 proposal that subsequently passed.[51] More recently, in 2010, the National Assembly approved a series of laws—such as the Organic Law of the Federal Council of Government, the Organic Law of the Communal

49. Venezuela, GO 39.140, Caracas, March 19, 2009.
50. Venezuela, GO 39.156, Caracas, April 13, 2009.
51. Venezuela, GO 5.993, Extraordinario, Caracas, August 18, 2010.

Councils, and the Organic Law of the Communes—that sought to move toward the consolidation of a communal state (*estado comunal*), yet another part of the proposal voted down in 2007 (though at the time it was called *poder popular*). The Chávez model of socialism consolidated the centralizing and authoritarian tendencies that were strengthened during the hegemonic struggle for power between 2001 and 2004 and bore similarities to twentieth-century social experiences in countries like the former Soviet Union and Cuba.

Because of oil income, the relative autonomy of the Venezuelan state vis-à-vis civil society enabled those who come to power during oil boom times to launch their political projects without the cumbersome process of negotiating among interest groups. In contrast, the undertaking that emerged in 1999 with the Chávez victory and the approval of the constitution—which took place in the context of low oil prices—had to be debated and a consensus had to be built. The CRBV gave legal expression to a series of demands and aspirations that dissimilar actors had been making since the 1980s, both through street protests and through work in institutional spaces such as the Comisión Presidencial para la Reforma del Estado (Presidential Commission for the Reform of the State). The same cannot be said of the twenty-first-century socialism of the second Chávez administration, which was imposed thanks to a combination of significant fiscal income from oil (a result of the 2004–8 oil boom), manipulated interpretations of law, and the immense prestige and confidence that the majority of the poor have in the president as a result of his first administration and the context of the conflict in which he found himself. Surveys have repeatedly shown that some key aspects of a socialist agenda, such as the weakening of private property or the implantation of Cuba-style institutions, do not have the support of the majority.[52] However, the symbolic kind of satisfaction generated with a discourse of revenge and social inclusion, the efforts made by the masses to keep Chávez in power during the difficult years of violent confrontation, the distribution of the enormous fiscal income that came from oil during the boom years through social policies such as the "missions," and the political weakness of the opposition allowed Chávez to force a transformation of Venezuelan society. It has yet to be seen, however, if this regime is viable in the midst of the unstable oil market of today. In 2009 and 2010 the decline and instability of fiscal income from oil was imme-

52. Datanálisis, 2009.

diately reflected in sociopolitical conflict and a decrease in the popularity of the president.[53] If revenues do not sufficiently recover to cover the public costs that the country's rentier socialism requires, the all-powerful and omnipresent figure of *el presidente* could be weakened, with consequences for Venezuelan society that will be unpredictable but certainly unfavorable in the short run.

In Venezuela, as in other countries, the adjective "populist" has been used to discredit all kinds of phenomena where the process of transformation is propelled by excluded social sectors mobilized directly by a charismatic leader with a polarizing discourse. This perspective does not make it possible to appreciate its merits as a useful instrument at a certain time—as Laclau points out—for building the basis of a new social vision that has great potential for mobilizing people and is capable of breaking an exclusionary and entrenched power structure that is blocking democratic progress in a society.[54] The temptation of the populist leader, however, is to hold on to the power he has attained, concentrating it at the risk of destroying the entire institutional fabric that permits a political order of dialogue and consensus building. The Venezuelan case shows clearly how once the conflict was resolved in favor of Bolivarianism, Chávez used his strength to modify the undertaking that had first given him legitimacy. The petro-state has facilitated the destruction of institutional checks and balances and the advancement of a mission that is no longer one of democratic deepening but rather of authoritarian tendencies.

Epilogue

Hugo Chávez was reelected for a third six-year term on October 7, 2012. His triumph served to give legitimacy to the effort to build a new kind of communal state as part of a project to build twenty-first-century socialism. Chávez defeated Henrique Capriles Radonski of the Mesa de la Unidad Democrática (Coalition for Democratic Unity), obtaining 8,191,132 votes (55.4 percent of valid votes) versus the 6,591,305 votes —or 44.5 percent—won by Capriles. Four additional presidential candi-

53. IVAD, 2010.
54. Ernesto Laclau, *La razón populista* (México: Fondo de Cultura Económica, 2005).

dates took less than 1 percent of valid votes. The 11-point difference between Chávez and Capriles was much smaller than in 2006, when the gap between Chávez and his opponent was 26 percent. The electorate, as in 2006, was extremely polarized. Those electoral institutions that were responsible for guaranteeing the fairness and equity of the campaign failed to do so. Nonetheless, the process of tabulating votes was meticulous and transparent; voting was secret, and all actors accepted the results of an election, in which fully 80.52 percent of eligible voters participated.

The 2012 election evidenced a number of the characteristics of earlier contests. But this time, the clarity as well as the crudeness of several features suggested the emergence of a different model of democracy quite distinct from liberal democracy. The use of public resources—transportation, buildings, the mass media, public funds—by the incumbent president and his party was visible, frequent, and massive. Electoral laws and regulations allowed each candidate three minutes of television time per day, and both Capriles and Chávez made use of this time. In addition, however, Chávez made massive use of mandatory presidential broadcasts (the so-called *cadenas presidenciales*) that totaled 43 hours and 17 minutes, an average of 29 minutes per day over the three months of official campaigning. This use of presidential broadcasts was four times higher than in 2006.

Moreover, the clientelist and paternalistic relations forged between Chávez and some sectors of the population intensified during the campaign. In addition to his permanent media presence, he used organizational networks such as the communal councils and the missions to channel state resources to his political base. The distribution of windfall profits from high oil prices, through the missions and especially the so-called great missions created in 2011, constituted a central element of Chávez's campaign and was possibly decisive to his victory. One mission that stands out is the Great Housing Mission (Gran Misión Vivienda), which was launched in 2011 to solve the acute shortage of housing for popular sectors. Another such mission, the Great Mission in Greater Love (Gran Misión en Amor Mayor), was formed in December 2011 to provide pensions to older citizens who did not have social security retirement funds. The My Furnished House Mission (Misión Mi Casa Bien Equipada) sold furniture and household electronic appliances at subsidized prices. And the Great Mission Sons and Daughters of Venezuela (Gran Misión Hijos e Hijas de Venezuela) gave financial support to teenage mothers, single mothers, and mothers with disabled children. These kinds of initiatives in the midst of a campaign made for a noticeable imbalance between Chávez and other candidates, even if their precise influence on the election's final results is hard to measure. The notorious inequity during the electoral process appears to have been accepted by most in society.

Recurring populist strategies over the course of more than fourteen years have led to the progressive weakening and destruction of Venezuela's liberal democratic institutional design, some of which was still present in the 1999 Constitution. Nonetheless, it might still be difficult for Chávez or *chavismo* to impose a custom-made socialist regime or communal state. Despite the prolific use of populist symbols, mechanisms, and strategy, and the mobilizing capacity of the PSUV's powerful electoral machinery, nearly half the Venezuelan electorate voted against Chávez in 2012. This substantial minority, which rejects both Chávez's leadership and the socialist project, poses governability challenges for Chávez or any leader who might succeed him. At the same time, the quasi-deification of Chávez as his health continued to fail meant that his persona would continue to be the central reference point of Venezuelan politics for the foreseeable future, even if the cohesion of his movement in a post-Chávez era was very much in question.

Chapter 10

From the MNR to the MAS: Populism, Parties, the State, and Social Movements in Bolivia since 1952

John Crabtree

The reelection in 2009 of Evo Morales Ayma as president of Bolivia for another five-year term invites reflection on the nature of political power in this country, and in particular the relationship between the state, party(ies), and a wide variety of social movements.[1] Much of the published literature on contemporary Bolivia reflects on how the country's ruling party, the Movimiento al Socialismo (MAS), first came to power in 2006, and the relationships it has had with social movements.[2]

1. Morales was reelected with 64 percent of the vote, considerably more than when he was first elected in 2005.
2. See, e.g., Deborah J. Yashar, *Contesting Citizenship in Latin America: The Rise of Indigenous Movements and the Post-Liberal Challenge* (New York: Cambridge University Press, 2005), 152–223; Donna Lee Van Cott, *From Movements to Parties in Latin America: The Evolution of Ethnic Politics* (New York: Cambridge University Press, 2005), 49–98; John Crabtree, *Patterns of Protest: Politics and Social Movements in Bolivia* (London: Latin America Bureau, 2005); Benjamin Kohl and Linda Farthing, *Impasse in Bolivia: Neoliberal Hegemony and Popular Resistance* (London: Zed Books, 2006); Forrest Hylton and Sinclair Thomson, *Revolutionary Horizons:*

Less has been written about the MAS as it has developed and how it has operated in governing the country in conjunction with these social movements. There is good reason for this; it is arguably premature to make hard and fast judgments about a political phenomenon that is still continuing to evolve and that embodies a number of ambiguities. But at the same time, the second term of the MAS government provides pointers as to the key features of how this government operates and how it relates to those who overwhelmingly endorsed it in the 2009 presidential and legislative elections.

The theme of this volume, however, invites one to think historically, comparing existing regimes in Latin America with earlier ones, in an attempt to define a little more closely what the word "populism" can usefully be taken to mean. How "populist" have past and present regimes been in Bolivia, particularly those that have sought to mobilize the popular movement in one way or another? There are no entirely new beginnings in history, and the MAS government—as we shall see—is embedded in long-running traditions of politics while, of course, contributing important new elements to these traditions that will make an important imprint on how politics is conducted in the future. The literature on populism involves a wide variety of definitions that sometimes cause the utility of the term to be brought into question. Indeed, problems in defining populism are almost as old as the concept itself. Here I prefer to highlight what I think are the main elements of these political traditions and then to discuss the extent to which they fit the various defining characteristics of populism. I hope that this will help enrich the discussion about populism rather than further muddy the waters.

A theme that runs through this chapter is the changing nature of the relationship between parties, the state, and social actors (or "movements") over a fairly long (sixty-years-plus) period, the space in which populist politics can be seen to emerge. I think that any discussion of Bolivian politics in this period has to take into account the achievements and limitations of the 1952 Revolution, an event that not only represents a decisive turning point in modern Bolivian history but also helps mark out some of the lasting differences between this country's politics and those of its neighbors. The legacy of 1952 has proved remarkably endur-

---

Past and Present in Bolivian Politics (London: Verso, 2007), 101–43; and Jim Shultz and Melissa Crane Draper, eds., *Dignity and Defiance: Stories from Bolivia's Challenge to Globalization* (Pontypool: Merlin Press, 2008).

ing, helping to establish the context in which politics have been discussed ever since. I therefore begin with a section that discusses the development of politics both before and after 1952, in particular how the state responded to the social pressures that expressed themselves within the Revolution itself and thereafter. I seek to measure this against the traits of classic populism as seen elsewhere. Then I move on to a consideration of the neoliberal period, after 1985, when the axis of Bolivian politics shifted substantially toward a model that many at the time applauded as a vindication of the principles of the Washington Consensus. This then provoked a sharp reaction in which, arguably, populist elements returned to the fore. Finally, I provide some thoughts on the nature of politics since 2006, and particularly on how the country's ruling party, the MAS, actually works and how it relates to social movements. To what extent can Morales and the MAS usefully be described as "populist"?

The MNR and Its Sequels

The 1952 Revolution was a product of the social changes that had taken place in Bolivia in the two previous decades, and how new social actors had entered the scene and begun to challenge the political control of a tiny elite, known in Bolivia as the *rosca*.[3] Not only did the 1940s see significant peasant mobilization and the formation of the mineworkers' union, the Federación Sindical de Trabajadores Mineros de Bolivia (FSTMB). They also saw the emergence of a nationalist political party, the Movimiento Nacionalista Revolucionario (MNR), which was influenced in no small part by European fascism and the example of Peronism in Argentina. The MNR provided a link between a small but developing middle class and more popularly based political currents with influence in the union movement. The MNR had first become an important force during the Villarroel presidency (1943–46), when it had sought to rally popular movements behind this nationalist and authoritarian

---

3. The breakdown in the traditional pattern of political domination had begun well before 1952, in the 1930s, particularly during the Toro and Busch governments. The 1938 Constitution introduced the idea of state intervention in many areas in pursuit of the common good, a radical departure from the liberal Constitution of 1880. See Herbert S. Klein, *A Concise History of Bolivia*, vol. 2 (Cambridge: Cambridge University Press, 2011), 192.

government with its pro-Axis sympathies.[4] More immediately, 1952 was a response to a political crisis provoked by the decision to overrule the results of the 1951 elections, in which MNR leader Víctor Paz Estenssoro had won an outright majority. The 1952 Revolution, therefore, was led primarily by middle-class reformists anxious to break with traditional oligarchic political control, but this involved the mobilization of a significant albeit shifting alliance of workers and peasants with a strong appeal to both national and popular sentiments, to *lo nacional* and *lo popular*.[5]

The Revolution therefore approximated to (and indeed was inspired by) the model of modernizing populism that had emerged with force in Latin America and elsewhere in the decades preceding 1952, particularly in Argentina. The ideology that emerged and was to remain dominant for the following thirty years was driven largely by nationalism and developmentalism.[6] The Revolution, of course, resulted in important structural reforms, notably the introduction of universal suffrage, the nationalization of the country's main mines, and the initiation of a process of agrarian reform. These were policies that reflected the interests of those who had participated actively in the Revolution, and indeed were "made" by them. For its part, the MNR's leadership quickly backtracked on its

4. In its origins, the MNR was largely a middle-class, urban force. However, it quickly realized that it needed to generate a social base for itself. Its opportunity came with Villarroel, whose Cabinet it entered in December 1943. It did so alongside Razón de Patria (Radepa), a group with strong fascist leanings. However, in the context of 1944, the MNR's leadership quickly realized that it needed to distance itself from such a categorization. The ideology of the MNR was grounded on nationalism, and while its rhetoric was multiclassist, its leadership was decidedly elitist. By the late 1940s it became conscious of the need to appeal to wide popular support if its nationalist agenda was to have hope of success. At that time, however, the labor movement was led by class-conscious radicals who viewed the MNR with suspicion. The growth of popular support for the MNR was largely through its ability to appeal to the leaders of popular movements rather than to their rank and file. See, e.g., Christopher Mitchell, *The Legacy of Populism in Bolivia: From the MNR to Military Rule* (New York: Praeger, 1977).

5. Still one of the best accounts of the Revolution and its aftermath is given by James M. Malloy and Richard S. Thorn, eds., *Beyond the Revolution: Bolivia since 1952* (Pittsburgh: University of Pittsburgh Press, 1972). For the genesis of 1952, see Herbert Klein, *Parties and Political Change in Bolivia* (Cambridge: Cambridge University Press, 2008). On the role of the miners in the revolution, see James Dunkerley, *Rebellion in the Veins* (London: Verso, 1984).

6. René Zavaleta, *Lo nacional-popular en Bolivia* (Mexico City: Siglo Veinteuno, 1986).

previously "revolutionary" discourse once the new government assumed office and found itself increasingly at odds with more radical social actors, particularly in the union movement.[7]

The revolutionary governments that followed built on the initial reforms, embarking on novel policies of national development that entailed a high degree of state participation in the economy (in the face of a very weak private sector) and the policies of nation building involved in the so-called *marcha hacia el oriente* (march to the East).[8] The colonization of the eastern lowlands by peasants from the highlands formed part of this project, providing an important opportunity for these governments to organize new sectors of the workforce. The year 1952 was therefore the moment when a new type of regime came into being based on much broader public support. However, the MNR governments found themselves first opposing the social agenda espoused by the mineworkers and other radical groups and then gripped in a financial crisis that preempted redistributive policies and pushed it increasingly into the hands of Washington and the International Monetary Fund.

The changes brought about by the Revolution helped empower those sectors of the population that had been involved, particularly the mineworkers and other incipient sectors of the small working class, along with many peasants who had occupied the lands they previously worked as peons, ejecting traditional landlords. The weakness of the central government provided ample space for autonomous mobilization that defied co-optation. The formation of the Central Obrera Boliviana (COB) in 1952, organized largely around the FSTMB, became the institutional expression of this bottom-up pressure. Conflicts were not slow in emerging, particularly because the MNR government sought to impose fiscal discipline on the newly nationalized mining industry. The key figure in this awkward and conflictive relationship was Juan Lechín Oquendo, who, with one foot within the regime and one foot outside, played an important role in managing relations between the new state and powerful sectors of the workforce.[9] The COB itself became a highly conten-

7. See Mitchell, *Legacy of Populism*, 52–55.

8. For the economic legacies of 1952, see Juan Antonio Morales, "Economic Vulnerability in Bolivia," in *Towards Democratic Viability: The Bolivian Experience*, edited by John Crabtree and Laurence Whitehead (Basingstoke, U.K.: Palgrave, 2001), 41–60.

9. S. Sándor John, *Bolivia's Radical Tradition: Permanent Revolution in the Andes* (Tucson: University of Arizona Press, 2009).

tious space between progovernment and antigovernment factions in the labor movement.

At the same time, and as the conflicts between the government and the FSTMB became more fraught, the MNR increasingly sought to build its own, independent power base. It turned initially to the peasant sector, creating a clientelist structure designed in part to counterbalance the power of the FSTMB and the COB. It did so with active support from the U.S. Embassy, and in particular from the U.S. Agency for International Development, which helped finance its agrarian policies under the aegis of what became the Alliance for Progress, specifically its colonization policies in the tropics of Cochabamba and Santa Cruz.[10] The MNR adopted policies designed to break down ethnic identities into a more homogenous "peasant" class and to integrate this into the regime.[11] To this end, it established a hierarchy of agrarian unions with corresponding branches at the local, provincial, departmental, and national levels. At least nominally providing a system of grassroots participation, the agrarian unions that developed in the 1950s and 1960s thus came to constitute more of a system of top-down control. This system of control became increasingly authoritarian after the MNR lost power in 1964 to the military, with the subsequent creation of the Pacto Militar Campesino.

Another area of state building related to the armed forces, which had been effectively destroyed in the 1952 Revolution. The rebuilding of the army during the 1950s—again with strong support from the United States in the context of Cold War superpower rivalries—came to represent the other main prop of the MNR's power base. The size of the military was greatly expanded and, under direct influence from Washington, its ideological stance became stridently anticommunist. The strength of the military was limited, but it lent itself to internal repression, particularly geared toward curbing the power of the more radical sectors of the union movement and putting down agrarian dissidence. By 1964, when the period of military governments began with the coup led by General René Barrientos (1964–69), the army had become a key political actor in its own right. It was able to dispense with the need to kowtow to the

10. Cole Blasier, "The United States and the Revolution," in *Beyond the Revolution*, ed. Malloy and Thorn, 53–110. The blueprint for economic diversification and the development of agribusiness in the eastern lowlands had been suggested as early on as 1941 by the Bohan Plan.

11. See Xavier Albó, "De MNRistas a kataristas: Campesinado, Estado y partidos, 1953–83," *Historia Boliviana* 5 (1985): 87–127.

MNR and civilian rule, while concentrating—through the Pacto Militar Campesino—on building up a social power base of its own. But its achievements in this respect were always limited. Even the relatively lengthy dictatorship of General Hugo Banzer Suárez in the 1970s failed to build a lasting institutional base of this sort. The circumstances under which the Banzer regime fell in 1978 showed that top-down political mobilization was a project based on weak foundations. Bolivia's return to democratic rule in 1978 was initiated with strikes in the mining camps and protests from other social sectors. The Pacto Militar Campesino did not outlive its creators.

So in what sense were the "National" Revolution and the governments of the MNR an exercise in populism? The MNR had gained prominence as a party built on corporatist lines, managing to mobilize popular sectors in ways that challenged the oligarchic status quo. Essentially middle-class in its leadership, it involved a progressive alliance that cut across social classes with a project dedicated to a new form of national development. It adopted a strongly nationalist discourse, appealing to *lo popular* but avoiding precise ideological definition. However, its rhetorical stance, as well as its praxis, switched fairly rapidly once in office, especially when its middle-class backers faced strong distributional challenges from below.

In terms of economics, the MNR's development model sought to diversify the economy and reduce its dependence on a single export commodity, tin. In its way, this model sought to promote industrialization, although the sort of import substitution as practiced elsewhere in Latin America remained elusive in a setting where the conditions for industrial growth were largely missing.[12] The role of the state in the economy was preponderant, reflecting the weakness of the private sector.[13] Nurtured on corporatist ideas, the MNR was never a "liberal" party, but the weakness of the state and its outreach meant that corporatism in Bolivia was always relative. Although it used the state's resources to mobilize support —giving a voice to previously excluded sectors—its ability to satisfy the

12. The MNR governments took some tentative steps toward promoting a metallurgical industry to increase the value added of exports. Bolivia cannot be said to have adopted the policies of import-substitution industrialization in vogue elsewhere in Latin America at the time.

13. Morales, "Economic Vulnerability," 52–53. Morales alleges that, Cuba apart, Bolivia was the most statist economy in Latin America in the 1960s and 1970s until it initiated the process of privatization in the 1980s.

needs of client groups was limited. Not only were there large parts of
Bolivia where the influence of the state was almost nonexistent, but also
after 1952 the MNR government encountered a fiscal crisis that forced it
into economic policies that were anything but *popular*.[14]

At the same time, important sectors of the politically active population consciously resisted attempts to co-opt or suborn them, and indeed
they were ready and willing to resist all attempts to clip their wings.[15]
Bolivia's class-conscious trade union movement—which was exceptional
by Latin American standards—proved remarkably resilient, although in
the process it suffered severe bouts of repression. Unlike its counterparts
elsewhere, the COB persisted as a single institution, encompassing the
ideological divides within its ranks but maintaining both its unity and a
large measure of autonomy from the Bolivian state. Whatever the populist intentions of postrevolutionary governments, the limited reach of the
state meant that they tended to fall short in reality.

Economic and Political Liberalization
and the Popular Reaction

If 1952 represented one watershed in Bolivia's recent economic and
political development, 1985 represented another. And just as it was the
MNR that brought in the changes that followed 1952, it was the MNR
again—indeed under the very same leadership of Víctor Paz Estenssoro—
that set about undoing many of the structures created by the National
Revolution. The New Economic Policy of 1985, introduced by the recently reelected Paz, set in motion a series of policies designed drastically
to reduce the scale of state intervention in Bolivia and free up the economy to market forces. These were the policies pursued with different
degrees of intensity and conviction both by Paz himself and his successors
—Jaime Paz Zamora (1989–93), Gonzalo Sánchez de Lozada (1993–97),
Hugo Banzer (1997–2001), Jorge Quiroga (2001–2), and Sánchez de

14. The stabilization crisis of 1956 involved the Siles Zuazo government having
to accept tight conditions imposed on it, at Washington's behest, by the International Monetary Fund. Among other things, it slashed food subsidies to the miners and public-sector wages.

15. The history of the FSTMB from the 1950s to the 1970s showed the degree to
which the mineworkers managed to survive savage bouts of repression and attempts
by successive governments to bring them to heel. See John, *Bolivia's Radical Tradition*.

Lozada again (2002–3). In the political sphere, a party system of sorts came into being, in which three main parties (the MNR; the Movimiento de la Izquierda Revolucionaria, MIR; and Acción Democratica Nacionalista, ADN) shared power in various combinations for nearly twenty years, along with smaller, less formal groupings like Conciencia de Patria (Condepa) and the Unión Cívica Solidaridad (UCS). Bolivia enjoyed a period of unusual political stability, and for a while this seemed to provide a powerful vindication for the sort of liberalizing reforms advocated by the Washington Consensus.[16]

It was indeed a period of considerable political as well as economic change. The New Economic Policy, among other things, dealt a heavy blow to the trade union movement (which only a few years previously had helped bring down the Banzer dictatorship) by closing down the vast majority of public-sector mines. Some 27,000 mineworkers lost their jobs between 1985 and 1988. The FSTMB, and with it the COB, found themselves bereft of most of their organized and militant members. Then, subsequently, the policies of privatization, pensions reform, and labor liberalization being pursued by Sánchez de Lozada also further reduced the unions' capacity in other sectors. The mineworkers, with all their class consciousness and independence, found themselves disarticulated and physically dispersed to other parts of Bolivia in the search for alternative livelihoods. With the demise of the mineworkers, other social forces lacked the sort of protagonistic leadership that the miners had provided over the years, both through the COB and more indirectly. At the same time, the armed forces found themselves politically weakened, following their involvement in cocaine production and trafficking during the governments of General Luis García Meza and his immediate successors (1980–82). As drugs replaced the Cold War as a key preoccupation in Washington, U.S. foreign policy shifted from its previous unwavering support for the Bolivian military.[17]

As we have seen, between 1985 and 2003, Bolivia was governed by a series of coalitions made up mainly of three main parties. Elections were

16. The Bolivian achievement of "second-generation" reforms was, e.g., much lauded by James Wolfensohn, president of the World Bank in early 1999. See James Wolfensohn, "Remarks at the Reinventing Government Conference," World Bank, Washington, January 15, 1999.

17. Indeed, in the Siles Zuazo administration that ensued (1982–85), Washington even tacitly accepted the participation of members of the Bolivian Communist Party (PCB) in the Cabinet.

held regularly and fairly, and—until at least 2001, when Banzer was forced to retire due to ill health—presidents managed to serve out their allotted terms of office. The parties that formed this new party system were a mixture of the old, like the MNR; the not so old, like ADN and the MIR; and the relatively new, like UCS and Condepa. But though the tonic here was one of consensus building and ideological convergence around a liberalizing economic credo, the parties increasingly failed to represent popular feelings or harness popular causes, except possibly at election times. Disaffection with party politics solidified around opposition to their clientelistic methods and patrimonial practices. The system was known as *cuoteo*, whereby party elites took turns dividing up the spoils of the public sector according to their electoral weight. The parties, which were run far from democratically, reflected the interests of new political elites, sidestepping the interests of those who had voted for them in elections. Even the so-called populist parties like Condepa and UCS—whose discourse was more attuned to the culture and interests of less-moneyed sectors of society—were seen to operate along the same logic. Although the institutionalization of political parties may have produced stability and facilitated technocratic policymaking, it was at the expense of representation and—ultimately—of democratic legitimacy.

However, during this period there were important institutional advances, which were designed to build bridges between the state and society.[18] Of these, the most important was Sánchez de Lozada's Law of Popular Participation of 1994 and his policies to decentralize public administration. The ostensible purpose of these was to extend the compass of the state, particularly in rural areas, by creating new institutions and using these as conduits to channel financial resources.[19] Although seek-

18. For a detailed and incisive analysis of the relationship between state and society over time, see George Gray Molina, ed., *El estado del Estado en Bolivia* (La Paz: PNUD, 2007).

19. The Law of Popular Participation, plus a law of administrative decentralization, established a large number of new rural municipalities, covering around two-thirds of the country's surface area. It established elected councils and oversight committees drawn from existing forms of social organization of different types. These were thus involved in setting priorities and supervising authorities through which substantial sums were to be channeled from central government. The structure created by Popular Participation subsequently was used by international donors to channel funds released from debt forgiveness into poverty relief. The structure introduced by Popular Participation proved durable and survived the political changes that took place subsequently.

ing to engage with popular organizations on the ground, this was very much a top-down initiative by an elitist and technocratic government with scant interest in strengthening popular organization. Skeptics at the time thought it was an elaborate piece of "neopopulism" designed to use public funds simply to build an electoral clientele for the MNR. In practice, such fears were not borne out. On the one hand, the MNR lost the 1997 elections to a megacoalition of opposing parties led by ADN; on the other hand, it helped prompt the unexpected revival of an autonomous popular organization, dissatisfied with the achievements of neoliberal policies, by creating new political spaces at the local level, giving local groups greater "voice" and providing them with more resources than they had had previously. The extent to which the Law of Popular Participation acted as a spur to grassroots organization and the appearance of new types of community leadership has been picked up and further clarified in recent studies.[20]

This, then, was the context for the sudden challenge to the existing political system that had erupted in the last few years of the twentieth century and the first ones of the twenty-first century in ways that were to once again transform the political landscape. This is not the place to detail the series of protests, beginning with the Cochabamba "water war" of 1999–2000 and culminating with the El Alto "gas war" of 2003, but simply to note how social movements of one sort or another reappeared after more than a decade of relative inactivity to impose themselves on the state and, finally, to oust an elected (albeit unpopular) president in October 2003.[21] This renewed activity was, of course, coincident with the rise of the Movimiento al Socialismo–Instrumento Político por la Soberanía de los Pueblos, to give the MAS's full name. The challenge to the *partidocracia* thus came from below, not from above, as was

20. E.g., see Roxana Liendo, *Participación Popular y el movimiento campesino aymara* (La Paz: CIPE / AIPE / Fundación Tierra, 2009).

21. The Cochabamba "water war" in 1999 and 2000 involved a largely spontaneous but cumulative sequence of protests against the privatization of water resources in and around Bolivia's third-largest city. It brought together a broad alliance of social actors and ultimately forced the Banzer government to annul its contract with the U.S. corporation Bechtel. It provided a catalyst for diverse protest movements elsewhere in the country. The 2003 "gas war" was, at least initially, a protest in El Alto against the Sánchez de Lozada government's plans to export Bolivian gas to the United States through a pipeline linking the Tarija gas fields to the Pacific through northern Chile. However, it ended up as an insurrection against the regime. For an account of both, see Crabtree, *Patterns of Protest*.

the case in some other countries of Latin America where neopopulism took root.

As is well known, the MAS arose out of the politics of the coca farmers (*cocaleros*) and their federations in the tropical Chapare region of Cochabamba, whose opposition to the coca eradication programs of successive governments led them to organize politically, taking advantage of some of the space created by the Law of Popular Participation in the mid-1990s. Influenced by the legacy of union organization—many of the fired miners from the highlands settled in the Chapare—the *cocaleros* sought to build their own political "instrument," which would be independent of the existing political parties whose acquiescence to U.S. demands for coca eradication further reinforced their conviction of the need to create a party of their own and to fight for their corner within the established political system. The coca leaf therefore became a symbol of national defiance as well as one that could be identified with the revaluation of indigenous culture. The electoral success of the MAS, first in the Chapare and then more generally in Cochabamba, showed that there was scope for new party alignments critical of the status quo and Bolivia's seeming subservience to pressures from the United States.[22]

The growing public disenchantment with the politics of "pacted democracy" became particularly evident after 1997, during the so-called megacoalition led by the then-president Hugo Banzer. The effect of the Cochabamba "water war" on the activities of social movements—long quiescent—was sustained and infectious. These movements, which were initially uncoordinated and had a variety of characteristics and agendas, gained force and exploited the political opportunities that presented themselves. They reignited deeply embedded Bolivian traditions of popular mobilization, and their methods involved a combination of direct action (protests, marches, road blockades, etc.) and engagement with the constituted political system. They took full advantage of the strong communitarian traditions in Bolivian political culture. The emergence of *indigenismo* as a potentially mobilizing force had been apparent from the late 1970s with the development of the Katarista movement, but it gained force in the late 1990s, partly as a consequence of the Law of Popular Participation and the educational reforms introduced by the Sánchez de Lozada government.[23]

22. The story is well told by Sven Harten, *The Rise of Evo Morales and the MAS* (London: Zed Books, 2011).

23. The educational reforms involved the introduction of bilingual education.

The success of the MAS was its ability to take full advantage of this mood of popular discontent with the workings of the traditional political system and the latter's estrangement from the concerns of grassroots politics. The MAS's choice to name itself an Instrumento Político (political instrument) was in itself revealing, because it did not wish to call itself a political party as such, although it chose to involve itself in electoral politics and to register officially as a party. Indeed, the loose way in which the MAS was organized—initially as a political instrument for the six federations of *cocaleros* in the Chapare tropics—was very different from how traditional parties did their business. Indeed, these local links to social movements and the idea that the movements provided the nucleus for organization, not the party, made the MAS a novel sort of party, characterized by decentralization and active participation at the grassroots level. The idea was to create a party that would be at the service of social movements, beginning with the *cocaleros*.

The phenomenal growth of the MAS as a political choice between 1997 and 2002—when it only narrowly missed winning the presidential elections—was evidence of the political vacuum. However, it also owed much to the party's ability to transcend its origins and broaden its appeal to a mass electorate. Within this five-year period, the MAS went from being a one-issue party in the Chapare to developing a discourse that encompassed the views of a wide range of voters across the country.[24] It managed to join together into a coherent platform a number of different issues: hostility toward coca eradication, the need for land reform, opposition to privatization, opposition to trade liberalization with the United States, antagonism toward multinational companies, and the desire to improve ordinary people's living standards. In short, the MAS was able to articulate a latent hostility toward the politics of the Washington Consensus in general and the politics of the United States in particular, and to weld this into a political movement with strong support, not just in Cochabamba but also in most other parts of the country.[25] At the same time, the MAS was able not just to appeal to the de-

---

The Sánchez de Lozada administration thus provided a stimulus to ethnic demands. See Xavier Albó, *Y de kataristas a MNRistas? La sorprendiente y audaz alianza entre aymaras y neoliberales en Bolivia* (La Paz: CEDOIN/UNITAS, 1993).

24. The electoral development of the MAS from 1997 onward is analyzed by John Crabtree, "Electoral Validation for Morales and the MAS," in *Evo Morales and the Movimiento al Socialismo in Bolivia: The First Term in Context, 2006–2010*, edited by Adrian J. Pearce (London: Institute for the Study of the Americas, 2011).

25. Sven Harten, *Rise of Evo Morales.*

fense of indigenous values but also to link these to wider issues such as the defense of the country's natural resources and ecology. While retaining its rural base, the MAS was therefore able to build up an alliance of constituencies and to highlight the common threads that would hold them together. Its experience thus contrasted vividly with the politics of the *indigenista* Movimiento Indígena Pachakuti (MIP), led by Felipe Quispe, one of Morales's chief rivals within the pro-indigenous movement. Rather than build a broad movement, the MIP sought to mobilize around strictly indigenous issues among the Aymara peoples of rural La Paz. As an electoral movement, its support ended up being narrowly constrained.

In what sense, then, can this political reaction against the politics of pacted democracy be called populist? In one sense, it seems to be quintessentially populist if we take as a definition of populism that offered by Ernesto Laclau and his colleagues.[26] It was the ability to move from a particularist to a more universal claim, and by so doing to create a new hegemonic discourse, that marked out the MAS. Its growth was, indeed, a story of creating a "chain of equivalence." The story of the MAS was also built around antagonism toward the status quo, involving an appeal to a marginalized and underenfranchised population that was largely ignored by the existing political institutions, which Francisco Panizza has emphasized as a defining criterion of populism.[27] However, taking other definitions of what populism can mean, one can reach rather different conclusions. If, for example, one interprets populism essentially as a top-down mode of mobilization to rally support for policies of structural reform of one sort or another, involving the incorporation of new sectors of the population as political participants, then the story of the MAS would not appear to be so populist. Indeed, it would seem to be quintessentially a bottom-up movement that, in the process of challenging the established elite, gained widespread political traction. Nor is this the story of political elites seeking to bypass representative institutions in a direct appeal to *el pueblo*; rather, it seems to be a self-conscious attempt to build new institutions that represent popular interests in a more genuine way within established institutions. A distinc-

26. Ernesto Laclau, "Populism: What's in a Name?" in *Populism and the Mirror of Democracy*, edited by Francisco Panizza (London: Verso, 2005), 32–49.

27. Francisco Panizza, *Contemporary Latin America: Development and Democracy beyond the Washington Consensus* (London: Zed Books, 2009): 174–76.

tion needs to be drawn here between the MAS in Bolivia and the movements spearheaded by Hugo Chávez in Venezuela or even Rafael Correa in Ecuador. But this will become clearer as I now seek to make sense of what the MAS is and how it has evolved since its landslide election victory in December 2005.

The MAS and Its Experience in Government

As we have seen, the MAS is a party that stands out compared with many others in Latin America for the strength of its origins in grassroots social movements. Possibly the closest parallel here is to be found in the origins and growth of the Partido dos Trabalhadores (Workers' Party) in Brazil. In no sense is the MAS to be characterized as a traditional or elite party. In what follows, I seek to elucidate the relationship between party, president, and social movements within the dynamic of power relations as these have developed since 2006. As mentioned above, the process of change has not all been in one direction. Policy has zigzagged in response to a variety of pressures, once again demonstrating the relative weakness of the state vis-à-vis society.

The nature and strength of Bolivia's social movements vary considerably from place to place, reflecting the country's heterogeneity as a whole, including its social structures and ethnic makeup. However, two powerful organizational traditions persist: the union tradition, and that of the indigenous or ethnic community. The structures of the agrarian *sindicato*, many of which came into existence in the wake of the 1953 agrarian reform, still prevail in much of the country, influenced by the forms of union organization pioneered by the mineworkers in the 1940s and 1950s. At the same time, the indigenous community has persisted, especially in the highlands; and with the resurgence in the salience of indigenous politics since the 1980s, some communities have reverted to time-honored forms of organization.[28] In the eastern lowlands, too, indigenous movements have emerged as strident and articulate defenders of their interests. New forms of popular organizations have also sprung up that have reflected the process of urbanization in cities like El Alto,

---

28. Frequently, these forms of organization take similar form, though the nomenclature may differ. Previously union-based forms of peasant organization have sought to reconstitute themselves in the highlands as traditional *ayllus*.

where neighborhood committees (*juntas vecinales*) and other forms of local organization have become key actors.[29]

Despite their differences, these social movements have important unifying characteristics. One is the persistence of a strong communitarian tradition, with problems discussed and decisions taken collectively. Among most social movements, there is a strong culture of active participation and adherence to decisions. There is also strong pressure on leaders (*dirigentes*)—whether elected officials or traditionally chosen community elders—to be held accountable to those (the *base*) who put them in positions of authority. In rural areas, in particular, there is a tradition of the rotation of positions of responsibility. Of course, these characteristics vary according to circumstances, and decisionmaking is not always as participatory as this would suggest; in practice, a good deal of clientelism and patronage are involved in community politics. But these participatory principles continue to provide an important framework for how decisions are made and how power is delegated. Chains of representation—from the local level, to the provincial level, to the departmental level, and finally to the national level—inevitably involve the delegation of authority, but they also create important lines of accountability whereby *dirigentes* are judged and sometimes recalled.

The MAS has matured infused with this culture of delegation and accountability, which—in the eyes of many—was vitiated and ignored by the traditional parties through their ostensible quest for money and jobs (*cuoteo* or *prebendalismo*). Notions of direct democracy arguably owe more to these traditions than to abstract critiques of liberal democracy. But such participatory principles can run counter to the efficacy of government, particularly where the central government is concerned. When the MAS took office in January 2006, it seemed quite likely that the practicalities of governing the country—in which local interests tended to be subsumed to wider concerns—would lead to a process of institutionalization within it. These would force the MAS to become more structured, bureaucratic, and "top-down," responding to a variety of interests and not just those of social movements. Perhaps echoing the experiences of the early 1950s, the bottom-up politics of *protesta* would thus give way to a top-down logic of governance in which the interests of social movements would be marginalized by other political or economic demands.

29. On social organization, the state, identity, and politics in El Alto, see Sian Lazar, *El Alto, Rebel City* (Durham, N.C.: Duke University Press, 2008).

Seven years after the MAS took office, and following its reelection for a further five-year term in 2009, it is possible to reach some preliminary judgments about the nature of the MAS in government and the extent to which it has undergone this sort of change. This is of some relevance to the discussion about populism. On balance, it would seem that the Morales government has remained surprisingly responsive to its grassroots constituency and has not sacrificed its original social links on the altars of political pluralism and governmental efficiency.

Indicative of this has been Morales's choice of Cabinet ministers. Many in 2006 came from humble—some would say plebeian—origins; people with little or no experience in government who rose to political prominence through leadership roles within (or accompanying) social movements. These were a far cry from the technocratic elites who had served in previous administrations or, indeed, the middle-class cadres promoted by the MNR after 1952. The same was true of those who took their seats in Congress, particularly members elected as uninominal deputies who hitherto had been mostly unknown figures in national politics. Although some were "appointed" from above, the majority emerged from a complex nomination procedure involving different echelons within the social movements.[30] Likewise, most of the candidates put forward by the MAS for the election to the Constituent Assembly in July 2006 were drawn from the leadership of social movements; the president of the Assembly, Silvia Lazarte (derided for her popular origins by some opposition figures), was typical of the involvement of ordinary people of indigenous origin who formed a large part of the assembly. The Plurinational Legislative Assembly (as Congress was called under the new Constitution), which was elected in 2009, was also composed of large numbers of members who had never before held public office, most of whom were drawn from and chosen by social movements.[31]

30. The personal narratives of members of Congress elected in 2005 are given by Moira Suazo, *Cómo nació el MAS: La ruralización de la política en Bolivia* (La Paz: Friedrich Ebert Stiftung, 2008). This provides some valuable first-hand evidence of how MAS candidates were selected, how the MAS works in practice, and the sort of organizational weaknesses that exist within the MAS. While it is true that in 2005 the MAS opened its doors to candidates from other backgrounds (especially middle-class and professional ones), this appears to have been less the case in 2009.

31. This was particularly the case of "uninominal" candidates to the Chamber of Deputies. The degree of rotation of seats on the MAS benches was very high from the previous legislature.

Since first taking office, Morales has given great importance to maintaining the links between the party "apparatus" in government and the social movements that (loosely) constitute the MAS's social base.[32] He has thus sought to avoid the same pitfalls that beset the traditional parties whose legitimacy dwindled as they lost touch with their base of support. Morales has also been concerned to avoid the emergence of possible rivals on the left. Much, if not most, of his time has been given up to meeting delegations from social movements or to making flying visits to communities across the country. Such linkages helped reaffirm his political leadership, but they also served to provide channels for articulation.[33] Among the most difficult issues for him have been the (fairly frequent) instances in which social movements have found themselves in conflict with one another, often vying for control over natural resources. The armed confrontation in November 2006 between the unionized mineworkers of Huanuni and the large numbers of informal miners working in cooperatives was one particularly difficult instance, but there have also been many others. And there have been many cases of social movements clashing with the government over aspects of policy in which the former feel that their interests have not been properly taken into account. Instances of this became more frequent following Morales's reelection in 2009, again showing the weakness of the state in imposing solutions at the local level. In 2011, there were widespread protests against the government's policies to raise fuel prices, there were demonstrations against wage restraints, and there was a march by indigenous peoples from the lowlands protesting against the government's plans to build a road through their territory. In each case, the govern-

32. These include the peasant confederation, the Confederación Sindical Única de Trabajadores Campesinos de Bolivia (CSUTCB); the women's peasant federation, the Federación Nacional de Mujeres Campesinas Bartolina Sisa; the Confederación Sindical de Colonizadores de Bolivia (CSCB) (recently renamed "Interculturales"); and the federations of *cocaleros*. These formed an alliance in 2003, the Unity Pact (Pacto de Unidad) with the indigenous confederations of the lowlands, the Confederación de Pueblos Indígenas del Oriente Boliviana (CIDOB), and of the highlands, the Consejo Nacional de Ayllus y Markas de Q'ollasuyo (CONAMAQ). By 2011, the Pacto de Unidad had broken down, with sectors of CIDOB and CONAMAQ moving into opposition against the government.

33. The daily agenda of the president, usually beginning well before daybreak, is unrelenting and a source of strain for those around him. This is well conveyed by Martín Sivak, *Jefazo: Retrato íntimo de Evo Morales* (Santa Cruz: Editorial Sudamericana, 2008).

ment found itself having to bow to popular pressures at considerable political cost.

Under Morales, the presidency has become the point at which such disputes and discrepancies tend to resolve themselves, rather than at lower levels of the state bureaucracy. This preeminence has been enhanced by the lack of structure within the ruling party and the subordinate standing of its elected representatives. Several institutional innovations, however, have helped provide something of a structure for the relationship between the executive and the social movements. One of the more important of these was the Coordinadora Nacional para el Cambio (Conalcam), an organization originally set up in 2007 to provide a semi-institutionalized space where policy issues could be discussed between government and the social movements. This was an initiative taken by the MAS deputies in Congress, who were concerned by the lack of institutionalized mechanisms of mediation between state and civil society. Although there were subsequently significant defections, Conalcam initially involved twenty-seven national-level organizations, including representatives from the Central Obrera Boliviana, peasant unions, women's organizations, and various labor sectors. As well as facilitating bottom-up dialogue, it proved a useful instrument for mobilizing the government's supporters against its adversaries, particularly in 2008, when political elites in the eastern departments (or *media luna*) threatened secession. However, in no sense has it been a structure with a permanent existence or life of its own, and by 2011 its importance as a mediating body between government and social movements had declined.

Although the MAS remains loose and unstructured in the way it works, its decisionmaking is centralized in the person of the president, albeit in consultation with social movements and a small inner group of trusted colleagues (who are often the target of criticism from those in the party who do not belong to it). It is difficult to overstate the importance of Morales within the political system as presently constituted. Not only does he stand head and shoulders above all others within the MAS, but he still commands extraordinary legitimacy in the eyes of those in the street simply because of who he is—Bolivia's first-ever *popular* and indigenous head of state, and a person of humble origins who symbolizes the sorts of values and practices that are widely shared among the poor and indigenous majority of Bolivian voters. That he received nearly two-thirds support in the August 2008 recall referendum and only just under this (against a variety of candidates) in the 2009 presidential election reflects this public standing.

But whereas decisionmaking is centralized in the figure of the president —frequently bypassing elected institutions like the Congress—Morales's power is by no means absolute. As we have seen, this has become particularly evident since his reelection in 2009. As well as having to yield to pressures from his opponents on the right—not least in the tussles leading up to the ratification of the new Constitution in January 2009—he also had to cede to pressures from social movements and organizations with agendas of their own. He has been keenly aware that neither he nor the MAS can dictate to the social movements that sustain them politically. So though he may use the political resources at his disposal to influence the leaders or members of social movements, these cannot be construed as being subservient to him or other leaders of the MAS. Although a degree of institutionalization may have crept into the way the party works, the relationship between leaders and the grass roots remains essentially fluid.

When it took office in 2006, the MAS saw itself as building a political system that supplanted what it saw as a corrupted system of liberal democracy, creating a more participative polity with strong elements of direct democracy. As it emerged, the new Constitution sought to increase levels of participation while maintaining older and well-established forms of representative government.[34] Some of the more radical provisions—such as creating a "fourth power" in which social movements would exert primacy over the other powers of the state—were dropped in the negotiations with the opposition in return for their acquiescence over holding the necessary referendum to approve the Constitution. As finally agreed to, the constitutional text highlighted the need for greater public participation and accountability. It introduced a system of indigenous and other autonomies also designed to enhance participation. At the time of writing at least, these new spaces for participation had not been firmly established.

Aspects of direct democracy were already in place under the old constitutional arrangements. Referendums and *consultas* on key aspects of policy had already been used well before the new Constitution came into force. Indeed, the previous four years had been ones of nonstop electoral

34. For an analysis of the 2009 Constitution, see Willem Assies, "Bolivia's New Constitution and Its Implications," in *Evo Morales*, ed. Pearce.

activity of one sort or another, something that helped sustain Morales's political stock and contain that of the opposition. The rule on referendums predated the Morales administration,[35] with President Carlos Mesa holding the first one in July 2004 on gas policy.[36] The use of the *consulta* to remove or ratify those in public office had been used in 2008, when the president submitted himself to a recall vote, along with the prefects of the nine departments.[37]

Still, the evolution of politics under Morales has arguably seen aspects of liberal pluralism eroded. The MAS has adopted a deliberately antagonistic discourse toward its enemies, real or imagined. These include variously the U.S. administration, the "*oligarquía*" of Santa Cruz, the traditional political parties and their leaders, and the presence of transnational companies. This has been a way of orchestrating unity among a heterogeneous political public in ways that create a community of interest among its supporters, although in practice policy often diverged from the discourse. The cost here has been to reduce spaces for active opposition, at both national and regional levels, a trend that appeared to become more obvious during the government's second term, when it exercised control over both houses of the legislature.[38] The government's critics have repeatedly drawn attention to what they see as the desire of Morales and the MAS to eliminate all sources of opposition and to heighten the powers of the executive at the expense of the legislature and the judiciary. Although ostensibly designed to open the system

35. The use of referendums was first mooted in proposals made by the Banzer government in 2001. They were included in a constitutional reform law the following year. See Eduardo Rodríguez Veltzé, "The Development of Constituent Power in Bolivia," in *Unresolved Tensions: Bolivia Past and Present*, edited by John Crabtree and Laurence Whitehead (Pittsburgh: University of Pittsburgh Press, 2008), 149–50.

36. Other referendums held during Morales's first period in government (2006–10) included the July 2006 referendum on regional autonomies, the August 2008 recall referendum for prefects and the president, the January 2009 referendum on the Constitution, and the referendum held at the same time on imposing a maximum upward limit on landholding. In April 2010, there were also local referendums on regional autonomies in those departments that had voted "no" in July 2006.

37. As we have seen, Morales was ratified with a large majority. The two prefects who were not ratified were both opponents of the government: Manfred Reyes Villa (Cochabamba) and José Luis Paredes (La Paz).

38. In the elections of December 2009, the MAS won slightly more than two-thirds of the seats in the Plurinational Legislative Assembly. As a consequence of the April 2010 regional elections, the MAS won six of the nine governorships and had a working majority in all but one (Santa Cruz) of the regional legislative assemblies.

of choosing senior judges, the 2011 elections to this end (involving the preselection of candidates by the legislature) were seen by some as reinforcing partisan control through the MAS's majority in both houses of the Plurinational Legislative Assembly. The Morales government was thus accused of undermining respect for the rule of law.[39]

The Morales government therefore clearly exemplifies some of the characteristics that can be seen as populist. Its discourse involves a strongly anti–status quo appeal, aimed at those who feel that they have been inadequately represented in the past within the Bolivian political system. This constantly highlights *lo popular*, and this is evidently an important aspect of defending its legitimacy. There are certainly elements of charismatic leadership and the use of notions of the nation and social inclusion in such a way as to create a strong community of interest. There are few institutional checks and balances to restrain that leadership. The government's public discourse also tends to highlight perceived enemies in such a way as to underscore that community of interest. Representative institutions, though present, are not always at the center of decisionmaking. A great deal of presidential time and energy goes into cultivating the support that the government enjoys. The MAS government has espoused a system of direct democracy that responds to the critique of the workings of liberal representative democracy.

At the same time, however, it would be misleading to suggest that Morales's appeal to the *pueblo* is simply a top-down maneuver to control the popular movement or that it has used the resources of the state in a profligate manner to this end.[40] Within the social movements and in their relation with government and the state, there are powerful bottom-up influences with and to which Morales has been permanently at pains to

---

39. One of the provisions of the new Constitution concerned the use of popular elections to ratify senior judicial appointments, including the Supreme Court. Elections were held in October 2011. Countering these criticisms, the MAS argued that the elections served to end the previous influence of elite groups to influence judicial appointments. Those elections certainly broadened the composition of the judiciary, with a substantial number of women and people of indigenous origin elected for the first time.

40. It has been frequently pointed out, not least by officials of the International Monetary Fund, that the Morales administration has not pursued "populist" policies in the sense of irresponsible fiscal and/or monetary management. Indeed, its macroeconomic policies proved fairly orthodox. Fear of stimulating the sort of hyperinflation that characterized the early 1980s may have been a powerful constraining factor.

connect and listen. On occasions, government policy has had to be jettisoned because it simply did not meet with popular approval. Although clearly decisions come from the top, the extent of popular participation in Bolivian politics has increased, and the social movements—to varying degrees—maintain their own agendas and seek to ensure that the government complies with them. They are not necessarily subservient or quiescent clienteles. The MAS does not control them as such; indeed, even though it may wish to impose control from above, the state lacks the power and reach to be able to manipulate social movements to its own ends. In this sense, at least, the populist label may be less appropriate.

Conclusion

The history of social movements, political parties, and the state in Bolivia during the last sixty years provides fertile terrain for examining how these interact. Bolivia stands out in Latin America as a country where the state remains relatively weak in outreach, and where social movements (partly as a consequence) have developed in ways that have given them greater power and autonomy than in other parts of Latin America. Meanwhile, political parties have demonstrated their limitations in providing a bridge between the state and society. Although ties of clientelism and top-down control are by no means absent from the Bolivian story, particularly in some parts of the country, there is a potent tradition of bottom-up mobilization. This is, at least in part, a legacy of 1952.

Of course, as we have seen, the relationship between these elements has fluctuated over time. During the post-1952 period, a new state came into being as a result of the mobilizations of the previous period, and it sought to impose order on the activities of social movements. The MNR, the party that had emerged in defiance of the old order, sought to organize the relationship between an interventionist state on one hand and society on the other hand, at once channeling popular demands and seeking to control them. After 1964, the armed forces tried to create a new institutional structure to replace the MNR, particularly in articulating social demands. The period of neoliberal hegemony in the 1980s and 1990s sought to restructure this relationship between state and society, offering greater space to political parties to institutionalize politics. Their failure to create new, lasting representative structures partly led to a political vacuum where resurgent social movements were able to assert

themselves. The MAS gave these movements political leadership, and
after 2006 it sought once again to restructure the relationship between
state, party, and social movements.

The achievements of 1952 cast a long shadow over the decades that
followed, deeply affecting political culture in Bolivia. Although the rise
of the MAS was due to much more proximate factors, there can be little
doubt that the National Revolution—as it continues to called in Bolivia
—exerts considerable influence. For some, the MAS has picked up the
agenda that the MNR failed to pursue in the 1950s, in translating
the promise of citizenship into reality and in creating a nation where the
principles of popular sovereignty prevail. At the same time, however, the
project of the MAS differs considerably from that of the MNR, particularly with respect to ethnic affirmation. The MAS sees itself as not just
picking up where the MNR left off but as pursuing a project of transforming a neocolonial state (of which the MNR was a part) that was
based on ethnic exclusion. The extent to which it has been successful in
this objective is open to discussion, and there has been a constant tension
in the discourse of the MAS between these two objectives—the nationalist and the indigenous.

The legacy of 1952 is also powerful in legitimizing popular protest, a
tradition of mobilization with roots stretching back to colonial days.
The memory of the miners and the COB still acts as a powerful trigger
for popular mobilization today. However, this tradition exists alongside
one of top-down mobilization by the state. The two traditions continue
into the present period, with the MAS at once involved in top-down
mobilization, as well as responding to mobilization from the bottom up.
However, what makes the Bolivian experience unusual is the importance
of participation within social movements and the responsiveness and
accountability of the *dirigentes*. As a *dirigente*, Morales sees the need to
make himself accountable to them, as well as to use their backing for his
own political purposes.

There is, as I have suggested, a strong legacy of populism derived
from the National Revolution and the project of the MNR, albeit a populism constrained by a vibrant society and the limitations of a relatively
weak state. The MAS government inherits some of these traits, not least
that of appealing to *lo popular*. It is still too early to say whether Morales
and the MAS will end up permanently changing the relationship between
society and the state. Certainly, however, the MAS has sought to make
the state more inclusive by bringing within the political system those

who were previously at the margins. This may have the effect of strengthening the state, changing thereby its relationship with social actors and movements. But seven years after first taking office, this was at most an incipient process. Although they may reveal typically populist traits, in governing Morales and the MAS remain constrained by the strength of social organization and social pressures from below. Bolivia's traditions of popular organization and participatory politics still set it apart from most other countries in Latin America.

Chapter 11

Rafael Correa and His Plebiscitary Citizens' Revolution

César Montúfar

The emergence of populist governments in the Andes poses several questions concerning democracy and its present status in the region. On one hand, it raises important doubts about the validity of viewing populism as a passing phase, as a transitory phenomenon, in the modern history of Andean societies. On the other hand, it brings into discussion whether populism is a path for the inclusion of excluded groups, an opportunity to generate symbolic, political, economic, and social-democratizing trends; or whether it is a phenomenon that leads to the institutionalization of authoritarian regimes aimed at concentrating power, limiting civil liberties, and implementing a political dynamic contrary to pluralism and democratic coexistence.

A Hypothesis for Understanding Correa's Populism

Regardless of the theoretical perspective one chooses for interpreting contemporary populism—for instance, a focus that understands populism as a set of strategies for gaining access to power, or an approach that interprets it as a peculiar political logic[1]—the existing literature provides several common characteristics: the cult of strong and charismatic leaders, the prevalence of a polarizing discourse, a rejection of the principles of democratic representation, and an anti-institutional character.[2] Despite these common elements, drawing on chapter 1, one may distinguish at least three historical subtypes of populism in Latin America: the classical populism of the 1930s and 1940s, which was associated with import-substitution industrialization policies and other inclusive agendas; the neopopulist movements of the 1990s, which pursued neoliberal reforms throughout the continent; and the contemporary radical populism predominant in the Andean countries, which embrace, among other elements, the so-called twenty-first-century socialist project.[3]

My point is that a crucial trait of all three subtypes of populism is a double movement toward promoting intense deinstitutionalization processes while simultaneously creating new institutions. Regime change is a central characteristic of Latin American populism, in general. However, the radicalization of such an institutional impulse constitutes the dominant element of contemporary radical populist movements. Much more so than in previous populist experiences, Andean radical populists incorporate a theological and refoundational dimension into their political project; and thus they call for a militant attitude toward creating entirely new societies and states, by means of profound constitutional transformations.

In fact, if one looks closely at the political strategies of Chávez, Morales, and Correa, they have very effectively advanced their political projects not only through the use of conventional populist techniques but also through processes of radical reinstitutionalization, which began with the writing of new constitutions. The constitutional dimension has been fundamental for the consolidation of their leadership and political hege-

---

1. Kurt Weyland, "Clarificando un concepto cuestionado: El populismo en el estudio de la política latinoamericana," in *Releer los Populismos*, edited by Kurt Weyland (Quito: CAAP, 2004); Flavia Friedenberg, *La tentación populista: Una vía al poder en América Latina* (Madrid: Síntesis, 2007).

2. Ernesto Laclau, *La razón populista* (Buenos Aires: FCE, 2008).

3. See chapter 1 of the present volume and Carlos de la Torre, "The History of a Controversy: Populism in Latin American Politics," draft paper prepared for the conference "Populism of the Twenty-First Century," Woodrow Wilson International Center for Scholars, Washington, 2009.

mony. In this sense, I argue that the success of radical populist leaders depends on the effectiveness of their strategies for demolishing the institutions of the old regime while putting together a new constitutional order.

This element differentiates contemporary radical populism from neo-populist leaders in the region. It is true that, in the 1990s, neoliberal neopopulists like Menem and Fujimori put forward important constitutional amendments to facilitate structural adjustment, privatization, and policies geared to the concentration of power. Nevertheless, neither of them made reforming the Constitution the heart of a refoundational project. In this respect, contemporary radical populism is more closely similar to classical populism, at least in its ambition to deeply transform societies and political systems. The scope of the revolution sought by Andean radical populists can be compared with Argentine Peronism or the Brazilian Estado Novo in its refoundational inspiration. Thus, in both classical and contemporary radical populism, one finds that what is at stake is a passionate struggle to construct a brand new future for their respective countries.

Without doubt, Rafael Correa's political movement could be inscribed as part of the radical populist trend in the Andes, due both to the adoption of the twenty-first-century socialist ideology and the enactment of a global institutional strategy. This assertion obliges one to analyze the different resources, both material and symbolic, used by Correa to institutionalize a new political regime predicated upon a model of plebiscitary legitimacy. As this chapter seeks to explain, *correísmo* has brought into Ecuadorian politics a vertiginous process of regime change that has implied the total destruction of the previous regime—the so-called *partidocracia*.[4] By *partidocracia*, I mean the political regime born in Ecuador when the country returned to democracy in 1979.[5] This regime confronted a long period of crisis, marked by extreme political

4. Actually, Correa borrowed the word *partidocracia* from Lucio Gutiérrez, who was the first to use it in contemporary Ecuadorian political discourse.

5. The *partidocracia* regime was run by the political parties that governed the country between 1979, when Ecuador returned to democracy, and 2007. These were the Social Christian Party (Partido Social Cristiano), the Christian Democratic (Democracia Popular), the Social-Democratic (Izquierda Democrática), and other populist parties headed by caudillos like Abdalá Bucaram, Lucio Gutiérrez, and Álvaro Noboa. Left-oriented groups like the Socialist Party or the Popular Democratic Movement were also part of the *partidocracia*, although they never won the presidency.

fragmentation and instability. In the period 1996–2007, six different governments ruled the country and none of the elected presidents could finish his term. Correa's radical populism put an end to this trend, inaugurating not only another presidency but also a new historical epoch in Ecuador.

In short, to correctly interpret radical populist movements like Rafael Correa's Citizens' Revolution, one should study the strategies put into effect to provoke rapid regime change and the creation of a new model of political legitimacy. Deinstitutionalization and reinstitutionalization processes should be given equal consideration in this analysis. Therein, the remaking of the Constitution should be seen as a crucial dimension. However, other more traditional populist mechanisms—such as discourse, communication, and propaganda, as well as redistributive policies—should also be taken into account to obtain a complete picture of this political phenomenon.

Along these lines, this chapter answers the following questions:

1. What successful mechanisms has Rafael Correa employed to construct his overwhelmingly popular political project?
2. Through what strategies has he managed to provide legitimacy to his refoundational agenda?
3. What type of political regime is the Citizens' Revolution aiming at institutionalizing in Ecuador, and how does it differ from the previous regime, the *partidocracia*?

These questions place us in the field of *how* the Correa administration has proceeded; *what kind* of political leadership sustains it; and *what new forms* of political legitimacy, authority, and institutionalization are under construction. Toward the end of the chapter, I explore the legitimizing dynamics that have been put in practice by the Correa administration, and the extent to which one can talk of a double plebiscitary legitimacy, built upon both indirect and direct forms of political participation.

This chapter examines the birth and consolidation of the Citizens' Revolution, beginning in January 2007, when Rafael Correa took office, through September 30, 2010, the date on which the government confronted a severe political crisis triggered by a police revolt. I argue that after this date, Correa's strategy changed radically, modifying its character. Herein, I present an interpretation of the Citizens' Revolution only applicable to its initial moment.

Four Features of Correa's Radical Populism

Because the national and international images of Correa's Citizens' Revolution are full of flaws and misconceptions, before tackling the questions posed above, it is important to describe its four principal features. First, *correísmo* is a top-down—not a bottom-up, social, or truly citizens'—revolution; Rafael Correa's political success has not come from mobilizing organized sectors of society. Instead, it derives from a three-layered political strategy whereby he has managed to build a new electoral majority that, in itself, has nothing to do with an underground, bottom-up social mobilization process. In October 2006, then–presidential candidate Rafael Correa placed second in the first round of the presidential election with 22 percent of the vote. One month later, in November 2006, he won the runoff election, and the presidency, with 56 percent of the vote, capitalizing on the large number of Ecuadorians who viewed his opponent negatively. His political movement, Alianza País, lacks organic links with social movements or other organized social groups and, moreover, it has not been a space for processing citizens' demands, such as those from consumers, public service users, and environmentalists. And this is true in spite of the fact that Correa's discourse has incorporated very popular issues, and has included ideological claims raised by the leftist middle sectors, young citizens, artists, intellectuals, and the like. These groups have been easily seduced by Correa's anti-American rhetoric, his rejection of the International Monetary Fund's and World Bank's conditions, and his denunciation of traditional elite politics in general. Without organic ties to any social sector, however, PAÍS has consolidated its effectiveness as an electoral machine that is very efficient in organizing electoral campaigns and performing proselytizing tasks—but is unable to articulate concrete social and economic interests, demands, or specific proposals from organized social sectors. In this strict sense, Correa's movement is not a citizens' revolution—it is not a movement emerging from below; instead, it is a revolution from above, a revolution created by the executive branch.[6]

Second, *correísmo* is an international and regional movement; Correa's revolution, as conceived by its leader, is not merely a local or national political project but part of a continental or even global movement:

6. See César Montúfar, "El gobierno de Rafael Correa," Working Paper, Diálogo Interamericano, Washington, 2008.

twenty-first-century socialism. Correa identifies his Citizens' Revolution with similar political projects, such as those of Hugo Chávez in Venezuela and Evo Morales in Bolivia. Thus, Correa views the historic projection of his administration as the expression of a regional trend aimed at redefining international politics, one that should change Ecuador's geopolitical alignment as a whole. Toward this end, Correa's government has pursued close diplomatic ties with Iran, Russia, and, especially, China, and it has actively promoted alternative regional integration initiatives such as the Alianza Bolivariana para los Pueblos de Nuestra América (known as ALBA; Bolivarian Alliance for the Peoples of Our America), the Banco del Sur, and the Unión de Naciones Suramericanas (known as UNASUR; Union of South American Nations). As mentioned above, his international approach has been very critical of multilateral organizations like the World Bank and the International Monetary Fund, and he has placed little priority on traditional integration initiatives such as the Andean Community and the Organization of American States. He perceives his political project as part of a global geopolitical shift toward the creation of a new international order.

Despite these connections with Chávez's Bolivarian Revolution, Correa's project differs from it in the fact that Ecuador is not as rich or dependent on oil revenues as is Venezuela. Also, the Citizens' Revolution has not stressed the grassroots organizations, communal councils, and other mechanisms of participatory democracy on which the Bolivarian Revolution has focused. Moreover, Correa, a civilian leader with academic credentials, is very different from Hugo Chávez with his military persona.

Likewise, Ecuador's Citizens' Revolution is significantly different from the Bolivian experience. The latter clearly represents a political movement built from below—a process whereby myriad social movements have taken state power through elections. Moreover, the Movimiento al Socialismo (known as the MAS) in Bolivia cannot be properly defined as a typical electoral apparatus, as PAÍS can, but as a coalition of different social movements and political organizations. Finally, Morales incorporates indigenous claims as an essential part of his political project, whereas *correísmo* has systematically excluded any organic linkage with social and indigenous movements.

All in all, Correa's model of twenty-first-century socialism is more similar to its Venezuelan counterpart. Quite possibly, this has to do with the petro-state context shared by Venezuela and Ecuador, and with the sharp distance between the leader's political project and the agenda of indigenous movements. Both elements mark an evident contrast with one of the central traits of the Bolivian multicultural Revolution.

Third, *correísmo* represents an innovation, but within the Ecuadorian populist tradition: Correa's leadership presents us with a continuation of Ecuadorian populism.[7] Correa's discourse and practices are undeniably similar to the populist features of recent neoliberal populist leaders, the so-called neopopulists, such as Abdalá Bucaram and Lucio Gutiérrez.[8] Yet, besides its leftist ideological profile, Correa's populism also brings in several new elements to the populist tradition, which are compared in table 11.1.

In spite of their common populist core, Correa, quite differently from his neopopulist predecessors, has successfully built a new state and political regime. Populist leaders, like Bucaram and Gutiérrez, were ousted from power long before completing the terms to which they were elected. Still, Correa's leadership, his polarizing moral discourse, the cult of his personality, and his confrontation with the status quo cleary show his affinity for the classical populist matrix. This is even more evident if one compares Correa with other populist leaders, for instance, José María Velasco Ibarra, the quintessential Ecuadorian populist, who was elected to five terms as president and dominated the country's politics between the 1930s and the 1970s.[9]

7. For a recapitulation of the debate on populism in Ecuador, see Felipe Burbano and Carlos de la Torre, "Reflexiones sobre el estudio del populismo en el Ecuador," in *El populismo en el Ecuador*, by Felipe Burbano and Carlos de la Torre (Quito: ILDIS, 1989). For recent research, see Flavia Friedenberg, "El flautista de Hammelin: Liderazgo y populismo en la democracia ecuatoriana," in *El retorno del pueblo: Populismo y nuevas democracias en América Latina*, edited by Carlos de la Torre and Enrique Peruzzotti (Quito: FLACSO, 2008); and Hernán Ibarra, "El populismo en la política ecuatoriana contemporánea," in *Releer los populismos*, ed. Weyland.

8. For interpretations of Bucaram's populism, see Carlos de la Torre, *Un solo toque: Populismo y cultura política en el Ecuador* (Quito: CAAP, 1996); Flavia Friedenberg, *Jama, caleta y camello: Las estrategias de Abdalá Bucaram y el PRE para ganar las elecciones* (Quito: Universidad Andina Simón Bolívar, 2003); and Catherine Conaghan, "Bucaram en Panamá," in *Retorno del pueblo*, ed. de la Torre and Peruzzotti. For a study of Lucio Gutiérrez's populism, see César Montúfar, "El populismo intermitente de Lucio Gutiérrez," in *Retorno del pueblo*, ed. de la Torre and Peruzzotti.

9. The studies of *velasquismo* are abundant in the Ecuadorian social sciences. The most influential works have been by Agustín Cueva, *El proceso de dominación política del Ecuador* (Havana: Casa de las Américas, 1972); Pablo Cuvi, *Velasco*

Table 11.1. A Comparison of the New Elements Brought into the Populist Tradition by Correa's Populism

	Abdalá Bucaram, August 1996–February 1997:	Lucio Gutiérrez, January 2003–April 2005:	Rafael Correa: January 2007–Present:
Dominant Tendency	Neopopulist	Neopopulist	Radical Populist
Main political actor	The poor	Honest patriots	Citizenry/people/clients
Caudillo's self-definition	"The loving madman"; "El loco que ama"	Dictócrata: a dictator for the rich and a democrat for the people	A revolutionary; a citizen impassioned for the Patria
Charismatic profile	Abdalá is one of us	Lucio is a military hero and a patriot	Correa is an extraordinary man; a secular saint
Social support base	Urban marginalized population	Middle-level campesinos	Middle class urban sectors plus a multi-class coalition
Regional support base	Coast/Highlands/Amazon Region	Amazon Region/Highlands/Coast	Highlands/Coast/Amazon Region
Slogan that defines the political process	"The strength of the poor" ("La fuerza de los pobres")	"A single force" ("Una sola fuerza")	"The Homeland is now for everyone"; "La Patria ya es de todos"
Sociopolitical trend of the ruling party	Assimilation into the status quo	Assimilation into the status quo	Concentration of power and construction of new ruling elite
Social profile administrative staff	Political-entrepreneurial	Military-technocratic	Revolutionary-technocratic
Ethnic identity	Cholo/Lebanese	Cholo/Indian	Mestizo
Economic policy	Neoliberal	Neoliberal	Sumak Kausay, inward growth and state centered; post developmentalism
Political organization	Partido Roldosista Ecuatoriano (PRE): From electoral machine to client-based party	Partido Sociedad Patriótica (PSP): From electoral machine to client-based party	Alianza País (PAIS): From electoral machine to client-based political movement
Enemy	Aniñados: "childish" oligarchy	Oligarchy, bankers and "corrupt" political parties	Partidocracia: party establishment; pelucones: upper class elites; the oligarchy, the mass media, the banking system, foreign powers
Ideology	Center-left	From left to center right	Radical left: twenty-first-century socialism
Political project	Incorporation to the existing power structures; no moral nor ethical claims	New political regime; no moral nor ethical claims	Refoundation of the country; new political regime; moral reform

In fact, there are important continuities between Velasco's and Correa's varieties of populism. De la Torre (1994), Cuvi (1977), and Ibarra (2004) have argued that one of the main traits of *velasquismo*, especially during its apogee during the 1940s, was the claim to moral reform, the emphasis on moral redemption. For Velasco Ibarra, politics desperately needed an indispensable ethical dimension that would favor the *pueblo* or the *chusma*. Furthermore, Velasco's politics had a lot to do with a moral crusade against the alleged corruption of elites, political parties, and the so-called oligarchy. In this regard, one can find obvious similarities with the strong ethical overtones of the Citizens' Revolution. For Correa, citizens possess all the civic virtues needed for the refoundation of the country, best expressed by the phrase "*volver a tener patria*" (returning to having a homeland).[10] Regaining the homeland is both a political and moral project conceived against neoliberalism and its worst moral defects: selfish individualism, interest-based behavior, and the privatization of the state.

To reverse the neoliberal moral project, Correa argues for the concentration and centralization of state power, primarily in the hands of the executive. This requires not only dismantling neoliberal policies but also constructing an all-too-powerful state with the capacity to refound the nation. For Correa, the rupture with the past at which the Citizens' Revolution aims implies a moral break with neoliberalism's economic and political elites and their worldview. Unlike neoliberals, who presented the market as the only positive paradigm, *correísmo* proposes that the state should become the unique moral referent of society. The president, at the center of the state apparatus, should perform the role of the principal actor of such ethical and moral revolutions. Therein, Correa is the secular saint incarnating the required extraordinary character and will. Interestingly, Velasco Ibarra, to a greater extent than other leaders, also represented the figure of a secular saint before the Ecuadorian people. Moreover, despite once having defined himself as a liberal, Velasco repeatedly fought for a strong state and a stronger presi-

---

Ibarra: El último caudillo de la oligarquía (Quito: Instituto de Investigaciones Económicas, 1977); Rafael Quintero, *El mito del populismo en el Ecuador* (Quito: FLACSO, 1980); and Carlos de la Torre, *La seducción velasquista* (Quito: Ediciones Libri Mundi, 1994).

10. Pablo Andrade conceives Rafael Correa's revolution as a republican project against neoliberalism. See Pablo Andrade, *La era neoliberal y el proyecto republicano* (Quito: Universidad Andina Simón Bolívar, 2009).

dency.[11] Correa's populism is heavily indebted to Velasco's pretensions of moral reform and state-centered conception of governance. He is the fresh representation of an old tradition—a tradition that the Citizens' Revolution has renovated using the communications strategies of politics in the twenty-first century.

Fourth, and finally, *correísmo* is a project aimed at refounding Ecuadorian society as a whole; it is not a political project alone, but a global crusade aiming at the transformation of every realm of society: Correa's administration understands itself not as another government, subject to democratic alternation, but as a new political regime that will endure over time, opening a new epoch in Ecuadorian history. This new regime results from the demolition of the political structures associated with the so-called *partidocracia*. In this way, Correa's administration is presented as an irreversible historical process endlessly threatened by reactionary forces. It is, in fact, not merely another presidency but a revolutionary movement involving a radical transformation of economic, social, and even cultural realms of society. The Citizens' Revolution proposes a new model of development anchored in the concept of *sumak kausay*, meaning *buen vivir*—good living.[12] The installation of the Constitutional Assembly in November 2009 was the starting point for the rebirth of Ecuador. The new Constitution, and later the new legal framework (approximately sixty new laws approved in the first three years), points toward a radical redefinition of all existing institutions and norms. The Citizens' Revolution is not solely a political project but also a global movement geared to transforming the social, economic, and cultural realms of society and the geopolitical balance of the whole continent.

How Was Correa's Radical Populism Constructed?

Having described the four basic traits of the Citizens' Revolution, I now turn to analyzing the construction of Rafael Correa's radical populist regime in the first phase of his mandate, from January 2007, when he

11. Hernán Ibarra, "El populismo en la política ecuatoriana contemporánea," in *Releer los populismos*, ed. Weyland, 141.
12. Alberto Acosta, "La Constitución de Montecristi, medio y fin para cambios estructurales," in *Nuevas instituciones del derecho constitucional ecuatoriano*, edited by Juan Pablo Aguilar (Quito: INREDH, 2009), 12–13.

took office, until the police revolt of September 30, 2010. My argument is that during this initial phase, Correa achieved his political goals through three concurrent mechanisms: the permanent campaign, the direct transfer of subsidies, and the constitutional reform process. With this three-fold strategy, the group in power has been able to defeat the *partidocracia* and dismantle all forms of opposition, create a new electoral majority, redirect state resources toward the consolidation of a new client base, and establish a hyperpresidential regime built upon plebiscitary procedures. Table 11.2 synthesizes Correa's strategy geared toward provoking a rapid regime change in Ecuador.

The outcome of Correa's threefold political strategy has been the construction of a new model of legitimacy that presents worrisome plebiscitary features. It is the case that, despite incorporating some democratic elements (regular elections, controlled people's participation in decision-making processes, the use of polls and surveys to monitor public opinion, etc.), *correísmo* involves the weakening of representation and a consequent disintermediation of political relations. This is a regime predicated upon clear antidemocratic elements: demobilization of autonomous civil society, a growing personalization of the political arena, an aggressive concentration of power in the hands of the executive, and a systemic erosion of the independence of the branches of state power. The logic of Correa's project, the route of regime change that *correísmo* has put forward in Ecuador, can be simply defined as the demolition of the *partidocracia* and its replacement by a semidemocratic regime built upon the bedrock of plebiscitary legitimacy. Let us now look at the three mechanisms of Correa's political strategy and its institutional consequences.

Table 11.2. Correa's Strategy for Provoking Rapid Regime Change in Ecuador

Political Goal	Mechanism	Institutional Result
Defeating the *partidocracia* and dismantling the opposition	Permanent campaign	Forming a new electoral majority
Redirection of public resources	Direct transfer of subsidies to the poor	Consolidation of a new client base
Demolishing the institutions of the old political regime, i.e., the *partidocracia*	Constitutional remaking; drafting and approval of a new Constitution	Construction of a hyperpresidential regime and a plebiscitary democracy

The Permanent Campaign

One of the pillars of Correa's success is his administration's systematic application of marketing techniques to sustain and enhance high levels of presidential approval. This type of governance implies a systematic fusion of administrative acts with political marketing to form the pattern of a "permanent campaign," which involves systematically using polling and communications strategies to monitor and control all government decisions. Thereby, the main goal of all government actions becomes achieving high approval ratings for the president's performance. As has been the case in other countries, the incorporation of these permanent campaign techniques strengthens tendencies toward the personalization of the political regime and the consolidation of a plebiscitary presidency.[13]

On the basis of this definition, Conaghan and de la Torre argue that during the last decade, extreme versions of plebiscitary presidencies have consolidated in the cases of Hugo Chávez, Evo Morales, and Rafael Correa.[14] In the Ecuadorian case, marketing tools and communications strategies have been very effective in winning repeated elections, in which Correa and PAÍS have managed to gain wide and unprecedented popular support, as shown in table 11.3.

An essential element of Correa's permanent campaign is his communications strategy. His discourse is based upon a polarizing, zero-sum view of the political arena, where "the enemy" is played by the political parties, private mass media, business groups, and all political adversaries. In particular, the president has made the press one of his administration's main political opponents. Presidential discourse treats independent journalists as political actors, whose work is distorted by illegitimate interests. In fact, the president himself has sued several journalists and newspapers, arguing in the courts that his honor has been affected. The most notorious cases have been the trial against *El Universo*, the biggest Ecuadorian newspaper, and the suit against the authors of *El gran hermano*, a book based on research that presents undisputed evidence of illegal government contracts favoring Correa's brother. In Correa's view, the privately owned media lack the political legitimacy to inform society.

13. Catherine Conaghan and Carlos de la Torre, "The Permanent Campaign of Rafael Correa: Making Ecuador's Plebiscitary Presidency," *International Journal of Press/Politics* 13 (2008): 267.

14. Ibid., 269.

Table 11.3. Correa's Electoral Results, 2006–9

Date	Election	National Percentage
October 2006	First presidential round	22.89
November 2006	Second presidential round	56.67
April 2007	Plebiscite calling for a Constitutional Assembly	81.72
September 2008	Referendum approving the Constitution	63.93
April 2009	First presidential round	51.99

Note: This table does not include the November 2007 election of members of the Constitutional Assembly because President Correa did not participate directly.

Source: Compiled by the author based on statistics from the Consejo Nacional Electoral.

Accordingly, his administration has sought to displace private media with newly established state-owned media, under direct government control. State-owned media entities include TVEcuador, Radio Pública, *El Telégrafo* newspaper, and many other television and radio stations throughout the country. The goal is to permeate public opinion with an official version on each issue and to impose on society the president's position on every possible subject.

The government's communications strategy also includes an unlimited use of paid radio and TV spots, as well as mandated national broadcasts. Correa has also instituted televised monologues every Saturday, during which he not only informs citizens of all his activities but also directly intervenes in the political debate by attacking his adversaries and insulting anyone who expresses different views. For example, in 2008 alone (similar events have occurred in the other years since he took office), he was on the air for 174 hours and 40 minutes, as shown in table 11.4. And this does not include government-paid radio and TV ads, which also have an important on-air presence on national and regional radio and television stations.

Table 11.4. Mandated National Broadcasts and Saturday Presidential Broadcasts, 2008

Type of Broadcast	Number	Time/Week	Time/Month	Annual Time
Mandated national broadcasts	176	35 minutes	2 hours, 40 minutes	30 hours, 40 minutes
Saturday presidential broadcasts	52	3 hours	12 hours	144 hours
Total	228	3 hours, 35 minutes	14 hours, 40 minutes	174 hours, 40 minutes

Source: Compiled by the author based on statistics from the Consejo Nacional Electoral.

National broadcasts of the president's monologues are mandatory for all the country's national, regional, and local radio and television stations, which add up to approximately 1,300 radio and 300 TV outlets. In addition, the discretionary distribution of the government's advertisements is enough of an incentive for many radio stations to broadcast and rebroadcast the monologues, not only on Saturdays but also on Sundays, at various times.

With such an enormous media presence, President Correa has become the single political actor on the national and local stages. His communications strategy dominates the Ecuadorian political debate without competition. One should note that the account given here does not include government-paid advertisements, that is, the plentiful radio and TV spots "informing" about government policies and untiringly pounding out the government's slogans and propaganda.[15] Naturally, in addition to all the above, the government's media exposure includes news coverage of the president's actions and government policies by the private press, where the administration's initiatives are, by and large, the main topic of media coverage.

The result has been a complete transformation of the Ecuadorian political and mass media scene. This is a critical element in explaining the high levels of popular support for the president and his policies. Ever since the 1990s, all Ecuadorian presidents faced approval levels lower than 30 percent, ostensibly diminishing their margins of governability. The only brief exception was Jamil Mahuad at the moment at which he signed the peace treaty with Peru. By contrast, because of the meticulous application of permanent campaign techniques, President Correa has governed with approval ratings that have not dipped below 50 percent, at times even surging above 70 percent, as shown in table 11.5.

Correa's communications strategy has succeeded in blocking the emergence of an articulated opposition or even any substantial criticism of the government's policies. Simply put, public opinion has been neutralized by the administration's communications strategy. As a consequence, the presidential message has emerged as the only credible reference point for a majority of Ecuadorians. Since Correa took office, political discourse in Ecuador has become completely centered on the president. No other political figure has had the chance to open an alternative space.

15. Hernán Ramos, "El nuevo gran actor en la comunicación: El Estado," in *La palabra rota*, edited by César Ricaurte (Quito: FUNDAMEDIOS, 2010).

Table 11.5. Correa's Approval and Credibility Ratings, 2007–10 (percent)

Rating	January 2007	April 2008	June 2009	August 2010
Approval	73	58	52	53
Credibility	68	53	50	51

Source: Cedatos-Gallup, www.cedatos.com.ec.

As a central piece of this strategy, since September 2009, the National Assembly has been debating a Communications Law, which, from the administration's perspective, should include restrictions on the independent press and would allow the government, through a Regulatory Council under the influence of the president, to establish limitations on free speech. The goal is to consolidate the government's control of public opinion and the independent press, to block free access to public information, and to establish a state monopoly over the information available to citizens.

Communications hegemony has been crucial for the consolidation of a new electoral majority. In less than four years, between 2006 and 2009, Ecuador ceased to be a country with severe political fragmentation and became one where representation is vastly concentrated in a single political force, the ruling party. As noted above, during this period Correa's supporters grew from 22 percent of the electorate in the first round of the 2006 presidential election to a political force that easily surpasses 50 percent of the electorate, with an even greater proportion of popularity and support for Correa himself. Permanent campaign techniques have thus proven to be extremely effective in dramatically changing Ecuadorian politics. Today, Correa reigns over the political scenario and monopolizes public debate. This hegemony over public opinion has been his major objective.

Direct Transfers of Subsidies to the Poor

Complementing its permanent campaign techniques, another mechanism used by the Citizens' Revolution is the direction of economic transfers to particular sectors of society, especially the poor. A legacy of neoliberal policies, this trend could not have occurred without the dramatic increase in the revenue raised by the Ecuadorian state, partly due to a highly extractive tax policy but principally to the rise in international oil prices. The amount of oil revenues received by the Ecuadorian state during the first three years of Correa's presidential term—that is, from 2007 to 2009—reached $25 billion. This was only slightly less than the total oil revenues received by the state between 2000 and 2006, and more than twice the amount the country received in the 1990s.[16] This oil bonanza can only be compared with the early 1970s, when oil exports began in Ecuador.

Taking full advantage of such a positive fiscal environment, from the very moment Correa came to power, the government dramatically increased public spending. During his first three years in power, he spent more than the amount in the previous six-year period, between 2000 and 2006, and substantially more than the government had spent during the entire decade of the 1990s, as shown in table 11.6. The 2010 budget alone represented an increase of 29 percent.

The growth of the government's budget translates into a significant increase in its social spending and direct transfers to the population's poorest sectors. These take place mainly through the human development and housing bonuses and the electricity subsidy. It is worth noting that these economic transfers are universally distributed among the poor, not only directed to the government's supporters—as shown in table 11.7.

The human development bonus (HDB) was first implemented during the government of Jamil Mahuad in 1999 as a subsidy directed to citizens living below the poverty line. Correa raised the number of HDB recipients from 1.176 million in 2006 to 1.650 million in 2009, as shown in table 11.8, and 1.899 in 2012. The administration also increased the amount of the HDB from $20 to $35 a month. Great effort has been made in favor of disabled citizens with a special program, the Manuela Espejo Mission, which was launched with enormous impact by the vice president. The housing bonus was a creation of the Correa administration as a direct transfer to citizens who plan to buy their first house or intend to improve their old one. No available information exists regarding the exact number of beneficiaries of this bonus. Along the same lines, the Correa administration reorganized the existing subsidy to provide cheap electricity to 3.3 million households. In 2010, the government created the so-called Electric Dignity Fare, through which 2.1 million families pay half the price of their electricity bill. In addition, the administra-

16. Jaime Carrera, "Economía y sociedad: Costosas oportunidades perdidas," November 2009, 4.

Table 11.6. Oil Revenues and State Spending, 1990–2010 (millions of dollars)

Period	Exports of Oil and Derivatives	State Spending
2007–9	25,000	60,000
2000–6	26,000	51,000
1990–99	14,000	41,000

Source: Jaime Carrera, "Observatorio de la Política Fiscal," 2009.

Table 11.7. Social Spending and Direct Subsidies, 2006–10 (millions of dollars)

Type of Spending or Subsidy	2006	2007	2008	2009	2010
Social spending	2,200	2,600	3,700	5,000	5,700
Direct subsidies	160	332	544	720	808
Electricity subsidy	230	30	230	240	256

Note: Social spending includes public health and education and social security pensions, among others. Direct subsidies include the human development and housing bonuses.

Sources: Central Bank of Ecuador; Ministry of Economy and Finance.

Table 11.8. Beneficiaries of the Human Development Bonus, 2006–10 (millions of beneficiaries)

2006	2007	2008	2009	2010
1.176	1.237	1.305	1.650	1.754

Source: Ministry of Social Inclusion.

tion has made an enormous effort to improve the database that lists all bonus recipients, along with making its delivery faster and "friendlier."

Although direct subsidy transfers to the poor do not amount to a coherent social policy—one that would succeed in reversing structural social problems over time—they surely create a sense of community— the sense of a caring community linking a leader, the government, and his base. If permanent campaign techniques aim at broadening Correa's nationwide popularity, direct subsidy transfers seek, very effectively, to consolidate a solid and focused clientelistic base of support. This social base easily develops strong connections, both instrumental and symbolic, with the leader. Subsidy transfers to particular social groups do generate a path for political inclusion, as well as obligations from both sides. It may not be the best way of institutionalizing a coherent social policy, but it certainly produces rapid political and economic effects.

Although different, the permanent campaign and direct cash transfers complement each other. In what follows, I seek to explain how a third mechanism, the constitutional reform process, has contributed to creating the necessary institutions to establish the new regime and a new model of legitimacy.

The Process of Remaking the Constitution

The third mechanism used by the Correa government to consolidate its political project has to do with the drafting of a new Constitution to create the basis for a new state.[17] As mentioned above, the administration's political project involves the opening of a new institutional era, a goal with quasi-theological overtones. In the words of one of its initial ideologues, Alberto Acosta, the new Constitution was to be the "means and end for structural changes"; it would crystallize the accumulated history of multiple social struggles and resistances and overcome market-centered, neoliberal, and neodevelopmental concepts of economic progress; it would transcend the "capitalist Western lifestyle" and bring about a "new coexistence pact" expressed in the Quechua concept of *sumak kausay*, meaning *buen vivir*, or good living.[18]

The 2008 Constitution was drafted by a Constitutional Assembly that assumed "full powers." In one of its first decisions, the assembly dissolved the Congress that had been democratically elected in 1996, along with Rafael Correa, and partially suspended the 1998 Constitution. In nine months, the assembly promulgated several laws and wrote an entirely new Constitution, which was ratified via referendum, with 63 percent of the votes, on September 30, 2008.

All in all, the 2008 constitutional structure rests on three pillars: (1) a broad catalogue of constitutional rights and the development of constitutional guarantees for their application; (2) a hyperpresidential political system; and (3) a plebiscitary model of democracy operating via elections and a variety of direct participatory mechanisms.

The new list of constitutional rights, which even recognizes the so-called rights of nature (*derechos de la naturaleza*), breaks with the tradi-

17. This section summarizes the thesis I develop in another work; see César Montúfar, *Constitución 2009: Estado presidencial y democracia plebiscitaria* (Quito: Universidad Andina Simón Bolívar, 2013).
18. Alberto Acosta, "La Constitución de Montecristi, medio y fin para cambios estructurales," in *Nuevas instituciones*, ed. Aguilar, 7–8, 10, 12.

tional model of civil, political, and social rights and proposes a different approach based on the concept of *buen vivir*. In addition, the Constitution emphasizes the collective rights of minorities as well as the plurinational character of the state, at the expense of the more traditional preeminence of individual guarantees. Simply put, the new constitutional model subordinates the protection of traditional individual rights to collective and social rights. It proclaims a new "constitutional state" that aims to transcend the liberal or welfare state.

The second feature of the constitutional model is hyperpresidentialism. Historically, Ecuador has had a robust presidential tradition. The enhanced presidentialism of the 2008 Constitution can be seen as yet another attempt to impose the will of the president on fragmented and conflictive legislatures, along the same lines as the 1983, 1994, and 1998 constitutional reforms.[19] Nonetheless, the last constitutional transformation outdid its presidential inclinations and created a political regime in which the executive branch is able to (1) subjugate the legislative branch and place restrictions on its oversight powers, (2) attain administrative and financial influence over local governments via the centralization of fiscal resources and their mandatory inclusion under a national planning system, (3) exert massive state intervention in the economy, beginning with the executive branch's control of so-called strategic sectors and the overextension of national planning, and (4) establish a system of political control over civil society through a variety of participation plans to incorporate and subordinate social groups to the government's administrative apparatus.

The creation of such a hyperpresidential system has been not without obstacles. In fact, the National Assembly installed in August 2009, in which PAÍS came close to obtaining a majority (it won 57 out of 124 seats), has become the main arena of political struggle over various critical laws ordered by the new Constitution. Therein, one needs to mention laws governing communications, water resources, basic and higher education, public service, and culture, among others. This legal structure aims at weakening the influence of organized groups within each sector, generally reinforcing the trend, already present in the Constitution, toward the concentration of power in the hands of the president.

19. For analyses of executive-legislative relations in Ecuador, see Andrés Mejía, *Gobernabilidad democratica* (Quito: Konrad Adenauer Stiftung, 2002); and Francisco Sánchez, *¿Democracia no lograda o democracia malograda?* (Quito: FLACSO, 2008).

As could have been expected, the government's legislative agenda has been strongly opposed by many organized groups in society: the indigenous movement, university students, journalists and the mass media, public servants, and others. In the government's discourse, social resistance to its proposed legislation is merely an expression of illegitimate groups attempting to protect their privileges. However, this has created an opportunity for opposition groups within the National Assembly to articulate some initiatives, partially diluting the government's legislative agenda. That does not mean, however, that the opposition in the legislative branch has been able to put a hold on Correa's power-enhancing process. In other areas of the state beyond the executive branch, Correa's influence and command are even clearer. The Supreme Court has been restructured twice, in 2009 and 2011, to adapt the judiciary to the political needs of the group in power. The Constitutional Court and the newly created Social Control and Social Participation Authority are no different. In sum, except for small pockets of opposition in the National Assembly, the executive determines the agenda, priorities, and pace of all branches of the state and autonomous public institutions. And with no elections set until 2013, one should expect no substantial changes in the current balance of power.

At a theoretical level, hyperpresidentialism is justified on the basis that that it is necessary to strengthen the state apparatus in order to guarantee the effectiveness of recognized rights. *Correísmo* uses the protection of recognized rights as an excuse to justify the expansion and strengthening of the state bureaucracy and the concentration of power in the hands of the president. Through this process, the state has become an end in itself. The underlying purpose of this model is to do away with the two pillars of the liberal state: the division of power into three branches, and democratic representation.[20] The break with the three-branch structure of the liberal state involves the addition of two branches to the traditional legislative, executive, and judicial powers. The new Constitution established the Transparency and Social Control Branch, which would incorporate citizens' direct participation in the structure of the state, and the Electoral Branch, which would be in charge of organizing elections

20. Albert Noguera Fernández, "Participación, Función Electoral y Función de Transparencia y Control Social," in *Desafíos constitucionales*, edited by Ramiro Ávila Santamaría, Agustín Grijalva, and Rubén Martínez (Quito: Ministerio de Justicia y Derechos Humanos del Ecuador, 2008), 137.

and plebiscitary processes. According to one of its ideologues, "the new Ecuadorian Constitution forms a political system that is authentically democratic because it breaks down the boundaries of bourgeois liberal representation and the three branches of power and . . . achieves a democracy that is directly exercised by the people in a process undergoing a permanent construction, based on the power of the citizens."[21]

There is a third pillar complementing the model: the generation of a plebiscitary democracy that operates through (1) direct and selective incorporation of social groups into the decisionmaking process; and (2) systematic calls for plebiscitary events focused on renewing popular support for the president. Under this model, the predominance of the executive branch over civil society, political society, decentralized autonomous governments, and market actors reinforces the president as the only point of reference—he thus is in a predominant position not only above all levels of the state but also above society and the market. Citizen participation is reduced to a selective inclusion of social organizations in the state apparatus, for the purpose of street and electoral mobilization. Here one finds a scheme for state co-optation of society and nothing that would indicate government interaction with an autonomous civil society.

In sum, far from promoting the active involvement of citizens or social movements in making public policy, or the free participation of civil society groups, or even the establishment of effective channels for social accountability, the Correa administration has consolidated a new model of legitimacy based upon repeated electoral victories, state co-optation of social groups, and systematic acclamation of the president. Traditional political mediations and autonomous social organizations have been left behind; the Citizens' Revolution considers them simply as the expressions of illegitimate interests, and as incompatible with the totalizing and all-correct vision of the leader.

Correa's Model of Plebiscitary Legitimacy

Permanent campaign techniques, direct transfers to the poor, and constitutional reform have institutionalized a new political regime in Ecuador, based upon a peculiar model of legitimacy. Focusing on the concept of

21. Ibid., 157.

legitimacy allows one to examine the dynamic relationship between leaders and their followers, and the ties that leaders construct in order that their rule be accepted and obeyed.[22] Using Max Weber's concept, one can argue that Correa's model of legitimacy combines elements that are both rational (rewriting the Constitution's appeals to a political order based upon citizen rights) and material (predicated upon the establishment of direct transfers of resources to clients seeking to consolidate a broad community of interests). Correa incorporates—albeit not without tension—both sources of legitimacy, something that, far from weakening his appeal, broadens his authority. In addition, his leadership is based on charisma, his "extraordinary dedication to saintliness, heroism or exemplary acts."[23] This is confirmed by his brave and firm confrontation with the "privileges of the past," that is, the alleged corruption of the *partidocracia*, the press, and economic elites; his everyday struggle for an egalitarian and just society; and his absolute dedication to the historical mission of the Citizens' Revolution.

The implementation of this dual model of legitimacy requires an army of public officials and administrative personnel loyal to the goals of the government and the will of the president.[24] According to the analyst Jaime Carrera, between 2006 and 2009, approximately 95,000 new bureaucrats entered the public administration, reaching a total of 454,000, most of whom were in the executive branch.[25] This growth created an impressive force of new public officials and government employees ready to implement Correa's revolution. Among these new administrative personnel are political personnel with technical and formal qualifications applicable to rational domination models, along with bureaucrats exhibiting absolute obedience to the president and an embrace of his mission.[26] Ultimately, the members of the administrative apparatus of the Correa

22. I use Max Weber's concept of legitimacy as the probability that a political order is recognized as valid and the ruler's commands are accepted as mandatory for the members of society. See Max Weber, *Economía y sociedad* (Mexico City: Fondo de Cultura Económica, 2002), 27.

23. Ibid., 172.

24. According to Weber, all domination models function through an administrative staff, the leader's immediate followers, who serve as a transmission belt for legitimation processes. Administrative officials are as important as the leaders themselves because they generate the institutional channels upon which the people's obedience is processed. See Ibid., 170.

25. Carrera, "Economía y sociedad," 4.

26. Weber, *Economía y sociedad*, 195.

government act as "commissioned missionaries" of the leader's political project, although they also provide proof of their skills and confirm their professional and ethical merits. The crucial element for belonging to the group of administrative officials is the recognition they get from the leader, and the leader's trust in their loyalty and obedience. It is a matter of charismatic trust creating duty.[27] In sum, Correa's political success departs from traditional patterns of legitimation based on privilege, property, or belonging to elite groups, which were dominant in previous regimes. The association of the *partidocracia* with the era of privilege, perks, and traditional benefits constitutes a crucial element of the legitimation of the new group in power. Correa's radical rejection of the past and his strong links to a revolutionary mission have allowed the government to hire thousands of public officials that exhibit an unquestionable commitment to the aims of the Citizens' Revolution. In this manner, Correa has opened the path to regime change in Ecuador, for the construction of an entirely new state apparatus run by an army of loyal bureaucrats.

This regime change has resulted in a new organization of the country's political space, structured through the traditional friend/enemy dichotomy. The "friend" field includes administrative officials at all levels of the government; the PAÍS movement, which has merged with the government bureaucracy; the allies from other parties who have supported the president from the outset, the political clients who receive direct subsidies from the administration, and Correa's supporters and voters in the broadest sense. The "enemy" field is made up of opposition parties, "*pelucones*," business and financial sectors, private media, unions, citizens who are not followers of Correa, and, finally, the so-called foreign powers, that is, U.S. imperialism.[28]

Correa is the single and unique reference point on this new chessboard of power. The leader acts as the tiebreaker in all strategic decisions, and bases his reputation on having extraordinary personal skills. He is the prophet of a coming revolutionary era, the authority for which has been granted by the people directly at the ballot box or through public opinion polls. If conflicts arise, the president is the only one who can resolve them because of his intellectual profile, academic background,

---

27. Ibid.
28. "*Pelucones*," a Correa neologism, are meant to be upper-class citizens accustomed to exploiting and abusing lower-income people.

moral character, and, fundamentally, his popular appeal. What matters is that the people, whether in elections or in polls, have transferred to the leader indisputable authority over the entire country, his followers, comrades, and staff. In this sense, enhancing plebiscitary legitimacy in favor of the president becomes the only goal of government actions, the strategic objective of every decision at all levels. This is a systematic and ongoing process, an uninterrupted and self-referencing circle, as shown in figure 11.1.

In figure 11.1, when A is high, B will work well, and vice versa. The three actors in the circle of plebiscitary legitimacy—the leader, administrative personnel, and people/citizens/clients—are linked in a constant relationship. The circle of plebiscitary legitimacy is a self-referencing process devoid of any political negotiation or attention to a democratic logic of conflict and consensus. Institutional balances and electoral counterweights cease to operate. The political process is solely based upon the leader's support and popular acceptance emerging from polling and landslide electoral triumphs. This constant relegitimation process, as measured by the peoples' support for the president, guarantees the loyalty of his operators at all levels, and serves to justify the complete

Figure 11.1. The Circle of Correa's Plebiscitary Legitimacy

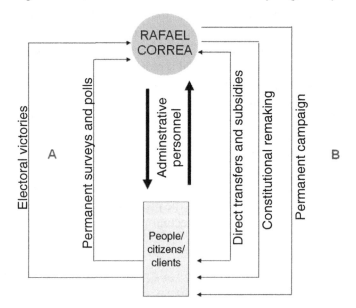

rejection of internal criticism or of opposition groups as valid speakers. An all-popular, academic, ethical president rules the political arena; none has the right to oppose or challenge him, because he expresses the will of the people.

Conclusion: Correa's Radical Populism in Perspective

The description of Correa's populism clearly differentiates it both from the classical populism of the 1940s and 1960s and from the so-called neo-liberal neopopulism of the 1990s. Correa's radical populism defines itself as revolutionary and citizen-based—humanistic, twenty-first-century socialist, utopian, and mestizo—and headed by a charismatic leader of extraordinary character. Correa has constructed his political project "with infinite love," "with passion for the Country," against the *pelucones*, corrupt bankers, foreign powers, and the mediocre press.

In spite of its rhetoric, the Citizens' Revolution is not a social or grass-roots movement but a revolution from above: a revolution generated from the government downward and outward. Correa's political project simply lacks organizational ties to any social movement, social class, or elite group. Furthermore, this revolution is not an isolated phenomenon but part of a regional trend, linked to Hugo Chávez's Bolivarian project, attempting to transform the traditional pro–United States alignment of the Western Hemisphere. Correa proposes a revolution not limited to rapid political reform or geopolitical realignment, but committed to the country's economic, social, and even cultural transformation. His project is a theological one; he and the Citizens' Revolution aim to wholly refound Ecuador. Consequently, despite its undeniable and evident continuation of Ecuadorian and Latin American populist traditions, this revolution is not conceived as another administration within a process of democratic alternation but as a new regime that will endure over time, for it represents "a new historical period."

Correa's political project has come together and consolidated itself in a very short time. Correa burst onto the Ecuadorian political scene as recently as 2005, when President Alfredo Palacio appointed him minister of the economy. Since then, in just a few years, in a country that had fallen victim to extreme political fragmentation and uncontrollable political instability, Correa has achieved a broad and overwhelming political majority. And not just that— in this period, the Correa government has demolished the institutions of the old regime and begun the construction of an entirely new state, featuring a very high concentration of power and a new legitimacy model with plebiscitary characteristics. This rapid process of regime change was made possible by the execution of a threefold political strategy consisting of permanent campaign techniques, direct transfers to the poor, and constitutional reform. This new regime places its leader at the pinnacle, above all actors; it makes him the supreme political, economic, and social point of reference. Correa's is a hyperpresidential regime, based on a model of plebiscitary legitimacy, which depends on a strong and extraordinary leader ruling over very weak state institutions, the economy, and society.

In a way, Correa's project can be interpreted as a successful response to the moment of the previous regime's sharp political delegitimation. At first, Correa appeared to be a transitional figure, who could lead a departure from instability, fragmentation, and crisis.[29] It is important to stress, however, that the collapse of the *partidocracia*, the regime built around structural adjustment and neoliberal policies, occurred at the political level and had to do with a deep crisis of political legitimacy in Ecuador. The end of the so-called neoliberal night did not come about due to an economic crisis or a social explosion. In fact, since the financial crisis of 1999, when the national currency—the *sucre*—collapsed and was replaced by the American dollar, inflation was brought under control and the economy recovered at a small but sustained rate, an average of 3 percent of the gross domestic product. Economic stability produced positive results in several social aspects. The poverty index declined 14 percent between 1999 and 2006; unemployment rates also improved during the first decade of the new century.[30] It was not the economy or social problems that produced the death of the previous regime; its political weakness, its legitimacy deficit, brought it down. The successful process of regime change brought on by *correísmo* was a product of a political breakdown, not economic or social crises.

But Correa represents more than a break from the past. Beyond a phenomenon arising from a historical rupture, his success indicates that

29. Following Roberts's analysis, Correa's, Chávez's, and Morales's radical populism would represent a departure from the crisis unleashed by the exhaustion of neoliberal policies. See Kenneth Roberts, "El resurgimiento del populismo latino-americano," in *Retorno del pueblo*, ed. de la Torre and Peruzzotti.

30. Ecuador Volunteer, "Statistics," http://www.ecuadorvolunteer.org/es/infor macion_ecuador/estadisticas.html.

populism is a predominant trait in Ecuadorian politics. It may be called an inherent ingredient of its political "normalcy," and thus it needs to be studied in all its complexity. Indeed, his discourse and practices express very similar strategies to those executed by past Ecuadorian populist leaders like Abdalá Bucaram, Lucio Gutiérrez, and, especially, Velasco Ibarra. In this sense, and certainly paradoxically, Correa represents both an exceptional departure from a historical crisis defined by political instability and fragmentation, and a crude repetition of a recurring populist tradition in Ecuadorian politics.

However, the most important exception is that, like other radical populists in the Andes, Correa's populism has gone beyond the demolition of the institutions of the old regime and has promoted the construction of a new state, a new Constitution, and a new model of legitimacy. In the Citizens' Revolution, one can find both a deep anti-institutional eagerness and a powerful institutionalizing trend. That is *correísmo*'s main source of strength against all its opponents. With a speed that has immobilized and defeated all his political adversaries, Correa has cleared the road toward a new institutional structure, in which he rules without checks, balances, or opposition.

Nevertheless, despite its apparent solvency and forcefulness, Correa's project is also quite fragile. Its plebiscitary character makes it completely dependent on high levels of popular support. The very moment when he were to become unpopular, or when citizens simply would turn their backs on him, his political castle would collapse. That could occur with the same speed as it has been put together, but could be prevented as long as the government has sufficient oil resources to finance permanent campaign mechanisms and direct subsidies to its clients. At the same time, such a possibility could also be ruled out as long as Ecuadorians in general continue dreaming that their country is approaching the dawn of a new historical epoch, that the past is fading away, that the *patria* is being regained, that Ecuador is being refounded by a messianic leader.

Chapter 12

Politicizing Insecurity: Uribe's Instrumental Use of Populism

Ana María Bejarano

Colombia stands out when compared with the rest of Latin America in many regards—one of them being the historical absence of a successful populist experience. This is all the more reason to see the populist style and discourse deployed by President Álvaro Uribe during his long mandate (2002–10) as a visible anomaly in the country's history. But just how populist was Uribe? This chapter argues that while he strategically called forth some aspects of the populist tradition, his government did not classify as a case of populism, radical or otherwise. Rather, it exemplified a particularly instrumental use of populism in order to consolidate an extremely conservative political project that emerged in the wake of the

The original version of this chapter was prepared as a paper for the conference on "Populism of the Twenty-First Century," held at the Woodrow Wilson International Center for Scholars, Washington, October 8, 2009. I wish to thank Cindy Arnson and Carlos de la Torre, as well as two anonymous readers, who contributed insightful comments and multiple suggestions for improvement of the chapter's previous drafts. The author also gratefully acknowledges research assistance from Luisa Fernanda Suárez Rozo.

country's worst security crisis since "La Violencia." With rising crime rates and publics ever more concerned about criminal violence throughout Latin America, the Colombian case illustrates the perils that come with the exploitation, for political ends, of citizens' fear of insecurity.

Colombia: The Absence of Populism

Unlike the majority of countries in the region, Colombia lacks a long or deeply rooted populist tradition. In this sense, the populist overtones characteristic of the "Uribe phenomenon"[1] presented a deviation from Colombia's traditional political patterns and stood out as anomalous vis-à-vis the country's political history.[2]

Throughout the twentieth century, Colombia saw the ascent of two populist movements only to see them prematurely aborted. The first one was the soaring rise of Jorge Eliécer Gaitán as a dissident leader within the Liberal Party during the late 1930s and the 1940s—after giving up on his intention to create a different party, the Union Nacional Izquierdista Revolucionaria, in the early 1930s. Gaitán is, no doubt, the most salient populist politician in all of Colombia's history. His effort to mobilize the dispossessed against oligarchic domination, his attempts to incorporate the excluded, first within the Liberal Party and, through it, into the broader political arena, produced one of the deepest and most enduring cleavages in Colombia's political history, a polarization that led not only to his assassination on April 9, 1948, but also to a decade of bloodshed

1. I say the "Uribe phenomenon"—rather than just "Uribe," or "Uribe's government"—to point to a reality that went beyond the person of the president and his immediate entourage. The majority of the Colombian electorate systematically favored him with overwhelming support not only during the two presidential elections he handily won (in 2002 and 2006), thus avoiding a runoff election on both occasions, but also stood by him, offering record popularity ratings of over 70 percent until the end of his mandate in August 2010.

2. Three keen observers of Colombian politics have put forth arguments regarding the country's exceptionalism with regards to populism. They are Daniel Pécaut, "Populismo imposible y violencia: El caso colombiano," *Estudios Políticos* 16 (2000): 45–70; Marco Palacios, "Presencia y ausencia de populismo: Un contrapunto colombo-venezolano," *Análisis Político* 39 (2000): 33–54; and Fernán González, "El retorno de los caudillos en Iberoamérica," in *Estado, democracia y populismo en América Latina*, edited by A. Chaparro, C. Galindo, and A. M. Sallenave (Bogotá: Editorial Universidad del Rosario–CLACSO, 2008), 51–115.

between Liberals and Conservatives simply known as "La Violencia."[3] Encouraged by these incorporation efforts through the Liberal Party in the 1930s, Colombia's workers and the urban poor participated enthusiastically in the Gaitanista movement.[4] After his assassination, they also participated in the wave of violence that first erupted in the cities (the dramatic Bogotazo was followed by popular upheavals in other urban centers), spreading later throughout the nation's territory. Alas, they came out of that experience divided and defeated.

The second populist experiment in Colombia's recent history happened during the last few years of a short-lived military dictatorship, led by Gustavo Rojas Pinilla, from 1953 until 1957. Following closely in the steps of the Peronist model and depending on the support of the urban working classes, it faced opposition from the two traditional parties, the Liberals and the Conservatives. These two parties, challenged by the threat of a populist military leader staying in power, found ways to overcome their enmity and put an end to the military government, quickly recovering the reins of power, together with their capacity to control the electorate. After ten long years of unbridled urban and rural violence (1948–58), they finally came to an agreement, successfully mobilized against Rojas, and achieved not only his downfall but also the return to a semicompetitive regime dominated by the parties. The Frente Nacional (National Front) bipartisan agreement decisively put an end to the second populist experiment in Colombia.[5]

Later on, in the 1960s, Rojas Pinilla staged a political comeback, and his rapidly growing movement, the Alianza Nacional Popular (ANAPO),

3. To understand Gaitán's appeal and the implications of his violent death, see Daniel Pecaut, *Orden y Violencia: Colombia 1930–1954* (Bogotá: Siglo XXI Editories and CEREC, 1987); and Herbert Braun, *The Assassination of Gaitán: Public Life and Urban Violence in Colombia* (Madison: University of Wisconsin Press, 1985).

4. See the sections devoted to Colombia in *Shaping the Political Arena: Critical Junctures, the Labor Movement, and Regime Dynamics in Latin America*, by Ruth B. Collier and David Collier (Princeton, N.J.: Princeton University Press, 1991).

5. On Rojas Pinilla's dictatorship, see Carlos Horacio Urán, *Rojas y la manipulación del poder* (Bogotá: Carlos Valencia Editores, 1983). On the Frente Nacional, see Jonathan Hartlyn, *The Politics of Coalition Rule in Colombia* (Cambridge: Cambridge University Press, 1988); Andrés Dávila, *Democracia pactada: El Frente Nacional y el proceso constituyente del 91* (Bogotá: Universidad de Los Andes, CESO, Departamento de Ciencia Política–Alfaomega–IFEA, 2002); and A. M. Bejarano, *Precarious Democracies: Understanding Regime Stability and Change in Colombia and Venezuela* (Notre Dame, Ind.: University of Notre Dame Press, 2011).

heralded a new burst of populism. This time, support for ANAPO was widened by widespread resentment against the two traditional parties, coming from all quarters—from the military, which had been displaced by the Frente Nacional agreements; from the left, which had been excluded from the new institutional arrangement; and from emerging social sectors (especially the new urban lower and middle classes), whose members found their interests and demands underrepresented in the restricted political space available under the Frente Nacional regime. The 1970 elections pitted the Frente Nacional establishment against the fledging populist contenders grouped around Rojas Pinilla and organized in ANAPO. The voting resulted in a virtual tie. However, when the government decided to deny Rojas Pinilla his alleged electoral victory, the movement backed down without much resistance. ANAPO was unable to either engineer a protest movement from above or to stage a nationwide showdown from below.[6] The significant political force it had managed to amass throughout the 1960s fizzled out in the early 1970s and was finally reduced to a small emerging guerrilla group, the Movimiento 19 de Abril (M-19; April 19th Movement)—which owed its name to the date of the disputed election.[7]

From then on, populist discourse in Colombia became monopolized by the guerrillas. Starting in the mid-1960s, the Fuerzas Armadas Revolucionarias de Colombia (FARC; Revolutionary Armed Forces of Colombia) gave voice to a radical discourse on the part of the peasantry, which had been cornered and displaced by a long history of land maldistribution that became even worse during the Violencia years; after ANAPO's disappearance from the political scene, the M-19 appropriated a popular nationalist discourse, promising to rescue Colombia's democracy from oligarchic control; finally, in the 1970s and 1980s the Ejército de Liberación Nacional (ELN; National Liberation Army) took up the banner of national sovereignty over natural resources (especially oil) against imperialist exploitation by foreign capital embodied in the presence of the multinational corporations on Colombia's territo-

6. On the life and times of ANAPO, see the work of César Augusto Ayala Diago, *Resistencia y oposición al establecimiento del Frente Nacional: Los orígenes de la Alianza Nacional Popular (ANAPO)—Colombia 1953–1964* (Bogotá: COLCIENCIAS and CINDEC, 1996).

7. On the origins of M-19, see Patricia Lara, *Siembra Vientos y Cosecharás Tempestades* (Bogotá: Editorial Punto de Partida, 1982).

ry.[8] For more than three decades, from the early 1970s until the election of Álvaro Uribe to the presidency in 2002, populism became the exclusive province of the revolutionary leftist movements that proliferated during the 1970s and 1980s.[9]

In sum, despite the emergence of some populist movements and a couple of failed attempts to gain or retain power on their part, Colombia skipped the golden age of classic populism in Latin America. Throughout the twentieth century, the country did not witness the formation of a national populist coalition between the industrial bourgeoisie and a strongly organized labor movement, nor did a redistributive welfare state ever take root. Gaitán's assassination in 1948 cut short the first and strongest populist impulse, and the military's populist experiment under Rojas Pinilla did not even take off. The efforts on the part of ANAPO to gain power through elections culminated in the alleged electoral "fraud" staged against it in 1970, and populist discourse became marginalized, in the hands of revolutionary guerrilla groups or, worse, in those of organized crime, starting in the mid-1970s.

This chapter, of course, is not the place to develop a full explanation of this atypical historical outcome, and yet one can briefly venture two hypotheses. The first one has to do with the social, economic, and political power that the landowning elites still retain in Colombia. If populism springs from a multiclass coalition of newly emerging social forces (the workers, the industrial bourgeoisie, new urban middle classes, etc.) against the old, traditional, landowning elite, its absence in Colombia signals that the balance of social power never quite tilted in favor of those newer classes but rather remained heavily slanted in favor of the few who own

8. For a history of the Colombian left, see Gustavo Gallón Giraldo, ed., *Entre movimientos y caudillos: 50 años de bipartidismo, izquierda y alternativas populares en Colombia* (Bogotá: CINEP and CEREC, 1989); on the guerrilla groups, see Eduardo Pizarro, *Insurgencia sin Revolución: La guerrilla en Colombia en una perspectiva comparada* (Bogotá: Tercer Mundo Editores and IEPRI, 1996).

9. It should be noted, however, that the drug lords also attempted to take the populist banners from the left and make them theirs. In particular, the movement founded by Carlos Lehder before his extradition to the United States (Quindío Libre) and the violent campaign carried out by the "Extraditables" (those included in a list to be extradited and judged in the United States for charges related to drug trafficking, led by Pablo Escobar) had increasing populist overtones; they allegedly represented the struggle of the poor in Colombia's society and the fight for a national solution to Colombia's problems away from the imperialist solutions imposed by the United States—what some, quite appropriately, labeled "narco-nacionalismo."

the land. Throughout the twentieth century, Colombia's economy stayed anchored in the production of coffee for export; in consequence, the transformation from a traditional, agrarian society into a more industrialized, urban, and modern one was slow, gradual, and protracted. Thus, the social bases of classical populism were either absent or much weaker in Colombia than in other Latin American cases.

Second, beginning in the mid–nineteenth century Colombia witnessed the emergence of two powerful political parties, the Liberals and the Conservatives, which were able to express, channel, and represent many (if not all) social conflicts, interests and demands—until the second half of the twentieth century. The absence of populism is related, in particular, to the Liberal Party's ability to take in and accommodate, among its various factions, a radical leftist wing, which somehow expressed the demands of the have-nots, the workers, and the excluded.[10] Simultaneous with (and partly as a consequence of) the strength of the two traditional parties, the Colombian state remained relatively small and weak.[11] This meant that it was unable to compete with the parties for the allegiance of the lower classes, much less try to mobilize and organize them as part of a populist experiment directed from above.

The Year 2002: The Turning Point

So what happened in 2002? How did Colombia go from the absence or marginalization of populist discourse to its apparent reemergence under Uribe? What I have called the "Uribe phenomenon" is, like most other populist experiences, the outcome of a crisis. However, unlike Argentina, for example, which was "battered by economic recession, hyperinflation, the crumbling of the middle classes and the specter of unemployment,"[12] at the turn of the twenty-first century, Colombia confronted a deep security crisis, reaching the worst crime rates (in terms of homicides, kidnap-

10. See Pécaut, "Populismo imposible"; Collier and Collier, *Shaping the Political Arena*; Marco Palacios, *Parábola del Liberalismo* (Bogotá: Grupo Editorial Norma, 1999); and Francisco Gutiérrez, *¿Lo que el viento se llevó? Los partidos políticos y la democracia en Colombia, 1958–2002* (Bogotá: Grupo Editorial Norma, 2007).
11. On the weakness of the Colombian state and its relation to the strength of the two traditional parties, see Bejarano, *Precarious Democracies*, esp. chap. 2.
12. Felipe Burbano de Lara, "A modo de introducción, el impertinente populismo," in *El fantasma del populismo: Aproximación a un tema [siempre] actual*, edited by F. Burbano de Lara (Caracas: Editorial Nueva Sociedad, ILDIS Ecuador, and FLACSO Ecuador, 1998), 14.

pings, and all kinds of threats against citizens' safety) since the times of La Violencia.[13] Unlike other countries, where a host of socioeconomic issues may be at the root of the crisis that gives way to populist mobilization, in Colombia insecurity became the main axis of polarization within society and the central issue around which new political loyalties came to be articulated since 2002.[14] Throughout the first decade of the twenty-first century, the most salient issues in Colombia's public debate were not inequality, poverty, the need for a new social policy, or more social spending.[15] Rather, the issues mobilizing the Colombian electorate at the time were all related to the topic of security: the war against terrorism, the war against drugs, and the war against "los violentos."[16] Unlike other cases in Latin American, where populism offered a vehicle to mobilize newly emerging social identities in contexts of socioeconomic crisis, the reemergence of populist discourse in Colombia came rather as a consequence of the nation's exasperation with the spiral of violence suffered since the mid-1980s.

Uribe was not the personification of a mobilized people but rather of a terrorized one. His election by a clear majority (53 percent) of voters during the first round of presidential elections in 2002 amounted to a

13. According to official information, 2000 was the worst year in terms of homicides and kidnappings since the mid-1980s. For the data, see Ministerio de Defensa, República de Colombia, "Consolidación de la Seguridad Democrática: Un esfuerzo con decisión y resultados, julio 2006–mayo 2009," http://www.mindefensa.gov.co/descargas/Documentos_Home/Gestion_Min_Santos.pdf; Observatorio del Programa Presidencial para los Derechos Humanos y el Derecho Internacional Humanitario, Vicepresidencia de la República, "Geografía de las tasas de homicidios 1998–2008," electronic publication, 2008; Observatorio del programa presidencial de DDHH y DIH, Vicepresidencia de la República, "Indicadores sobre derechos humanos y DIH Colombia: Año 2008," 2008; and Observatorio del Programa Presidencial de DDHH y DIH, Vicepresidencia de la República, "Dinámica espacial del secuestro en Colombia, 1996–2007," 2009.

14. For a similar reflection on changes in the party system, see Jonathan Hartlyn, "Democratization in Colombia: Reflections on the Role of the National Front," paper presented at the conference "50 años de regreso a la democracia: Nuevas miradas sobre el Frente Nacional," Escuela de Gobierno, Universidad de los Andes and Centro de Estudios Históricos, Universidad Externado de Colombia, Bogotá, September 29–October 1, 2009, 5.

15. This is of course not meant to diminish their importance. The point is rather to signal their lack of centrality in Colombia's public debate.

16. "Los violentos" (literally translated as "the violent ones") is a euphemism widely used in the country to name all those involved in acts of violence without having to name names, thus avoiding the attribution of responsibility to specific individuals or groups of actors.

plebiscite against the failed attempts at negotiating with a powerful recalcitrant guerrilla group, the FARC, during the previous presidential
term of Andrés Pastrana (1998–2002). In a context of declining party
loyalties, the electorate had become exhausted by all the previous attempts to end the country's armed conflict through negotiations, and
it was ready to put its trust in the hands of a strong leader who, claiming to be an outsider, promised to bring peace through military might
alone. The government of Uribe Vélez rapidly embarked on an effort
to strengthen the military's capacity to combat the guerrillas, funded
through a greater domestic fiscal effort but also, and fundamentally, by
a dramatic increase in military aid provided by the United States beginning in 2000 under Plan Colombia.[17] Since 2003, it had also initiated a
very controversial negotiation process with the paramilitary groups,
which nevertheless failed to root out these criminal organizations from
the national territory.

In May 2006, President Uribe was reelected with an even higher proportion of votes, 62.3 percent, also in the first round—40 points ahead of
the candidate with the second-highest number of votes, Carlos Gaviria,
from the leftist Polo Democrático Alternativo (Alternative Democratic
Pole), who obtained 22 percent. A solid majority of Colombians favored
the president's reelection mainly because his heavy-handed policies delivered. Between 2002 and 2006, Colombia experienced a speedy recovery of most security indicators: The numbers of killings and kidnappings
dropped significantly; attacks from both guerrillas and paramilitaries
against small rural hamlets declined; and, for the first time in decades,
Colombians felt free to travel out of the cities thanks to the strong presence of the armed forces along the country's main roads and highways.[18]
Simultaneously, in part due to this renewed sense of internal security,
but also due to higher international prices for commodities, the economy
witnessed a steady recovery from the low point of the late 1990s, when
the country had suffered the worst recession in a century.

Uribe was the first Colombian president to be reelected for a second
term in more than a century, because running for a second term had

17. Since the introduction of Plan Colombia in 2000, Colombia has received
more than $8 billion in security aid from the United States to fight guerrillas and
drug traffickers, making it the largest recipient of U.S. military aid outside the Middle East (and far below Iraq and Afghanistan). This figure comes from *The Economist*, December 11, 2010, 49.

18. In terms of the "war on drugs"—allegedly the main goal of U.S. military aid
—the results were far more disappointing.

been banned since the early 1900s. The fact that he got away with amending the Constitution to allow him to run again is a measure of the political power he had managed to marshal. In addition, during the congressional elections of March 2006, a coalition of four pro-Uribe parties (the traditional Conservative Party plus three newly created parties: the Partido de la Unidad Nacional, Cambio Radical, and the Movimiento Alas / Equipo Colombia) obtained comfortable majorities in both chambers of Congress. The stage was set for an increasing concentration of power in the president's hands. A former Liberal, Uribe astutely used a divide-and-conquer strategy vis-à-vis his old party comrades, with dire consequences for the latter. Thus the Liberal Party, which historically had dominated the Colombian political landscape, garnered a dismal 12 percent in the presidential contest of 2006, a distant third from the victor and lagging far behind the Polo Democrático Alternativo, a new party of the left that became the main source of opposition to Uribe's policies.

During his second presidential term (2006–10), Uribe delivered more of the same: a tough stand against the FARC, a softer hand for the paramilitary armies—in favor of which the government presented and gained approval for a generous piece of legislation, the Peace and Justice Law—and a close relationship with the United States in matters related to drugs, security, and trade.

In short, at the turn of the twenty-first century, a deepening security crisis and a profound "negotiation fatigue," in the context of the party system's increasing weakness (but not collapse), led Colombians to vote for and reelect a dissident member of the Liberal Party who ran on a platform promising order and security.[19] It is against the backdrop of Colombia's profound and desperate weariness with both war and the fruitless efforts to end it that we may explain not only Uribe's election in 2002 and reelection in 2006 but also his sustained popularity (hovering between 60 and 70 percent) throughout the eight years of his mandate. If it had not been for the Constitutional Court's decision to stand in the way of a second reelection,[20] it is quite probable that he would have eas-

19. The apt expression "negotiation fatigue" comes from Cynthia Arnson and Teresa Whitfield, "Third Parties and Intractable Conflicts: The Case of Colombia," in *Grasping the Nettle: Analyzing Cases of Intractable Conflict*, edited by Chester Crocker, Fen Osler Hampson, and Pamela Aall (Washington, D.C.: U.S. Institute of Peace Press, 2005), 231–67.

20. On February 26, 2010, Colombia's constitutional court ruled as unconstitutional the law that called for a national referendum to put to the people the question

ily won a third mandate.[21] The question is whether, beyond being extremely popular, one can also consider Uribe to have been a populist. The following pages tackle this very question.

Uribe 2002–10: The Instrumental Uses of Populism

In an article published in 2003 (less than a year after Uribe won his first election), John Dugas argued against classifying the president as a populist; nothing in his private or public personae, previous political career, campaign strategy (in 2002), or ideological outlook would have caused people to suspect him of being a "populist"—a term that Uribe himself despised and rejected.[22] Yet, in the following pages I argue that during his long tenure as president (2002–10), Uribe made active use of a populist style and a populist discourse, based on the politicization of citizens' fear of insecurity, as part of a strategy to concentrate power in his hands while trying to retain the presidency. Sociologist Carlos de la Torre has argued that, rather than an immutable essence, populism is best seen as a strategy and a discourse.[23] This certainly proved to be the case with Uribe's instrumental borrowing of several elements from the populist tradition. However, other central elements of this same tradition were sorely missing in this case: the emphasis on class divisions as the central social cleavage; the effort to incorporate the masses and offer some mea-

of whether or not to allow President Uribe to run for a third consecutive term. On the importance of this controversial decision, see Felipe Botero, "Flash Report: A Key Decision in Colombia," Andean Democracy Research Network, Centre for the Study of Democratic Institutions, University of British Columbia, Vancouver, March 2010, available at www.blogs.ubc.ca/andeandemocracy.

21. In 2009, seven years after his first election, 63 percent of those polled were still willing to vote for him—an incredible degree of popular support for most presidents in Latin America. IPSOS-Napoleón Franco opinion poll carried out on September 28–29, 2009, and published by the radio stations LA FM and RCN and *Semana* magazine on October 2, 2009.

22. See John C. Dugas, "The Emergence of Neopopulism in Colombia? The Case of Alvaro Uribe," *Third World Quarterly* 24, no. 6 (2003): 1117–36.

23. See Carlos de la Torre, "Populismo, ciudadanía y estado de derecho," ponencia presentada en el Congreso Latinoamericano y Caribeño de Ciencias Sociales, FLACSO-Ecuador, Quito, October 31, 2007; Carlos de la Torre, "The Resurgence of Radical Populism in Latin America," *Constellations* 14, no. 3 (2007): 384–97; and Carlos de la Torre, "Populismo Radical y Democracia en los Andes," *Journal of Democracy en Español*, 2009, 24–37.

sure of redistributive justice; and the intention to use the central state as a vigorous instrument of redistribution and incorporation. There was nothing of this in Uribe's government (2002–10)—forcing us to conclude that this was a particularly "hollow" instance of populist discourse that never went beyond its quite apparent instrumental and strategic use.

Politicizing Insecurity:
A Polarizing Discourse and a Costly Policy

Pido a los compatriotas que no cedamos ante el terrorismo, que no aflojemos en la decisión de derrotarlo . . . que la decisión sea una sola: Sin vacilación a derrotar a los violentos.[24]

Carlos de la Torre proposes to conceive populism "as a discourse that produces a deep political polarization in two camps confronting each other in an antagonistic and Manichaean fashion: the people against the oligarchy."[25] In the radical populist experiments described by de la Torre, "politics is lived as confrontation between antagonistic projects of society," and thus rivals are conceived of as "enemies of the leader, the fatherland, and history."[26] Uribe's double-term presidency shared a number of characteristics with de la Torre's description; politics was indeed conceived as a confrontation between antagonistic projects of society, and the rivals of the president were often seen as enemies rather than political adversaries. Yet Uribe's rhetoric also differed from the radical populism pictured by de la Torre in important ways, for even while reflecting (and fostering) a profound division of society into two camps, the division proposed by Uribe did not refer to class cleavages at all, and neither did it propose to include or incorporate those excluded, nor to set the people against the oligarchy. The social division pictured in Uribe's discourse and his reactionary rhetoric was instead based on moral categories such as "good against evil" and order against chaos.[27]

24. President Uribe's declaration after the attack against a private club (El Nogal) in Bogotá on February 7, 2003, quoted by Paola Holguín and Carolina Escamilla, *Uribe de carne y hueso* (Bogotá: Editorial Norma, 2009), 138.
25. De la Torre, "Populismo Radical," 24.
26. Ibid., 25.
27. On the topic of reactionary rhetoric, see Albert O. Hirschman, *The Rhetoric of Reaction: Perversity, Futility, Jeopardy* (Cambridge, Mass.: Harvard University Press, 1991).

Uribe's invocation of "enemy versus friend" echoed the divisiveness of populist discourse, thereby adding to an already polarized society. But his conception of "us versus them" was not predicated on socio-economic distinctions or class identities; rather, his division hinged on separating the good citizens from the "violent ones" or the "terrorists." With time, the notion of the enemy grew to encompass not just the members of the FARC and ELN guerrillas, recalcitrant paramilitary groups, and drug dealers but also almost anybody who opposed the president, his government, or his policies—including nongovernmental organizations focused on human rights, journalists and intellectuals, opposition politicians, and even some state officials, such as the justices of the Supreme Court.[28]

Through the symbolic power of his polarizing discourse, Uribe captured and contributed to reproducing and deepening a profound cleavage in Colombia's society. The division in this case, however, was not between rich and poor, the people and the oligarchy, but between those who upheld a certain order and those who were willing to question or challenge it. It was an appealing discourse because it helped to simplify the heterogeneity and complexity of Colombian society, turning it into a black-and-white picture. The combat against the violent elements of society ("los violentos" or, more frequently, "the terrorists") was not only a struggle for material security or the defense of private property; it was mainly cast as a moral combat of good against evil. Uribe's discourse displayed a highly moral and religious content; there was a constant effort to draw a line between good and evil, very much in line with President George W. Bush's post–September 11 discourse. The highly moralistic and religious content of Uribe's discourse cleverly spoke to the profound religiosity of the Colombian people. But rather than calling forth a reflexive sense of religiosity, it played on the populations' most elemental and basic religious sentiments.

De la Torre also argues that "populism is based on the activation and mobilization of the excluded sectors from the political system," whose members live democratization as the "expression of popular will in mass actions and plebiscites."[29] During Uribe's term in office, however, there were no mass mobilizations against the oligarchy, no efforts to mobilize

28. See Ramiro Bejarano, "La justicia sitiada," in *Las perlas uribistas*, edited by Iván Cepeda (Bogotá: Random House Mondadori, 2010), 11–24.
29. De la Torre, "Populismo Radical," 24.

the excluded in order to incorporate them; and there were only a few plebiscitary demonstrations of support for the government.[30] Elections were useful, of course, not as episodes of popular mobilization but rather as opportunities to ratify the power vested in the leader and the subjugation of society to his will. Uribe's appeals to direct democracy (a failed example of which was putting forth a comprehensive package of political reforms as a referendum in the fall of 2003) were not intended to stir participation or to widen or deepen democracy. They represented, rather, a way of bypassing other institutions of representation (mainly Congress and the political parties) that stood in the way of the president's will.

Unlike other instances of populism, which have sought to challenge established elites and promote change, nothing in Uribe's platform suggested that he would use popular support to introduce radical social transformations; the intention was rather to avoid radical reform, to eliminate any questioning of the status quo. The profoundly conservative discourse deployed by Uribe sought rather to perpetuate the state of things, to retain power in the hands of those who already had it, and to silence and eventually eliminate any glimpse of opposition or alternative project for change.

Uribe's discourse was not inclusionary; nor was it nationalist, anti-imperialist, or anti–United States in content. It thus bore little resemblance to the features commonly associated with populist discourse. The president did not present himself as the leader of the poor (as did Bucaram in Ecuador), or of the "*descamisados*" (literally, the shirtless, as did Perón in Argentina), or of the excluded (as have done Chávez in Venezuela, Correa in Ecuador, and Morales in Bolivia). Instead, Uribe represented a project of reassertion of the landed elites, an opportunity to reaffirm their right to rule over society.[31] Despite his dressing up as an

30. A well-attended march along the streets of Colombia's cities and towns—which took place on February 4, 2008—was ostensibly organized against the FARC and its practice of kidnapping for ransom; it was also, quite clearly, a demonstration in support of the government's tough security policies. The mobilization to collect 4 million signatures in favor of a referendum that would have allowed Uribe to stand for a second reelection also classifies as a plebiscitary mobilization.

31. Uribe's social background is best reflected in a comment by his own wife. In an interview with the journalist María Isabel Rueda, Mrs. Uribe commented that she "started going out with a cattle rancher and ended up married to a politician [Yo empecé a salir con un ganadero y terminé casada con un político]." See Lina Moreno de Uribe's interview with María Isabel Rueda, *Semana*, June 19, 2006, 37.

"arriero paisa" (typical Antioqueño peasant), his image remained closer to that of the hacienda owner, the big landlord, the paterfamilias. Through his discourse, he delineated a relationship with the people that resembled that of an authoritarian father with his children—paternalistic and dominant. In his own words: "I have come to see my compatriots with the responsibility of a family father."[32] The father/leader does not represent his children; he rules over them. He is there to protect them from outsiders as well as from themselves, from their own mistakes, from their immaturity. He makes decisions for them while they obediently thank him, without protesting. Uribe became the leader of many terrorized Colombians, who sought in him a sense of order and security at any cost. He provided them with the image of a protective father who would save them from their own fear of violence. Politics thus disappeared as a space for collective deliberation and decisionmaking, reduced to the people's passive acquiescence to and cheering support for a leader who knew better, who was wiser, omnipotent and omnipresent, almost a demigod.[33]

For their part, the pro-Uribe parties (which emerged during his tenure as president and may disappear) were nothing close to "the party of the poor," as Peronism had once claimed to be; rather, they represented the most conservative interests in Colombian politics. These interests encompassed the traditional Conservative Party—which became a steadfast supporter of Uribe in Congress—and also two new parties, which represented little more than two right-leaning factions of the Liberal Party—Cambio Radical (headed by German Vargas Lleras), and the Partido de la Unidad Nacional (led by then-minister Juan Manuel Santos)—and extended all the way to the darkest presences in Colombian politics, those representing the unholy alliance of big landowners, regional politicians, and drug barons who stood together behind the armed project of the paramilitary groups during the last two decades of the twentieth century.[34] Their discourse, and Uribe's, did not side with the people against

32. "He aprendido a mirar a mis compatriotas con la responsabilidad de padre de familia," Álvaro Uribe, quoted by Holguín and Escamilla, *Uribe de carne*, 135.
33. For a taste of this, see the op-ed columns by José Obdulio Gaviria, the president's counselor throughout his eight years in power, in *El Tiempo* (www.eltiempo.com); and the op-ed columns by Alfredo Rangel, a supporter of the president, in *Revista Semana* (www.semana.com).
34. These now seem to be grouped under the Partido de Integración Nacional (PIN).

the elites; on the contrary, it placed the latter back on their pedestal, ruling from which they would know better than the people how to direct them and how to look after their interests—the landed oligarchy suddenly redeemed by the enlightened leader. In this inverted version of populist discourse, there was no glorification of the people but rather of "the leader" (in the singular); it was the glorification of the leader as the messiah, the country's savior.

But it was not just his highly conservative, moralistic, patriarchal, and divisive rhetoric that gave Uribe a strong grip on power throughout his eight years as president. His discourse was meant to accompany the central piece of his government, his "democratic security" policy—a controversial effort that delivered undeniable security gains between 2002 and 2010, when almost every indicator—from homicide rates, to the number of kidnappings, to the number of attacks by armed actors against small towns, all except for urban crime—showed signs of subsiding under Uribe's watch. His democratic security policy focused on strengthening the military's response to Colombia's conflict involving leftist guerrillas, right-wing paramilitaries, and the state's own armed forces. Initiatives included "a near doubling of the security forces' size, their deployment in much greater numbers among the general population, the use of paid citizen informants, and negotiations to secure the demobilization of pro-government paramilitary bands."[35]

It is now widely recognized that Uribe's internal security policy reduced murders, kidnappings, infrastructure attacks, and guerrilla activity. Between 2002 and 2008, according to the security analyst Alfredo Rangel, kidnappings went down 89 percent, while attacks on electrical towers went from 483 to 138, and the number of murders (per year) dropped from 28,837 to 16,140.[36] However, as Isaacson's review is quick to point out, Rangel leaves out some less comfortable statistics: "There is no mention of the 21,000 combatants and at least 14,000 civilians killed by the conflict since 2002, the 2.2 million forcibly displaced during that period, or the fact that no paramilitary leaders have been convicted of war crimes."[37] In fact, human rights and civil liberties advocates, local

35. See Adam Isaacson's review of Alfredo Rangel and Pedro Medellín, *Política de seguridad democrática,* in *Americas Quarterly,* Summer 2010, http://www.americas quarterly.org/node/1722.

36. Alfredo Rangel and Pedro Medellín, *Política de seguridad democrática* (Bogotá: Editorial Norma and Revista Semana, 2010).

37. Isacson, "Política de seguridad democrática."

as well as international, have persistently denounced the policy as leading to a perilous concentration of executive and military power, which is clearly inimical to democracy. Some also argue that it failed to address—in fact, it may have strengthened—the power of paramilitary and organized crime networks beyond the main cities. Despite its questionable means and associated costs, the security gains delivered by Uribe's democratic security policy won him the overwhelming support of Colombia's voters for eight years in a row and were clearly behind the election of his successor to the presidency, ex–defense minister Juan Manuel Santos, by a landslide in June 2010. Undeniably, however, it also had a deleterious impact on Colombia's democratic institutions, not to mention its cost in terms of the lives of those civilians caught in the crossfire—including the shocking scandal involving extrajudicial killings (dubbed the "*falsos positivos*") and the persistent abuses of power by the internal security police (DAS).[38]

Undermining Democracy from Within: Playing the Role of the "Outsider" with an Antipolitics Discourse

Uribe gradually assumed the messianic tone and discourse typical of populist leaders, but he was far from being a political outsider. The image of him as an outsider was one of the many myths that were actively pursued, carefully built, and strategically displayed by the president and his entourage. They successfully portrayed him as someone who did not come from the political parties, nor belonged to the political class that he so actively tried to eliminate and replace. However, one only needs to read his biography to see how far this was from the truth:[39] coming from a Liberal family, at the age of twenty-eight years he had already held three public administration positions, first in Medellín's Public Utilities Corporation (Empresas Públicas de Medellín) in 1976, then as secretary-

38. For more on the costs of Uribe's democratic security policy, see Felipe Zuleta Lleras, "Los 'falsos positivos': Crímenes de lesa humanidad," and León Valencia, "Lo que ocultó Uribe en la negociación con los paramilitares," both in *Perlas uribistas*, ed. Cepeda; and Claudia López Hernández, ed., *Y refundaron la patria . . .: De cómo mafiosos y políticos reconfiguraron el Estado colombiano* (Bogotá: Corporación Nuevo Arco Iris and Random House Mondadori, 2010).

39. This was available on the presidency's Web page, http://web.presidencia.gov.co. A detailed account of Uribe's political career is given by Dugas, "Emergence of Neopopulism?"

general of the Labor Department (in 1978, during López Michelsen's government), and last as national director of the civil aviation agency, AEROCIVIL (1980). In 1982 (when he was thirty years old) Uribe was appointed mayor of Medellín, a position that he held only for a few months. He owed these appointments to his participation in the party machine of a regional Liberal boss, Bernardo Guerra Serna.

In 1984, candidate Uribe competed for elected office for the first time and obtained a seat on Medellín's municipal council as head of the group presented by the Liberal faction led by Guerra Serna. In 1986, he broke off from Guerra Serna's faction and formed his own regional movement, Sector Democrático, putting his weight behind a national-level movement, Poder Popular, led by a then-young emerging politician, Ernesto Samper (who later became president). Uribe was thereafter elected on three occasions to the Senate: in 1986, in 1990 (a mandate that was cut short by the 1991 Constituent Assembly's decision to dismiss Congress and call new elections), and again in late 1991. During his tenure as senator, he took an active part in drafting a series of laws (the Pensions Act, or Law 71, of 1988; the Labor Reform Act, or Law 50, of 1990; and the Social Security Reform Act, or Law 100, of 1993) that have been considered by their critics to be markedly neoliberal. I would therefore agree with Dugas in that, if populism entails "the mobilization of a broad multiclass coalition with significant appeal to the lower classes," it was hard to see any evidence of a populist leaning in Uribe's legislative record during his years in the Colombian Senate.[40]

In 1994, Uribe was elected governor of his native department, Antioquia, for a three-year period (1995–97). It was during his tenure as governor that he developed the public image that would carry him all the way to the presidency—that of a sober, disciplined, and austere politician who avoided demagogy and favored ceaseless work; above all, one who would not hesitate to confront security challenges head on.[41] During his years as governor of Antioquia, one of the country's most violent regions, he inaugurated his micromanagement style, holding a Security Council meeting every day at 7 a.m. He based his security policy on the creation and promotion of "security cooperatives," the infamous

40. Dugas, "Emergence of Neopopulism?"1123.
41. During his tenure as governor of Antioquia, Uribe decreased the number of public employees in the department's public administration by two-thirds; the number of employees went down from 14,061 to 5,499. *Semana*, 2002; the same figure appears in Holguín and Escamilla, *Uribe de carne*.

CONVIVIR or "Asociaciones Comunitarias de Vigilancia y Seguridad Rural" (Community Associations for Rural Surveillance and Security). These were supposed to be a kind of civil defense group recognized and sanctioned by the state, designed to provide information and support to the armed forces. Instead, they received training and offensive weapons and eventually turned into the allies—or worse, the seedlings—of paramilitary forces. Governor Uribe defended these controversial associations as examples of cooperation between the state and society. On the ground, however, they became the clearest example of how a strategy to delegate state functions to private hands only helped to feed the ongoing spiral of violence in both Antioquia and the rest of the country.[42] Despite the dubious effects of his regional security strategy, Uribe's tough stand vis-à-vis the guerrillas and his promotion of these semiprivate counterinsurgency groups launched him onto the national political scene; they would eventually get him elected to the presidency of the republic five years later, in 2002.

Upon leaving the post of governor of Antioquia, Uribe supported the Liberal Party's candidate for the presidency, Horacio Serpa, in 1998. After Serpa's defeat by Andrés Pastrana (a Conservative), Uribe opted for all-out opposition to the negotiation strategy promoted by President Pastrana with the FARC. In early 2002, the Liberal Party again chose Serpa as its presidential candidate. It was then that Uribe broke off from the Liberal Party to found a new electoral movement, Primero Colombia (Colombia First), which appealed to liberals, conservatives, and independents alike. In the first of many populist gestures to come, Uribe declared: "I had to leave the Liberal Party in order to present my candidacy directly to the people."[43]

This electoral tactic was not new; two previous conservative candidates, Belisario Betancur (1982) and Andrés Pastrana (1998), had reached the presidency riding on a supraparty coalition that enabled them to compete with the majority Liberal Party. In the case of Uribe, the goal was not to form an antioligarchic mass movement (as in Gaitán's previous efforts) or to bring about a new form of doing politics (as Luis Carlos Galán had attempted to do twenty years earlier with his Nuevo Liberalismo, or New Liberalism). It was a case, rather, of using the tra-

42. Dugas states that political violence in Antioquia intensified during this period and that the rate of political noncombat killings doubled, reaching a peak of 1,431 victims in 1996. Dugas, "Emergence of Neopopulism?" 1124.
43. "Tuve que dejar el Partido Liberal para presentar directamente al pueblo mi candidatura," Álvaro Uribe, quoted by Holguín and Escamilla, *Uribe de carne*, 108.

ditional forms of electoral mobilization to garner support for the "*mano dura*" (literally, tough hand) policies that he cultivated during his tenure as governor. This strategy proved successful; a little while after he broke from the Liberal Party, the Conservatives decided to support his candidacy. Some postelectoral polls of self-identified voters indicated that 81 percent of Conservatives voted for Uribe, compared with 49.2 percent of Liberals.[44] Primero Colombia was the vehicle that brought him to the presidency in May 2002.

After this first electoral success, Uribe deepened his antipolitical discourse as he realized that the attack against the known vices of the Colombian political class made for a good campaign strategy. In his discourse against the political class and its traditional practices, what he called "*la corrupción y la politiquería*" (corruption and politicking), he found a point of coincidence with a widespread disdain for professional politicians, Congress, parties, and, in general, the institutions of democratic representation. Nevertheless, his proposed referendum against "*la corrupcion y la politiqueria*" was defeated in October 2003. This was a significant turning point; after this failed attempt at rallying the popular vote against the parties, he quickly learned to negotiate with that same political class. Over the years, he managed to amass a significant amount of legislative support from an array of parties mostly located on the right side of the political spectrum.

Despite Uribe's aggressive antipolitical discourse and his posing as an outsider, it was rather thanks to his experience and abilities as a tried politician that he managed to pass significant pieces of legislation, including the constitutional reform that allowed him to stand for a second election in 2006 as well as the law calling for a referendum that would have allowed him to run in a third consecutive election. Still, his insurgency against the Colombian political class and representative system was purely instrumental; rather than inaugurating a different form of doing politics, he used the purchasing power of an antipolitics discourse to get elected and remain in power, thanks to a constant discrediting of the parties, especially those in the opposition, and of politicians, especially those who attempted to compete against him.

Despite his personal history as part of the political and party establishment, Uribe cleverly used the arsenal of the critique against political parties and the political class to stay in power while minimizing the abil-

44. G. Hoskin, M. García, and R. Masías, unpublished manuscript, Universidad de los Andes, Bogotá, 2003, cited by Dugas, "Emergence of Neopopulism?" 1129.

ity of the opposition, as well as that of his own followers, to mount any significant challenge to his personal control. Tragically for his own political fate, he also prevented the formation of a solid and capable Uribista party that would uphold and defend his political project after his departure. In his efforts to be reelected once again, he continuously played his divide-and-rule tactics, thus fragmenting his own basis of support and thereby impeding the emergence of a leader who could succeed him.[45] Unlike other populist situations where charismatic leadership is eventually replaced and becomes routinized through a political party (e.g., the Partido Justicialista in Argentina after Perón, the Partido Revolucionario Institucional in Mexico after Cárdenas), at the end of Uribe's term there was no institutionalized pro-Uribe party to succeed him.[46]

Instead of working toward the institutionalization of a new party that would uphold and continue his political project, Uribe kept busy presenting himself as the only possible candidate, turning his job as president into a permanent campaign. His own words are quite telling in this respect: "For democracy it would be best if one's government could be a 'reality show.' If at any minute the country could know live—what they now call in real time—everything the government does or thinks."[47] In addition to a deft utilization of the mass media (especially television), Uribe inaugurated a new form of communication with the masses, the Consejos Comunales de Gobierno (CCGs; Communal Councils of Government) to create and recreate the illusion of a direct link between the president and the local communities. The president and his Cabinet

45. There were a couple of them, of course. When the Constitutional Court decided that Uribe could not stand for a third term, they fought bitterly to the end, with Juan Manuel Santos (arguably not Uribe's chosen heir) winning the upper hand after Andrés Felipe Arias (his favorite) lost the Conservative Party's nomination as its presidential candidate.

46. If anything, since taking office in mid-2010, President Santos has quite consciously sought to distance himself and his government from the former president and the worst legacies from his time in office. Meanwhile, some of the previously divided Liberal factions that formed part of Uribe's majority in Congress seemed to be coming together in what looked like a probable revival of the traditional Liberal Party. For the news of a possible merging of Cambio Radical and the Liberal Party, see http://www.eltiempo.com/politica/liberales-y-cambio-radical-se-encaminan-hacia-una-posible-integracion_8608664-4.

47. "Lo mejor para la democracia es que el gobierno de uno fuera un reality. Que cada minuto el país conociera en vivo y en directo—lo que se llama ahora en tiempo real—todo lo que dice y piensa el gobierno." Álvaro Uribe, quoted by Holguín and Escamilla, *Uribe de carne*, 136.

traveled tirelessly throughout the territory to meet with governors, mayors, and the local communities; to address all kinds of regional and local problems; and to promise all kinds of quick fixes. From 2002 until 2009, 249 CCGs took place (at an average of 35 per year or one every week and a half), both in the big cities as well as in some of the most remote villages of the national territory. The CCGs were carried out on Saturdays and were broadcasted via radio and television through the state's own stations and channels.

According to the Alta Consejería para la Competitividad y las Regiones (ACCR; Office of the High Commissioner for Competitiveness and Regions), which was in charge of organizing these events, "each CCG's agenda is prepared before the meeting by the Office of the High Commissioner for the Regions at the Presidency of the Republic, based on the notions put forth by the President of the Republic in his 'Democratic Manifesto,' in particular, the seven tools to build social justice: an education revolution, social security, fostering a solidarity economy, social management of the countryside and of public utilities, small enterprises development and quality of urban life, in addition to the specific projects in each region."[48] Despite their participatory appearance, the CCGs were carefully staged and tightly controlled events. Previous to each CCG, a rigorous selection of the participants was carried out by the ACCR and other government entities. In addition, security forces collected information on all those attending the CCG; there were also some topics not allowed on the agenda, such as public order, democratic security, and extradition. Finally, those willing to participate in the discussion during the CCG needed to register before the event and announce the topic they were going to raise beforehand.[49] The CCGs thus fell short of offering true opportunities for participation; rather, they turned into occasions to advertise the government's agenda while sidelining the regional and local levels of government and creating the illusion of a direct relationship between the president and the people. As part of a populist strategy, the CCGs worked extremely well—they became a big hit with the population that felt recognized and included (if only symbolically) and cheered on "their president," though he used them effectively to

48. Alta Consejería para la Competitividad y las Regiones, http://regiones.presi dencia.gov.co/regiones/como-se-realizan.asp.

49. Adolfo Atehortúa Cruz, *Las banderas del presidente Uribe: Estado comunitario, seguridad democrática, revolución educativa* (Medellín: La Carreta Editores, 2007), 34.

cement his own popularity while bypassing every institution of representation not only at the national but also at the local and regional levels.

The CCGs were a crucial part of Uribe's permanent electoral campaign; indeed, they formed a clever strategy to use state resources to promote the president as a perpetual candidate. It would not be far-fetched to say that, in this regard, Uribe's strategy was not very different from that displayed by Fujimori in Peru, or from Chávez's famous *Aló Presidente* chain broadcasts in Venezuela. Given the CCGs' coverage of the national territory, if Uribe had been allowed to run for a third term, it would have been very difficult for any political rival to match the CCGs as a campaign strategy.

The flattening of the political landscape, the sidelining of political parties, and the attempts to eliminate any institutional mediation between the leader and the people are part and parcel of populist leaders' distrust and disdain for the institutions of liberal democracy. In a simplistic understanding of democracy as majority rule, populism tends to undermine the complex institutional arrangements that make representative democracy possible. It offers, instead, the illusion of direct participation without intermediaries, assuming the existence of one single, known, homogeneous popular will; it usually ends by assimilating this to the will and interests of the leader. In doing so, it denies the existence of the multiple interests present in society, the need to represent them in all their diversity, and the need to protect those groups, sectors, or individuals that are not part of the dominant majority. Constitutional limits on presidential power are usually treated as an unnecessary nuisance and are often overlooked or openly attacked in an effort to expand the leader's power. In this sense, Uribe had much in common with other populist leaders. Apart from a persistent effort to reduce the influence of political parties and Congress, Uribe's government attempted to control every agency of horizontal accountability, and it protagonized an almost ceaseless confrontation with the judicial branch, especially with the Supreme Court of Justice (CSJ).[50] The confrontation only deepened after the CSJ unveiled the so-called *parapolítica* scandal—as the result of which at least one-third of the members of Congress (a majority of whom were affiliated

---

50. On this, see M. García Villegas and J. E. Revelo Rebolledo, eds., *Mayorías sin democracia: Desequilibro de poderes y Estado de derecho en Colombia, 2002–2009* (Bogotá: Centro de Estudios de Derecho, Justicia y Sociedad, and DeJusticia, 2009).

with pro-Uribe parties) became the object of judicial investigations to determine their role in the promotion of paramilitary groups. Despite Uribe's many attempts to discredit the CSJ, or to constrain its power to investigate the members of Congress, the CSJ persisted in its battle against the unholy alliance between paramilitary armies, drug dealers, and regional politicians, which called into question the democratic nature of Colombia's electoral process and representative institutions.[51]

The efforts on the part of Uribe's government to undermine the authority of the courts and their capacity to place limits on the use of executive power added a new source of threats against Colombia's democratic institutions, which was magnified by the president's high and persistent levels of popularity (hovering around 70 percent) throughout his mandate.[52] And yet, in a tribute to the resilience of Colombia's democratic institutions—despite decades of violence and the more recent attacks coming from the seat of executive power—the courts were able to withstand the blow and stood up in defense of constitutional democracy. Nowhere was this more visible than in the debate about the eventual and ultimately impossible reelection of Uribe to a third consecutive term as president. In 2004, he engineered a constitutional reform that allowed him to run for reelection in 2006. With his tacit approval, his supporters tried to open the door to a second reelection by requesting that Congress consider a referendum law in 2008.[53] On February 26, 2010, the Constitutional Court ruled unconstitutional the law that called for a national referendum to put to the people the question of whether or not to allow President Uribe to run for a third consecutive term, thus restoring faith in the institutional balance of power established by the Constitution of 1991, which had been so badly battered and bruised during Uribe's mandate.[54]

---

51. On the conflict between Uribe and the Courts, see Bejarano, "Justicia sitiada."

52. For more on the tensions and conflicts between Uribe and the courts, see A. M. Bejarano, H. Alviar, F. Botero, G. Hoskin, and M. Pachón, "Colombia: Democracia amenazada," in *Democracia en la región andina*, edited by Max Cameron and Juan Pablo Luna (Lima: Instituto de Estudios Peruanos, 2010), 101–64.

53. Promoters of the referendum law collected close to 4 million signatures, which obliged Congress to initiate legislation on the issue between 2008 and 2009. Nevertheless, several procedural flaws—including flagrant violations of legal limitations on such activities plus Congress's disregard of proper procedure—prompted the Court's decision against the referendum law. For more details, see Botero, "Flash Report."

54. For a thorough analysis of the Court's ruling, see ibid.

Thus, like the old and new populist leaders of Latin America, Uribe shared a disdain for the institutions typical of liberal democracy. Nevertheless, unlike many of the cases included in this volume, Colombia's democratic institutions (especially the courts, but also the opposition parties in Congress, supported by the press and civil society organizations, both national and international) showed an outstanding degree of resilience and were finally able to constrain even this very powerful executive branch. This victory of institutions over the personal ambitions of a powerful president certainly makes Colombia a unique case in the region.

Conclusion

Uribe's government (2002–10) cannot be classified as a case of populism in the full sense of the word. I have argued, instead, that it used a number of populist tactics in a conscious and obviously instrumental strategy to gain and retain power. Thus Uribe represented a rather hollow version of populism—the tactics and the gestures were there, but without the content.

In contrast to both classic and radical versions of populism, Uribe's project was not one of incorporation of the subaltern classes, the poor, or the excluded into society and politics. Neither was it a project for socioeconomic redistribution calling for an expansive and interventionist role for the state. Neither his discourse nor his policies were nationalistic or anti-imperialist in content. Rather, his economic project kept important continuities with the economic liberalization policies of the 1980s and 1990s; it did not represent a break with the economic orthodoxy of those decades, and yet it was not radically neoliberal, as Fujimori's and Menem's had once been. It instead ratified Colombia's tradition of seeking a middle ground between opposite development models while preserving a leading role for the private sector in the economy, together with a state that plays a limited role in stimulating and orienting (rather than directing) economic activities. Nothing in his economic policies is reminiscent of the classic populism of the 1940s and 1950s, and its distance from the neostatist and nationalist projects typical of the new radical populism is quite glaring.

Uribe was not a great believer in the role of the state; throughout his tenure as president, he insisted on the desired goal of a state reduced in size and scope, with the sole exception of the armed forces and military expenditures. His government advocated a rather technocratic view of the state, according to which it should be conceived as a resource administrator rather than a political actor. His discourse (if not always his policies) insisted on reducing the size of the state, the number of public employees, and the amount of public expenditures. His view of the so-called communitarian state conceived of a minimum state that delegates to society and the market most functions not directly linked to the provision of security and the protection of private property. The idea was to move toward a smaller and leaner state, deeply rooted at the local level, efficient in the provision of services, but not necessarily interested in mobilizing the population, much less in directing the economy or shaping social outcomes.[55] There was just one single and important exception: Starting with his first Development Plan (presented in 2003), Uribe's government clearly stated the need to strengthen the military and set to increase the portion of the national budget devoted to internal security and defense.

Uribe's understanding of social policy was necessarily limited by his minimal view of the role of the state. This is not the place to attempt a thorough analysis of social policy during his term as president. His critics have argued that the targeted poverty alleviation programs (Familias en Acción and Red Juntos) were not only insufficient but were also used for political ends. This is nothing new; rather, it builds on Colombia's tradition whereby the limited resources available for social purposes trickle down through government and party structures, in a selective fashion, reaching only those who are connected to the state via extended networks of political clienteles and patronage. Perhaps the novelty during Uribe's eight years in power was that rather than distributing these resources through the party networks, they were channeled to a great extent (some say upward of 80 percent) directly through the executive branch.[56]

55. On Uribe's conception of the "communitarian" state, see Ingrid J. Bolivar, "El Estado comunitario: Más administración y menos política," *Revista Foro* 46 (Bogotá), December 2002–January 2003, 18–24.

56. Two cases spring to mind as cases of targeted, selective social policies with obvious political purposes: One is the selective granting of agrarian subsidies to big landowners (as opposed to peasants with small and medium-sized farms), who in turn allegedly helped finance the political campaign of Uribe's minister of agriculture and potential successor (Andrés Felipe Arias) in what has come to be known as the "Agro-Ingreso Seguro" scandal. The second is the persistent allegations by the opposition that the targeted family grants program known as Familias en Acción was

Judging from the outcomes, it becomes quite evident that during Uribe's term in office, there was no dramatic change in the historical patterns of social inequality and exclusion that have plagued Colombia for centuries. As of 2009, poverty stood at 46 percent of the population, the richest 20 percent of the population continued to receive 62 percent of the national income, and the Gini coefficient (which measures inequality) increased to 0.59 (which made Colombia one of the most unequal countries in Latin America).[57] In terms of the allocation of resources, there is no question that social expenditures never grew at the same pace as military and defense outlays. Finally, and not surprisingly, there were no attempts to promote or even discuss some fundamental social reforms such as land reform. Needless to say, given his social origins and political outlook, Uribe's government did nothing to address the country's highly unequal land tenure pattern, which has been historically tied up with much of the violence in the country. In short, a cursory look at social policy during the Uribe administration tends to confirm the view that there was no intention or attempt to put forward a comprehensive package or major overhaul of social policy in order to operate any meaningful redistribution of wealth and income among Colombians, therefore including or incorporating the hitherto excluded.

This chapter has argued that the apparent reemergence of populism in Colombia under Uribe was mostly limited to the government's discourse, which was quite clearly used in an instrumental and strategic fashion to cement the president's hold on power. Given the country's historical absence of populism, Uribe's introduction of a personalistic style of governance and his efforts to weaken the traditional vehicles of democratic representation and accountability may have seemed at first a radical departure from the country's tradition. However, on close inspection, it boiled down to an instrumental use of populist rhetoric and gestures with the sole aim of concentrating and preserving a hold on power—a hollowed-out version of populism that has very little in common with those cases where a more substantive version of populism has been tried.

---

repeatedly used to obtain the recipients' signatures in the referendum petition, as well as their votes in the 2010 presidential election.

57. These data come from a study written by Ricardo Bonilla, a researcher at the Research Centre for Development (CID) at the National University, and published by *El Espectador*, December 25, 2009, http://www.elespectador.com/economia/articulo179073-pobre-resultado-de-politica-social-muestra-gobierno-de-uribe-revela-informe.

Still, despite its emptiness, the "Uribe phenomenon" may be a harbinger of things to come for the rest of the region: As they face rising crime rates that tend to trigger citizens' rising fears, many countries in Latin America may become fertile terrain for the emergence of personalistic leaders who accumulate power and thrive based on the politicization of insecurity.

Chapter 13

Conclusion: The Meaning and Future of Latin American Populism

Cynthia J. Arnson
and Carlos de la Torre

We began our exploration of contemporary populism in Latin America by asking several basic questions: about how to define populism, how to explain its revival in light of earlier populist manifestations (particularly the period of "classical populism" in the 1930s and 1940s), and how to understand more deeply the ambiguous and at times antagonistic relationship between populism and representative democracy. Although it still may not be possible to come to definitive and undisputable responses to these broad questions, we believe that the rich empirical and theoretical material in this volume allows us to approximate answers in novel and important ways.

At the level of definitions, Leslie Bethell reminds us that in the study of Latin American political history and contemporary politics, "populism has been, and continues to be, an elusive concept that is notoriously difficult to define and is highly contested." Our contributors do not always agree with one another: Is populist mobilization by definition "top-down?" or can it also be "bottom-up?" Is it confined to only one historical period—that of the 1930s and 1940s—or is it a recurrent phenomenon, with leftist as well as rightist manifestations, eclectic ideology, and neoliberal as well as expansionist and statist approaches to social and economic policy? Can governments embody some elements of populism and not others, thus qualifying any search for a unique prototype? Does it make more sense to refer to populist interventions rather than populist actors or regimes—in that, as Francisco Panizza puts it, "populism is never an encompassing totality that completely defines a leader, a party, or a regime"?

Although these debates will be ongoing, the contributors to this book illustrate how the strategic and discursive aspects of populism can be integrated as part of a multidimensional definition that facilitates nuanced comparisons among populist movements and regimes. As a political phenomenon, Bethell emphasizes that populism encompasses movements, parties, and leaders who reach, retain, and exercise power through direct or quasi-direct, unmediated relationships with previously unorganized and excluded sections of the population. Kurt Weyland similarly emphasizes populism as a strategy to achieve and maintain power in which "personalistic, plebiscitarian leaders" govern "on behalf of the people," by overcoming structural and institutional constraints—thus exercising leadership as a form of "unbounded agency." Populist leaders, according to Weyland, "command considerable autonomy, zealously concentrate power, seek to escape from institutional checks and balances, and bend or break constraints." López Maya and Panzarelli show how in Venezuela, populist "direct democracy" has privileged the connection between leader and social base, rejecting and/or replacing the mediating institutions of representative democracy. This bypassing of institutions has profound implications for constitutional democracy, a theme to which we return later in this chapter.

Similarly, in discussing the Ecuadorian and Bolivian cases, César Montúfar and John Crabtree, respectively, emphasize not only populism's skirting or undermining of existing institutions but also the coupling of processes of de-institutionalization with efforts to create new institutions that re-found the state based on a new constitutional order. Their arguments recall Kenneth Roberts's conceptualization of populism as a force of "creative destruction" whose goal is to "break down, realign, and (potentially) rebuild more institutionalized forms of mass political representation." Although some measure of institutional or constitutional reformism has frequently characterized Latin American populism, it is the radicalization of this impulse that, Montúfar argues, distinguishes contemporary "populism of the twenty-first century" from previous manifestations. As he notes in chapter 11, for Andean populists, "the constitutional dimension has been fundamental" to the consolidation of leadership and political hegemony.

In addition to populism's institutional and strategic aspects, recurrent throughout these chapters is the importance attached to its discursive and rhetorical dimensions. If "the people" are the fundamental referent of populist politics, populist discourse is marked by the invocation of fundamental and irreconcilable antagonisms between "the people"—the underprivileged majority—and the corrupt, predatory "elites" or "oligarchies"—the privileged few who have benefited from past political and socioeconomic arrangements. Populist discourse strategically invokes and politicizes these dichotomies, imbuing them with moral, absolutist values and thereby setting in motion or deepening processes of profound political, social, economic, and cultural polarization. Conceiving of politics as a moral, redemptive crusade and a zero-sum confrontation both justifies and hastens the attack on the status quo.

Kenneth Roberts underscores that, even if populism represents the "quintessential expression of outsider politics," the polarizing discourse employed by populist leaders has differing effects, depending on the way antagonisms are constructed. He argues that when elites are identified in economic terms (the "oligarchy"), populism tends to lean to the left and generate class-based cleavages, whereas a discourse that takes aim at a corrupt political establishment or *partidocracia* tends to generate populism of the right, protecting economic elites while attacking, undermining, and even abolishing political institutions. In recent years, the degree of party institutionalization and the extent of contestation of neoliberal economic orthodoxy have been key determinants of the type of regime that has emerged from a period of crisis.

Populism's Supply and Demand

Given the central role of charismatic leaders, it is tempting to focus on their actions and rhetoric at the risk of ignoring deeper contextual factors that give rise to populism. In other words, without denying the crucial importance of leadership, we need to better define the institutional and structural conditions that lead to the emergence of populist regimes.

As various authors in this volume have indicated, populism can emerge in times both of crisis and noncrisis. César Montúfar goes as far as to say that in Ecuador, populism is part of the country's political "normalcy," and Cynthia McClintock traces the evolution of "serial populism" in Peru over a period of close to half a century. That said, populism in Latin America has most often been associated with crises of political, socioeconomic, or ethnic inclusion/exclusion. These exclusions can be intertwined, and reducing populism's emergence to one or another aspect can be artificial and even misleading.

Numerous chapters in this book have pointed to the key role of institutions in determining whether pressures for inclusion lead to populist ruptures. Reverberating throughout the case studies in this book are the ways that the weakness, ineffectiveness, or collapse of representative institutions, especially parties (see chapter 2), the malfunctioning of mechanisms of political mediation (chapter 3), and the deficits of legitimacy provide a fertile context in which populists come to power. Without these facilitating institutional weaknesses, populist leaders or movements claiming to represent the interests of "the people" are confined to the margins of the political system. Most, but not all, populist leaders are political outsiders who win elections by running against the system. Almost by definition, they have not been socialized into the constitutional rules of the game; hence, when they attain office they exhibit little interest in the preservation of existing institutions, especially those that would constrain their power and discretion. When existing institutions are considered to be "instruments of an exclusionary political establishment that was oblivious to the needs of marginalized groups in their own societies," the incentive is to ignore, replace, or destroy them.[1] The conditions are then ripe for transformational projects that concentrate power in the executive, establish direct, vertical connections between the leader and his or her followers, and substitute some version of "real" or "authentic," nonmediated democracy for the dysfunctional system of liberal democracy.

If weak institutions provide one breeding ground for populist ruptures, conditions of socioeconomic privation and exclusion magnify popu-

1. The quotation is from Steven Levitsky and Kenneth Roberts, "Democracy, Development, and the Left," in *The Resurgence of the Latin American Left*, edited by Steven Levitsky and Kenneth M. Roberts (Baltimore: Johns Hopkins University Press, 2011), 407.

lism's appeal. Despite significant progress in Latin America since the beginning of the 2000s in expanding the middle class and reducing poverty, along with some success in reducing inequality, Latin America remains the most highly unequal region in the world and is marked by deep class, ethnic, and gender disparities, the severity of which varies from country to country.[2] Notwithstanding improvements in the labor market, as much as a third to half of the labor force in many countries works in the informal sector, without steady incomes and with only precarious and spotty inclusion in social protection schemes such as pensions and health care.[3] Despite some improvements, public education in many countries remains underfunded and of poor quality, and private education is financially out of reach for the majority.

In addition, millions in Latin America are, in the words of the late Argentine social scientist Guillermo O'Donnell, "legally poor."[4] There is a duality between the enshrinement of rights in constitutions and in official discourse and the limited upholding of rights or the enforcement of rules in everyday life. The rule of law is tenuous at best; at worst, the law appears to serve only the interests of the powerful few. Latin American states "may be described as 'frustrated' because of the perma-

2. Between 2003 and 2008, levels of inequality in several Latin American countries improved, sometimes dramatically, with the most notable reductions in Venezuela and in urban areas in Argentina, Panama, and Bolivia. Brazil, Chile, Ecuador, Nicaragua, and Paraguay also registered significant advances, but fully half the countries of the region made no significant progress. Income distribution worsened during this period in Colombia, the Dominican Republic, and Guatemala. For the region as a whole, social expenditures as a percentage of GDP increased more than 5 percent between 1990 and 2008, and per capita social spending almost doubled between 1990–91 and 2006–7. See United Nations Economic Commission on Latin America and the Caribbean, *Time for Equality: Closing Gaps, Opening Trails* (Santiago: United Nations, 2010), 172; United Nations, *Millennium Development Goals: Achieving the Millennium Development Goals with Equality in Latin America and the Caribbean, Progress and Challenges* (Santiago: United Nations, 2010), 5, 178; Cynthia J. Arnson and Marcelo Bergman, "Introduction," in *Taxation and Equality in Latin America*, edited by Cynthia J. Arnson, Marcelo Bergman, and Tasha Fairfield, Update on the Americas (Washington, D.C.: Latin American Program, Woodrow Wilson International Center for Scholars, 2012), 1–2, http://wilsoncenter.org/sites/default/files/Taxation.pdf.

3. Juan Pablo Jiménez et al., eds., *Evasión y equidad en América Latina* (Santiago: Comisión Económica para América Latina y el Caribe, 2010), cited in *Taxation and Equality*, ed. Arnson, Bergman, and Fairfield.

4. Guillermo O'Donnell, "Reflections on Contemporary South American Democracies," *Journal of Latin American Studies* 33, no. 3 (2001): 602.

nent contradiction between the voluminous paper regulations that they spawn and their inability to enforce them in practice."[5] A vast social science literature has explored these "deficits" in the quality of democracy in Latin America, the truncated nature of citizenship, and the difficulties of democratic deepening once democracy's electoral dimensions have been established. Not all forms of legal, political, or socioeconomic exclusion give rise to populism. But in the absence or discrediting of mechanisms of political mediation and institutions of representation, populist interventions that give name to and politicize people's daily experiences of marginalization and humiliation remain a constant possibility.

Several of the chapters in this book also indicate the ways that crises of security can open spaces for populist appeals. Alberto Fujimori came to power in Peru amid rampant hyperinflation (official figures put it at more than 7,000 percent in 1990) along with the seemingly uncontrollable violence by the brutal Maoist insurgent group Shining Path. Fujimori's "self-coup" (*autogolpe*) of April 1992 shut down the Congress, abolished regional governments, and intervened in the judiciary, and he governed with the support of the armed forces and intelligence services. The decimation and eventual "strategic defeat" of the guerrillas—in tandem with antipoverty programs aimed at the informal sector—consolidated popular support for Fujimori's authoritarian government. (His government collapsed in 2000, following massive protests against electoral fraud and amid a corruption scandal for which he was ultimately tried and convicted in 2009.)[6]

Like Fujimori, Álvaro Uribe was elected in Colombia in the midst of a profound security crisis and the public's demand for a hard-line response to guerrilla violence after a collapsed peace process. As Ana María Bejarano demonstrates in chapter 12, "Uribe was not the personification of a mobilized people but rather of a terrorized one." His polar-

---

5. Miguel Ángel Centeno and Alejandro Portes, "The Informal Economy in the Shadow of the State," in *Out of the Shadows: Political Action and the Informal Economy in Latin America*, edited by Patricia Fernández-Kelly and Jon Shefner (University Park: Pennsylvania State University Press, 2006), 28.
6. The conviction was also for human rights violations in addition to corruption. See Carlos Basombrío Iglesias, "Peace in Peru, but Unresolved Tasks," and Carlos Iván Degregori, "Commentary—'Eppur Si Muove'—Truth and Justice in Peru after the Truth and Reconciliation Commission," in *In the Wake of War: Democratization and Internal Armed Conflict in Latin America*, edited by Cynthia J. Arnson (Washington, D.C. and Stanford, Calif.: Woodrow Wilson Center Press and Stanford University Press, 2012), 215–38, 373–84.

izing discourse distinguished between "good citizens" and "terrorists," a category that over time broadened to include anyone—Supreme Court justices, journalists, opposition politicians, nongovernmental organizations—critical of his policies. Uribe's effort to concentrate power was ultimately constrained by Colombia's institutions. But his and Fujimori's politicization of insecurity may signal a new variant of populist expression in a region where crime, violence, and insecurity are becoming ever more prominent concerns of the citizenry.[7]

Populism and Democracy

We admitted in the introduction to this book that an analytic approach to the study of populism was not devoid of normative judgments, none more laden than that which concerns populism's relationship to democracy. It is important to note at the outset that both populism and liberal democracy base their legitimacy on the notion of popular sovereignty. But the notion of a sovereign people is defined in sharply divergent ways; whereas populism "stresses the collective rights of the people" in antagonism with the status quo, constitutional liberalism emphasizes "the importance of individual rights, checks and balances, and the toleration of differences."[8] As Enrique Peruzzotti points out in chapter 3, tensions and ambiguities in the notion of what constitutes democracy create the

7. According to the Santiago-based polling firm Latinobarómetro, when citizens were asked in 2011 what they consider to be the most important problem in their country, citizens in eleven of the eighteen countries polled (the eleven were Venezuela, Costa Rica, El Salvador, Mexico, Uruguay, Argentina, Panama, Ecuador, Guatemala, Honduras, and Peru) responded that crime and public security (not economic issues such as unemployment) ranked as their greatest concern. In addition, fully 83 percent of the citizens polled believed that crime had increased. See Marta Lagos and Lucía Dammert, *La Seguridad Ciudadana: El problema principal de América Latina* (Santiago: Corporación Latinobarómetro, 2012), 5, available at www.latinobarometro.org. The overtaking of economic concerns by concerns for personal security are also reflected in Latinobarómetro's annual opinion surveys in the region. The results of Vanderbilt University's Latin American Public Opinion Project (LAPOP) demonstrate further that crime victimization and the perception of insecurity negatively impact citizen support for democratic systems and respect for the rule of law. See LAPOP, "Americas Barometer / Barómetro de la Américas, Political Culture of Democracy, 2010," 78–86, available at www.lapopsurveys.org.

8. Francisco Panizza and Romina Miorelli, "Populism and Democracy in Latin America," *Ethics and International Affairs*, Spring 2009, 39–46.

conditions in which populism is viewed either as "an obstacle to the development and consolidation of democratic institutions" or as "the very expression of democracy and of politics itself: . . . a necessary antidote to the ills of representative politics" as well as a "healthy countervailing force against the elitist tendencies" of liberal democracy.

What are the ambiguous relationships between populism and constitutional democracy? Leslie Bethell maintains in chapter 7 that populist leaders "for the most part have been authoritarian, and impatient with existing democratic institutions" that are regarded as "fundamentally hostile to the interests of the 'people.'" At the same time, Bethell acknowledges that populist leaders have in some cases "fostered radical experiments in direct, participatory forms of democracy—but at the cost, it could be argued, of weakening, even destroying, representative democracy." Building on the debate between the political theorists Benjamin Arditi and Margaret Canovan, Peruzzotti argues that populism is a specter that accompanies and renews democracy while simultaneously haunting it as an authoritarian possibility.[9]

As our contributors illustrate, the democratizing credentials of populism lie, first and foremost, in the political, economic, and symbolic inclusion of the excluded: "By giving voice to popular grievances against the status quo, populism can under certain conditions contribute to the renewal and enlargement of democracy."[10]

Margaret Canovan has argued that populists democratize their societies by reasserting the notion that political power ought "to be taken from politicians and 'given back to the people.'"[11] In her view, populism constitutes the redemptive phase of democracy.[12] Historically, populism has not been an inherent threat to constitutional democracy. Under classical populism in Brazil and Argentina, Leslie Bethell and Hector Schamis illustrate how rapid economic and social changes from the 1930s onward threw oligarchic regimes into crisis, contributing to a redefinition of the relationship between the state, the working class, and white-collar, lower-middle-class public employees in urban areas. The expansion of

9. Benjamin Arditi, *Politics on the Edges of Liberalism: Difference, Populism, Revolution, Agitation* (Edinburgh: Edinburgh University Press, 2007); Margaret Canovan, "Trust the People! Populism and the Two Faces of Democracy," *Political Studies* 47 (1999): 2–16.

10. Panizza and Miorelli, "Populism and Democracy," 45.

11. Margaret Canovan, *The People* (Cambridge: Polity Press, 2005), 1.

12. Canovan, "Trust the People!"

the right to vote intersected with the broader distribution of socio-economic resources to sectors of the population that had not previously benefited. The organized working and lower middle classes were materially, politically, and culturally recognized as the essence of their nations. Juan Domingo Perón, for example, transformed the despised *cabecitas negras* and *descamisados* into the very soul of the Argentine nation; as a political and electoral force, different currents of Peronism have defined Argentine politics since the 1930s.[13]

In subsequent decades neopopulists such as Peru's Alberto Fujimori appealed to the politically unorganized and informal sectors of the population, pursuing neoliberal economic policies while establishing clientelistic networks to redistribute the profits from the sale of state-owned enterprises. Kurt Weyland illustrates in chapter 5 how Fujimori's policies bypassed the organized formal working and middle classes, benefiting instead previously ignored groups in the *pueblos jóvenes* of Lima as well as in remote areas of the countryside. Fujimori's neoliberal neopopulism served to renovate political and economic elites without, as Cynthia McClintock shows, establishing a more participatory regime. Fujimorismo relied not on the mobilization of mass constituencies but on public opinion polls and electoral coalitions constructed through clientelism.

In terms of economic inclusion, radical populists such as Chávez, Morales, and Correa have distributed windfall rents from the commodity and hydrocarbons sectors to millions of poor people, many of whom suffered dramatic setbacks during periods of neoliberal restructuring. Argentina under the Kirchners also expanded social protection programs and subsidies, spending billions of dollars made available by, among others, the takeover of private pension funds and increased agricultural exports, principally to China. As noted below, the expansion of economic and social rights is a fundamental, but not the only, ingredient that explains the popularity of these leaders. And whereas earlier studies of populist economics posited that the poor would ultimately suffer as a result of gross economic mismanagement and incompetence by the state,[14]

---

13. The endurance of Peronism in a context of persistent institutional weakness and instability is discussed by Steven Levitsky and María Victoria Murillo, eds., *Argentine Democracy: The Politics of Institutional Weakness* (University Park: Pennsylvania State University Press, 2005), esp. chap. 9.

14. Rudiger Dornbusch and Sebastian Edwards, eds., *The Macroeconomics of Populism in Latin America* (Chicago: University of Chicago Press, 1991).

the sheer magnitude of state spending—based on high global prices for commodities throughout the first decade of the twenty-first century— has benefited the poor in ways that offset the deleterious consequences of macroeconomic distortions that have produced inflation, shortages of basic goods (including energy), and the weakening of the manufacturing sector. Furthermore, twenty-first-century populists have demystified assertions regarding the technical neutrality of neoliberal experts or international financial institutions such as the International Monetary Fund, politicizing the economy as a *political* economy.

Andean populism has also fostered ethnic inclusion. Evo Morales, as Bolivia's first indigenous president, represents the symbolic and actual empowerment and inclusion of nonwhites, restoring the dignity of indigenous peoples who have suffered discrimination and marginalization in Bolivia for centuries.[15] In the words of Bolivian vice president Álvaro García Linera, "We have put indigenous people in the government in record numbers and appointed them to positions they never held before. . . . Now an indigenous person can be anything from president to a construction worker."[16] Morales's electoral campaigns implicitly and explicitly redefined the category of "the people" to mean indigenous people, despite the imprecision of ethnic and racial categories as well as individual self-identification within them.

Studies of democratic participation at the local level demonstrate not only the complexity of how democratization and authoritarianism are intertwined but also the differences in the social bases of contemporary radical populist regimes and the nature of linkages between leader and society. In chapter 9, Margarita López Maya and Alexandra Panzarelli show how the Chávez regime created sociopolitical organizations that mobilized the underprivileged from the top down, reinforcing a vertical power structure linked to the persona of Chávez. At the same time, the creation of new institutions of participatory democracy at the local and neighborhood levels—community water committees, land committees, health committees, and the like—"drove a significant 'bottom-up' dynamic" for access to public services that helps explain the support and

15. Esteban Ticona Alejo, "El racismo intelectual en el Pachakuti: Algunas consideraciones simbólicas del ascenso de Evo Morales a la Presidencia de Bolivia," in *El Pachakuti ha empezado (Pachakutixa Qalltiwa): Democracia y cultura política en Bolivia*, edited by Alejo Ticona (La Paz: Corte Nacional Electoral, 2006), 155–91.

16. Linda Farthing, "Controlling State Power: An Interview with Vice President Álvaro García Linera," *Latin American Perspectives* 37, no. 4 (2010): 31.

enthusiasm for Chávez among poor Venezuelans. López Maya and Panzarelli also argue that, following his election to a second term, Chávez began to displace these community organizations in the effort to construct socialism, using his charismatic leadership to neutralize autonomous grassroots expression. Although more research is needed, politics at the local level reveals that the tensions between arenas of popular empowerment and vertical notions of populist power are constantly at play.[17]

In Bolivia, John Crabtree shows how the Morales government "has remained surprisingly responsive to its grassroots constituency and has not sacrificed its original social links on the altars of political pluralism and governmental efficiency." Bolivia's strong social movements constitute powerful bottom-up influences with which Morales constantly negotiates. In part as a legacy of a strong communitarian tradition, Crabtree argues that "there is also strong pressure on leaders (*dirigentes*) —whether elected officials or traditionally chosen community elders—to be held accountable to those (the *base*) who put them in positions of authority." Hence, Morales's power is by no means absolute.

César Montúfar shows that the Ecuadorian case constitutes an exception. "Without organic ties to any social sector," Correa's movement "is not a citizens' revolution" from below, but rather, "a revolution from above"; like Chávez, Correa is adhering to the classical populist model of building a movement of loyal followers from the top down. Unlike in Venezuela, participatory institutions have not been created at the local level. And in contrast to Bolivia, Ecuador's indigenous movement opposes a self-described leftist administration. Correa's government is composed of experts who claim to enact policies on behalf of the nation, particularly the poor, but who do not involve popular organizations in the discussion and planning of that new nation. Unlike Morales, who was elected as a result of his deep connections with social movements,

17. Sujatha Fernandes, "Barrio Women and Popular Politics in Chávez's Venezuela," *Latin American Politics and Society* 49, no. 3 (2007): 97–127; Sujatha Fernandes, *Who Can Stop the Drums? Urban Social Movements in Chávez's Venezuela* (Durham, N.C.: Duke University Press, 2010); Kirk Hawkins, *Venezuela's Chavismo and Populism in Comparative Perspective* (Cambridge: Cambridge University Press, 2010); Kirk Hawkins, "Who Mobilizes? Participatory Democracy in Chávez's Bolivarian Revolution," *Latin American Politics and Society* 52, no. 3 (2010): 31–66; David Smilde and Daniel Hellinger, eds., *Venezuela's Bolivarian Democracy: Participation, Politics, and Culture under Chávez* (Durham, N.C.: Duke University Press, 2011).

Correa came to power without them. He was elected when the indigenous movement's mobilizational strength had diminished. Moreover, because the indigenous movement previously participated in the overthrow of elected presidents, it was perceived as a destabilizing and dangerous force.

What are the authoritarian traits of these regimes? Focusing on questions of institutional design, most studies of radical populism agree that the regimes of Chávez, Morales, and Correa are undermining or destroying liberal democracy in the name of fulfilling popular aspirations. In chapter 3, Peruzzotti lays out the rationale:

> The popularly elected president appears as the institutional power that directly expresses the democratic will of the people, whereas the legislative and judicial powers represent constitutional constraints on the majority. To preserve its democratic substance, the president must always keep direct contact with the people, and this usually leads to the establishment of forms of communication that bypass representative channels of opinion formation and aggregation. Elections, the mass media, and mass mobilizations are the prominent mechanisms that a leader has at hand to stay in constant connection with the people, and they all play a central role in populist regimes.

López Maya and Panzarelli argue that Venezuela's petro-state "has facilitated the destruction of institutional checks and balances and the advancement of a mission that is no longer one of democratic deepening but rather of authoritarian tendencies." In Bolivia, Crabtree shows how aspects of liberal pluralism under Morales have been eroded. Real or imagined enemies—agencies of the U.S. government, the *oligarquía* of Santa Cruz, the traditional political parties and their leaders, transnational companies—have proliferated. Crabtree shows how the construction of enemies allows the Morales administration to seek unity among a heterogeneous political public in ways that create a community of interest among the regime's supporters. "But the cost here has been to reduce spaces for active opposition, at both national and regional levels," a trend that accelerated during Morales's second term in office. Similarly, Montúfar identifies as the Correa administration's antidemocratic elements the "demobilization of autonomous civil society, a growing personalization of the political arena, an aggressive concentration of power in the hands of the executive, a systemic erosion of the independence of the branches of state power."

Democratic erosion is also evident in Argentina. Although, as chapter 4 indicates, the institutional and societal foundations of pluralism are stronger there than in Venezuela, Bolivia, or Ecuador, in chapter 6 Hector Schamis demonstrates how presidents Néstor Kirchner and Cristina Fernández de Kirchner embraced populism's legacy; they took advantage of fragile institutions and political party fragmentation to concentrate power in the executive branch, rule by decree, reduce Congress whenever possible "to a mere appendix" of the presidency, and blatantly use government resources "to grease the wheels of Peronist party politics." The "bellicose and nationalistic" rhetoric by the husband-and-wife team fostered confrontation at home; and street demonstrations— by both supporters and opponents of the regime—became the dominant form of political expression.

Schamis illustrates how Cristina Fernández de Kirchner strategically and liturgically used the death of her husband in 2010 to articulate a utopian vision around which to construct a long-term political movement. Néstor Kirchner's "political canonization" resurrected his wife's presidency and propelled her to a landslide reelection in 2011. In her second term, Fernández de Kirchner's government moved sharply to the left, confiscating the Spanish firm Repsol's majority stake in the Argentine oil company YPF, marginalizing key allies, and relying for support increasingly on the left-wing Peronist youth movement headed by her son, Máximo.[18] Meanwhile, governors, legislators, and other officials sympathetic to the government floated the idea of introducing a constitutional reform to allow Fernández de Kirchner to extend her mandate into a third term in office. As the economy stalled and her approval ratings plummeted in late 2012, it was unclear whether she would be able to muster the two-thirds congressional majority needed to alter the constitution.

The growing authoritarianism of populist regimes in Latin America is not characterized by the repression and massive human rights violations of bureaucratic authoritarian military regimes of decades past; rather, it is reflected in the ways that power is held and exercised. To varying degrees and most significantly in the Andes, today's populist regimes are focused on transformational or revolutionary projects that concentrate

---

18. To capitalize on her support among young people, Fernández de Kirchner promoted legislation to lower the voting age to sixteen years, a measure approved by the Argentine Senate in October 2012. Brazil, Ecuador, and Nicaragua are other Latin American countries that have lowered the voting age to sixteen.

power in the executive and do not envision ceding power to political opponents.[19] Even if leaders continue to enjoy strong popular support and to convene and win elections that are technically carried out without fraud, the institutions and legal frameworks that constrain the unfettered exercise of power have been systematically eroded. Constitutional reforms that do away with limits on presidential terms are one factor in that erosion; the weakening or elimination of checks and balances and mechanisms of horizontal accountability, through the packing of institutions such as the judiciary or electoral councils, are another. The polarization of society is fostered from above; politics is lived not as a process of bargaining within shared rules of the game but as a full-blown confrontation between irreconcilable interests whose defense rests on the utter vanquishing of the other. The public sphere and civil society have become less civil, impeding democratic dialogue and exchange. The fostering of polarization is not unique to populist regimes; indeed, all politics rests to some extent on the confrontation of ideologies and personalities and the mobilization of mass followings behind a particular leader. What matters is the institutional framework within which power is contested and exercised; whether those institutions serve to constrain "unfettered agency" and permit or prohibit peaceful alternation; and whether a vast array of rights, from media freedoms to individual civil and political rights, are upheld by the rule of law.

The attacks on press freedoms in Venezuela, Ecuador, and to a lesser extent Argentina, constitute troubling indicators of democratic erosion. Press freedoms have deteriorated in many countries of Latin America; in countries from Mexico to Honduras to Brazil, journalists covering issues of drug trafficking and organized crime have been threatened, physically assaulted, and murdered as a result of their reporting. Although these attacks reflect a state failure to protect citizens and, more generally, to uphold the rule of law and overcome impunity, criminal groups, not the state, are for the most part responsible. By contrast, the pressures on independent media under contemporary populist regimes are less violent but nonetheless explicit, state-directed policies, aimed at harassing and

19. As the October 2012 presidential election in Venezuela appeared more competitive, senior government officials, including the defense minister, made ambiguous and ominous statements about what would happen in the event of an opposition victory; and Chávez himself warned of the dangers of instability and even civil war if the opposition won the election. The fear that Chávez would not leave office even if he lost did not appear to be widely shared within the opposition.

punishing critics and limiting the free flow of information. The pressures are most severe in Venezuela, where the Chávez regime "blocked critical coverage, closed broadcasters, sued reporters for defamation, excluded those it deems unfriendly from official events and harassed—with the help of government allies and state-run media—critical journalists."[20] Simultaneously, the "building up of a vast state-run media empire"[21] and the requirement that radio and television stations carry Chávez's speeches ensured that his appearances and messaging saturated the airwaves.[22] In Ecuador, the Correa administration has seized private media outlets, sued journalists and editors who have criticized his policies, and interrupted broadcasts to allow government spokespersons to rebut unflattering news reports.[23] In Argentina, the government of Cristina Fernández de Kirchner has used tax audits to harass critics, including *Clarín*, the most widely circulated newspaper. In defiance of a Supreme Court ruling, the government has used the state advertising budget to reward supportive media and punish outlets critical of the government; fined economists for publishing inflation statistics at odds with the government's figures; and brought the sole newsprint manufacturer under government regulation, a company in which the two largest papers sharply

20. Monica Campbell, *Venezuela's Private Media Wither under Chávez Assault* (New York: Committee to Protect Journalists, 2012), 4.

21. Ibid.

22. Between 1999 and June 2012, Chávez appeared more than 2,300 times in broadcasts (*cadenas*) that radio and television stations were obliged by law to transmit. That translated into one *cadena* every other day for thirteen years; the average length of the broadcasts was 45 minutes. See Genaro Arriagada and José Woldenberg, "Informe Sobre las Elecciones del 7 de Octubre en Venezuela," Woodrow Wilson Center Latin American Program and International IDEA, September 2012, 4, http://www.wilsoncenter.org/sites/default/files/Elecciones_Venezolanos_Informe.pdf.

23. The most notorious case involved an editor and three board members of the largest privately owned newspaper, *El Universo*, who were convicted of defamation and sentenced to three-year terms for publishing an editorial titled "No a las mentiras" ("No to Lies"); the paper was also fined $40 million. All four of those convicted were pardoned in early 2012. See Catalina Botero, *Annual Report of the Office of the Special Rapporteur for Freedom of Expression 2011*, OEA/Ser.L/V/II, Doc. 69 (Washington, D.C.: Organization of American States, 2011), 78–80; Juan Forero, "In Tiny Ecuador, A Populist President Restrains the Press," *Washington Post*, January 24, 2012; Carlos Lauría, "State-Owned Media and the Public Interest," *Americas Quarterly*, April 25, 2012, http://www.americasquarterly.org/state-owned-media-and-the-public-interest. For a book-length treatment of the pressures on independent media in Ecuador, see César Ricuarte, ed., *La Palabra Rota: Seis investigaciones sobre el periodismo ecuatoriano* (Quito: Fundamedios, 2010).

critical of the government—*Clarín* and *La Nación*—owned a majority stake.[24] The restrictions and pressures on independent media point to the efforts of today's radical populists to establish what Chávez has explicitly called "communications hegemony" at the expense of opposing points of view.[25]

Restrictions on the media have gone hand-in-hand with other measures that move the political system toward greater authoritarianism. The political scientists Steven Levitsky and Lucan Way coined the term "competitive authoritarianism" to describe the ways in which leaders combined democratic rules with authoritarian governance, winning elections in which the voting was technically fair but the electoral playing field was skewed in ways that overwhelmingly and systematically favored the incumbent.[26] Taking issue with the democratization bias of studies of regime change in the post–Cold War world, Levitsky and Way

24. The government accused *La Nación* and *Clarín* of collusion with the military dictatorship in acquiring ownership of the company, Papel Prensa. Under antitrust provisions of a controversial 2009 media law, the government also ordered *Clarín* in late 2012 to sell its extensive holdings of cable, radio, and television stations. See "Argentina to Opposition Media Group: Divest by Dec. 7 or Face Forced Sale of Cable Stations," *Washington Post*, September 22, 2012; Nathan Gill, "Argentina Insists on Clarín Media Breakup Ahead of Court Ruling," Bloomberg News, September 24, 2012; "Knock, Knock: The Government Unleashes the Tax Agency against Its Opponents," *The Economist*, July 21, 2012; Botero, *Annual Report*, 24–32; Committee to Protect Journalists, "Attacks on the Press 2011: Argentina," http://cpj.org/2012/02/attacks-on-the-press-in-2011-argentina.php.

25. A study of media coverage during the 2012 presidential campaign in Venezueala found that print, television, and radio coverage of the opposition candidate Henrique Capriles Radonski was far more extensive than that of Hugo Chávez. Some of the difference can be attributed to the ways that Chávez's illness limited his ability to campaign actively. See the weekly reports on campaign media coverage compiled by the Universidad Católica Andrés Bello, *Monior Electoral Presidencial 2012*, http://www.monitorelectoral.org.ve/?q=perfilcoberturaactorescampana.

26. According to Levitsky and Way, "competitive authoritarian regimes are civilian regimes in which formal democratic institutions exist and are widely viewed as the primary means of gaining power, but in which incumbents' abuse of the state places them at a significant advantage vis-à-vis their opponents. Such regimes are competitive in that opposition parties use democratic institutions to contest seriously for power, but they are not democratic because the playing field is heavily skewed in favor of incumbents. Competition is thus real but unfair." See Steven Levitsky and Lucan Way, *Competitive Authoritarianism: Hybrid Regimes after the Cold War* (Cambridge: Cambridge University Press, 2010), 5. See also Steven Levitsky and Lucan A. Way, "The Rise of Competitive Authoritarianism," *Journal of Democracy* 13, no. 2 (2002): 51–65.

argued that competitive authoritarianism was a distinct, nondemocratic regime type, not the result of an incomplete or flawed process of democratic transition. More recently, scholars have sought to explore populism's impact not only on processes of democratic transitions and deepening but also on processes of *de-democratization*; in one formulation, competitive authoritarianism appears midway on a continuum between the erosion of liberal democracy and the establishment of a fully repressive, authoritarian regime.[27]

These concepts are useful for speculating about the future of twenty-first-century populist regimes, the prospects for peaceful alternation, and the possibility for the diffusion of populism to other countries of the region.

On the one hand, Andean populist regimes appear stable. As of this writing in late 2012, Chávez had been in power longer than Perón or any other populist president in the history of Latin America; only issues of physical health following his reelection by a wide margin in October 2012 cast doubt on his ability to remain in office, and plans for succession were under way. In Bolivia and Ecuador, Morales and Correa brought political stability to nations where cycles of popular protest kept a sequence of presidents from finishing their terms in office.[28] In Argentina, Cristina Fernández de Kirchner crushed her opponents in the 2011 presidential elections, winning more votes than her two closest competitors combined. Although her approval ratings remained volatile as the economy floundered, the weakened state of the opposition meant that various factions of the Peronist movement would be decisive in defining future political outcomes.

Moreover, the high commodity and energy prices that sustained and allowed populist governments to consolidate showed only modest declines, even in the face of protracted recession in the United States and Western Europe and economic slowdown in China. Thus, in political economy terms, the natural resource–based, distributionist schemes at

27. Cas Mudde and Cristóbal Rovira Kaltwasser, "Populism and (De)Democratization: A Theoretical Framework and Research Agenda," draft paper prepared for the annual conference of the American Political Science Association, August 30–September 2, 2012, 1–34.

28. Bolivia had six governments in six years and Ecuador had seven governments in ten years in the late 1990s and early 2000s. See Ignacio Walker, *Democracy and Populism in Latin America*, Working Paper 347 (Notre Dame, Ind.: Kellogg Institute for International Studies, University of Notre Dame, 2008), 12–13.

the core of contemporary radical populism seemed likely to be sustained for the foreseeable future—even intensified during electoral periods—despite their inefficiencies.

Conversely, the story of commodity, and especially oil, prices during the last century is one of booms and busts, and the degrees of economic and related political dependency on commodities create vulnerabilities for countries from Argentina to Venezuela. César Montúfar has shown how, even though Ecuador is less dependent than Venezuela on oil revenues, commodity rents nonetheless finance permanent political campaigns and subsidies distributed in clientelistic fashion. However, the plebiscitary character of the Correa regime, the absence of, and indeed conflict with, grassroots organizations, and the reliance on middle-class technocrats and public opinion also create fragilities that could cause the regime to implode as quickly as it arose from the political chaos of the early 2000s.

In responding to crises—whether brought on by a dramatic decline in commodity prices or some other unforeseen combination of events—the type of regime suggests different capacities and strategies for staying in power. Referring to the kind of economic crisis provoked by a fall in oil prices, the political scientist Javier Corrales has argued that, whereas a democracy might collapse, hybrid regimes[29]—those that combine elements of democracy as well as authoritarianism—can survive by intensifying the regime's authoritarian features.[30] Given that populists have already achieved some level of control or co-optation of key institutions (including through corruption and cronyism), maintaining control in a crisis means counting on the loyalty of armed forces and the police to quell popular protest, alone or in coordination with armed militias loyal to the regime. Although we need to know much more about the armed forces and their relation to populist regimes in the Andes, it appears that only in Venezuela, with its armed popular militias and "cooperatives"

29. For a seminial work on hybrid regimes, see Terry Lynn Karl, "The Hybrid Regimes of Central America," *Journal of Democracy* 6 (July 1995): 72–86.

30. Javier Corrales, "The Repeating Revolution: Chávez's New Politics and Old Economics," in *Leftist Governments in Latin America: Successes and Shortcomings,* edited by Kurt Weyland, Raúl Madrid, and Wendy Hunter (Cambridge: Cambridge University Press, 2010), 28–56. For a comparative historical analysis of the effects of extreme financial instability on the survival of democratic regimes, see Francisco E. González, *Creative Destruction? Economic Crises and Democracy in Latin America* (Baltimore: Johns Hopkins University Press, 2012).

and a military that over time has been purged of anti-Chávez leaders, would such a capacity even theoretically exist. By contrast, Argentina lived through the trauma of repressive military dictatorship and (as underscored in chapter 3) the revaluation of civil and political rights following the return to democracy. Although violent protest could erupt in a variety of scenarios, intensifying the repressive capacity of the state as a strategy for retaining power appears far less likely than the fall of the government and the convening of new elections, as occurred at the peak of the economic crisis in the early 2000s.

In speculating about the future of populist regimes, it is important to separate tangible economic benefits from other sources of popular support and legitimacy. In the case of Venezuela, for example, López Maya and Panzarelli as well as others demonstrate that *chavismo* is not just based on material distribution in exchange for political loyalty. Chávez has enormous personal charisma and established profound emotional connections with large segments of the electorate. Chávez's destiny, as Kirk Hawkins argues, is "determined by much more than the economy";[31] his goal was to create a new Venezuela, "a comprehensive moral and spiritual revolution" to demolish "the old values of individualism, capitalism, and selfishness."[32] In undertaking this effort, Chávez created political identities, cleavages, and a sense of empowerment among the poor that will outlast his rule, and his followers will not easily be demobilized. In this sense, *chavismo*—as a political phenomenon based on but transcending a particular ruler—is similar to Peronism in Argentina or *aprismo* in Peru. In Bolivia as well, Morales and the MAS have empowered indigenous and poor mestizos, as individuals and especially as collective actors organized in powerful social movements. These movements will not be easily deactivated in the event that Morales himself loses legitimacy in the eyes of his followers.

In explaining populism's reappearance in Latin America and in speculating about populism's future, the contributors to this book have combined structuralist (political economy) arguments with an analysis of representative institutions—parties and party systems. Kurt Weyland and others, for example, have underscored the critical role of commodity rents in giving rise to and sustaining twenty-first-century populism; among

31. Hawkins, *Venezuela's Chavismo and Populism*, 243.
32. José Pedro Zuquete, "The Missionary Politics of Hugo Chávez," *Latin American Politics and Society* 50, no. 1 (2008).

these writers there is skepticism that populist regimes could emerge in countries without similar economic structures.[33] Those focusing on institutions conclude that as long as political systems function and foster inclusion, they can deter the rise of populism.

As Ana María Bejarano argues in the case of Colombia, the absence of populism was related to the two-party system and to the ability of the Liberal Party in particular "to take in and accommodate, among its various factions, a radical leftist wing, which somehow expressed the demands of the have-nots, the workers, and the excluded." At the same, the party system did not process all demands for political and socioeconomic inclusion, giving rise to powerful guerrilla movements whose political demands were intermingled with (and some say, superseded by) involvement in narco-trafficking and other criminal activity. With respect to demands for inclusion, the Colombian historian Marco Palacios has argued that populism and revolutionary warfare are, in fact, different sides of the same coin, and that the failure or absence of populism in places such as Colombia (along with some Central American countries) helps explain the emergence of revolutionary, armed challenges to the status quo.[34]

Combining structuralist and institutional approaches, it might seem that the possibilities of diffusion of twenty-first-century radical populism are indeed slim. The 2011 presidential elections in Peru, in which Keiko Fujimori and Ollanta Humala—two outsiders of dubious democratic credentials—competed in a runoff, would seem to illustrate that calls to "re-found the nation" are not as appealing as they were only a few years ago. In the mid-2000s, Chávez was at the peak of his power, generously distributing petro-dollars and attempting to consolidate an alternative model of hemispheric leadership that was statist, militarist, antiglobalization, and anti–United States. The *chavista* model of political transformation, centered on the creation of a new hegemonic group that displaces political parties via the convening of a Constitutional Assembly to write a new Constitution, inspired and was partially emulated by the MAS in Bolivia and by Correa in Ecuador. However, when Ollanta

33. See chapter 5 in the present volume. See also Kurt Weyland, "The Rise of Latin America's Two Lefts: Insights from Rentier State Theory," *Comparative Politics* 41, no. 2 (2009): 145–64; and "The Left: Destroyer or Saviour of the Market Model?" in *Resurgence of the Latin American Left*, ed. Levitsky and Roberts, 71–93.

34. Marco Palacio, ed., *Populistas: El poder de las palabras—Estudios de política* (Bogotá: Universidad Nacional, 2011), cited by Arnson, *In the Wake of War*, 12.

Humala made his second bid for the presidency in 2011, Chávez's influence was waning. The Venezuelan economy was in crisis, and Chávez's image throughout the region in tatters.[35] Leftist leaders from Paraguay to El Salvador took pains to distance themselves from Chávez's model of political transformation. Ollanta Humala explicitly stated in 2011 that it had been "an error" to have allied himself so closely with Chávez during the 2006 presidential campaign.[36] As Cynthia McClintock demonstrates in chapter 8, Humala

> reiterated that he would not upend the economic policies that had facilitated Peru's growth . . . [and] swore an "Oath for Democracy," promising to respect the Constitution, the separation of powers, human rights, freedom of speech, and term limits. With these economic and political shifts, Humala was able to gain the support of key establishment leaders, including Mario Vargas Llosa and Alejandro Toledo.

Finally, Humala invoked the prestige of Brazil's Lula, turning to advisers from the Partido Dos Trabalhadores to redesign his campaign, focusing against the legacy of Fujimori's authoritarianism. The Peruvian analyst Martín Tanaka concluded that "the key to Humala's success in 2011 was his recently adopted moderate stance, not the anti-system radicalism that had propelled him to the second round in 2006."[37]

35. In a study of the image of the United States in Latin America on the eve of President Barack Obama's March 2011 trip to the region, the polling firm Latinobarómetro asked respondents in eighteen countries to rank U.S. and Latin American leaders on a scale of 1 to 10 (with 10 being the highest score). President Obama and Brazilian President Luis Inácio Lula da Silva tied for first place, with a score of 6.3. Fidel Castro ranked the lowest (with a score of 3.8); second from last was President Hugo Chávez (with a score of 3.9). In a separate study on Latin American attitudes, Latinobarómetro found that majorities in only two countries—Venezuela and the Dominican Republic—believed that Venezuela's impact in Latin America was positive. By contrast, majorities in all but two countries—Argentina and Paraguay—believed that the U.S. role in the region was positive. See Corporación Latinobarómetro, "The Obama Era? The Image of the United States in Latin America 1996–2010," March 2011, 20, available at www.latinobarometro.org; and Corporación Latinobarómetro, "América Latina Mira al Mundo: La globalización y las relaciones con otros países del mundo," June 2010, 20–21, available at www.latinobarometro.org.

36. Juan Forero, "Chávez's Influence Wanes in Latin America," *Washington Post*, May 17, 2011.

37. Martín Tanaka, "A Vote for Moderate Change," *Journal of Democracy* 22, no. 4 (2011): 81.

Humala's election could signal the end of the diffusion and the attraction of the *chavista* model of re-foundation.[38] The same could be said of the 2009 coup in Honduras against President Manuel Zelaya, a Chávez ally who was ousted when Honduran elites backed by the armed forces became convinced that he aspired to a transformation of Honduras's Constitution that would set the country on a path similar to Venezuela's. Elsewhere in Central America, however, the specter of *chavismo* continued to hover. The political scientist Shelley McConnell has shown how Daniel Ortega in Nicaragua manifested some aspects of neopopulism but not others.[39] Opportunism, she argues, underlay "the pact" in Nicaragua that virtually eliminated horizontal accountability among branches of government and made its political system one of the most exclusionary in Latin America. As president, Ortega "relied on elections as a device for mass mobilization while his party was diminished to a personal vehicle."[40] Assistance from Venezuela constituted almost a fourth of the national budget in certain years, facilitating clientelistic distribution through citizen power councils composed largely of the Sandinista support base. Ortega aligned himself with Chávez and other members of the Alianza Bolivariana para los Pueblos de Nuestra América (Bolivarian Alliance for the Peoples of Our America) on issues of foreign policy, including relations with Iran.[41]

38. See Steven Levitsky, "A Surprising Left Turn," *Journal of Democracy* 22, no. 4 (2011): 84–94.

39. McConnell discusses, among others, the manipulation of the Constitution by the Supreme Court in 2009 to permit Ortega's candidacy as an indication of "illiberal democracy" in Nicaragua. She considers certain aspects of the case for populism in Nicaragua less than compelling, including features of Ortega's successful 2006 bid for the presidency. She notes that the party system, distorted as it was by the pact of convenience between the Sandinista and Liberal parties, was not discarded in favor of "direct democracy without parties." See Shelley A. McConnell, "Nicaragua's Pacted Democracy," in *In the Wake of War*, ed. Arnson, 139–73.

40. Ibid., 140.

41. See Instituto de Estudios Estratégicos y Política Pública, "Política exterior, defensa y seguridad: ¿Hacia dónde vamos?" August 15, 2010, http://www.ieepp.org/index.php/politica-exterior-defensa-y-seguridad-hacia-donde-vamos/; and Javier Meléndez and Félix Maradiaga, "Iranian-Nicaraguan Relations Under the Sandinista Government: Rhetoric or Anti-Establishment Foreign Policy?" in *Iran in Latin America: Threat or "Axis of Annoyance"?* Reports on the Americas 23, edited by Cynthia J. Arnson, Haleh Esfandiari, and Adam Stubits (Washington, D.C.: Latin American Program, Woodrow Wilson International Center for Scholars, 2010), 65–81.

Questions for Further Research

Sparked by the Venezuelan example and by movements and regimes that some consider a threat to democracy and others its corrective, the scholarship on populism is burgeoning. The resurgence of the left in Latin America in the 2000s and the sharp contrasts between the contestatory and the moderate left paths to power have also contributed to the revival of the debates on populism.[42] Scholars thus far have focused primarily on political systems and institutions. To a lesser extent, they have studied the relationships (whether "top-down" or "bottom-up") between populist figures and social movements, the nature of populist leadership and discourse, and the ways that populism's emergence and consolidation are linked to broader structural factors such as windfall rents from minerals and other natural resources. The contributors to this volume illustrate the advantage of combining the analysis of political economy with institutions and discourses. Even though, in the heat of conceptual debates, scholars try to reduce the core of populism to political economy, discourse, or political strategy, we have endeavored to show how combining these approaches leads to more complex and subtle analyses.[43] Instead of trying to opt for one explanation over others, we encourage future studies to integrate the study of structures, institutions, political strategies, and discourses.

Despite the significant amount of scholarship focusing on institutions, we know far less about how people live the ambiguities between authoritarianism and democratization as they participate in mass rallies, redistributive social programs, or newly created grassroots institutions. The prevailing wisdom is that followers are passive or are manipulated

---

42. According to the formulation set out by Kurt Weyland, the moderate left pursues goals prudently, "respecting economic constraints and political opposition." The contestatory left, he argues, is less radical than the Marxist left of the 1960s and 1970s with respect to capitalist property relations, but feels an urge to "contest" with enemies such as the private sector or political opponents in order to strengthen a mass following. See Kurt Weyland, "The Performance of Leftist Governments in Latin America: Conceptual and Theoretical Issues," in *Leftist Governments*, ed. Weyland, Madrid, and Hunter, 3.

43. In their book *Re-Inventing the Italian Right*, Carlo Ruzza and Stefano Fella also illustrate the advantages of combining the study of political institutions and political opportunities with that of culture and discourse. See Carlo Ruzza and Stefano Fella, *Re-Inventing the Italian Right: Territorial Politics, Populism and "Post-Fascism"* (London: Routledge, 2009).

from above. Many use the term "clientelism" without explaining the subtleties of these exchanges. The rich literature on political clientelism demonstrates that what from above is perceived as the instrumental exchange of votes for favors has different meanings for the actors involved.[44] We need further research to analyze how and to what extent the support for populist regimes is based merely or even principally on strategic exchanges. If populism offers more than economic rewards, we need to know more about the symbolic dimensions of populist interactions. If these exchanges have to do with notions of morality and feelings of humiliation, revenge, or empowerment, more research is needed to understand their different and ambiguous meanings.

Similarly, the wealth of scholarship about populism's discursive aspects has not addressed the social conditions of reception. Why do populist appeals appear more credible than those based on class? Why are such appeals more compelling than liberal democracy's focus on pluralism and individual rights and freedoms? Why do some outsiders fail to connect with a broad electorate, their populist rhetoric appearing hollow and empty, whereas at other times outsiders succeed in politicizing society into antagonistic camps? Do followers accept the leader's discourse as valid, or do they use it instrumentally to advance their own agendas?

As Cynthia McClintock indicates, more research is also needed about the relationship of the armed forces to contemporary radical populism and to politics in general. Has the military retained its institutional autonomy, or has that been compromised by successive purges and other efforts to ensure loyalty to the president or to a project of revolutionary transformation? How would the armed forces respond to the electoral defeat of a populist leader—by defending the Constitution or with the continuation of the revolutionary project? Although the emphasis in studies of democratic transitions has been on the military's return to the barracks and its subordination to civilian rule—a framework still useful in explaining the Argentine case—it is not clear that this paradigm captures the dynamics of the military's mission or role in society under populist leadership. Related to this issue is the need for more research about the international relations of today's populist regimes, in particular about the ways that their search for sovereignty has led to an array of linkages with countries such as Iran. In the United States, debates over the security aspects of this relationship have be-

44. See, e.g., Javier Auyero, *Poor People's Politics* (Durham, N.C.: Duke University Press, 2001).

come politically divisive, with partisans on both sides accusing the other of either minimizing or exaggerating the threat. Understanding the true dimensions of the security and intelligence relationship is difficult under any circumstances, but even more so given the lack of transparency that characterizes most aspects of decisionmaking and governance in today's populist regimes.

Conceptualizations of populism as a political strategy or as a discourse do allow for comparative research to illuminate the peculiarities of populism's different manifestations.[45] Populist appeals in Western Europe have rarely led to the establishment of populist regimes; only when institutions have been permissible, as in Italy after the breakdown of the political system and the establishment of new electoral rules in 1993, did populist politicians win power as partners of coalition governments. Outside Latin America, populist regimes have been relegated to the margins of the political system. In Europe, populism tends to be linked to nativism, an ideology that holds that "states should be inhabited exclusively by members of a native group ('the nation') and that nonnative elements (persons and ideas) are fundamentally threatening to the homogeneous nation-state."[46] These movements are exclusionary, and their appeal to the "real people" is frequently xenophobic and racist. Unlike their Latin American classical and radical counterparts who embraced statist redistributive policies, European populists—like Latin American neopopulists—advocate for a leaner and smaller state and are thus more exclusionary in economic terms. But like their Latin American counterparts, populists elsewhere politicize issues of exclusion and mobilize those who perceive the political system to be closed and unresponsive. Right-wing populism in Europe is also based on the promise to establish real and unmediated democracy.[47] These democratizing promises are, of course, in tension with nativist appeals.

45. An innovative work in this direction is by Cas Mudde and Cristóbal Rovira Kaltwasser, *Voices of the Peoples: Populism in Europe and Latin America Compared*, Working Paper 378 (Notre Dame, Ind.: Kellogg Institute for International Studies, University of Notre Dame, 2011). See also Cas Mudde and Cristóbal Rovira Kaltwasser, "Populism and (Liberal) Democracy: A Framework for Analysis," in *Populism in Europe and the Americas*, edited by Cas Mudde and Cristóbal Rovira Kaltwasser (Cambridge: Cambridge University Press, 2012), 1–27.

46. Cas Mudde, "The Populist Radical Right: A Pathological Normalcy," *West European Politics* 33, no. 6 (2010): 1173.

47. Charles Lindhlom and José Pedro Zúquete, *The Struggle for the World: Liberation Movements of the 21st Century* (Stanford, Calif.: Stanford University Press, 2010), 76.

As noted in chapter 6, the current and future challenge for democratization in the region is how to reconcile "the substantive goals of inclusion and equality" with the equally substantive goals of "robust procedures and institutions." Chapter 3 emphasizes that the unmediated processes of popular identification will take priority over "the mediated politics of representative government" unless the political system finds ways to respond more effectively to citizen demands. The challenges of democratic deepening have rightly focused on improving political procedures and institutions, to make political participation meaningful, to improve the capacity of the state to respond effectively and with transparency to citizens' demands, and to reinforce the rule of law. Issues of socioeconomic, ethnic, and symbolic inclusion have largely been treated as secondary—questions to be taken up in the sphere of public policy, with redress subject to the effectiveness and capacity of governance institutions. The chapters in this book serve as powerful reminders that the "voice of the people" is often heard most insistently with respect to these other, nonpolitical demands for inclusion. How this voice finds expression, and who listens and through which channels, determines its potential to destroy or reinforce the potential for representative democracy.

Contributors

Cynthia J. Arnson is director of the Latin American Program at the Woodrow Wilson International Center for Scholars. She is the coordinator of the Latin American Program's three-year project on democratic governance and the "new left" in Latin America, which culminates with this volume. She is editor of *In the Wake of War: Democratization and Internal Armed Conflict in Latin America* (2012); editor of *Comparative Peace Processes in Latin America* (1999); and author of *Crossroads: Congress, the President, and Central America, 1976–1993* (1993); among other works. She is a member of the editorial advisory board of *Foreign Affairs Latinoamérica* and of the advisory boards of Human Rights Watch/Americas and the Social Science Research Council's Conflict Prevention and Peace Forum. She writes and lectures frequently on Latin American politics, and on U.S. policy toward the region, particularly Colombia and Central America. She received an M.A. and Ph.D. in international relations from the Paul H. Nitze School of Advanced International Studies at Johns Hopkins University.

Ana María Bejarano is associate professor of political science at the University of Toronto. She previously taught at the Universidad de los Andes in Bogotá, where she also directed the Center for Social and Legal Studies. She coedited *The Crisis of Democratic Representation in the Andes* (2006) and is the author of *Precarious Democracies: Understanding Regime Stability and Change in Colombia and Venezuela* (2011). Her current research explores the sources of constitutional choice in five Andean countries—Bolivia, Colombia, Ecuador, Peru, and Venezuela—as well as the impact of recent constitutional innovations on the prospects for democracy in the Andes. She received a Ph.D. in political science from Columbia University.

Leslie Bethell is emeritus professor of Latin American History at the University of London, emeritus fellow at St. Antony's College, Oxford, and senior scholar at the Woodrow Wilson Center. He was formerly director of the University of London's Institute of Latin American Studies and the University of Oxford's Centre for Brazilian Studies. His research has been principally in the field of nineteenth- and twentieth-century Latin American—and especially Brazilian—political, social, and cultural history. His numerous publications include *Latin America between the Second World War and the Cold War* (with Ian Roxborough) and the twelve-volume *Cambridge History of Latin America* (editor).

John Crabtree is research associate at the Latin American Centre at Oxford University and a senior member of St. Antony's College. He has written widely on Andean politics, particularly on Peru and Bolivia. His most recent coedited book is *Unresolved Tensions: Bolivia Past and Present*. He also published *Patterns of Protest: Politics and Social Movements in Bolivia*, and is coauthoring a sequel on contemporary Bolivian politics to be published in 2013. Aside from teaching and writing on Latin American politics, he works as a consultant. He received a B.Phil from Liverpool University and a Ph.D. from Oxford Brookes University.

Carlos de la Torre is director of international studies and professor of sociology at the University of Kentucky, Lexington, and former professor of political studies at the Latin American Faculty for Social Sciences (FLACSO-Ecuador). He was previously associate professor of sociology at Northeastern University and at Drew University, and was a fellow at the Woodrow Wilson International Center for Scholars in 2008–9. He is the author of five books and many articles and book chapters, most of which focus on two main research areas: populism and populist movements in Latin America, and racism and ethnic/racial movements in Ecuador. He received a Ph.D. in sociology from the New School for Social Research.

Margarita López Maya is senior professor at the Center for Development Studies (Centro de Estudios para el Desarrollo) of the Central University of Venezuela. Her areas of expertise include Venezuela's contemporary history and politics, political parties, and popular protests; and participatory innovations in "Bolivarian" Caracas. She has served on the Board of Directors of the Consejo Latinoamericano de Ciencias Sociales and has held numerous fellowships at such institutions as the University of Notre Dame, Oxford University, Columbia University, and the Woodrow Wilson International Center for Scholars. Her major publications include *Del viernes negro al referendo revocatorio* (2006); *Protesta y cultura en Venezuela: Los marcos de acción colectiva en 1999* (2002); and *EEUU en Venezuela: 1945–1948* (1996). She received her undergraduate degree in history and a Ph.D. in social sciences from the Central University of Venezuela.

Cynthia McClintock is professor of political science and international affairs at George Washington University. She was previously a fellow at the Woodrow Wilson International Center for Scholars and president of the Latin American Studies Association. Her most recent book is *The United States and Peru: Cooperation—at a Cost*. Her previous publications include *Revolutionary Movements in Latin America: El Salvador's FMLN and Peru's Shining Path* and *Peasant Cooperatives and Political Change in Peru*.

César Montúfar is a professor at the Universidad Andina Simón Bolívar in Quito and a member of the National Assembly of Ecuador. His areas of expertise include Ecuadorian and Latin American politics, international development, and international security. He received a Ph.D. in political science from the New School for Social Research, where he won an award for the best doctoral dissertation by a foreign student. He is the author of *Hacia Donde Llevan las Banderas* (2011), *Gobernabilidad y*

Participación (2004), *Hacia una teoría de la asistencia internacional del desarrollo* (2002), and *La Reconstrucción Neoliberal* (2000), among other publications.

Francisco Panizza is reader in Latin American politics at the London School of Economics and Political Science. He has taught in universities in Argentina, Brazil, Mexico, Spain, Switzerland, and Uruguay. His main research interests are populism, the politics of economic reform, and the relationship between ideas and institutions. Among his recent publications are *The Triumph of Politics: The Return of the Left in Venezueula, Bolivia, and Ecuador; Contemporary Latin America: Development and Democracy Beyond the Washington Consensus; Populism and the Mirror of Democracy;* and *Unarmed Utopia Revisited: The Resurgence of Left-of-Centre Politics in Latin America.* He received a law degree from the Universidad de la República of Uruguay and a Ph.D. in political science from the University of Essex.

Alexandra Panzarelli is adviser to the Canadian Embassy in Venezuela and lecturer at the Escuela de Estudios Políticos de la Universidad Central de Venezuela. She previously served as a consultant to Gobernación de Miranda in Caracas and was program assistant at the Joint United Nations Program on AIDS/HIV (UNAIDS) country office in Venezuela. She has also published several articles concerning electoral policies and social movements. She received a degree in political and administrative sciences from Universidad Central de Venezuela, a postgraduate degree in public management from the Universidad Metropolitana, and a master's in politics from New York University, which was supported by a Fulbright scholarship.

Enrique Peruzzotti is associate professor in the Department of Political Science and International Studies at Torcuato Di Tella University, Argentina, and researcher at Consejo Nacional de Investigaciones Científicas y Técnicas. He was a visiting researcher at the United Nations Research Institute for Social Development in Geneva and a 2009–10 Simon Guggenheim Memorial Foundation Fellow. He has written numerous articles and book chapters on civil society and democratization in Latin America, and has coedited books on the rule of law, populism, and democracy Latin America. His most recent publication is the coedited volume (with Martin Plot) *Critical Theory and Democracy: Civil Society,*

Dictatorship, and Constitutionalism in Andrew Arato's Democratic Theory (2012).

Kenneth M. Roberts is professor of government and senior associate dean of the College of Arts and Sciences at Cornell University. He is the author of *Deepening Democracy? The Modern Left and Social Movements in Chile and Peru* and coeditor of *The Diffusion of Social Movements* as well as *The Resurgence of the Latin American Left.* His current work explores the transformation of party systems in Latin America's neoliberal era. His research on political parties, populism, and labor and social movements has been published in a number of scholarly journals, including *American Political Science Review, World Politics, Comparative Political Studies, Comparative Politics, Latin American Politics and Society,* and *Studies in Comparative International Development.* He received his Ph.D. from Stanford University.

Hector E. Schamis teaches at the Center for Latin American Studies at Georgetown University. He was previously a fellow at the Woodrow Wilson Center. He has published articles on comparative political economy and democratization in journals such as *Comparative Politics, World Politics,* and *Journal of Democracy.* He is also the author of *Re-Forming the State: The Politics of Privatization in Latin America and Europe.* His current research is on the historical evolution of populism, as well as on the relationship between political institutions and the persistence of boom/bust cycles in Latin America's development. He received his Ph.D. in political science from Columbia University.

Kurt Weyland is the Lozano Long Professor of Latin American Politics at the University of Texas at Austin. He has published many articles and book chapters on democratization, neoliberalism, populism, and social policy in Latin America, and his work has appeared in journals such as *World Politics, International Organization,* and *Journal of Democracy.* He is the author, most recently, of *Bounded Rationality and Policy Diffusion: Social Sector Reform in Latin America* (2007) and coeditor of *Leftist Governments in Latin America: Successes and Shortcomings.* His new project analyzes the wavelike diffusion of political regime changes across countries, starting with the explosive spread of the 1848 Revolution in Europe and Latin America.

Index

383

Made in the USA
Middletown, DE
23 April 2021

38202738R00235